Ian Gordon-Brown and *Barbara Somers*

The Raincloud of Knowable Things

A PRACTICAL GUIDE TO TRANSPERSONAL PSYCHOLOGY

Workshops   History   Method

292.

The Wisdom of the Transpersonal

Also in this series :

Journey in Depth : A Transpersonal Perspective
The Fires of Alchemy: A Transpersonal Viewpoint

Proposed future title :

Symptom as Symbol – Barbara Somers

For a full list and details of all our titles
please see our website at:

www.archivepublishing.co.uk

The Raincloud of Knowable Things

A PRACTICAL GUIDE TO TRANSPERSONAL PSYCHOLOGY

Workshops   History   Method

IAN GORDON-BROWN
with
BARBARA SOMERS

Edited by
HAZEL MARSHALL

Illustrations
IAN THORP

Original paintings
FRANCES CRAWFORD

2008

First published in Great Britain by
Archive Publishing
Dorset, England

Designed at Archive Publishing by Ian Thorp

© 2008 Archive Publishing
Text © Hazel Marshall, 2008

Barbara Somers and Ian Gordon-Brown assert the moral right to be
identified as the authors of this work

A CIP Record for this book is available from
The British Cataloguing in Publication data office

ISBN 978-1-906289-03-4 (Hardback)
ISBN 978-1-906289-02-7 (Paperback)

All rights reserved. No part of this publication may be reproduced, stored in
a retrieval system, or transmitted at any time or by any means electronic,
mechanical, photocopying, recording or otherwise, without the prior
permission of the publisher

Cover painting: 'Communion – Loanhead of Daviot' by Frances Crawford
and 'Moon's Rest – Loanhead of Daviot' - reproduced courtesy of the artist.
Allathumpach, Deskry-side, Strathdon, Aberdeenshire.
francescrawfordart@yahoo.com
also at www.archivepublishing.co.uk

Printed and bound in Latvia by
Dardedze Holography

'Moon's Rest – Loanhead of Daviot'

Frances Crawford

DEDICATION

With love and gratitude, this book is dedicated to

Barbara Somers

quicksilver at the heart of matter

CONTENTS

Dedication	viii
Contents	ix
Imaging Explorations	xiv
Illustrations	xvi
Acknowledgements	xix
Foreword	xx
Preface	xxii
Introduction	xxv

PART I: Introductory Workshops — 1

CHAPTER 1 — 3
APPROACHING THE SELF — WORKSHOP I
IAN GORDON-BROWN and BARBARA SOMERS

Introducing the workshop	3
Maps of the psyche	9
Two questions about myself – short exploration	17
The traveller on life's journey – exploration	18
Sub-personalities	20
Sub-personalities 1 – exploration	28
Sub-personalities 2 – exploration	30
Symbols and images	32
The four-ball map	41
Gestalt exploration	46
The four functions	48
Experiencing the transpersonal	59
The inner sanctuary – exploration	66

CHAPTER 2 — 68
THE MASCULINE & FEMININE WITHIN — WORKSHOP II
IAN GORDON-BROWN and BARBARA SOMERS

Introducing the workshop	68
The cup and sword – exploration	70
The feminine principle	73
The masculine principle	84
The coming together of masculine and feminine	91

The masculine and feminine met on the road – exploration	94
Marriage as a psychological relationship – (Container and contained and The four people at the wedding)	96
Developing intuition	104
Gestalt exploration	106
Symptom as symbol	109
Identity – 'Who am I?'	116
The grounding exercise – exploration	118

CHAPTER 3 — 121
CYCLES AND STAGES — WORKSHOP III
IAN GORDON-BROWN and BARBARA SOMERS

Introducing the workshop	121
Patterns and cycles of growth	121
The seven-year cycle	122
Short exploration, the pattern of your life	131
Self-image exploration	131
Projection	133
The shape of your life 1 – exploration	138
The shape of your life 2 – exploration	141
Control patterns, polarities	143
Change	145
The road of your life – exploration	151
Archetypal energies	152
Core energy – short exploration	161
Review of the three introductory workshops	162
The sanctuary – exploration	166

CHAPTER 4 — 168
INITIATION AND THE MYTH OF THE JOURNEY — WP IV
IAN GORDON-BROWN and BARBARA SOMERS

Introducing the workshop	168
The story of Buddha	170
Stages in the life of Christ	172
The door and the cave – exploration	188
Rites of passage	189
The water of emotions – exploration	207
Initiation and therapy	208

The myth of the journey – initiation in myth and legend	211
The hero's journey	213
The desert and the mountain – exploration	221
The initiates	223
Contemplation – exploration	225

CHAPTER 5 — 227
THE OTHER SELF — WORKSHOP V
BARBARA SOMERS and IAN GORDON-BROWN

Introducing the workshop	227
Singing stone	227
The journey through the four elements – exploration	229
Directions, elements and functions	230
The 'inferior' function	233
The door and the mirror – exploration	236
Alchemy and the elements	238
Journey to the other self – exploration	243
The other self	244

PART II: Intermezzo – Emphasizing the Practical — 251

CHAPTER 6 — 253
IMAGING AND THE TRANSPERSONAL
IAN GORDON-BROWN

Introduction – transpersonal psychology	253
Active imagination and psychology	254
More recent history	258
Mental imagery techniques in analysis and psychotherapy	259
Using guided imagery	261
A transpersonal use of spot imaging and the guided daydream with individuals	263
Spot imaging	265
The full guided daydream	266
Running transpersonal workshops	272
Designing imaging explorations	276

PART III: Advanced Workshops — 279

CHAPTER 7 — 281
   ARCHETYPES
      IAN GORDON-BROWN
   Introduction – of what stuff am I made? — 281
   Archetypal images – exploration — 283
   Mapping the archetypes — 284
   Archetypes of the self — 295
   Archetypes of the self – exploration — 297
   Archetypes and psychotherapy — 298
   Spirit of place – communities and locations — 300
   Life-cycles of groups and organisations — 301

CHAPTER 8 — 307
   THE CHAKRA SYSTEM
      IAN GORDON-BROWN
   Introduction – energy in the human body — 307
   Exploring the chakras – exploration — 322
   The opening of the chakras — 323
   Working with the chakras — 325
   The chakras and their symbols – exploration — 326
   Chakras and health – symptom as symbol — 327
   A first-aid exploration for panic, fear and anxiety — 331
   Chakras, places and organisations — 333

CHAPTER 9 — 337
   INTUITION, INSPIRATION AND THE WILL
      IAN GORDON-BROWN
   Introduction – energy-threads — 337
   Intuition, inspiration and will – exploration — 338
   Intuition – the consciousness thread — 339
   In search of your intuition – exploration — 342
   Inspiration – the creative thread — 343
   In search of your inspiration – exploration — 346
   Will – the life thread — 346
   In search of your will – exploration — 348

CHAPTER 10
THE RAINCLOUD OF KNOWABLE THINGS
IAN GORDON-BROWN

	351
Introduction – the personal and the planetary	351
Four explorations for groups	361
My personal place of creation – exploration	361
The group and the ashram – exploration	362
The temple in the sun – exploration	362
Orienting the Self – exploration	363
Some ways to the centre of life	363
The universal blessing of Buddhism – exploration	365

PART IV: Appendices 367
IAN GORDON-BROWN, unless otherwise indicated

1	Checklist for running Transpersonal workshops	369
2	Commentary on some of the workshop explorations	370
3	Writing up sub-personalities	376
4	Some roots of Transpersonal psychology	379
5	Suggested programmes for the first four workshops	381
6	Original reading lists for the first five workshops	386
7	Alternative projection exploration	391
8	Transcenders and actualisers	391
9	Some Buddhist teachings (Classic)	393
10	Six stages of discipleship (Alice Bailey)	393
11	Plato's myth of the cave (Classic)	394
12	Faiths of the Cheyenne people (Hyemeyohsts Storm)	395
13	Some pioneers (Ed.)	396
14	Guided imaging and fantasy techniques (Desoille, Leuner, Assagioli)	408
15	Some symbolic situations for guided imaging	411
16	Working with individuals: the structure of the journey	415
17	Masculine and feminine aspects in the archetypal context	420
18	Seven Archetypes, Seven Rays (Alice Bailey)	422
19	The Nations and the Rays (Alice Bailey)	426
20	The chakras and the glands	427

| ORIGINAL BIBLIOGRAPHY | 431 |
| INDEX | 441 |

IMAGING EXPLORATIONS

APPROACHING THE SELF
Two Questions about Myself	17
The Traveller on Life's Journey	18
Sub-Personalities 1	28
Sub-Personalities 2	30
Gestalt Exploration	46
The Inner Sanctuary	66

THE MASCULINE AND FEMININE WITHIN
The Cup and Sword	70
The Masculine and Feminine Met on the Road	94
Gestalt Exploration	106
The Grounding Exercise	118

CYCLES AND STAGES
The Pattern of Your Life	131
Self-Image Exploration	131
The Shape of Your Life 1	138
The Shape of Your Life 2	141
Travelling the Road of Your Life	151
Core Energy	161
The Sanctuary	166

INITIATION
The Door and the Cave	188
The Water of Emotions	207
The Desert and the Mountain	221
Contemplation	225

THE OTHER SELF
The Journey through the Four Elements	229
The Door and the Mirror	236
Journey to the Other Self	243

ARCHETYPES
Archetypal Images	283
Archetypes of the Self	297

THE CHAKRA SYSTEM
Exploring the Chakras	322
The Chakras and their Symbols	326
A First-aid Exploration for Panic, Fear & Anxiety	331

INTUITION, INSPIRATION AND THE WILL
Intuition, Inspiration and Will	338
In Search of your Intuition	342
In Search of your Inspiration	346
In Search of your Will	348

THE RAINCLOUD OF KNOWABLE THINGS
My Personal Place of Creation	361
The Group and the Ashram	362
The Temple in the Sun	362
Orienting the Self	363
The Universal Blessing of Buddhism	365

APPENDICES
Alternative Self-Image Exploration	391

ILLUSTRATIONS

Ian Gordon-Brown and Barbara Somers — ii
Frontispiece – 'Moon's Rest – Loanhead of Daviot' — vii
Facing Page to Chapters – Facsimiles, IGB and BS
Facing Page to Parts – Hand-rendered charts by Alison Gaffney

Workshop I
   1:01 – Splits — 6
   1:02 – Jung's Map 1 — 9
   1:03 – Jung's Map 2 — 10
   1:04 – Jung's Map 3 — 11
   1:05 – 'Assagioli's Egg' 1 — 13
   1:06 – 'Assagioli's Egg' 2 — 14
   1:07 – The Onion Map 1 — 15
   1:08 – Some Possible Sub-Personalities — 22
   1:09 – Some Feminine Sub-Personalities — 23
   1:10 – Some Masculine Sub-Personalities — 24
   1:11 – Levels of Consciousness 1 — 26
   1:12 – The Four-Ball Map 1, The Child — 41
   1:13 – The Four-Ball Map 2, The Average Adult — 43
   1:14 – The Four-Ball Map 3, The Mature Adult — 45
   1:15 – The Gestalt Exploration — 46
   1:16 – Introvert and Extravert — 49
   1:17 – Perception and Judgement — 50
   1:18 – Jung's Map with the Four Functions — 51
   1:19 – The Way of the Snake — 55
   1:20 – The Dynamic Turn-type — 57
   1:21 – The Transpersonal Experience — 60

Workshop II
   2:01 – Left and Right Brain — 74
   2:02 – The Feminine and the Chinese Tai Chi glyph — 75
   2:03 – The Eternal Feminine — 77
   2:04 – Levels of Consciousness 2 — 84
   2:05 – Some Archetypal Masculine Figures — 87
   2:06 – Symbols of the Masculine and Feminine — 91
   2:07 – Symbols of the Masculine — 92

2:08 – Symbols of the Feminine	93
2:09 – The Four People at the Wedding 1	99
2:10 – The Four People at the Wedding 2	102
2:11 – Body, Emotions and Mind	109
2:12 – Levels of Consciousness 3	116

Workshop III
3:01 – The Seven-Year Cycle	122
3:02 – The Shape of your Life Exploration 1	139
3:03 – The Shape of your Life Exploration 2	142
3:04 – Change	146
3:05 – Typical Archetypal Energies	153
3:06 – Some Archetypes of the Masculine Principle	154
3:07 – Four Archetypes of the Feminine Principle	159
3:08 – The Onion Map 2	163

Initiation
4:01 – Levels of Consciousness 4	169
4:02 – Stages in the Life of Christ	173
4:03 – Life-Stages	175
4:04 – Finding your Chosen Family	177
4:05 – The Temptation in the Desert	182
4:06 – The Transfiguration	184
4:07 – The Mountain of the Transfiguration	186
4:08 – The Seven Stages of Life	191
4:09 – The Human Function Curve	200
4:10 – The Time of the Elder	203
4:11 – The Hero's Journey	213
4:12 – The Labyrinth in Chartres Cathedral	216
4:13 – The Bridge and the Ladder	217
4:14 – The Myth of the Journey	218
4:15 – The World Axis	220

The Other Self
5:01 – The Four Directions	230
5:02 – The Four Functions	231
5:03 – Crisis and Nourishment	235
5:04 – The Spiral Way	248

The Chakra System
    8:01 – Map of the Chakras   309
    8:02 – Eight Chakras   310
    8:03 – Solar Plexus and Heart   316

Intuition, Inspiration and the Will
    9:01 – Three Threads of Energy   337
    9:02 – Links and Threads   355

Appendices
    11:01 – 'Assagioli's Egg' 3   379
    11:02 – The One   420
    11:03 – Major Endocrine Glands   427

ACKNOWLEDGEMENTS

My profound gratitude and respect to
Ian Gordon-Brown and
Barbara Somers
for the creation of their unique work
which has inspired and will inspire very many.

My warm thanks to those who have helped in the preparation
of this book.
They include the following,
and if I have missed anyone it is by mistake:

Sacha Abercorn, Dorothy Allen,
Pamela Allsop, Monica Anthony, Sarajane Aris,
Gina Barrs, Renita Barwell, Naona Beecher-Moore, Beata Bishop,
Julia Crabtree, Frances Crawford, Hossein Farhadi,
Alison Gaffney, Hazel Guest, Celia Gunn,
Adrian Marshall, Jonathan Meads,
Peter Merriott, Robert Patterson,
Anita Somers, Joan Swallow,
Anthony Thorley,
Ian Thorp,
Philippa Wallace (deceased),
Roger Walters, Ruth White, Lindsay Radermacher

Acknowledgement and thanks are due to the following publisher for permission to quote from 'The Four Quartets' by TS. Eliot:
Faber & Faber Ltd. London

FOREWORD

This is the third book in the series on the Wisdom of the Transpersonal so skilfully edited by Hazel Marshall, and even after the illumination we have received from 'Journey in Depth' and 'The Fires of Alchemy', for many, this latest volume will be seen as the book which really gets to the heart of the matter. For the unique teaching and synthesis of transpersonal psychology generated by Ian Gordon-Brown and Barbara Somers from the mid 1970s onwards was not a set of lectures or seminars, personal supervisions, academic papers or textbooks but the core of an oral tradition in the form of a set of brilliant participant workshops.

The problem about such workshops as a medium of communication is that they are so immediate and beguiling for participants but so elusive to tell your friends about or to recommend to colleagues; except to say, 'You'll have to go on one!' Many of us, of course, did just that.

How can I ever forget Ian's warm, reassuring patrician voice intoning, 'Find yourself in a field or a meadow. It need not be one you know….' The beginning of a long transpersonal journey which has shaped my own subsequent life and the lives of so many others. For Ian and Barbara it was the workshop and its spontaneous creativity which was the heart of the matter, and now through this book we are able to engage directly with that teaching: a precious piece of oral tradition in transpersonal psychology caught for posterity.

However, as an oral tradition and participant form of learning, this book is not a crafted textbook of cerebral instruction or a formally-written didactic account, but a guide to a practical tradition compiled from notes, diagrams, flipcharts and the heard and spoken experience. At the core of these workshops is a series of exercises in guided imaging, and through that potent technique, unconscious and transpersonal material becomes immanent and accessible for dialogue and understanding. The absence of that personal material as it is the experiential component, inevitably tempers the style of the book because at many levels it does not read like a conventional textbook. It is at best a set of guiding notes for the workshops that are described, and notes (even so eloquently extended as these) are bound to miss out the 'between the lines material' such as humour and reflective body language only known to the workshop facilitators and the participants.

But as an instructive guide it also contains a collection of jewellery and precious stones of wisdom which are priceless, so that at times you are almost overwhelmed by the originality and creativity of the authors. The range of sources: psychological, spiritual, historic, esoteric and cultural is amazing. The teaching seems to spring fully-formed into the world so that the natural question is where did all this integrated knowledge and carefully thought through material actually come from? Where are the predecessors of this finely wrought wisdom and refined technique? Books? Personal experience of therapy? Psychothera-peutic practice and the personal integration of (often painful) life events? Yes to all those things, but also more than a little genius borne from the authors' own deep personal acquaintance with the collective and transpersonal. The effect of reading this combination of wisdom and common sense practicality is so stimulating and personally catalysing not simply because it reflects the individual view and take of the authors (something rarely found in more conventional texts) but also because it carries refreshingly daring and unconventional insights.

So as a practical guide, it repays careful reading and many returns to read again and again. Like the reality of the workshops themselves needing good digestive intervals between each experience to allow cerebral and emotional composting, so this text can be re-visited (perhaps necessarily) in the same style. The book is not best approached as a straight-through read but more – dare I say it? – as a source like the energy of a great river to be dipped into, studied by the paragraph, worked on and contemplated. As such it is a great deal more than simply a guide to teaching workshops and should appeal equally to the curious new explorer as well as the experienced practitioner.

For those who want to use the book to organise transpersonal workshops (and indeed develop new ones) Ian and Barbara's teaching is precise and explicit, with many practical tips and hints and even timetables for organisation down to the last minute! We know in fact that these workshops in their original framework are being actively run today and that each year more and more people are becoming involved. So this volume is not only a record of history in the full flow of creativity but also a living contemporary tradition.

As I read through the various workshops and the guided image journeys, I came to realise how much this luminous and inspired teaching is a healthy form of twentieth-century mystery school albeit shrouded (or at least protected) by its modern handmaiden, psychology. Devoid of any accurate written accounts we can only speculate about the precise nature of the Eleusinian, Orphic and Druidic mystery schools, but here through this remarkable book we are able to enter into the real detail of a contemporary transpersonal mystery school tradition. And then I read in the extraordinary and most prescient final workshop first given in 1995, the 'Raincloud of Knowable Things', Ian Gordon-Brown's own revealing confession and perhaps the core essence of this unique book: 'So our work for the Raincloud is in preparation for the mystery schools of the twenty-first century. This is my personal goal, working in the area of heart-consciousness.'

Dr Anthony Thorley
Bath
February, 2008

PREFACE

The authors

Ian Gordon-Brown and Barbara Somers met at Dartington in 1970, united in their interest in producing a new way of therapy. Ian, who had been in industry, had previously visited the USA in his role as International President of the Lucis Trust. He went again, explored what was going on there and returned to London confirmed in his view that something Transpersonal and different was needed here. Barbara was a therapist who had been working with the Society of Authors. Their partnership sparked something new. They absorbed and adjusted their material and, wanting to make it known, set the scene by creating a series of workshops. They created them by running them (together they published very little). There was a free, initiating flow in those earlier years; to find yourself there was to be living in that creation. The workshops seemed to spring fully formed into the world; it was tremendously exciting.

How the book came about

The book presents an account of the core of those original Transpersonal workshops, and of some of the later ones, held by them in London in the nineteen-seventies and -eighties. Its aim is to anchor and make available the extraordinary inspiration of the authors, the outpouring of their first energy. It is built up from *notes*, many from the authors themselves (from Barbara Somers, a few flow-charts; from Ian Gordon-Brown, stacks of word-lists and phrases, mostly on the backs of elderly, discarded sheets of A4). Many people who attended those workshops have kindly made their own notes available. Yet other notes were mine; I attended each workshop except the last, many of them several times, and I wrote steadily. I have put them all together into a book which is, obviously, *my* idiosyncratic account of the teachings of two masters – a written version of an oral tradition. It is of the twentieth century and I have made no attempt to adapt it for the twenty-first; some of the wording, despite my best efforts, may at times appear a little outmoded. Ian Gordon-Brown said of the work: 'It will make sense only to those to whom it makes sense'. I believe this is true of the book also.

Why do I and others feel this material to be so important? It taps into something hard-wired and archetypal, contains timeless stuff. I believe it deserves a wider readership: it communicates to a new audience. I have personally found that, with no major modification, the workshops do not date but survive the test of time: in being run steadily over the years since Ian's death they have proved their continuing excellence, working well for participants. I felt they should be published as nearly as possible in their original form to preserve them for the future.

Structure

The book is in four main sections. Part I contains the material of the first three original workshops; this includes explanatory talks and themes for discussion as well as experiential sessions of active imagination. (Neither the notes nor the editing can do more than hint occasionally at the infectious humour with which the authors ran the workshops, and the way in which the feelings and participation of the people who came contributed to the effectiveness of the learning experience.) Workshop IV, 'Initiation' and V, 'The Other Self' follow, deepening the level again. Next, in Part II, you may wish to stop to water the horses at Chapter Six, based on Ian Gordon-Brown's weekend on 'How to run Transpersonal Psychology Workshops'. It presents some of the history and uses of imaging and offers the basics of working transpersonally, with individuals and with groups. In Part III we move through and beyond to explore 'Archetypes', 'Chakras', 'Intuition, Inspiration and the Will' and finally 'The Raincloud of Knowable Things', Ian's last four advanced workshops, which follow more esoteric themes. The appendices are in Part IV.

Scholarship

This book presents rich source material; it makes no claim to being academic, though referring whenever possible to works available to the authors (the bibliography more or less stops with Ian Gordon-Brown's death in 1996). However, those interested in Transpersonal Psychology as an academic discipline will be able to avail themselves of the wealth of original material here and take it into the world of comparative study. Its origins could be traced back way beyond Jung, Frankl, Maslow and Assagioli to Far Eastern and Aboriginal sources, to Greek and later Western teaching, to other great transpersonal pioneers of the twentieth century and forward into the twenty-first.

Who were the workshops for?

Anyone might attend. Open to all, the first five weekends were never restricted to those with any particular professional interest (though, of those who came, many who hadn't already been working with people did later take up, for example, counselling). The programme began with the three introductory workshops (which had to be taken in numerical order) and continued to deepen with 'Initiation' and 'The Other Self'. These *Trans*personal workshops offered ordinary people seeking *personal* growth the chance to explore their own inner worlds, gain insight into their unconscious patterns, work towards freedom from the control of those patterns and thus find more meaning in their lives. However, Ian said: 'No one should do the workshops unless they are on an inner, spiritual path, or quest, or pilgrimage – are seeking some sort of initiation.' It was made clear that it could be useful to have at least six months between workshops; galloping from stage to stage is not helpful. (So here, there is no need to hurry from chapter to chapter.) In these experiential weekends, active imagination was offered as the main technique for contacting the inner world.

Next, after nine months or a year of workshops followed by two more years of training, those who asked, 'How would I myself run such a workshop?' might have passed through the more coolly intellectual study presented in Chapter Six. Eventually they would encounter the subtler material of the last four chapters: 'Archetypes', 'Chakras', 'Intuition, Inspiration and the Will', and 'The Raincloud of Knowable Things'. (This was Ian's last workshop; he manifested the same ongoing creative process right into his later years.)

Who is the book for?

It is for the uninitiated. It is for those who did *not* attend the original workshops, nor any later, as well as for those who did. The whole thing is a path of initiation. It's a progression, a developmental process that confers freedom. It catches naturally into people's need – no one need bend themselves to fit. The material is, yes, for counsellors, therapists and those who work with people. But not only for them. It is, as originally conceived, for *anyone* drawn to it. First and foremost, it is for individuals at a personal level. It is also for those who might run the workshops themselves – adopt them for use in their own fields. I hope that it will speak particularly to those who were personally involved in the original weekends in London from the early years, and that they will allow and understand its now being given physical form. It is both for them and for those who might never have heard of the Transpersonal – those who are to come. So it will reach to the Collective.

Hazel Marshall
Cropston
February, 2008

INTRODUCTION

Transpersonal psychology

In the word 'trans-personal' the prefix *trans* means 'beyond' – beyond and including the personal. Transpersonal psychology takes account of the unexplained impulses, the unusual intuitions and ideas that rise up in very many people's experience and, not fitting a rational picture, puzzle them or fill them with strange longings. It is oriented towards the responsible implementation of findings relevant to spiritual paths. Theory is important, as are techniques of exploration. Personality structure is studied, the higher self and the continuum of consciousness.

Transpersonal psychology is about consciousness. It looks towards oneness, cosmic awareness and meta-needs, aiming towards essence, being rather than doing, transcendental exploration and a synergy both individual and species-wide. It is concerned with transcendence of the ego-self, with ultimate meaning and Self-actualisation. It embraces the mystical experience of unitive consciousness, including peak experiences, awe and wonder, ecstasy and bliss.

Transpersonal psychology is an umbrella term, covering a number of related approaches both Eastern and Western. It is interested in the combining of modern knowledge with ancient wisdom. Both the personality and the higher Self, the mechanistic and the depth approach, the masculine and feminine principles, here come together into a synthesis, a living relationship. The inside and the outside are one. It adopts practices for focusing awareness and studies theories of meditation, seeking ways towards wholeness, aiming to make everyday life sacred. It explores the freedom to grow, over against too much 'should-and-ought' morality. It notes transcendental phenomena. Its essence lies with ultimate or 'spiritual' values – compassion, humour and playfulness among them.

The Transpersonal Self

Outer impressions affect outer judgments and shape our thoughts and decisions, giving incentive to change – as advertisers know well. But we lack ideal images to raise our *inner* aims. Few heroes mark our inner crises of growth and change; few rituals or structures support us. Those who help other people don't easily find help or nourishment for themselves. We are not so much wrong as lopsided. And we are searching. The thrust of the inner world is towards wholeness. The *transpersonal Self*, of which we are unconscious, triggers the search: 'Am I just a fragment? Is my essence something more than this?' The Self is trying to help us, longing for us to find meaning, to move through the interplay of conscious and unconscious towards and into Self-knowledge, awareness, actualisation. To change, we need a realisation of this inner, transpersonal Self, this omega point. We seek a route to the centre. Mostly we discover our own way, our own strengths; become our own heroes.

The search

People have always reached into and explored the psyche in different ways. Not all are equally useful; it depends where a person is. Some have long practised astral projection and mediumship. Others employ drugs, including alcohol and hallucinogens. Some do it by hypnotism; some have gone the way of classical psychoanalysis and free association, or employed projective tests – Rorschach blots, word association, bio-feedback and other useful tools. Yet others invoke magnetism by physical means such as *mudras, mantras, tai chi, yoga*; by interpersonal means – behaviour therapy, gestalt, encounter; and by artistic means – sound, colour, writing. Many in the West are coming to fresh realisations by contemplation and meditation. Dreams offer universal symbols. *Creativity* is often a powerful way of vitalising the link with the unconscious. The Self may be made manifest through sculpture, painting, poetry, dance. Practical work earths the energy as we build and destroy. Being alive to music and sound makes a resonant channel between the worlds. Then there's the spoken word: talk yourself through, let there be light. 'How do I know what I think (or feel) till I hear what I say?' We hold conversations with the inner world, the dialogue increasing our self-understanding and informing our actions till our lives, and those of the people around us, are changed. Loving and nourishing ourselves and them, we are each enriched by it. So we build – what? Usable bridges, whether between abstract ideas or between people, becoming aligned in love, joy, compassion, serenity. We aim to disengage and so control negative feelings, changing and transforming the energy as we recognise that the inside and the outside are one. We learn to see ourselves more as others do, looking with honesty and openness, discovering what we are. Good and bad may be revealed; but good, bad or indifferent, we can accept this as fact. We know we can change.

These workshops explore mysteries

Workshop I examines mysteries of consciousness, identity and energy. It deals with the conscious ego and the outer world, understanding how the personality works and the relations between conscious and unconscious, ego and Self. It offers basic models of the structure and organisation of psychology, mapping consciousness and the dynamic interactions within the psyche, looking at common patterns and problems. We put 'I want' side by side with 'I need', sensing priorities, balancing the organism and the environment, the need for solitude and for participation in the world.

Workshop II looks at the contra-sexual sides of ourselves, the mysteries of polarity and relationship, projection and the impulse to become whole. We grapple with the duality implicit in our being. The workshop is not so much about women and men, as about the masculine and feminine present within each one of us. We claim and own not 'either this or that', but *both*. And we look at our own symptoms as symbols.

In Workshop III, patterns and cycles emerge, energies and qualities. We explore the mystery of archetypes (queen, father, ruler, priestess, priest-healer, philosopher, maiden, idealist, artist, magician, for instance), asking which of them affect our own lives. It's as if we put the map on the floor and stand on it – another dimension, this. It is a profounder, deeper journey. The first two workshops looked up and out, within and down: the self reaching towards the Self. In this third one, some descending lines have been established, down from the Transpersonal, back from the Self to us.

And on ...

Ian Gordon-Brown
1996

xxviii   THE RAINCLOUD OF KNOWABLE THINGS

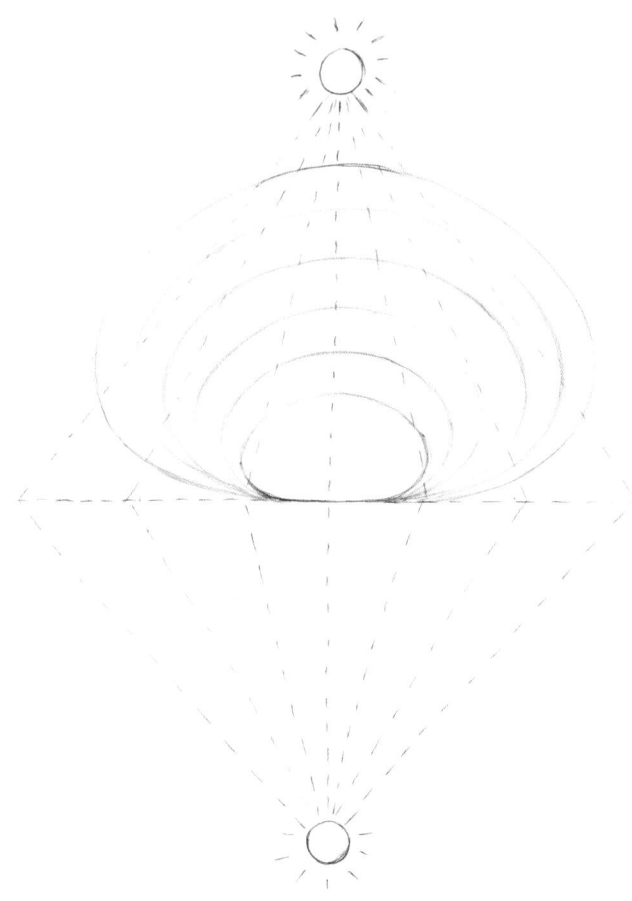

Hand-rendered drawing of the Onion Map: Alison Gaffney

PART I
Introductory Workshops

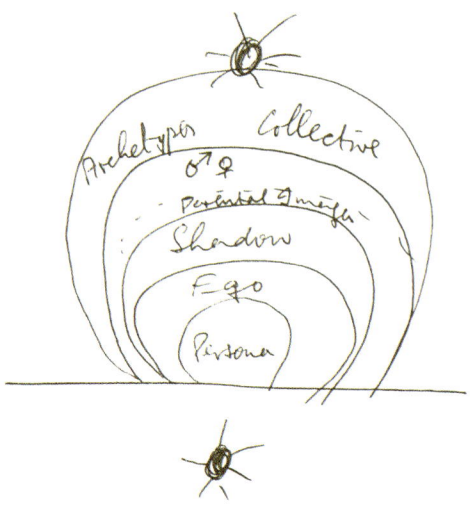

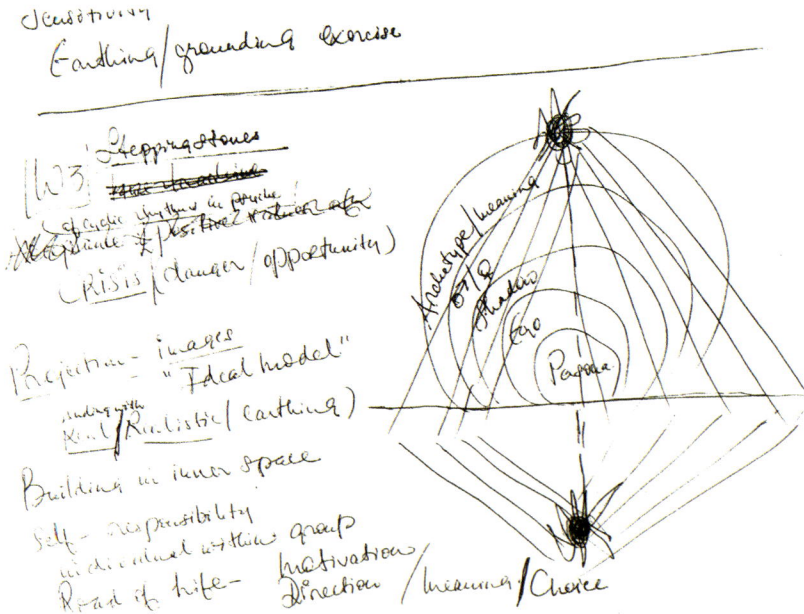

Facsimiles of notes – top: Ian Gordon-Brown, bottom: Barbara Somers.

CHAPTER ONE

Approaching The Self

Workshop I

Ian Gordon-Brown and Barbara Somers

We do have a transpersonal Self – or perhaps, indeed, it has us[1]

INTRODUCING THE WORKSHOP [2]

Three Mysteries

The mystery of consciousness. This first Workshop is about our relation to the unconscious. How far do we suppress, repress or censor what it brings up? Who controls us – is it in fact our conscious mind, as we like to believe? Freud, Jung, Assagioli would indicate that it is largely the *un*conscious. Consciousness, like an island in the ocean of the unconscious or, to change the metaphor, like the vast, submerged, invisible part of an iceberg, has many dimensions. Four main organs of consciousness are available to us: our bodies, our emotions, our minds and our intuition, that extra-sensory perception whose pervasive nature belongs not so much to the individual as to the collective. Beyond them in the unconscious lie the will, the spirit, and more. The psyche aims towards a full relationship, a flow between conscious and unconscious, until ultimately all is contained in the Self.

The mystery of identity. Who am I? We may see ourselves as parent or child, even as adult. However, we are more. Most of us have multiple identifications – with our bodies, our emotions, our minds. But, 'I am not my body, not my emotions, not my mind, though I often

---

1   These quotations at the heads of chapters and sections are from Ian Gordon-Brown or Barbara Somers throughout, unless otherwise indicated.
2   If those running the workshop are following the suggested programmes (pp.381-385), they need, at the outset, to remind people that (preferably) all the workshops make three fresh starts, Friday, Saturday and Sunday (it is well to make the start times '6 for 6.30 pm.' or '9.30 for 10 am.', and to begin very promptly). Endings are at 10 pm. 6 pm. and 2 pm. respectively. There are breaks for refreshment and change of energy, and time set aside for sharing material that comes up. Such sharing is always optional. You may wish to start with a short time of quiet, to light a candle if that suits your style, and to have time for brief personal introductions. Some notes on the running of aspects of this workshop are given in Appendices 1, 2 and 3. Ed.

identify with them. I am not even my intuition'. What am I? Perhaps I am a seed, growing into, becoming what life intends me to be, seeking form, structure, meaning, significance and spiritual utility. Happy those apple seeds planted among their own kind – for often a perfectly good apple tree finds itself growing up in a forest of oak.[3]

The mystery of energy. Consciousness is an energy, and energy is neutral. We are receivers, transformers, distributors, even generators of energy. Negative energies such as resentment, jealousy, doubt, anxiety, all have their positive manifestations. We can read anger as the energy of frustrated purpose; jealousy as thwarted love and the need for love; doubt as a desire for clear objectivity; fear as a necessary caution arising from heightened perception. Anxiety is excitement without the oxygen.

The unconscious speaks

We are each on a personal journey through life, starting before birth, going on after death. On this continuous journey the everyday personality moves as it were horizontally, establishing itself and assuming various different ways of being for different occasions – like different hats. For many people, this personal, *horizontal* journey seems to be enough. But for others, it is just not satisfactory. They are restless, seeking something, they don't know what. Experiencing the depth, or the height, of things, they long for a quality not found in the world around them. Profoundly touched by music, art, literature, religion, nature, they may resonate to myth, fairy tale, stories of height and of depth. They are seeking a *vertical* journey.

'Lift up your hearts!' we are enjoined. Sometimes we cannot. Weary of looking upwards towards the heavens, we may be forced *down* beneath the level surface of personal life into a depth of crisis – an accident perhaps, a loss, a failure of health or relationship. At these critical moments, 'breakdown' may be the sheer breaking up of everything we have known. And, for the less aware, things may remain broken up for a long time. However, if we trust the process, this break-up may turn into a breakthrough. Seeking a way back from the depths, we are taken through a passage and the future opens. The journey is now in a different dimension: towards the other Self, the Self with a capital S – the soul, the psyche, call it what you will.[4] The vertical line is that of the *trans*personal, unconscious inner Self. It meets and

---

3   See Somers & Gordon-Brown 2002, *Journey in Depth*, p. 26
4   Terms used interchangeably and freely are: the inner world, the higher Self, the inner Self, the other Self, the transpersonal Centre. Ed.

crosses with the personal, horizontal journey of the conscious ego. We are at the intersection.

How does the unconscious speak to us?

How does the internal voice of the transpersonal Self make itself heard? Often with difficulty. Throughout history, the unconscious psyche has spoken to humans in many ways. To understand the languages of the unconscious, we must return to the source. Modern Western man focuses on his body and his mind; here he has his being, this is what he thinks he is. Although this assumption is now being to an extent readjusted, we still need to learn, or relearn, some of the languages of the inner world. They are not only of the mind but of primitive instinct, of the body, emotion, intuition; not only of the masculine principle, but also, profoundly, of the feminine.

The unconscious speaks to us through our *body-language* – the body is a symbol of the psyche. Someone's foot taps as they deny their anger; another's head shakes even as they say, 'Yes, I agree!' Freud points to the *slip of the tongue* as manifestation of unconscious desires: 'I'm happy to declare this meeting closed – er, I'm sorry – open!' Embarrassingly we refer to, 'those half-baked – I mean, those heart-based mystics!'

Sometimes, again, we catch ourselves in the most *uncharacteristic behaviour*. Tidy people lose things, leave things behind. Those with elephant memories forget, the obsessive miss the train or leave the door open for the burglars. 'How could I?' we ask. 'I don't know what got into me!'

There are *repeating patterns*; once again we've chased the same type of unsuitable lover, or boss, or job. Outside events keep marking our lives – burglaries, redundancies, accidents. Things happening to the body may also make statements from the unconscious. To break your Achilles tendon if you are a dancer seems like tragedy, but for one colleague it sounded a note of freedom, heralding a welcome change.

Illness and pain are sometimes experienced not as the disasters they appear from outside, even if they end in death, but as the kindly hand of fate introducing us to a different, richer and more profound relationship with the world. 'Nothing better could have happened to me,' said one woman, who died a few weeks later.

Our *hunches*, expressions of intuition, the unknown wisdom of the Self, may urge us to act, and only much later do we see the sense.

Sometimes the unconscious speaks directly through *fate*. Indeed,

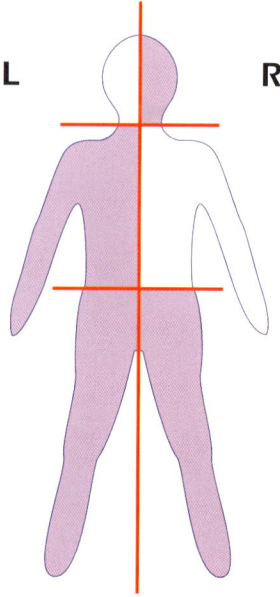

Chart 1:01 – Splits

there seems to be a law: when a conflict is unconscious, it acts on us from the outside, like destiny. Those who narrowly escape terrible disasters, natural or man-made, are often convinced fate saved them.

Many people are as it were *split*. Happily unconscious, some are split across the middle. Assuming all is taboo below, they may remain largely unconscious of it and scarcely move their hips, which become thick and solid. Others live *only* there. Some are split at the neck; existing only above it, they are completely unaware of their bodies, which dangle along purely to keep their heads up. They barely know what their bodies feel like, or when they are cold or tired, hungry or uncomfortable. One person said, 'I feel I'm this computer – and I'm sitting above a pain in the neck!' Yet others are split down the middle, their rationally thinking right hands and left brains divorced from their intuitively feeling left hands and right brains.[5] They may remain unaware of the less dominant side, till they try drawing or writing with their least favourite hand. We are largely unconscious of all these shadowy parts of our bodies.

---

5   See Chart 2:01, Left and Right Brain, p. 74.

Dreams express the unconscious particularly vividly; they need processing, incubating and containing – and not to be exposed too readily to the light of day. If dark and frightening figures emerge, remember that psychological forces are neutral, or tending towards the light. Behind the negative there will lie the positive. Anyway, such triggers operate only when we are ready, so fear is out of place. Rather than running away, turn and face it in imagination and it may transform into an astonishingly life-affirming instrument of the psyche. Instead of escaping into the light, seek to take light down into the darkness.

Symbols often speak to us from the unconscious. Frogs and princes, stunted figures, magicians, wise women and helpful animals emerge from myths, legends and fairy tales. Symbolic images appear, indicating transitions towards wholeness, relating the lower to the higher: circles, squares, flowers – the rose, the lotus. Truly transpersonal symbols – the divine child, for instance – may come up. Inwardly we test their significance: from what level do they come, and with what energy? They usually have highly specific meanings – and not always the ones given in the books. Note the age and life-condition of the person whose symbol it is. The symbol is not (always) the reality. Distinguish between archetype and stereotype. Test its truth through visualising it; name and define it and eventually begin to crystallise its energy.

The unconscious also speaks through *transcendent experiences* – of power, of light, of love. In these peak experiences, the little 'me' fades out (without effort, for *it* does it). All at once the barriers fall; through some different organ of perception we glimpse the universe as a beneficent, integrated whole. Detached from everyday reality, we become one with all, temporarily losing our separate identity. In this receptive state we are amazed by such at-one-ness with the unity of the cosmos. Such times are a sharing, a *participation mystique*. From this perspective the cosmos is seen as good in its own right, evil a mere temporary limitation. Polarities and splits are left behind, negative emotions fade out and are lost, time and space transcended. Briefly, we are in touch with the transpersonal Self. Life has purpose. Things fall into place. Such timeless moments of full attention can change our lives, bringing profound after-effects. Meaning becomes clear and we are full of awe, wonder and joy. These experiences are their own justification. And they are much more usual than we may think.

And, as we've seen, it's also through the mundane events of *everyday life* that the Self reaches towards us and speaks.

How do we speak to the unconscious?

It's not all one-way. If we listen, dialogue, use imagination, develop an attentive sensitivity within the moment, then is there not a mutual communication? Aware of our bodies, we sense into our energy levels, posture, movement, any pressures, tensions or symptoms. Aware of our feelings, we first identify and then begin to dis-identify with our emotional centre. Through our minds – receptive, reflective, creative as they are – we may reach towards the inner world. Through our intuition we pay attention, listening to its symbols. We are encouraged by four things: firstly, we can learn to *listen*; secondly, to acknowledge the possibility of an *inner* as well as an outer journey, recognising the thresholds and frontiers, plateaux, oceans, mountains and valleys of the inner world; thirdly, to become aware of the *positive* thrust of the unconscious; and finally, to understand that we do have a *transpersonal Self* – or perhaps, indeed, *it has us*.

In this workshop we shall explore our own relation to the unconscious – a little and gently. How does the inner world speak to *me*? Through my instincts, body, emotions, mind? Am I in tune with my intuition? If it should speak, what may be done about it? For many of us, habitually motivated by what we think we *should* be doing, 'I ought to, it's my duty!' has long been all-pervasive. In excess, this leads to the repression, suppression and censoring of a great deal of what we are. Polarised, trapped between the opposites, our legitimate energy is drained away. Nothing need be regarded as 'bad'. There is no judgment, no blame. Rather – have a go, let go, find joy in discovery.

Throughout, introspection will be invited by the use of *active imagination* or guided daydream, drawing on our power to create images. The exercises offered are powerful tools for accelerating development; they invite archetypal symbols – water, earth, mountain, rock, tree, cup, sword – to illuminate theory and help towards self-discovery. Be prepared for a confrontation with the Self within. It may generate negative figures, which lead in turn not only to positive figures, but to consciousness and meaning. So, listen, hear, love and accept what is being said – and, if it is appropriate, do something about it. We have times for general and small group discussion, aiming to relate theory and practice in personal terms. You are invited to share with each other if it feels right for you – although the primary

APPROACHING THE SELF

encounter is with yourself and you can of course decline to disclose. There is absolutely no pressure – life is pressure enough. The Self knows best about this; trust it.

MAPS OF THE PSYCHE

The map is not the country

The Transpersonal is an attitude to the possibility of living in several dimensions at once. For the journey of self-discovery towards and into these other dimensions, maps are useful; though, while sound theory is essential, it's well to remember that the map is not the country. A map is like a bridge; we assume there is land over the bridge and we need to know, at least a bit, what it is like. Our present maps are crude, like the early world-maps; but, though primitive and inadequate, they're

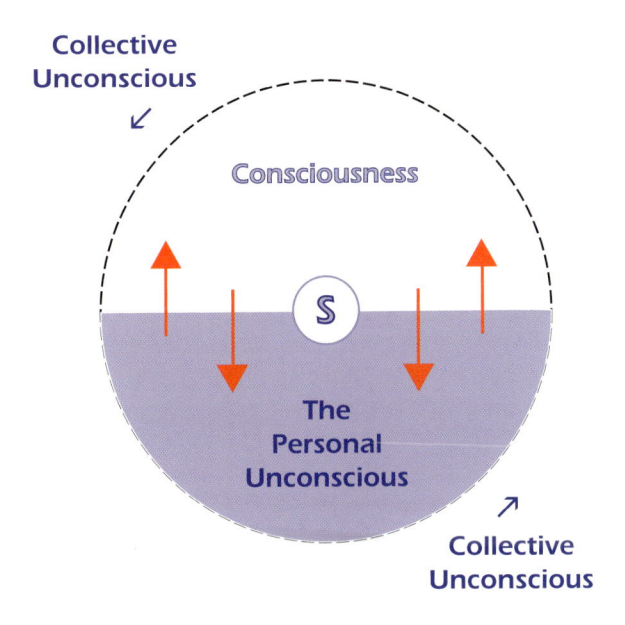

Chart 1:02 – Jung's Map 1

useful – after all, though aiming for India we did find America.

Jung's Map

People generally come into counselling with a presenting problem. From this they can move many ways, for there are many paths of growth. Some will take a religious path, some a more mystical one, others will follow a course of action. Many will go in, go deep, go down. Based on the work of Carl Jung, this map of the Self, like the following ones, charts the territory. It shows the depths and the heights, consciousness above, the unconscious below. The collective unconscious surrounds the map, indicating that far more is unconscious than conscious. It is not that we have an unconscious, but that *the unconscious has us*. Racial, tribal memories and archetypes are in the lower half; the Self is in the centre and within, largely engulfed by the personal unconscious. Remember this Other in the core and heart of us, this Self. It has a mediating function in the ever-changing

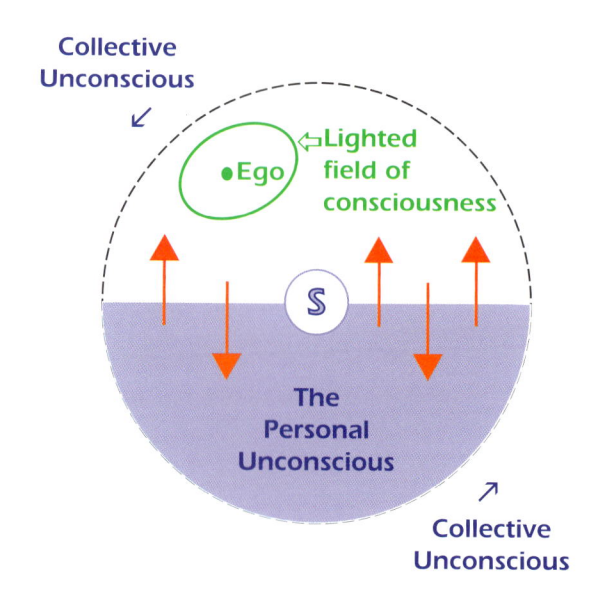

Chart 1:03 – Jung's Map 2

circle; for the psyche has to keep in movement, and it is the Self which regulates its constant flow. The whole map radiates like a sun.

The map shows the little 'ego' as separate from the Self, a small island near the top. Jung said that consciousness is a lighted field on which the ego floats, as on an ocean. The Self and other forces try to get through from the unconscious – 'the sea upon which the ego rides like a ship'. But the primordial world of the psyche is not lost; as the sea laps the continents round like islands, so our individual consciousness is pressed around by original unconsciousness.[6] In the Self, a tremendous thrust to wholeness and completeness is apparent. It seems to abhor lopsidedness: focus too much up and outwards, and we get warnings to look within; too much in and downwards, warnings come the other way. If we are on treadmills, we have symptoms which tell us to stop; if we become too other-worldly, we are made to anchor

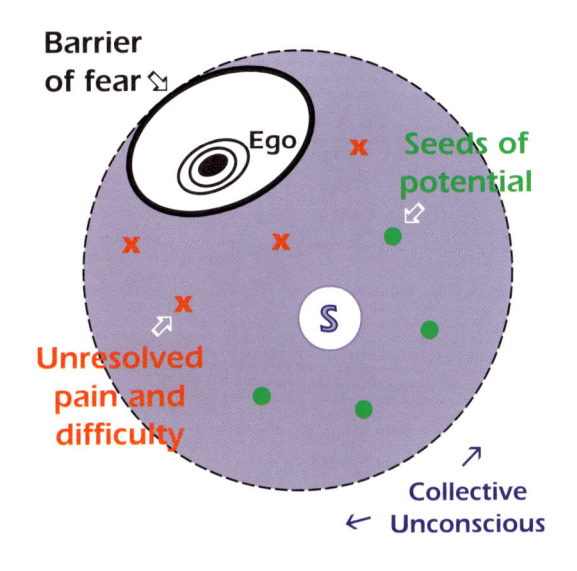

Chart 1:04 – Jung's Map 3

---

6   See Jung 1933-1934, *The Meaning of Psychology for Modern Man*. CW 10, para 285.

and ground ourselves. The art of living is to listen to the images, crises and physical effects that come from the inner world; then, instead of 'either this or that', we learn to say, 'both this and that'.

Jung's map very often gets distorted, at least in the modern Western world. The small ego becomes the recognised centre, the unconscious spreads by repression and the Self is lost in the unconscious. A barrier of fear comes to surround the small field of consciousness, protecting it against the unconscious, which has become full of unresolved pain and difficulty; we are unaware of the seeds of potential within it. Yet, like a shy animal, the personal psyche runs spiral-wise round this central point, frightened yet fascinated, always in flight yet drawing steadily closer to this virtually unknowable centre, whose qualities become ever more distinct. Like a magnet, it draws the disparate parts of the unconscious, gradually capturing them as in a crystal lattice. Then all our intensely personal troubles seem nothing but complications, petty excuses for our hesitant timidity as we shrink from facing this uncanny crystallisation with all its final strangeness.[7]

Assagioli's Egg Map

This map is taken from Roberto Assagioli. Around the 'egg' of the psyche the boundaries are permeable, allowing energy in and out. Again, the collective unconscious of the race lies around the outside. The dot in the middle indicates a point of pure consciousness, and the field of everyday awareness and experience lies around it like the buckle on a belt.

Assagioli talks more about *levels* of the unconscious than Jung does, positing a lower, middle and upper unconscious. The immediate or *middle unconscious* takes up the whole of the central 'belt' section; this is where we find our delayed-action surface memory, accessible with a time-lag.

Below is the *lower unconscious*. According to Freud, this is where material too painful, too irrelevant, too unacceptable is stored. Through repression, we are likely to make the line dividing this area from the field of everyday awareness become impermeable. Indeed, the lower unconscious has often been thought of as 'the dustbin of the psyche', full of expendable stuff locked away; and certainly we do sometimes need to look back at our shadow. However, once

---

7   See Jung 1944, *Psychology and Alchemy*, CW 12, para 325-6.

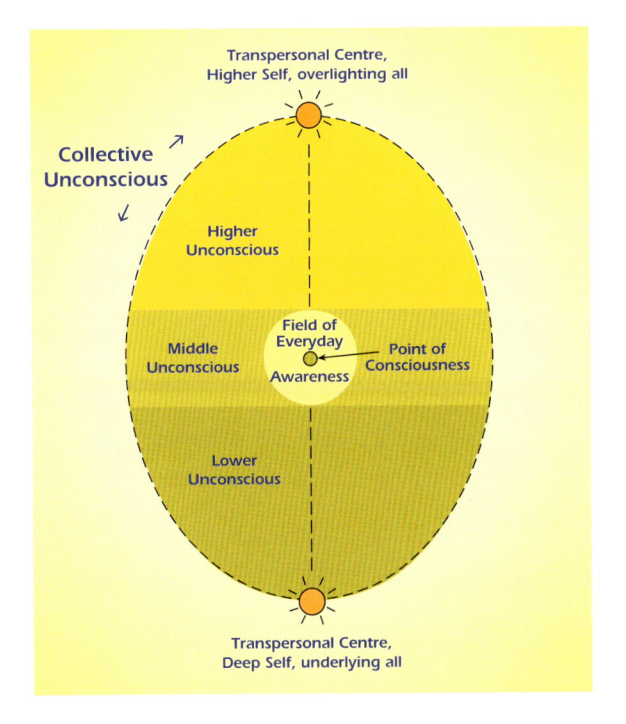

Chart 1:05 – Assagioli's Egg 1

communication is established it becomes a compost heap and, as we saw in Jung's map, its richness can nurture the seeds of our future creative potential.

The *higher unconscious* is the seedbed from which come inspiration, intuitive flashes, future knowledge. This upper, or deeper, *supra-conscious*, level, overlying and underlying all, doesn't just lie on the top but permeates through. This is where we could put *samadhi*.[8] It is the inner area from which come flashes of intuition. It holds our future potential, that which lies just beyond reach, the evolution of consciousness. Here we meet Patanjali's 'raincloud of knowable things' being processed in the present and moving back into the past.[9] But we remember that this map too is not the country.

Assagioli placed a symbol for *the Self* above even this. Here at the top of the egg, with the sun indicating the mystery of the Other, *nirvana* could be mapped.

---

8 Samadhi: a Vedic/Indian/Sanscrit term: a non-dualistic, one-pointed state where the consciousness of the experiencing subject becomes one with the object experienced.
9 Bailey 1927, *The Light of the Soul: The Yoga Sutras of Patanjali*, Book IV, Sutra 29, p. 425. See n. 291 below.

However, Transpersonal psychology adds to Assagioli's map. Unlike some other psychologies, it holds that in each one of us the Self – that which chooses the life – both knows and intervenes. So we map the transpersonal Self not only at the top, but also *down* below the bottom of the egg. Thus we map the link both up from and *down to* the Self – from 'me', the little everyday ego. The Self is about the deep; it goes into the depths. We need to be clear about the difference between the two centres: the small, personal 'I' in the middle, and the higher Self, here mapped at top *and* bottom.

Chart 1:06 – Assagioli's Egg 2

Our first task is to develop the field of everyday consciousness in the middle of the diagram; very creative people are much wider than most in the area of their immediate awareness – take Leonardo da Vinci, or Teilhard de Chardin. Then the process of individuation is about making an inner bridge at will, from 'me' to the transpersonal

Self, journeying along the path between till finally, in Christ, and Buddha, and Krishna, the higher Self has taken over and radiates on all mankind (as in the lower part of the map).

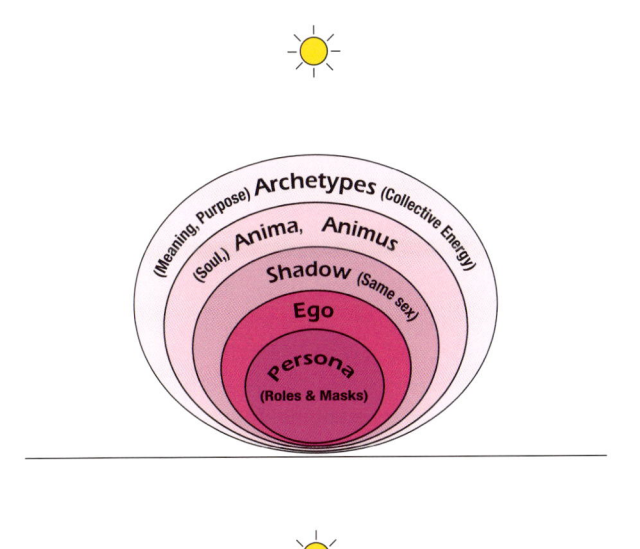

Chart 1:07 – The Onion Map 1

This map shows onion-like growth-rings in the dynamics of the personality. The conscious ego emerges upward from behind a mask, holds the unconscious at bay and begins to integrate the more consciously-functioning aspects of the psyche – again, like the rings in a tree trunk. These images are seen by us, not imposed from outside. To assume they have meaning and that, by evoking them, we may come to a deeper sense of meaning in life at large, is to start to know who we are. Talking with them, befriending them, we can be led back closer to our own basic purpose. We take the layers of the onion from the inside out:

> *The Persona.* The inside layer is about roles and masks. 'Persona' comes from *per sonare*, referring to the ancient Greek actors who held theatre masks in front of their faces and 'sounded through' them. A well-functioning *persona* deals with social interchange. When we have to compromise between inner needs and outer demands, the persona aids our adaptation. We need more than one persona for different occasions. They

need to fit, accommodating to how the inner person likes to appear outwardly, bearing on our ideal model of ourselves. They should be relevant to our physical and psychological capacities and limitations. Functioning well – flexible, adaptable – they defend our inner vulnerability. We need them. With no mask, the pure and living spirit would be unbearable: Arjuna asked Sri Krishna to drop his veil, and he did, and there was chaos. Swiftly Arjuna asked for the veil back.

However, they must be removable at will. Get stuck in them and they become rigid, so that our inner potential may atrophy, risking disorder. The rigidity of the mask can be a key to psychological health. Someone riveted in a job-persona – a teacher, say – may never leave it; locked in, trapped, they see only through the role, looking at everyone else as if they too were just masks. Some masks are inadequate or inappropriate: someone stuck behind a persona that is always 'nice' and good-natured is left with their hidden rage and violence. They need help to see that 'good and bad' are less important than light and dark, inner and outer, and that both are acceptable. What does the mask conceal, hide, protect? 'If you didn't have the power to hate, you wouldn't have the power to love.'

The Ego. If images followed the map, it would be very simple; but they come from all levels and in any order. However, to take the next onion-layer: the Self incarnates as this 'I', this 'me myself', this *ego* constellated in the world. Behind the masks and roles of the persona, this is the one who supports and wears the masks. In its turn it is responsive to the layers of the unconscious above, sensing the shadow, the masculine and feminine, even the archetypal energies around. And the Self itself.

The ego may try to hold the unconscious altogether at bay, turning only towards the everyday world; yet, if it become aware, the unconscious can dance together with consciousness. Looking both ways, it can arbitrate and make a bridge between objective and subjective. We can talk of having established a personality when we have an ego-centre broadly capable of managing our reactions both to the outer world and to the emerging unconscious forces. This *ego-personality* is my self with a small s, an aspect or partial expression of the Self, its instrument, the means by which the Self relates to the world of conscious living.

The Shadow. That which is not in the light of consciousness may be a bright shadow; but it's rarely bright at first. When in our inner exploration we pass through and from the outer world, we often see a dark face looking from the mirror. Gradually we come to realise that this is really our projection of the Self. In the meantime, it can be bewildering, shaming and very shaking. We need someone to give us care and respect, standing midway between conscious and unconscious, holding it for us, trusting the process – and always with humour.

Parental Images. For every child, the parents were gods. From this we gained our sense of masculine and feminine. Then, like dragon-gods, they began to hold us back. We often need help to face them now and confront how we actually felt. The *image* of mother is wider and more collective than the mother herself. No matter how much we love our real parents, the womb is the devouring sea-monster and the image of father is as ogre and tyrant. Duty, love and despair constellate. Our relationships carry it. Again, we hope to meet someone who will stand and hold it, someone able to say, 'It's all right to be like that.' Then in the end we come to see our parents as – just people.

Archetypal Levels. Beyond the parents lies this collective layer. We must not identify with an archetype, but relate to it, which is a different matter (otherwise a person might feel they had actually *become* for example the Christ or the goddess). There may be a further permeable ring outside even that, away into the unconscious above.

The journey towards the centre is not only about the search for the Self; it is also about how the Self uses the person in the world. And that is generally after some mid-life crisis.

SHORT EXPLORATION
TWO QUESTIONS ABOUT MYSELF
(10 minutes)

[Now follows the first example of imaging. It introduces, or re-introduces, people to the process of contacting their own inner world, and of sharing with someone else. Those running the workshop need to emphasise that the sharing is optional. Invite people to sit comfortably and symmetrically, close their eyes, relinquish 'thinking about' things, and allow whatever emerges. The two questions each need to be repeated. Ed.]

You are invited now to go inside yourself and reflect on these two questions:
> What has led you to look deeper and explore beyond the surface of life?
> At times of crisis, what has brought you through?
> (The crisis itself? A dream, an image, a person, a symptom? Or?)

You may wish to write it down, and perhaps share what came up with someone else.

[This is a good place for a break; important for changing the energies. The exploration which now follows needs enough space for people to lie down. They need materials for drawing to hand, and to know in advance about the timing: each question will be given about six minutes, including time for them to record, in pictures preferably, and also in words. Ed.]

EXPLORATION
THE TRAVELLER ON LIFE'S JOURNEY
(45 minutes)

The hero or heroine, pilgrim or explorer, sees life as a quest.

The main question behind this exploration is, *Where are you going?* We shall use *imaging*. It is helpful to understand the difference between *imaging* (the use of 'active imagination' or the 'guided daydream') and *visualisation*, which is focusing the attention on something given. If, say, you are asked to imagine a blue cow – and you can do it – then that's visualisation. Imaging, on the other hand, is a relaxed, receptive, attentive state, a conscious daydream, letting your *own* images come to you.[10]

Trust the imaging process, then images will come. Take the first image that appears, without censoring. Whatever comes up is not a fixed state but a cut across the inner world now, today. *Negative figures* are good to have; till you are ready to meet them, they do not present themselves. The energy locked up with them can be released into your life.

---

10 Commentary on the Traveller exploration, Appendix 2. Imaging and visualisation in general, Chapter 6, p. 256.

The speed with which you get a response to the input doesn't matter – some will inevitably find it too fast and others too slow. *How* do you get your answers? As pictures; as a word or phrase; a body movement, a kick in the solar plexus, a tension in the head? If *nothing* comes, gently ask the help of your mind. Later, it may be appropriate to draw the 'nothing', to record it. In any case, record your response when you get it, preferably in pictures, words too if you wish, noting any body sensations or emotions that arise. You may later wish to share whatever comes up; if not, honour your feeling; things too tender or newborn for the light of day positively should not be shared.

If the light of the reason is the sun, we now need moonlight and stars. So abandon clarity and go into the dimness of your inner world, rich with symbols. Put your logical mind aside and, lying down, centre down, let your body unwind and feel it giving way, relaxing in your own special way. Again, trust the process; the Self knows best and there is time and space now to let it work its magic.

Take about six minutes to ask yourself each question, and as soon as you get an answer, sit up and record it. First, have an image of yourself as a traveller. You are on life's journey. You may see yourself as a pilgrim or explorer – a heroine or hero – setting out on life's quest.

The seven questions:

[Each point may be repeated more than once to enable participants to hold the question or instruction with clarity. This is true of all the imaging explorations in the book.]

Minutes[11]

  6 1.   First, invite an image for yourself as an explorer travelling through life. What is your name, how are you dressed, and what do you sense to be your most essential quality, or qualities?

  6 2.   As you set out from now, all that has been is past. What are you most glad to leave behind? What do you most wish to bring forward with you?

  6 3.   Where, as traveller, do you really want to go? What is your true quest or goal?

  6 4.   What most prevents you, the traveller, from going where

---

11 It is important to allow the full time suggested; give a reminder a minute or so before moving on. Insights often emerge during the final minute.

you really want to go; what is your major obstacle at this time? Note any feelings or body sensations which that question arouses.

6 5. What do you need to develop within yourself to get you where you really want to go?

6 6. On the journey of life, the traveller often changes without realising it. Go deep within and ask yourself: 'Who am I?'

6 7. Now be more deeply in touch with your own Self. There is one final question: Recognising who you are, and who you might become, see if there is some small next step on the journey of your life which you might decide to take.

You may find it helpful to go into the foetal position. Yawn and stretch, change your energies first; then sit up. Number your responses, and we'll give you the questions again to remind you. There will be the chance to share tomorrow. This is the first opportunity to dialogue with yourself. On Saturday it's about meeting a 'wise person'. On Sunday you *become* the wise observer.

SUB-PERSONALITIES

*If something has been locked in the coal-cellar for years,
it will naturally be somewhat shadowy and annoyed when released*

How do we think about our own and other people's self-images? Where once we observed traits and humours, now we measure psychological characteristics and adopt theories about types. Note George Kelley, who asked, 'How do you construct yourself?'[12] Later we shall look at Jung's 'Four Functions' model, noting how we perceive and judge the world through sensation, feeling, thinking and intuition, and how these may be associated with different kinds of people.[13]

One perspective is that our self-image is constructed from our *sub-personalities*. These are semi-autonomous 'beings' or compensatory functions from the unconscious. They usually represent unlived portions of our lives. Every person is, as it were, an assemblage of these sub-personalities. Discussion never ceases among them. Many

---
12 George Kelley also said, 'If you want to know what's wrong with a person, why not ask him?' Kelley's Personal Construct theory, see Appendices 4 and 13.
13 The Four Functions, p. 48. Ways of mapping the personality, Appendix 4.

are apparently negative in energy; they are not usually permitted to be either positive or creative. Indeed, each may be an interior image of anti-serenity, repeating its message, often a composite of parental scripts, over and over again. When they are in play, we find ourselves asking, 'Is this truly me – what am I doing this *for*? What do I *really* want to do – what in all this is worth keeping?'

Sub-personalities are usually incomplete; for instance, they may show as being largely physical rather than emotional, or vice versa. They arise in a variety of ways. Some of them come from the roles we play (for example, brother, nurse, boss); new roles arise with new circumstances. Sometimes they come straight from our immediate *personal unconscious*. The question, 'Whatever came over me?' may arise and trigger something here: 'Why on earth am I doing this *again*?'

The sub-personalities may represent inner or outer *conflicts*; for instance, the doctor within a person may be at war with the wife or the artist who is also in that person. Feeling fragmented and torn, we oscillate between the demands of each. Or, if we stop this dithering, it's only because we have become stuck in the role of one or the other. Stereotypically, we settle for being either this *or* that. The well-balanced person, on the other hand, is the one who will flow, who adopts roles and relinquishes them as necessary – who has them but *is not* them. The true person within each of us can say, 'Yes. Both this *and* that.'

Sub-personalities may emerge less as real people than as *fantasy images*, figures not necessarily rooted in everyday life at all: superman, good fairy, bad wolf.

Or again, a deep archetypal pattern may emerge from the *collective unconscious* – a legendary figure: Medusa, the Serpent, Leviathan. They're not all negative: Psyche, the Earth Mother, the feminine Muse may come up, or Pegasus, or the archetypal masculine Master-builder. Maybe a wise counsellor will appear, or a gardener; or perhaps one with an all-seeing, visionary eye – a profound, transpersonal figure, male or female.

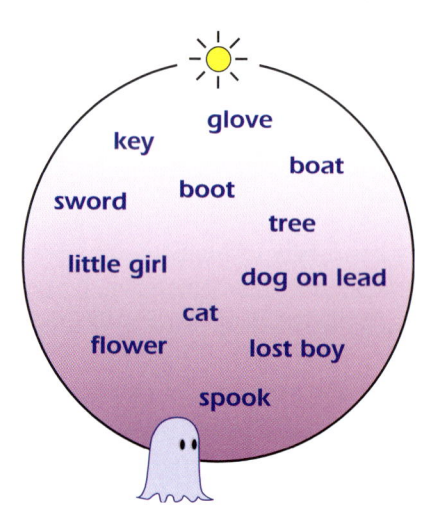

Chart 1:08 – Some Possible Sub-Personalities

Our sub-personalities are *symbols*. They do not necessarily emerge as people; they may well show as objects – a key, a sword, a boat, stone, fence, tree, flower, a wall, a cup. They often appear as animals, so you might have a bird, say, or a dog on a lead, a cat, a wolf, a snake. A spook may well appear – indeed, any of these inner, semi-autonomous figures can be dark and a bit scary. Dark figures which come up from the lower unconscious represent something not yet known: if something has been locked in the coal-cellar for years, it will naturally be somewhat grubby and annoyed when released. It is not necessarily horrible. Try to find out what it is about. Welcome its appearing. Let it out; say 'Thank God!' instead of spending energy on keeping it in captivity. Turn and face difficult figures and they often transform themselves into helpers. And so we are filled with energy.

The feminine is mapped in the round.[14] It needs a circular artist's palette, while a list, ordered and straight, better suits the masculine. The Self in the centre is circled by some sub-personalities that may be around for men as well as women – we can all find ourselves being run by one or other of them. Each except the last has a positive and a negative aspect:

---

14 More detail in Chapter 2, Chart 2:03, The Eternal Feminine, p. 77.

Chart 1:09 – Some Feminine Sub-Personalities

There's the *little girl* who has never really grown up. Though naturally playful, joyous, innocent, spontaneous, alive and free, yet she may become the unhappy child if things have gone wrong in her relationship with her mother; then, kicking against the feminine, she doesn't grow up but remains around – manipulative, demanding, 'me first', perhaps very angry.

The maiden if all is well will be aesthetic, tender, with a deep knowledge of earth. However, if things have gone wrong with her father she may become a tease, a siren, seductress, temptress. As a sub-personality she will remain young and stay around, perhaps as sensual, sexual playmate, emerging on suitable or unsuitable occasions.

The *vocational* or *career woman*, often very intelligent, is companion and co-builder with other people. If things are well she remains linear, well-focused, organised, brotherly. However, majoring in this to the exclusion of other feminine aspects, this sub-personality can become aggressive, offering opinions in a harsh, tinny voice; loving power, she might fight *against*, not *for*, people and causes.

Then there's the *mother*, the enabler, tender nurturer, all-nourishing one. However, someone believing she is *only* maternal is bereft, like the grieving goddess Demeter, as her children leave home. This sub-personality cannot live fully while her child is lost; if she becomes bitter, she will makes her husband impotent, de-feminise her daughters and capture her sons.

Psyche is a mysterious goddess. Inspirer, muse and leader-forth of men, she is Ariadne to Theseus, showing him the way in the dark. She is Beatrice to Dante. She is intuitive soul, inner guide. Things can go wrong with her too; as sub-personality, she may become the alluring deceptrice – the witch – full of murky hunches, leading men astray with siren's song.

The *wise woman* is a composite figure, a reflection of the Centre. Androgynous midwife, healer, village herbalist and layer-out of the dead, she leads people deep into their inner world, helping them discover their most hidden and essential part. Beautiful, mature, humorous and grounded, archetypal – more than a sub-personality – she has no dark side. She has gone beyond the feminine to the earth; and yet the sun shines on her.

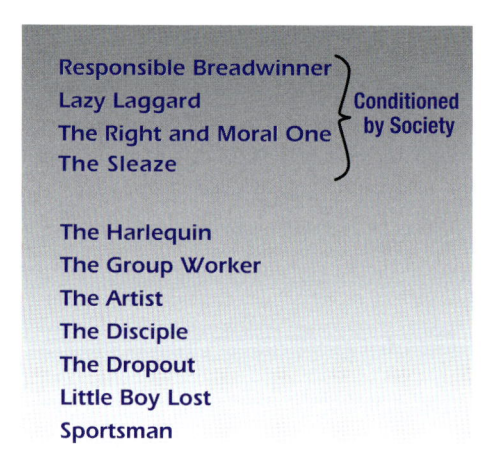

Responsible Breadwinner ⎫
Lazy Laggard   ⎬ Conditioned
The Right and Moral One ⎭ by Society
The Sleaze

The Harlequin
The Group Worker
The Artist
The Disciple
The Dropout
Little Boy Lost
Sportsman

Chart 1:10 – Some Masculine Sub-Personalities

Unlike the feminine ones, these may be set out in linear mode. The first four conditioned, stereotypical images often emerge among the sub-personalities of a middle-aged man. The son of average, middle-of-the-road parents, let's say, he was brought up to *achieve* at all costs, especially without appearing to try – and to do it through the mind. Thus at school, at least as a boy, he found that being good meant doing well – and doing well meant being loved. Growing up, he realised it is hard to love an unsuccessful child, so part of him remained centred in *becoming* something. Desiring to do better meant guilt, which led to altruism. Now, since only positive feelings were allowed the child, so no negative feelings are allowed the adult.

Several sub-personalities may dominate this man. Unaware that all this is only a part of him, he believes he *is* the *responsible breadwinner*, motivated towards mental achievement, having only positive feelings. Embarrassingly, however, this character won't stay around. It oscillates with the *laggard*, who lives in the country, lies about and is full of dry wit – which responsible breadwinners aren't. Favouring leisure, characterised by a half-conscious sadness and not keen on doing anything much, this lazy one is content with being. The man's wife chases him for his idleness; inner as well as outer conflict follows. And while he oscillates between the two, his gut is being torn apart. There may also be a middle-class *moralist*, keen to do what is right, with religious feelings founded in fear – not true religion, this, but dread and guilt. The cheerful *sleaze* comes out on men-only occasions (one such aptly named himself the Happy Bastard); such a character may also be characterised by cynicism, sexuality, rebellion, anger, sensuality.

Other half-familiar sub-personalities may appear: the *little boy lost*, torn between positive and negative feelings, racked with fear and guilt, full of the need for love and understanding; also the *critic*, the *pedant*, the *know-all*, each representing scripts into which the person has been trapped, each to do with becoming, not with being. To be run by them is to live the provisional life.

Where is the feminine side? And what about the son of this middle-aged person? Still led by the mind, perhaps, still critical and depressed, his being majoring in introspection? But during leisure periods this young man will be able to contact his intuition. His anger is his creative energy. Is there a *dropout* – a rebel with or without a cause? Or a *disciple*, full of spiritual impulse and, perhaps, religious feeling? Or a *group worker*, whose motivation, like his father's, lies in achievement – altruistic, yet his sense of reality gives rise to his cynicism and his very joy leads him into sadness? Will an *artist* appear, characterised by spontaneity, sex and sensuality closely linked with aesthetic values? Or not, giving rise to a *Don Juan* character thriving on conquest?

Into and among them all may leap some symbol all unexpected, some *harlequin* telling of his suppressed sadness and melancholy, yes, but bringing music, feeling, spontaneity, humour. This figure links body and mind to emotions and heart, and runs right up through them to intuition.

And is there some *wise old person*, full of humour and warmth, a friend in the dark?

Working with sub-personalities

Generally, about six sub-personalities emerge at first in the exploration that follows (p. 28), though none may appear at all. This is not a cause for concern. They come into consciousness because the seed of their potential is ready to grow. Maybe they would have appeared before, offering opportunity for change, but we resisted them. They can be hard to identify: 'What *is* this sensation in my solar plexus?'

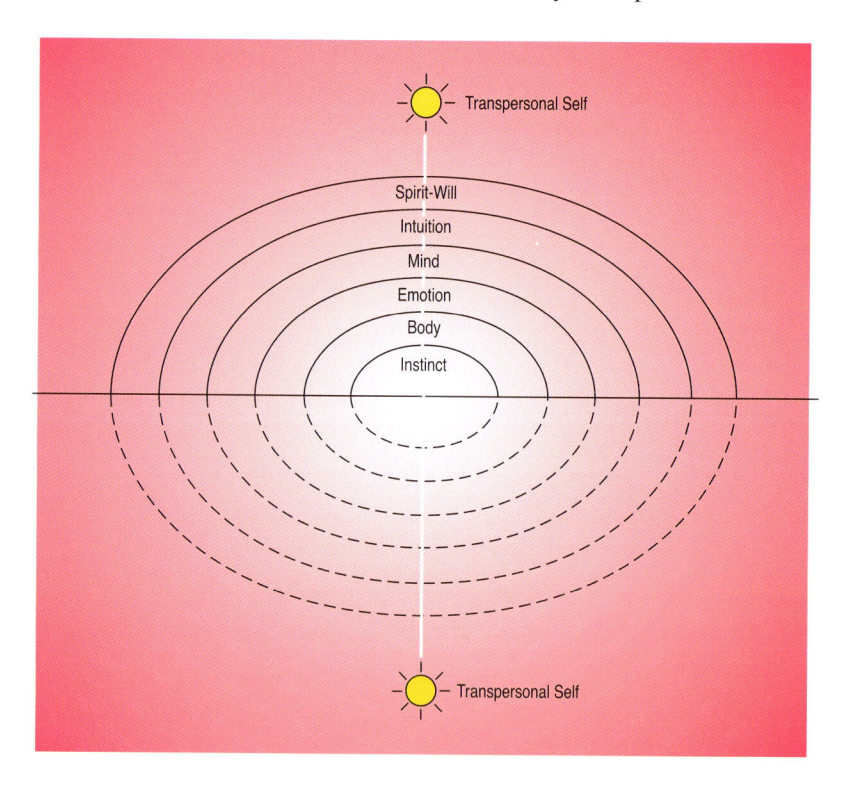

Chart 1:11 – Levels of Consciousness 1

The sub-personalities can be plotted on to these levels of consciousness (to be read from below). As our awareness widens, new ones emerge for old. Given the right food for their natural growth, there will be no distortion or danger; unless our motivation is off-course, for example, if we want to make ourselves more interesting. If we intend to grow and develop, we are protected against triviality. What comes is today's; the pattern that emerges is not fixed for ever, but a snapshot of the present. The whole thing is changing and flowing.

Imaging requires time, allowing, gentleness. We aim to reclaim our *centre*, not any one of the sub-personalities alone. But, exploring them, we discover any conflicts among them; also, the balance of masculine with feminine. Very often the feminine is missing, both for women and for men. Women in particular may need to bring it out – but in their own way.

First we *recognise* a sub-personality: 'It's an aspect of myself – but in a strange guise'. Then we hope to *accept* it, no longer being identified with it: 'I run it, it doesn't run me'. We may even *befriend* it. It does belong to us and it needs our friendliness; its development depends on the value we place on it. When sub-personalities know we love them, they change. Seeing how they relate to each other as well as to ourselves, we begin to *co-ordinate* them: 'How do they live together as individuals? Could one not help another?' So the bereft mother within may take on the lost child, and both find fulfilment. Being brought together in new ways, transformations occur: the hungry baby turns out to be the magical boy. Later we *integrate* them into ourselves, letting them belong with us and each other. Eventually they are *synthesized*, we see them collectively as a group and their energy is released into our lives.

Reviewing them, whether daily, monthly or yearly, does help. Keeping a workbook or journal, recording by writing, is a very exact way, and creative expression can use other materials. Holding dialogues with and between our sub-personalities, we reflect on their quality, value them, offer them warmth and praise. Observe them; rather than re-living their ways of being, build in their desired qualities. Help the exhausted ones to move toward the leisure they need, the over-controlled ones to let their hair down a bit, the frustrated ones to move towards freedom. Revising our attitude to these parts of us, these images, we attend to where they want to go; then our *instinctual* side may want more contact with the natural world. Our *bodies* may need to dance, to run, to rest. Gradually we come to feel all of our *feelings*, which move from anxious, pained 'solar plexus' energy to the energy of the heart. We cultivate serenity for our *minds*. Our *intuitive* nature may require artistic expression, moving through action to creation and so to service.

[A key exploration now follows. It is in two parts separated by a coffee break. Again, people need to lie down. Materials for drawing will be needed at the end of each of the two parts. It is probably best not to discuss during the break whatever came up in the first half, as it is still only partially cooked. Sharing will follow in the afternoon. Ed.]

EXPLORATION
SUB-PERSONALITIES 1
(45 minutes)

Be invited to relax and, lying down or sitting as you prefer, to enter your inner space. It is generally true that if you lie out on your back you will go deeper, while if you sit up you will remain more in control. Either may be appropriate in different circumstances or for different people.[15]

Minutes
- 3 Find yourself in a field or meadow. It need not be one that you know. It is summer and all is green. On the edge of the meadow you see a house or dwelling. Spend the next two or three minutes being in the meadow, orienting yourself to it and getting the feel of it, with its sights and sounds, and the scents of summer time.
- 7 When you are ready, move towards the house. What kind of house is it? You know it is the home or dwelling of your sub-personalities. You hear voices inside. These are the voices of some of your sub-personalities; but at this moment you don't meet them. Explore around the outside of the house. In your own time, enter the house or dwelling and spend the next few minutes exploring in and around it, seeing what it contains, sensing its atmosphere. You do not yet meet your sub-personalities, but you know they are behind a closed door.
- 10 Coming out of the house, move some distance away, maybe twenty or thirty yards. Face the house, and invite the sub-

---

15 See Chapter 6, pp. 370-371.

personalities you know best, perhaps four or five of them, to come out separately and join you. See them stand before you and talk with you. Greet each one; invite a symbol or image and a name for each. Get a clear picture and a feeling of the quality of each.

5   Now turn and face the house. The door will open again and one or more sub-personalities whom you know very little, or not at all, may come separately out of the house. As before, give a greeting. Take a good look, aiming for a clear picture. Sense their quality, and invite a name, and a symbol or image, for each of these unknown sub-personalities.

6   Now, take two of your sub-personalities who get on least well together. They have difficulty in understanding or communicating with each other. Take them away to the centre of the meadow to talk. Can you discover the nature of the difference? Is there anything that can be done about it, either by you, or one or other of them? Do they want anything of each other? Is there any way to help them live together more harmoniously, getting some better understanding between them? Listen to *them*, let them tell you.

4   Begin now to bring the discussion to a resolution. Invite an image or symbol for the resolution itself. When you are ready, return to the other sub-personalities. See them all go back into the house, and the door close behind them. You may wish to go into the foetal position as you return to this room in your own time.

Anchoring in the body. This is a very important part of imaging. You are invited to stand, keeping in the feeling of the exploration.

10 Choose one of the two sub-personalities you took into the meadow away from the others. Keeping your eyes closed, let your body adopt the posture, the feeling and energy of that chosen sub-personality; let your body *become* it, moving with any movement or gestures belonging to it.

Explore the second one in the same way through the body, sensing how it is and feels and lives inside you. Feel the shift in energies as you move from one to the other.

Return to the posture of the first one. Is there anything different in its energy now? Know that you will recognise this sub-personality when it comes up in your life.

Do the same with the second one, so that you will recognise and know it.

Lastly, if you found a symbol for some resolution between them, let your body take on the shape of the symbol. If not, see if your body can offer some clue as to what that resolution might be. Let your body really feel it. Is this particular posture found in your life in the world? What would happen if you allowed it to be more prominent?

It is suggested that you record the exploration so far by drawing your images of the sub-personalities, perhaps placing each in a segment of a circle, with the Self at the centre. Indicate the house, too. And that you remain in the spirit of the exploration over the break.

EXPLORATION
SUB-PERSONALITIES 2
(35 minutes)

Relax, re-enter your inner space; let the ground take your weight.[16]

Minutes

4 Return once more to your meadow and give yourself a moment to enjoy it. Find yourself standing a little way away from the house – it may have changed. You are in the centre spot of a large circle in the meadow, about twenty yards across, the size of a large room or larger. It is a special circle on the ground: maybe the grass is a lighter colour – the feeling of it is light, a circle of light.

10 Standing on this centre spot, invite each of your sub-personalities out in turn to join you. There may be new ones; that's all right. Greet each. With those you know best, ask each in turn if there is anything they want of you, and tell them what you would like of them. With the less-known ones, those you haven't met before, spend time getting to know them better. Why have they come into your life at this time? What is their meaning or message for you?

3 If you feel there might be another sub-personality, known or

---

16 Commentary on the Sub-personality exploration, Appendix 2. Guidelines for writing up sub-personalities, Appendix 3.

unknown, still inside, you may wish to go back into the house; but do not try to insist that it come out.

4 When you have talked with each sub-personality, bring the conversation to a close. See them standing round the perimeter of the circle, with yourself in the centre. Then see a column of white light coming down into the centre of the circle where you are standing. Ascend the column of light. When you are some way up, at about tree top height, look down and see what your sub-personalities are doing.

10 Now you ascend much further. As you do so, a wise person or presence, or a feeling, may come to meet you; or it may be a place where wisdom is to be found. Is there anything you would like to ask the wise person? They may have something to say to you? With this person or presence, or in this place, explore the deeper, transcendental, transpersonal meanings of the sub-personalities you have seen. Explore also the possibilities for growth and transformation within them, now that you have them.

4 Soon, the meeting with the wise person or presence will come to an end. Thank them, if that's appropriate, and prepare to take your leave. When you are ready, descend the column of light back to the centre of the circle in the meadow. Say goodbye to your sub-personalities; see them go back into the house and the door close behind them. If any of them don't want to go into the house, leave them outside.

When you are ready, come back into this room, perhaps spending a few moments in the foetal position before you return to the present day and open your eyes. Draw and write if you wish.

SYMBOLS AND IMAGES

*Stretching over lands and across the aeons, symbolism contains
the dreams of the race and the thoughts of the ages.
Kindling our imagination in a few conventional lines,
it leads us to realms of wordless thought.*
Lin Yutang[17]

What are symbols?

Through the centuries, symbols have been new-minted for each generation, leading out of time into eternity, out of space into the spaceless. Older than time, fresh as tomorrow, they deal with practical issues, yet, imbued with flashes of significance, appeal to the non-rational areas of emotion and intuition. As Carl Jung said, symbolic words or images imply more than their immediate or obvious meanings and lead the mind to ideas beyond reason's grasp.[18] Jill Cooper pointed out that the symbol is key to a realm greater than the person who employs it, greater than itself.[19] It speaks the language of dreams and tales and once-known things – childhood things, forgotten, to be rediscovered. It is the language of *and*, not *or*. It holds the paradox: 'Yes and no – both at once and both are true.'

There is a difference between *signs* and *symbols*. *Signs* such as traffic lights give clear and unambiguous messages to all. The Aborigines cross sticks as a *sign*: 'Be alert: the gods are nearby'. *Symbols* are less straightforward, though they are also placed at crossroads where crucial meetings occur and time and eternity coincide. Criminals are buried here, in limbo, spirit and matter interacting in one reality, vertical lines crossing the horizontal. The external and the internal meet at similar crunch points in our own work and relationships.

Facing different ways at once, symbols are Janus-faced, both dark and light. Primary and most ancient expressions of the unconscious, they unite everyone, pointing to meaning, to a godhead. As the sun obliterates the night sky, so the light of reason blots out the stars and galaxies of our inner space – perhaps as vast and as mysterious. And symbols are like constellations in that inner space. Since they cannot

---

17 See Lin Yutang, b. 1895, d. Hong Kong 1975, quoted in J. C. Cooper's Encyclopaedia of Symbols, p. 7.
18 See Jung 1961, *Man and His Symbols*, p. 4.
19 Cooper 1978, ibid.

be approached rationally, it is when we let the sun of our intellect sink down and set that we may re-learn their language, asking, as we depart on our voyage of exploration, 'Why this symbol and not another? What does this feeling, this atmosphere, remind me of?'

Your sub-personalities are symbols

They have emerged via your images from the unconscious into clarity. Are they valid? We rightly value what mind and hand can measure, often fearing the rest is 'only imagination'. 'I just made it up,' we say. 'It's nonsense!' But why did *this* come to mind? Why *these* images among a myriad? Boxed into our heads (our left-brains, anyway), if we say that *only* what can be weighed and quantified is valid, then we're lopsided and losing half of life's reality. Feelings, instincts and intuitions inform our thoughts and choices more than we realise. The non-rational world cannot be denied. Our heart, our *being*, insists on being heard, befriended and paid attention to. The total psyche is more than outer reality, more than knowledge and the conscious mind, more than what *is*, in the present. It includes inner reality, unconscious factors, what is past and what is in process of becoming. It involves head *and* heart, doing and being, outer and inner, light and dark, left hand and right hand.

Approaching our sub-personalities requires delicacy, courtesy, time – love. The problem is that many of us dislike parts of ourselves. Those parts often make their reactions felt through the body, appearing as psychosomatic disorders: thus we are heavy-hearted, have the world on our shoulders; we drive with the brakes on, live with a pain in the neck, can't stomach it. Wholeness includes both health and illness, solitude and relationship. Instead of blocking those parts, get to know them. Love them – and let them know it.

Symbols come from different levels. Entering the house from the meadow, we pass out of the conscious to unconsciousness. The house: is it a home – or a prison? An upper room or attic may have to do with higher consciousness, and a basement with the unconscious. The large pale circle in the field symbolises the field of consciousness, and the meadow around it the middle unconscious. The column of light is the link between the personal and transpersonal centres. Tree-top height gives another perspective – we see things differently. The wise being stands in for the transpersonal Self. Listen... Symbols have emotions.

Explore them, through painting, dancing, writing. On the horns of some dilemma, paralysed or yoyo-ing between the poles? A transcendent, transforming symbol may arise now to bring freedom. Trust, allow and acknowledge the process.

Our sub-personalities are symbols emerging *today*; but they will be fulfilled, worked out, in the future. Allow them time; it may take years. We evoked them, they are our own. We can safely act on anything they say so long as it seems valid. Does each have enough space and time? Which of them is currently running us? What minor adjustments could we make for them? Even the tiniest modifications can bring about major transformations. Become that transformation. Our symbols contain our energy; listen to the inner language of life's experiences, and it can be released within us.[20]

The language of images and symbols

So this is a language of the total psyche. Marvellously evocative, it imbues the commonplace prose of our lives with a deeper resonance. No matter how we demand of ourselves, 'Be predictable, reasonable, sensible, practical, balanced!' yet (fortunately) other responses also move us.

Unconsciously and spontaneously, we produce symbols. Most of us favour particular smells, colours, flavours, have special places and things which resonate, filling our intuition and our dreams. Natural patterns move us: hills, clouds, sea, sunlight, moonlight, starlight. A half-heard snatch of music tantalises, the stirrings of love or repulsion bypass our logic. After all, what *use* is a violin concerto, a painting, a kiss? When so evoked, images rise all by themselves in response. Religions all employ symbols: from Celtic or Christian crosses to Japanese lanterns in gardens, stupas, temples, mosques, cathedrals; all carry a powerful energy. Some people are themselves symbolic – J. F. Kennedy, Marilyn Monroe, Nelson Mandela, Mother Theresa – having an important place in the general imagination. There's only one Shakespeare or Goethe or Mozart, one Gioconda's smile; yet generation after generation stirs inwardly on connecting with the rich inheritance of shared human experience encapsulated in their symbols.

Is the scientific community 'against' symbols? Symbols live on, alive and celebrated; and as much in scientists themselves as in artists

---

20 Guidelines for writing up sub-personalities, Appendix 3.

and song-makers, poets, dancers and dreamers. It was the intuition and imaging of physicists, as well as their thinking, that leapt the gap from the known to the possible – to black holes, quantum theory and quarks. Only later were these proved by mathematics and then measured. Indeed, in the world of sub-particle physics only symbolic, *mythical* language will do. Like space fiction, modern physics sounds like myth-making. Classical mythology was itself the philosophy, the psychology and the science of its day, and we would be naïve to think that the science, philosophy and psychology of our own day will not in their turn come to be seen as forms of myth.

We need non-rational, romantic fiction, to do with the heart and the imagination. Until the seventeenth and eighteenth centuries, *fairy stories* were winter entertainment for both adults and children, dealing with 'otherness', instinct, feeling, intuition, with the subjective. Indeed, there is a resurgence of symbol in our recent literature. Legends take on new life as modern myths are created, fresh journeys through the elements of earth, water, air and fire. Story-tellers keep the language alive. From the creation myths of aboriginal tribes to our modern myths (not only Coleridge with his Ancient Mariner, not only J. R. R. Tolkien, C. S. Lewis with Narnia, Mervyn Peake with Gormenghast; but Star Wars, Close Encounters and many more), a wealth of 'new' legends are being published, filmed, recognised and taken to our collective heart.

The symbols in dreams

A major symbolic language of the psyche, dreams open an even more direct channel to the unconscious. It is well worth noting them down.[21] Hearts and intuition, as well as heads, are needed to understand their meaning and unlock and make available their energy. There seems to be a sense of love in them, something behind them that bends over backwards to help us. Our dreams are befriending us. This lovely befriending by our own nature is always there, ready to meet us and lead us through (although probably not *out of*) situations – if we will heed it. The pattern shapes itself. We don't have an unconscious, our unconscious has us. All we can do is flow with it, let it be, listen to it and learn to balance the different aspects of our own deepest nature.

One man dreamed he was at a potter's wheel, trying to shape something extremely beautiful and elegant. However, he couldn't get

---

21 And see Somers 1999, 'Dreaming in Depth', chapter in Wellings & McCormick 2000 (Eds.), *Transpersonal Psychotherapy*.

the hang of it and the clay kept dropping thickly down. At last, it insisted upon becoming a beer mug. Later, his chagrin turned to delight: this 'mere mug' meant for him friendship, fun, the ordinary. The dream helped lead him out from the influence of his over-ambitious wife, wrong job and inappropriate value system.

Symbols have their light and their dark sides, as we have seen, and the dark side may well emerge first. Never be afraid of the dark; it's only the other side of the light. Trying to tell us something, our own wise inner centre is quite likely to lead down through the negative. As people tend to shout at foreigners, so our symbols sometimes shout at us in 'nightmare'. They want dialogue, not monologue. They want us to understand and reach the positive on the other side. Symbols speak through such images and dream figures, far-ranging, yet explicitly relevant to the dreamer.

Never know first and never know best.[22] Each person's dream symbols are particular to them. Do not try to interpret them for the dreamer, who needs to gather his or her own sensing of the dream. Tree, mother, home, sailing boat – all mean different things to different people. First, seek the dreamer's personal *associations:* 'What does your dream mean to *you*, its word, image, symptom? What was the feeling? What did the place, the atmosphere remind you of?' Important questions: 'How old was that character?' and, 'How old were you in the dream?' leading often straight back to areas that need further exploration.

Only when their associations have been thoroughly explored may it be appropriate to offer some more collective *amplification*. For instance, frogs typically suggest transformation (always remembering that *this* frog – the dreamer's frog – may not). Wild animals may indicate untamed instinct, the earth the feminine, the mother. Amplify it tentatively from your own experience. With that proviso, here are some typical symbolic dream images, again plotted on to the Egg Map.

Dreams from the middle unconscious

Familiar, everyday dreams, a mish-mash of immediate events, are not of much significance. They arise in the Middle Unconscious, they include events from yesterday and tomorrow and involve people met recently.

---

22 This was frequently said by Barbara Somers. I believe it came from Jung, but the reference has proved elusive. (Ed.)

Dreams from the lower unconscious

Symbols of anxiety, stress and tension come from the lower part of the map. We view this as no mere dark cupboard of the soul nor dustbin of the unconscious, but rather as a rich and splendid compost heap where seeds of new potential may find fertile soil. Though dark, the Lower Unconscious is full of meaning. Here we encounter the shadow, the devil, our most intransigent problems. Modes of transport may feature here: cars, trains, bicycles, canoes, ships; and, of course, the missing of the bus or plane. Many people dream of shitting in public. Houses may appear, underground rooms or caves beneath them may indicate the Lower Unconscious. Jung described a very detailed dream he had at the age of three or four: he went down a stairway into a hole in the ground and found a great ritual phallus in a subterranean chamber. The many collective interpretations he discovered for these dream elements stayed with him for years.[23] From this lower region of the map come dreams of:

>*Lost values*
>*Rejected attitudes*
>*Unresolved conflicts*
>*Unlived life and thwarted growth*
>*Death and transformation*
>*Rejected potential*

Dreams of losing things – wallets, handbags, purses, tickets, passports, money – may have to do with *lost values*, lost libido. The value has been taken away.

Dreaming about thieves, drunks, tramps, dropouts may signify that some of our *rejected attitudes* need re-examining. Neglected children, animals or plants may appear: material unacceptable in consciousness has been held down by the dreamer. Are the animals wild or tame? How old are any children? What characterises old people or other figures?

Dreams arising from *unresolved conflicts* – perhaps such as we saw among our sub-personalities – can wake us up with a bang. Different bits of us are at war with each other. We are impotent to act, immobilised, caught into action, violence, persecution by thugs, rapists, terrorists, executioners, torturers, THEM. Here are attacking animals: for example, someone dreamt they spent the whole night

---

[23] See Jung 1963, *Memories, Dreams, Reflections*, p. 26 ff.

trying to close the windows and doors against a tiger. Later they saw that the house was the dreamer, the windows and doors were their senses, their awareness, and the tiger was their strong energy, creativity, anger. Dreams of erupting volcanoes may indicate the release of long-held emotions.

Unlived life and thwarted growth may also involve impotence to move, a more inertia-like paralysis. The dreamer feels helpless, in a desert. Deformed people, hunchbacks, dwarfs may appear; one person dreamed of a man's body with a child's head. Here the plants, animals and children may be not only neglected but cut back, cut off, maimed or dead.

Death and transformation. When tombs, skulls, skeletons, decaying corpses, images of dismemberment, come into our dreams, they rarely foretell a physical death of either the dreamer or of people close to him. Such transitional symbols as the coffin or the death's head seem rather to refer to old patterns and scripts. Due to die, they must be let go of, put away.

But it is the dream of *rejected potential* that brings the darkest symbols. This is the nightmare – the mare, the horse that rides at night bringing messages: 'Look to the Self!' Behind its dark aspect lies the bright face of new potential. If *depression is the aching of an unused talent*, we may find new life, peace and health behind our nightmares. Marie-Louise von Franz told of a rich businessman who, when ill, dreamt recurrently of an ill-tempered and filthy tramp who disgusted him. Persuaded to hold an inner dialogue with this revolting figure, he was told: 'I'm not getting enough attention – that's why I've made you ill. Dress in my clothes, go out into the country – and listen to me!' So the businessman did. Because of this, eventually he bought a horse to which he became devoted; he rode in the country each week and was no longer ill. The horse was the symbol made real in the world.[24]

Dreams from the higher unconscious

Some dreams and images have a special resonance that won't go away. Unforgettable, they flavour whole days or years, even a lifetime, with their essence. Like great art or poetry, they bring sudden and intense inner experiences. And they don't leave us. Coming from the Higher Unconscious, they talk about the future, bringing news of imminent

---

24 See von Franz 1971, *Jung's Typology*, p. 32.

breakthrough and of integration and individuation. Linked with outer events by synchronicity, they touch an inner trigger or chord – and it vibrates. Stunted, withered, deformed things straighten and start to grow again. Harmonisation of the opposites begins and *transitional symbols* appear – heralds of hope from the upper part of the map, sent perhaps by the Self. They include upper rooms, flights to mountains, to water, sea, rivers (does the river flow from left to right, or *vice versa*? Following it, is the dreamer travelling up- or down-stream?) Dreams of making love may come in here, as may mythical, legendary figures – gryphons, unicorns, winged horses. There may be dreams of:

>*Change*
>*Movement*
>*Emergence*
>*Awakening of new potential*
>*Transformation*

Change in our lives may involve dreams of boundaries, borders, thresholds; connecting symbols emerge – bridges and trees. We may dream of kitchens, laboratories, alchemists' dens, where substance is transformed and becomes life-bringing.

Dreams of *moving through an element* (fire-walking, swimming, flying, tunnelling) may also indicate some dynamism.

Emergence from one element into another, as we explode into an altogether new life, may be heralded by dreams of bursting cocoons and cracking eggs. Here are crabs, water-voles, otters, dragonflies, butterflies (and what a nervous breakdown the caterpillar goes through before its metamorphosis!) Here are kingfishers and all diving birds; winged creatures of the water. And how about the dragon itself, and the phoenix? A multitude of symbols of transit, of the movement from separateness to wholeness, from repression to release and growth.

Dream images symbolising the *awakening of new potential* in undeveloped parts of ourselves include clutches of eggs, newborn babies, young children, small animals, white horses, birds, pin-heads of light.

Symbols of *transformation* and wholeness include not only the egg breaking, the seed shooting, but light from darkness. Here in the dream garden are the rose, the lotus, the sunburst, the sun-dial. Three-fold figures are here transformed and made complete, yielding four-fold figures – the four-armed cross, the square in the circle – or the circle in the square – and the square that's round. Here are found the wheel or mandala and the jewel, pearl, crystal or diamond. The *lapis*, the Philosophers' Stone of the alchemists – even the divine child – may appear. These prime symbols of wholeness and completion are a living reality within the human psyche, releasing energy into life whether or not we fully understand them. Religious symbols in the deepest sense, they bring holiness, wholeness and healing.

What to do with dream symbols

They are life-enhancing. Relate to them. Draw, write, make things. Dialogue with them, listening as well as talking; act on what they say if it's appropriate, and so reclaim their essences. If negative, *evoke* them deliberately during the day; *recognise* and *accept* them; later *co-ordinate* them and begin to *integrate* them into yourself. Finally, *synthesise* them so that they work together and their energy becomes yours. Holding in your hands the crystal of life, dare to look into its faces and depths – joy and pain, crises and high points. Embracing the Buddhist *maitri*, that 'all-encompassing warmth and friendliness towards your own experiencing', begin to understand the essential meaning behind life's challenges. And so, *befriend* your experience

DISCUSSION AND SHARING IN SMALL GROUPS

Sharing.[25] The aim of the workshops is to encourage participants to have insights into their own unconscious programmes and patterns and, by increasing their understanding, to work towards freedom from being controlled by these patterns. Each individual is unique; no two people will gain exactly the same insights from any given workshop. And they are a private matter. Thus, while a participant shares the material from an imagery session, it is important that no one else should attempt to evaluate it. Interpretations must come from the person.

Sub-personalities. Individuals may be encouraged to follow them up at home – though probably *not* to repeat the whole exercise on their own, since several together can be a bit overwhelming. Fuller commentary is given in Appendices 1 and 2 below, and Appendix 3 has suggestions on writing them up.

---

25 And see Appendix 1.

THE FOUR-BALL MAP

*It is necessary to accept ourselves, imperfect though we are,
for we can only serve people out of our abundance;
there is no way we can serve them from our need.*
Joan Swallow [26]

We are not so much neurotic as lopsided. The psyche is trying to balance itself; dreams, images and crises call and urge us. Here is another map; it offers a way of looking at break-up, breakdown and breakthrough:

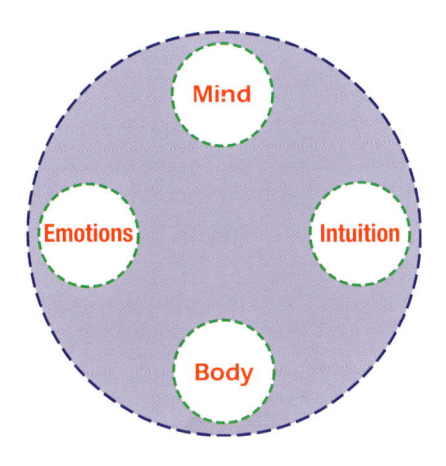

Chart 1:12 – The Four-Ball Map 1, The Child

This is a child too young to have any consciousness of himself. Children have a diffuse awareness. The unconscious is fluid; four islands of consciousness, areas of potential, rise out of it. They have permeable boundaries. There is no ego, no I, no centre.

Imagine a little boy – it could be a girl – playing on the beach; he is with his parents and he is digging in the sand, making a castle. His *mind* is totally absorbed, all his awareness is in what he is doing and creating. Suppose the sun goes behind a cloud. He begins to feel cold. Immediately he forgets the sand, the castle, his bucket and spade, and

---
26 Joan Swallow, a close colleague of Ian Gordon-Brown (IGB), who was on this occasion running the workshop with him.

becomes completely aware of his *body* and its coldness. He looks around for his mother, and for the moment he can't see her behind some other people. Now he totally forgets being cold; all he knows is that he *feels* lost and afraid. In immediate terror, complete panic, he yells his fear without embarrassment or restraint. When he sees and runs to his mother, his awareness oscillates between his body and his feelings, as he sobs and is cuddled and comforted. But quite soon he gets down and runs off in his warm jacket, awareness back in his body and his mind once again. His fright leaves no tail; it is all gone. The boundaries are fluid.[27]

The child's *intuition*, too, may develop at an early age. He knows without thinking, or even feeling, whom he can trust, and he will say so: 'That is not a nice person.' The lack of a sense of 'me' precludes all embarrassment. He will probably be soon prevented from pointing such things out: 'You must always tell the truth, but you must not say things like *that*'. And so he enters into the world into which he must grow up.

As the child develops, the boundaries become more impermeable. A centre, an 'I' appears in the middle of the map. Since our present-day education often gives little heed to feelings or intuition, his body and mind soon join up around this ego-centre, becoming an island with almost impermeable shores. In a way this is all right: he learns that his body is interesting and to be developed, though parts of it are certainly taboo; and using his mind is a key to praise and success. However, since the emotions are left out as definitely 'not OK', especially for a boy, he comes to think that he *is* his body and his mind. His intuition is by now all but non-existent. His own sense of self plays a part in this; the central island of ego, body and mind is now associated with consciousness. He is hardly aware of any feeling or intuition. So by, say, seven his *mind* will probably be excited, his *body* ambivalent, his *emotions* neglected and his *intuition* rejected.

All this could develop in the opposite way. Brought up in a family where people majored in their feelings and intuition instead of in their minds and bodies, a child would be conscious of emotions, with body and mind left outside. This is more rare in Western society. Either way, we grow up lopsided. The boundaries harden.

Approaching adolescence, the bodies of others are completely taboo. The young person loses awareness of his own, rejecting parts of

---

27 This analogy of the child on the beach came from Joan Swallow. See n. 26. Ed.

it altogether. (In later life, the cold bits of our bodies may be those that we rejected in this way. What to do with them? Love them.) He may need illnesses to give him time out from the stress of growth. He has also learnt that emotions, if felt at all, are best protected because they hurt. Positive ones are suppressed, negative ones always hidden. Vaguely ashamed of them all, he hardens them right off. His mind, meanwhile, may have remained excited if his education has been good enough. This area is usually considered all right, though girls sometimes feel they must not shine too much intellectually. The mind stays relatively open at first; but later, at university or at work, he finds it too has dangerous areas which must be shut off, at least partly. And the rejected intuition, irrational and therefore unacceptable, shrinks even further until it is largely atrophied.

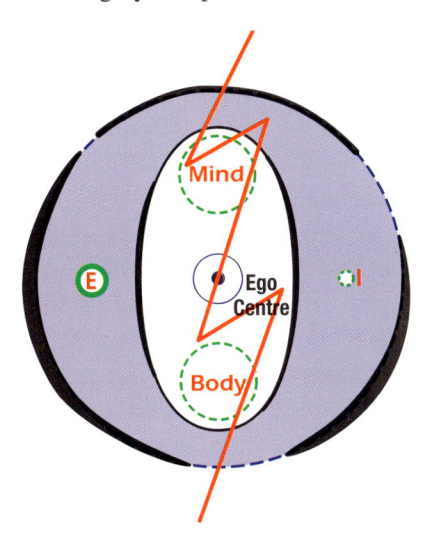

Chart 1:13 – The Four-Ball Map 2, The Average Adult

The average adult usually establishes only two functions: around *body* and *mind*, scar tissue hardens. A further almost impermeable barrier rings *emotions* too. *Intuition* is shut out. The child has become a lopsided adult. Much is unconscious and unused. Even being in love reaches his mind and his body – but not his feelings.

Note that these defences are highly necessary. Counselling does not try to strip them away; indeed it could be dangerous to do so. They form a pattern of personal pain, set up to protect the vulnerable parts. But now he is atrophying in it, merely coping, sinking in fear of any change: 'Be brave! Stick with it! Soldier on!' He needs a sanctuary.

What happens? The outer, damaged and scarred ring has to be broken up. It's to be hoped a lightning strike cuts through it. A mature person needs all four of those areas, but the strength to let the boundaries become open and permeable again cannot come from the old centre; it is a rare individual who has incorporated them all. Often, a midlife crisis ensues: bereavement, accident, redundancy, rejection, loss. Or we may read a particular book, meet a particular person. It feels extremely uncomfortable. The customary coping system won't work and chaos is looking at us. It is with pain and shock and agony that the chrysalis begins to break up. One part of our nature may react with a breakdown, another with a breakthrough.

Regression may follow, a break-up of old patterns leading to a desire to go *back*, to sink into the external support of childhood, into a womb. We want to be ill and cared for, free to look after our energies. This is quite natural, especially if not much personal centre has yet been developed. It is a shock like that of birth to break through the rigid walls of the average adult; we may go through complete breakdown before the hoped-for breakthrough to meaning and understanding takes place. No doubt the chrysalis also feels as if it's having a nervous breakdown. *Anxiety is one face of energy*. So, symptoms arise. Certainly, too long a breakdown into dependency is unhealthy and inappropriate but, instead of working with them, panic-stricken professionals may prescribe drugs, even hospital, and make into a clinical state that which is usually a natural process, rebalancing and rebirth.

For the Self begins to break through, with jolts big or small. Gradually or suddenly, a new centre coalesces, both from the ego and from a higher, deeper place within. Child-like, though not childish, it relates back to the little boy and his immediacy of experiencing. The four areas begin to relate and come together, impermeable barriers soften and yield. Fleetingly we glimpse it. This new centre is us and yet goes beyond us. It is intimately related to the other Self. We can afford to relate to that Self; awareness of it comes in short flashes and disappears again, sustaining us, offering an anchor which *goes beyond* the person. It is *trans*-personal.

So, like children, we are not childish; like the bamboo, we can bend in the gale. We ask, 'Where are you taking me? What is the meaning?' Dangerous areas are not seen as dangerous any more. We break out of our old constraints – the internalised voices of parents, society, the law, politics, economics. Old patterns of behaviour, assumptions of roles, are questioned and may be put aside. The religious maxims we have taken on board are looked at anew – are they still true for us in their original forms? Society, too; it cannot become conscious easily, but needs people to make the breakthrough at a personal level. As old skins crack and burst, a new wine, a new spirit, comes both to individual and collective.

'There's no growth without pain,' they say (though there's an awful lot of pain without growth). Given the hard walls we have mostly erected, few people do it without trauma. The *midwife of the spirit* is one who trusts the process, and the person, and herself. She knows it's a huge effort, a vital shock of life-giving proportions that requires not interference, but loving, confident attending and support. She helps the person confront their pain and fear, using drugs only as a last resort, encouraging, sustaining, comforting and being with the person; and as they go through the centre of the pain and shock, there they find comfort, love and a new life. For in the very depths, in the very heart of their grief, fear and doubt, is the transpersonal Self in the bottom of the egg, awaiting them with open arms.

A mature adult thus emerges, not yet in final form but able to grow, change and develop as required. A *true man or woman of no rank*, in

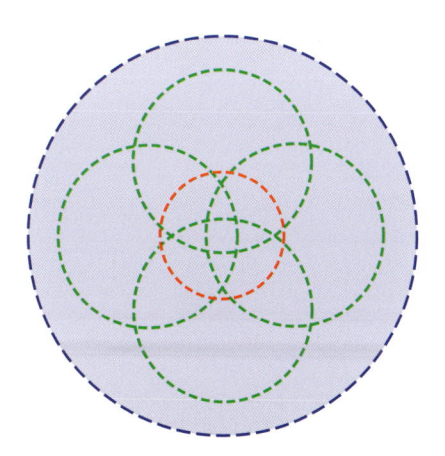

Chart 1:14 – The Four-Ball Map 3, The Mature Adult

touch with all aspects of their being, they observe their own inner lives with detachment. They are identified with none of the four areas: they feel, but are not taken over by feelings; they understand and treat their bodies better; their open minds are less attached to opinions and judgments; enjoying and delighting in intuition, they set aside time to flourish in it, knowing *change is how we allocate ourselves to time*. Instead of the walls which the child learnt to put up, they carry portable screens of light.

GESTALT EXPLORATION
(50 minutes)

[Each person needs a notebook and four chairs or cushions, placed in a diamond pattern and plainly and literally marked with pieces of paper: Body, Emotions, Mind and Observer. The fourth chair is for the non-judgmental, transpersonal Observer who, listening, provides the synthesising factor, external or internal: falling in love, an outside interest, a change, a challenge, a stimulus. The process of physically moving from place to place, each time facing the centre, clarifies which of them is speaking. Ed.[28]]

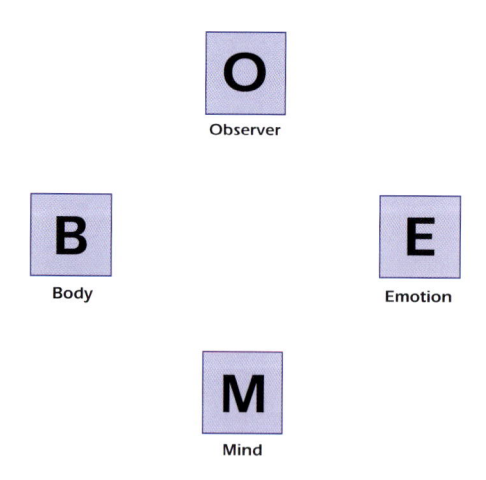

O
Observer

B
Body

E
Emotion

M
Mind

Chart 1:15 – The Gestalt Exploration

---

28 It is as well to explain this at the end of the previous evening. Commentary on this Gestalt exploration, Appendix 2.

Most time is spent as Observer. At the beginning you *dialogued* with the Self as the traveller on the journey of life. Then, with the sub-personalities, you *met* a wise being up a column of light. Now, you *become* the wise representative of the Self, the Observer, the highest you know, as nearly as possible the transpersonal Self, the true centre, the essence of being. Quite non-judgmental, compassionate, not sentimental, the wise Observer gives a view of your life in the round. It is not a judgment seat. Not the Self, yet it is in touch with the Self. Be in that mode as much as possible when in the Observer position. The exploration is in three parts:

Stage 1
Minutes

   3   Starting as Observer, centre yourself there and, without now making any note, consider and reflect on your life and daily round. What's it about? What is going on now? Be in touch with your work, relationships, with balance, meaning and purpose. Aim to see clearly and compassionately, without judgment, a picture of your life today. No one knows as much about it as you do.

   5   Move to the position of your Body. How does it feel, from head to toes, now: comfortable – tense – energised? Discover how your Body *senses* your life today. How does it regard your daily round and relationships? Hear and record your Body's answer to any questions you may have.

   3   Returning to the Observer position, clear your consciousness of the work you have just done with the Body, and centre again.

   5   Move to the position of your Feelings or Emotions. Explore with them how they *feel* about your life, daily round, relationships.

   3   Return to the Observer place to clear your consciousness of the work with your Emotions. Be in touch with your own Centre once again.

   5   Next, move to the position of your Mind. This superb instrument mediates what *is*, here and now, involving outer action, *doing*. It conditions your image of outer reality, your image of yourself and others, and your choice of action. It can analyse, verbalise and explain the outer world. Seek to get in touch with your mind; find out what it *thinks* about your life, daily round, relationships and your present lifestyle.

6 Finally, return and centre yourself in the Observer place, clearing your consciousness of the work just done with your Mind. Staying in the Observer position, imagine you are in a private place of your own choosing, where you might hold an intimate conversation. Spend a few minutes there with your Mind, Emotions and Body, obtaining an overview of the situation with them all, making any notes.

Stage 2

10 The second stage is, again by moving physically, to revisit your Body, Feelings and Mind, in your own time and in any order, and to ask them how they want you to develop. What changes in your lifestyle does each request? Between each, go back to the Observer position to clear your consciousness, and return there eventually.

Stage 3

10 Now, while staying in the Observer position, return to that place of intimate conversation and bring your Body, Feelings and Mind together. Consider together the crunch question, the Monday morning question: 'What are you going to *do* about all this?' What action might now follow, what decisions for change could be made? What energy, what creativity could be released by making these changes? And decide to contact them frequently and regularly and find out if they are all being nourished.

Take a moment to express your appropriate thanks to your Body, your Mind and your Emotions, and to be glad that you have them. Then rest quietly in the Observer position.

This is a good exploration to repeat at home, when it could be valuable to add places for Instinct and for Intuition.

THE FOUR FUNCTIONS

In earlier maps we examined some of the basic structures of the human psyche proposed and refined by Jung over a lifetime of clinical experiences, some with clients, many personal. Following his traumatic split with Freud, Jung had a near breakdown – a midlife crisis. Some years of introspection and observation led to his formulating this model of the psyche, which proposes the four 'functions': *sensation, feeling, thinking* and *intuition*. He further defined thinking and feeling as rational functions, while sensation and intuition are a-rational, or non-rational. They give rise to certain personality types.

The Extravert

Ego — Object

The Introvert

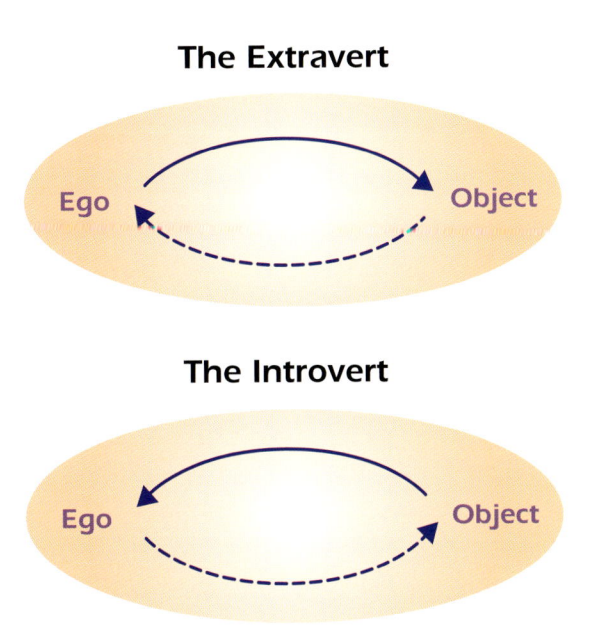

Ego — Object

Chart 1:16 – Introvert and Extravert

The terms *extravert* and *introvert* have become household words, yet many do not appreciate that it was Jung who defined them. They refer to two 'attitude types'. Less about whether we are quiet or noisy than about our fundamental flow-orientation, they are also to do with our timing. Introverts act more slowly. In the extravert, the conscious libido flows out *towards the object* (people, the world); secretly, however, an unconscious counter-action flows back *towards the subject* (themselves). Habitually attentive to people around them, they don't realise how profoundly influenced they are in turn by that outside world; for, unconsciously, they are introverted. Extraverts tend to meet new situations with *Yes!* – 'Oh good, yes, a party!' However, Jung pointed out that they say Yes for different reasons: self-confidence, lack of reflectiveness, desire for adventure, pleasure. Or because it's too much trouble to say No, or because they can see no viable alternative – indeed they may say Yes for no good reason at all. Their greatest fear is *isolation*.

Introverts, on the other hand, feel as if always having to pull back from an overwhelming object that wants to affect them, fall on them, drown them in impressions; but secretly they stimulate that outside world, borrowing its energy. The world piles in on introverts; yet at some unknown level they encourage it to do so since, all unconsciously, they are extraverted. They meet new situations with an unvoiced No! – 'Oh heavens no! A party!' Though they may still go – even enjoy it – the first reaction is, 'No way!' Is it second thoughts, an excess of reflection, fear, caution, laziness; can't be bothered, can't see the point? Or, as with the extravert, is it for no good reason at all? The greatest fear of the introvert is *chaos*.

That is, of course, a portrait of extremes; most of us are somewhere between the two.

Jung found extraverts and introverts irreconcilable. They just don't value each other, don't see the point, can't communicate; they talk from a different place and time. The extravert sees the introvert as selfish, inturned, navel-gazing, too-earnest-by-half, always analyzing

Ways of Relating to the World

Sensation Function ←→ **Perception** (a-rational) →→ Intuitive Function

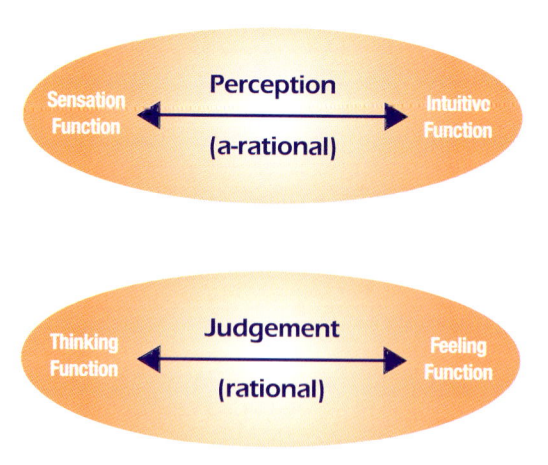

Thinking Function ←→ **Judgement** (rational) →→ Feeling Function

Chart 1:17 – Perception and Judgment

everything: 'You think too much!' The introvert sees the extravert as shallow, trivial, superficial, noisy: 'When in danger or in doubt, you run in circles and shout out!'

This distinction, however, was not enough for Jung. We also see the world at any given moment according either to rational evaluation, *judgment*; or to a-rational *perception*. Each gives rise to two 'functions'. The functions of judgment are *thinking* and *feeling*, the functions of perception *sensation* and *intuition*. Each person has all four available, though tending to favour just one of each pair. One end is easier, comes naturally, comes first; and the two ends are mutually exclusive at any given moment.[29]

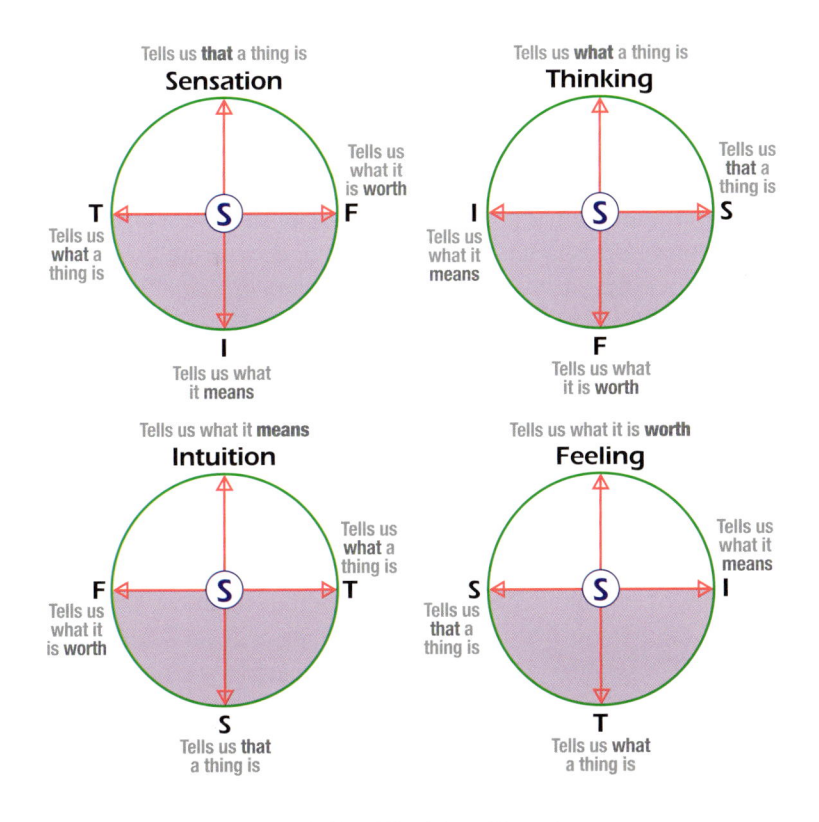

Chart 1:18 – The Four Functions

---

29 A further refinement looks at how each function may, in an individual, be either introverted or extraverted. See C. G. Jung 1921, *Psychological Types*. For a system based on this concept of Jung's, see Isabel Briggs Myers 1962, *The Myers-Briggs Type Indicator*. See also Keirsey & Bates 1984, *Please Understand Me*.

We may see the map as a dynamic wheel; the aim is to get it turning freely, as appropriate. The most differentiated, most comfortable, conscious function at any given moment is above, at twelve o'clock as it were. The least differentiated or 'inferior' one is down in the unconscious at six o'clock. One function at least is bound always to be below, in the dark.[30]

The Sensation function

Through our five senses, this function tells us *that* a thing is. It's on the Perception axis. We become aware of the fact: the song of a blackbird sounds – we hear it. People at ease with their Sensation function, acutely aware of facts and tangible reality *now*, don't easily get lost; they know the exact way again, with map and compass in their heads. They can handle practical matters and materials, knowing how something is made and its uses, asking, 'Can it be reproduced – now?' Repairs and do-it-yourself present few problems. They are artisans, craftspeople, farmers, technicians, interested in market values, making careers in engineering or design. Observant of physical details – places, clothes, furnishings – they are at home in their bodies, on earth, in the world. They may have a strongly aesthetic side but, readily accumulating facts, miss the subtler connections between those facts. They enjoy practical puzzles (such as those Rubik's cubes of 1974). They can be heavy, fixed, unyielding people, delighting in research designed to prove that the intuitive is getting it wrong.

The Thinking function

Moving the map around, we come to the Thinking function. This tells us *what* a thing is. It names, categorises, classifies, describes; it is one step removed from experience and is on the Judgment axis. A bird sings, and the person who majors in Thinking will no sooner hear it than name it: 'Ah, that's a blackbird.' Such people are rational in all situations; logical, objective, analytical, conceptual, judging things as right or wrong, true or false. They make quantitative evaluations, fixing things in time, giving them an extrinsic value, a date, a historical context. They become scientists, researchers, academics, analytic thinkers. They doubt and reason; they don't believe. Comfortable with concepts, discriminating their *feelings* is hard; ask, 'How do you feel?'

---

30 See also Jacobi 1942, *The Psychology of C. G. Jung*, pp. 10-26.

and they look puzzled, think hard, and reply, 'Feel? Me? Well, I *think* I feel.... ' They can name and define their feelings, but they don't actually *feel* their feelings, which are unconscious and, not being discriminated, are considered fearful, dangerous. Rage is kept hidden – unexplored, unexpressed, unexplained – until it blows up hugely. If deeply afflicted, rather than feeling grief they may become physically ill. So, leave the axis of Thinking and Feeling; reach buried feelings by going instead to Sensation and ask the *body* to help resolve powerful emotions; ask the Intuition. Thinking people can be blinkered and bigoted. They may become psychologists, seeking feelings vicariously through other people's experience.

The Feeling function

Moving across the map, we come to the Feeling function. Here, 'feeling' means not 'emotion' but *valuing*. When the blackbird sings, the Feeling function person exclaims, 'What a heavenly song!' Feeling function people are sensitive to quality; they judge a thing by its intrinsic worth, its beauty, its value, rather than by price or quantity or reasoned analysis. 'That's no good,' they declare, 'it's not worth following up', but they can't say why. They judge a person by whether or not they like them, feel them to be good or bad, pleasant or unpleasant, whether they give pleasure or pain. The *thinking* function is down in the dark, archaic, undifferentiated, slow. Unable to tell the difference between reasoned judgments and mere opinions, they commit to certain ideas and stick with them. They are true believers. Subject to sudden conversions they may, like St. Paul on the Damascus Road, be struck by a blinding light and their thinking system be transformed (and the conversion may take and last and be of benefit). They swallow it whole.

Again, like Jung as a boy in the Cathedral at Basel,[31] they may be tormented by elusive thoughts, trying desperately to hold at bay some half-conscious idea that seems dangerous and shocking to them. One person dreaded, yet with help managed to catch, the bird of thought: 'If my son-in-law died, my daughter would come back home.'[32] When such thoughts are caught as they fly they lose their harmful potential – though often, like birds, they are hard to capture. *Feeling* perfectly fine, these people's *thinking* – vague, fluid and diffuse – may be turned against themselves,

---
31 See Jung 1963, *Memories, Dreams, Reflections*, pp. 52-56.
32 Marie Louise von Franz. See von Franz & Hillman 1971, *Lectures on Jung's Typology*, pp. 45-46.

tormenting them with ideas of being worthless or bad. Feeling function people are good on social occasions, making comfortable, dealing effectively. Found in person-related fields (healthcare, therapy) yet they may become eternal students, repeatedly acquiring certificates to prove they can think, needing an astonishing number of diplomas and degrees before they dare begin to practise anything.

The Intuitive function

The function of Intuition is an internal perception of the 'within of things'. It tells us what something *means*, what the possibilities are; it sees round the corner and into the future. The blackbird sings and the Intuitive person says, 'Spring must be coming – let's sow the seed now.' Their perception of the world bypasses external reality and the normal five-sense process. They feel for the inner, trusting their imagination. Aware of possibilities and nuances, they pick up purposes. To other people, their hunches and divinations can be so accurate that it seems a miraculous faculty. Their intuitive flashes make them sensitive to individuals and their feelings. They don't put everything down to outward events. If someone's houseplants are drooping, they ask not, 'Is it the central heating?' but, 'Could it be that *you* aren't happy here?' Their ability to touch on the most sensitive spot makes them very good counsellors, and they may be excellent with animals. Seeking the spirit of things and their symbolic representation, they follow careers in fashion-designing, advertising, speculating. An intuitive person is good to have *behind* the company leader, seeing in flashes of inspiration how the business will go. At home with atmospheres and subtleties, they trip over their feet in the physical world. Material objects baffle them, presenting huge obstacles. They get distraught at filling a form or choosing a shirt. And change a plug? They can be too far out, too unearthed, not in time, *now*. With little sense of outer direction, maps become a mystery; one very intuitive person (lost and late again) reported, aggrieved, that her way had been marked by the parked Post Office van.

Sensation, Feeling, Thinking and Intuition may be dubbed respectively Hand, Heart, Head and Hunch. The functions usually develop by *the Way of the Snake*. The one naturally at the top of the map, our favourite, 'superior' function, is the least trouble, the most smooth-running and unobtrusive. Children tend to develop this one at

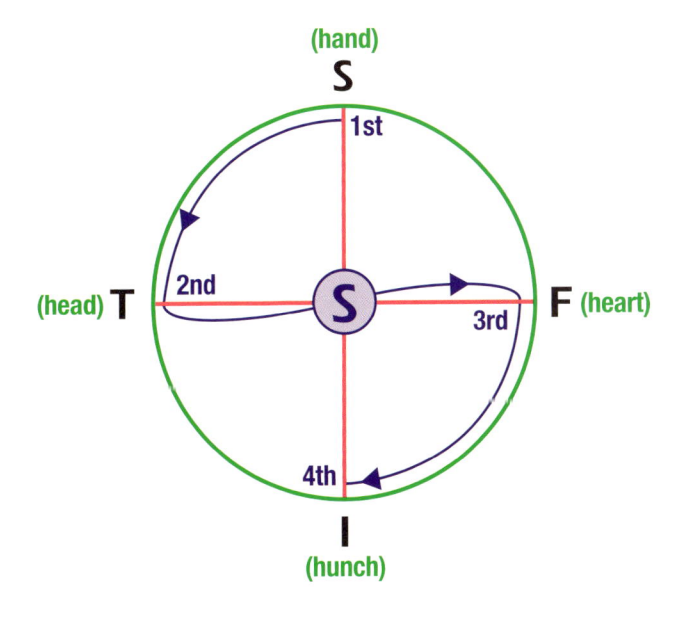

Chart 1:19 – The Way of the Snake

the expense of its opposite; they spend time doing what they do well – if possible – and leave the rest. So do most of us. Thus we grow up naturally into our own most differentiated function. Within families the types may be distributed, so that no one develops more than one or two functions. 'Dad's the practical one, leave it to him.' 'Ask your mother, she copes with teachers and people.' The marriage of opposites, often blissful at first, thus becomes difficult later. The children may also be pigeon-holed, one 'artistic and dreamy', another the 'brainy, bookish' one, leaving little room for development in other directions. In our society an academic, thoughtful child may develop thinking easily and neglect feeling. Another, good with their hands, may fail to understand meanings and subtleties.

While we usually also develop one or both of the secondary functions with relatively little trouble, 'by the Way of the Snake', the least differentiated one causes problems. For each of us it is down at 6 o'clock, associated with both our lowest depths and our highest aspirations.

The least differentiated ('Inferior') function[33]

In the stories, it's the divine fool who makes the hero's journey to the bottom of the world. There's often a king and his three sons – four in all. The youngest, the idiot hero – say, Dummling – is the divine fool. The king is ailing, the kingdom in trouble, so the smart eldest son takes the best horse and sets off to find the elixir of life for his father. However he fails to help little old ladies, birds and others who appeal to him, and so when he meets the dragon at the threshold of adventure there is none to help him and he perishes. The second son fares likewise. Only the despised youngest – who sets off on the old donkey, shares his dinner with the poor woman collecting sticks, binds up the bird's broken wing – is assisted in his turn at the threshold of adventure. So he crosses it; and he and his donkey continue to the bottom of the world, having many an adventure on the way. And there he meets the beautiful princess and finds the elixir of life, and they ride back home in time to save his father. But it is Dummling who now sits on the throne with his queen at his side.

So it is with the ridiculous and unadapted part of us, our fourth function, described by Jung as 'infantile and tyrannical.' Its very slowness means it should be developed later in life. For example, intuitive people may *dose* their bodies but they don't *listen* to their bodies; even to feel their heart beating is difficult. As they learn to do it, Sensation comes up; and through this least differentiated function the connection with the unconscious is built, the bridge to the symbolic world holding the secret key to their totality.

Most of us combine two functions. In Chart 1:20 the four functions map is set on the diagonal, so that any two functions are in consciousness at one time:

Sensation-Thinking people (centre), aware of the present, they are good at getting things done and handling the external world, *now*. Well hung together, technical and problem-solving, they tend to be polarised with:

Intuitive-Feeling people (top left and bottom right), who understand relationships and people. With a sense of the future, they make good counsellors and mediators.

Sensation-Feeling people (top right), often aesthetic, good at nursing,

---

[33] Jung regretted his original naming of the most and the least differentiated as the 'superior' and 'inferior' functions.

cooking, gardening; they need relationships in order to thrive. They too ask, 'What is *now*?' They are either drawn to or clash with their opposite:

Intuitive-Thinking people (bottom left), who add in a sense of the future. Some, aware of fashion trends, are found in advertising, economics and finance; others, more philosophic, are at home with ideas and abstractions, higher mathematics, quantum physics.

How to tell which we are? Which *axis* – judgment or perception – is most important? One probably dominates. To find our most and least differentiated *functions*, ask: 'What do I actually, habitually, characteristically *do* when there's nothing to do?' This may indicate the 'superior' function – and it's the doing, not the emotion about the doing, that counts. Our deepest *values* may tell our 'inferior' function, bringing us to the numinous with the pull and power of a god.

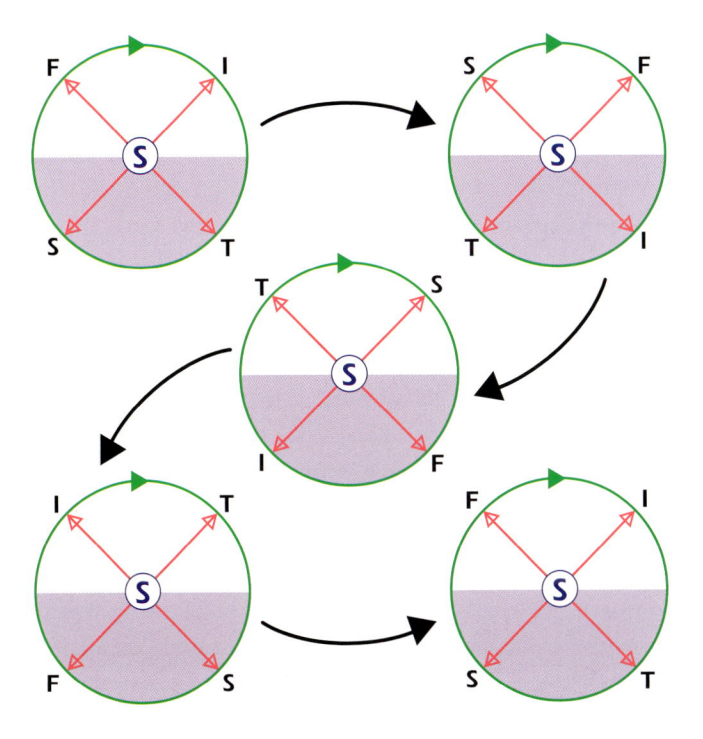

Chart 1:20 – The Turn-type

And you may be a *turn-type*. Did you grow up according to your naturally most differentiated function? In our society, as we have seen, education tends to develop Sensation and Thinking at the expense of Feeling and Intuition. Children born with Feeling and Intuition naturally dominant tend to be forced to the middle position at No. 3. Was the wheel so turned in your childhood? Did you have to develop your naturally least differentiated function first? This is very useful – those who start with easier lives will have to do it later to become whole. But in midlife you, like the old king, may become sick of the functions you have had to develop.

Such a child, with Intuition really superior and Feeling the second function, forced to develop Sensation and Thinking instead, feels alien, dropped in a strange place. Out of step, with a keen sense of nature, she picks up on subjective dreams and imaginings. She suffers from a gradual disillusionment. She knows what others don't know, and she's amazed that they don't. Surprised that they see the world differently, she defends herself against attack, adapting her own being to make it acceptable, quietening intuition, pushing it under, learning to trust few people with it – it will not be understood. She becomes practical, developing Sensation instead, living against the grain. It requires a conscious effort to do anything. Such people may be dyslexic – quick at first, dropping back in school. Having to pass exams brings up Thinking, leaving little time for Feeling. This is all right, for Feeling drops down to shed light in the unconscious. The wheel turns.

She – or he – feels a changeling, oddly lonely even if much loved because the love is not quite attuned to her. Intuition won't go away, nor Feeling – but both have dropped right out of sight. It feels like death, being put out of paradise, lost to God and man with no place on earth. Later she may turn to drink, schizophrenia, suicide – unless she can get the wheel turning again and find who she really is. As an apple tree in a forest of oaks,[34] if someone tells her, 'It's all right to be an apple tree' if they ask, 'What makes your heart sing?' if they say, 'Take heart: you may be a natural intuitive and not know it. Why always think; why always be doing? Feeling and intuition are all right too,' then she is redeemed. People who become redeemers of others get the wheel turning again. 'You once had a pearl and you lost it; re-find it now in a new way.' This kindred spirit hears her dreams: 'You, the

---

34 Also Somers & Gordon-Brown 2002, *Journey in Depth*, p. 26.

child, were once close to paradise. You went for years to a far country; you had to learn the language of the tribe. You yearned for your homeland.' Now she has met a stranger from that homeland who speaks her own language. She has come home.

So, the wheel begins to turn again. No longer, 'I never had a meaning', but, 'I once had a meaning and I lost it'. Will she die with the joy or live with the agony of it – this heaven and hell – as the wheel turns back and she finds the face she had before she was born. Hope in future will never die.

And now she can use all four functions. Our task is to develop them all. Perhaps the wheel turns many times (and with a spiral turning); perhaps we go by the Way of the Snake. In fact, it's usually both. And what rises from the depth of the unconscious, from that place of power, is charged with meaning.

EXPERIENCING THE TRANSPERSONAL

We embark on a voyage of discovery, accepting, befriending, and trusting the psyche;
it knows what it's about and we're in its safe hands.

Here is a paradox: transpersonal experience – what is it not? As we have seen, the Transpersonal is that which transcends the personal, acknowledging the existence of a unifying centre, the Self or Atman.[35] How to grow towards this centre? Introspection, contemplation, paths of formal religion all lead us towards clarity of consciousness. But also there is action; and what about science, what about analysis? Are these not also some of the many roads by which we travel towards love, the realm of the heart and of feeling?

The experience of the Transpersonal seems to involve detachment from immediate human concerns and the taking of a cosmic perspective. Transcending the little self, the person is centred in a larger whole. Those who have knowledge of it will recognise that the experience is generally of two kinds, which may be termed the *unitive* and the *dualistic*. In either case, what is required is total attention. The

---

35 Since people are different, some experience this as 'God', and they do so in different ways, responding to different aspects of the Deity – historically, recognising Vishnu, Zeus, Jehovah, Buddha, Allah, Christ.

> **Unitive Experience**
>   Oceanic
>   Void
>
> **Duality Experience**
>   Power / action / energy
>   Love / oneness
>   Light / illumination
>   Insight / revelation
>   Symbols
>   Creativity
>   Pressure to action
>   Crisis
>
> and – drop by drop by drop

Chart 1:21 – The Transpersonal Experience

experience has its own value in its own right and there is no need for justification. It seems to be about the end, rather than the means. It has a timeless quality in which the universe is perceived as sacred and meaningful, and this world as good and worthwhile. Evil is understood as limitation. The person's reaction is therefore one of compassionate understanding. A receptive rather than an assertive state of consciousness seems to be required. People report emotions of wonder, awe, worth, humility, joy; it is a kind of dying of the personal self. Polarities and dichotomies are transcended and there is complete loss of fear, anxiety or tension.

Unitive experiences

Language is altogether inadequate for these hugest, rarest, most ineffable experiences of the mystics. Imbued with a sense of the oneness of the universe and of our place in it, they arise in the supra-conscious in two forms, the *void* and the *oceanic*:

> *The Void experience.* Relatively uncommon, this is an expansion by going *inwards*, an instant 'witness' with everything, Nirvana.

There is an intense inner awareness or perception of being at the inside of everything, at the centre of a great emptiness, and the light within is the darkness of pure spirit. This is the resonating point at the centre of the dome of the cathedral; the person goes through until, *becoming* this most intense point, they also touch the farthest universe. The vault of heaven seems around and they at the centre, electrical, magnetic. There is a sense of immense distance. Time stands still. This state can creep up on a person, or it may be sudden, as if they were lifted up – or as if grace descended to their own centre from the transpersonal centre. Their 'I-ness' fades out. It is most intense concentration, as though all of the seas were focused in the one drop. This is a matter of degree, not quality; we all have glimpses, if rare, of the same thing.

The Oceanic experience. Again, those who know will recognise it. This is *samadhi*. Opposite to the void experience, this time the expansion is by going *outwards*. The drop becomes the ocean, the point becomes the circumference. It parallels the feminine principle; the seed swells, the egg hatches, the barriers break down and instantly the mystic is in touch with the underlying unity of the cosmos. The person becomes a drop in the ocean, and the drop cannot be got out – it is fundamentally transformed. The individual is lost in the Transpersonal – or the Transpersonal comes down and takes over – and the individual is lost. The person never forgets such an experience, but is permanently changed by it. He or she comes to *know*, and no more has to *believe*.

Dualistic experiences

These may be commoner and more within our reach; we normally live not with unity but with relationship. In them, we remain aware of our own personal I-consciousness; the separateness we still feel makes the duality. The flow of energy may be from the supra-conscious or from the personal centre. Dualistic experiences take several forms:

Power, Energy, Action. The person is caught in a very strong form of energy from the transpersonal centre, related to the Void described above. A great magnetic field overshadows them, pressing in through the highest head-centre. Or, again, it circles over the head like an electric sword, a current, a flying saucer above the head, and the person *becomes* the magnetic field. Great psychic energy is associated with this experience of *power*, of the ability to move mountains. Though it is power over self, not over others, it can be a somewhat repelling pressure – it is an energy of the will, giving the capacity to influence and to do. The magnetic field of a dynamo is directly proportional to the power passed through it; and a strong aura, a force-field, seems to come from outside with a steely, electric quality. Statesmen, politicians, businessmen and women may be no strangers to this; they have a single vision to pursue and create. Such people are uncomfortable to be with. This is different from Love's power.

Love and Oneness. An experience characterised by love and compassion, this is gentle but not weak – of heart rather than head. It is about identity and the oceanic unity of life. A golden, lambent light steals from the heart over the person, perhaps the radiance and energy of Christ flowing out and out and out like non-sticky honey. Felt sometimes as a 'tickle' in the heart chakra, gentle and sweet, a flow, inexhaustible and stealthy, it increases the more it's used. Those around experience it as magnetic; it is characterised by joy, passion and intensity of understanding.

Light and Illumination. The total vision is transformed, the world remade and the mind renewed. This happened for the Buddha. The experience is about perception: change our view, and our reality is different. We may undergo a sudden blinding, as did St. Paul on the road to Damascus, but it does not lead to darkness. Candidates for initiation were sometimes blindfolded, thereafter seeing the world altogether differently.

Insight or Revelation. More specific than light, this experience alters a person's view of a particular aspect of reality. It may come through a resonant dream or by an intuitive hunch. Examples of new understanding and breakthrough in specific areas can be found among scientists and philosophers whose flashes of inspiration have become famous: Archimedes – this is the Eureka moment; Newton; Kekulé and the Benzene Ring;[36] Einstein.

Experience of Symbols. Perhaps this is one of the best ways to experience the Transpersonal. Symbols – in our dreams, in myth,

---

36 August Kekulé, (1829 – 1896) German organic chemist; founded the theory of chemical structure, particularly benzene. See n. 89 pp. 105.

or the arts or in nature – mediate different levels of reality one to the other. We develop intuition through their study because they can hold *both* sides of a question, freeing us from 'either this or that'. Learning to read them with our whole being, not just with our minds, we find they lie beyond thought. It is as if the Self were facing in two directions at once, towards both the personal and the Trans-personal, and the symbol is the bridge between.

Creativity. Revelation comes through sculpture, painting, music, writing. It's as though it does it, not we ourselves, as we develop the ability to anchor our visions and bring them through. *I find not that inspiration breeds work, but that work breeds inspiration*, as Henry Moore is said to have remarked. Imagine a tank of creative water in the roof but the plumbing is rusty. By taking up pen or brush, chisel or bow, the tap is turned on and it may flow (or it may not, especially at first). But it certainly won't until we start clearing and keeping open the channel. Then, *it* can work through us. How after all do we know what we think till we hear what we say? *How* do we work? Mozart was sudden and quick, Beethoven more gradual. How could we possibly compare them; how ask which was greater? And our experiences in meditation – do they involve sudden illumination, or gradual percolation? The Transpersonal operates infinitely variably.

Pressure to Action. This is impulse. No light or vision or emotion or creativity are involved, just a push to do something, an insight, a hunch, a nudge from the unconscious. It's intuitive. We don't know why we did it till we've done it. Such non-rational impulses can be valid, as when, for example, they take us to see someone and we find them in need.

Crisis. This is how many of us do in fact experience the Transpersonal – the kick in the pants at our weakest spot, administering tests, blowing fuses, perhaps renewing our health. A researcher with a tank of ailing North Sea herring was advised to put a dogfish in with them. Reluctantly he did so, finding to his surprise that the gains from the bucking up of the shoal well outweighed any losses as the dogfish helped himself to his dinner. The Transpersonal knows we need sticks as well as carrots – knows when we are ready for the breakthrough engineered by the Self.

Whether sudden or gradual, whether positive or negative in its impact, it's to be hoped it increases our humanity and leads to expansion, humour, proportion and perspective; not inflation.

Drop by drop by drop. Some people may experience the Transpersonal in none of these ways. Rather, it may be imperceptible. Add colouring little by little even to a huge, house-sized tank of water, and you'll eventually change it. A drop a day of dye in all this clear water and, after many years, people will notice a difference. In the end you may well have become a radiant transpersonal being, trailing clouds of glory. Or something.

What next?

Heaven is within us and all around. Glimpsing unitive consciousness means knowing the oneness of sacred and secular, resolving the dichotomy of pride versus humility, Self versus not-self. The transpersonal experience leaves profound after-effects on people: it is therapeutic, integrating, unforgettable, leading to a revolution of attitude. Their friends tell how they became more loving, spontaneous, accepting, less demanding of themselves and others. Some comments:

> *It is about true Selfhood, 'becoming what thou art'.*
> *Giving up over-responsibility for other people.*
> *Growing more responsible as a person, freely choosing control over my own destiny – and anyway, the whole thing transcends any idea of 'my own destiny'.*
> *My experience is of being fortunate – I don't really deserve this.*
> *It's a car gliding quietly along in a power-drive, no longer struggling and roaring in the wrong gear.*
> *It's like beginning to drive with the brakes off.*
> *And don't push the river; it flows by itself.*

Marvellous experiences don't constitute the Transpersonal. We may be in touch with it without any of them. Certainly a long build-up may be followed by a sudden breakthrough but it is not all joy, peace and serenity – not all sweetness and light. Pain, struggle and difficulty may accompany us, everything may fall apart and take a long time to come together again. As Eliot said, to arrive where you are, you have to go by a way without ecstasy.[37] Paradoxically, the most negative teaching

---

37 See Eliot, *Four Quartets*, 'East Coker', line 137.

experiences are almost invariably the most useful. To recognise them as changes in our lives lets energy, creativity and compassion follow these apparent disasters. So we will find ourselves diving, not drowning.

There are hares and tortoises. People who hurry may fall. Being hyperactive, over-earnest or extra sensitive will not help; neither will overdoing meditation, or adopting unsatisfactory practices focused on an unhelpful centre. The task may be to reach the top of the mountain consciously and at will; but any difficulties may be telling us, 'Slow down. Have fun.'

And we are going to make mistakes. Be cautious. The energy of the Transpersonal is very powerful and may be negative at first, especially if we break the rules of common sense. Irritation, if it goes on too long, is a warning sign. Negative energies which generally blow the fuses in our circuits *can* be coped with in just a few moments when they occur. We *can* seize the moment, moving out of the situation in a transformed way – even if our deep breath has to wait till we are safe in the bathroom.

Be suspicious of too much drama – the Trickster can be at work. The psychic is indeed the psyche, but seen from the outside, not the inside. Go gradually, feet on the ground, developing discrimination on the way. Aim to rise out of the shadow not into perfection but into wholeness, into life in the round. Illusion is real and collective: depression and *idées fixes* take people over. They become inflated, fancying their own greatness – being Joan of Arc or Sir Percival – while inside they still have a very bad self-image. Thoughts are substance. Be careful what you think. A punishing thought will hurt someone. It may be you.

Growth is natural, but the collective seems to want something more than natural – some sort of accelerated growth. Loneliness is a feature of this work, at least at the beginning. It can also be there in the middle, and maybe at the end as well. But we find our friends, our group, our family, and then loneliness becomes something precious and creative – a needed solitude which may be hard to find.

Is the experience genuine? 'By their fruits' is the first and last test.[38] Is it transpersonal, or just fantasy? How do I react to deeper experience? Is there a change in energy, creativity, compassion? Is that change ongoing and beneficial? Do I enjoy my own humanness? Do I value play, laughter, humour? How is my sense of proportion, of perspective? The Transpersonal is collective and enlarges life

---

38 'Wherefore, by their fruits ye shall know them.' Matthew 7:20.

generally. To attend to myself may be extremely important, but the fundamental question is, 'Does it enlarge my life?'

EXPLORATION
THE INNER SANCTUARY
(10 minutes)

This short exercise in creating your inner psychic space is for every day, reserving room both inwardly and outwardly for the practice of awareness. It involves relaxation.

Be in touch with your image or mental picture of an ideal sanctuary, a place of regeneration and special retreat. It may be an actual scene, or one you have created inwardly, knowing it, or its development, through inner experience. Otherwise, begin now to create this inner space for yourself. Such an inner centre should fulfil several requirements:

> You will be able to find it in the Monday Morning world. Since it is a sanctuary, there will be none of the stresses of everyday life. It will be a place of wholeness, healing and holiness; a place especially for the recharging and regenerating of the whole of you, body, mind and emotion.
>
> It may be for creative gathering, a spiritual home where you can find those with whom you have a close spiritual affinity, your inner group. You can invite others – or not if it's not appropriate.
>
> It is a workroom where you can discover your own direction; also, any directives to serve your fellows.

So, a sanctuary which the cares of the world can't invade, where you may find solitude and, if appropriate, meet your inner group. Here you can be recharged on every level. Both seriousness and brightness and laughter can work here. Go there; see how it meets your requirements: a sanctuary, a place of wholeness, a spiritual home, and a workroom. Or build it so it becomes your own. Impress it on your heart. You can go there in future.[39]

---

39 Commentary on closing the workshop with the Inner Sanctuary, Appendix 2. Suggested programme and original reading list for the workshop, Appendices 5 and 6.

CHAPTER TWO

The Masculine and Feminine Within

Workshop II

Ian Gordon-Brown and Barbara Somers

*Learning to deal with the man or woman within us,
we can better get on with the actual person outside*

INTRODUCING THE WORKSHOP [40]

Two great energies

This workshop is not about men and women in general. It is about these two great principles within each one of us. Language is a problem; the terms 'masculine' and 'feminine' are descriptive, not evaluative. The search for alternatives offers positive and receptive, focused and diffuse, rational and a-rational, left and right sides. In myths and stories of all peoples since ancient times, the 'feminine' and the 'masculine' (in the East, the *yin* and the *yang*) have represented the major creative energies of life. Mother Earth and Father Spirit in their love-dance create the universe, sometimes struggling and competing, sometimes at one, ecstatically embraced in delight. They represent all polarities: heart and head, earth and spirit, inner and outer, dark and light, death and life. Images need clarifying or refurbishing for the future. This workshop explores how these two great energies work in us, in our world, our relationships and our own contra-sexual natures, and how our psychological gender and sexual preferences are affected.

Masculine dominance, feminine reaction

The patriarchal society of the last two to four thousand years, with its excess of male power and energy, has been responsible for many of the world's problems: the ruthless pursuit of power, the destructive exploitation of the natural world, the insanity of nuclear weapons,

---

40   Some notes on the running of aspects of this workshop are given in Appendices 1 and 2.

violence between nations, denigration of women, child abuse, racial oppression, lonely competitiveness and soul-less materialism. Patriarchy has created a raging monster, made captive by its own chains. We have assumed that to solve problems we need to be active, aggressive, scientific. But rational, logical, sequential thought is limited, though extremely useful in its place. It lacks inspiration, creativity, vision; it won't help us conceive the future of our dreams.

This masculine dominance has continued in the last era; even, perhaps particularly, in women themselves. The reaction is against intellect and 'head stuff'. The feminine is surfacing. Signs of its altering role have included dress, equal pay, Women's Liberation, Gay Liberation, the International Women's Day each year. There are fewer 'men' around today. The masculine has had to step back, whether voluntarily or by being pushed. It has not been getting a good press. With less potency and power, wielding less authority, men are having a painful time.[41] Male institutions are in disarray. This major collective and individual shift leaves men themselves in a strange place. Women too are extraordinarily conscious of... what? The move towards the feminine. But *is* it that?

Traditionally, in the first half of life men lived in and through their masculine side; their feminine was largely unconscious and so, from mid-life on, the task of men seeking to become whole was to discover and relate to the *anima*, their inner feminine side. Likewise women lived the first half of their lives through their feminine side and the masculine *animus* was largely unconscious; a woman seeking consciousness had therefore to search later for the masculine. Conversely now, though growing numbers of men and women are reverting to this traditional way, young women often have to live from their masculine side and must later, for wholeness, *rediscover* the feminine. And many men, through occupations which require a feminine touch, live through their *anima* for the first decades, so that later they must rediscover the masculine. This is true irrespective of an individual's sexual orientation; the issue is one of psychological gender.

The return of the feminine

We need the re-emergence of the feminine: co-operation, receptivity, sensitivity, imagination, emotionality, synthesis, conception, spiritual

---

[41] See the writings of Robert Bly, James Hillman and others.

awareness. Then we will see our challenges in a different way. Are we prepared to take leaps of faith, shake up our old perceptions, trust our intuition, live in harmony with each other and with the planet? Only the balance of masculine with feminine energy can unlock the vortex of power within. Only goddess energy can set us free. But feminine energy is not 'better' than masculine. Without masculine energy, the creative inspirations, hunches, desires and emotions, not to mention the compassion, empathy and love which spring from the feminine, would never be acted upon. They are complementary, both personally and globally.[42] We aim to learn to balance the two, valuing feeling as much as thought, intuition as much as rationality, imagination as understanding, receptivity as assertiveness, synthesis as analysis, being as much as doing. *Logos* must be given form through acceptance of vocation; *Eros* held and lived in human relatedness.

Feminine judgment rests on feeling, masculine on the mind and the law; yet the scales, the balance, are held by the goddess Athene. Where the *animus* is right in its judgment of large affairs, it is invariably wrong in its perception of relationships. The *anima* on the other hand, fallible over great matters, is infallible in relationships. It has been said that where the masculine is about the love of truth, the feminine values the truth of love. Are we moved by the love of authority, or by the authority of love? To change the world we must know ourselves. *This workshop is not primarily about any struggle between women and men.* It is about the individual, each man or woman. The encounter is within ourselves: finding the feminine in us; is it lost, dominant, playing a lesser role, overwhelming us? And it is about finding the masculine in us. Is it running our lives; or lost, bewildered, hurt? Again, the map is not the country. Though working through these two great primary channels, the Self transcends them both.

EXPLORATION
THE CUP AND SWORD
(35 minutes)

Since those who came to the first workshop will be familiar with the process of imaging, we start this second one as we mean to go on,

---

42 A dreamer told Jung of a dream-character who said that right and left go together in everyone. He said he was at one with himself when he saw each side as the mirror image of the other; there are only symmetrical people, and the lopsided ones who, still in a childhood state, can fulfil only one side of themselves. CW 12, para 227.

honouring the inner world in this way.[43]

This is an inner journey to find a cup and a sword, or chalice and staff. It addresses the balance of energies in yourself.

Find a comfortable space to lie down. Close your eyes, relax, let go of the day. Breathe out any thoughts; move from the mind's analysis to the perception of the dreamer or artist. Going inwards, allow whatever comes. What emerges relates to the present time in your life; if it seems different from the instructions, be open to *your* version of this inner journey. Note your feelings and reactions.

Minutes

4 Entering your inner space, become very quiet. The sounds of the everyday world fade away. You find yourself in a meadow. Be there clearly. A range of hills or mountains is nearby, or a view towards higher ground. Orienting yourself to the place, get the feeling of it.

3 Now leave the ground of the meadow and move toward the mountain or higher place. Travel towards, and into, and up, the lower slopes. Note your surroundings and how you feel. Take your time to become more aware of the day, the season, the sights and sounds and scents in the air. You know this is a special place.

7 The journey is about the discovery of a cup and a sword. For some, the cup may be a chalice and the sword a staff. Coming towards the higher ground, search for these two objects. You do not know which you will find first. One may be near the bottom, perhaps easy to find, perhaps hidden and difficult. And then look for the other on the way up the mountain. Take note of the circumstances in which you find each, its appearance and style – size, shape, colour, condition – and the feelings and associations it evokes for you. Does anything else seem important? In what order do you find them?

3 Taking them in your hands, carry on up the mountain. Find yourself at the top; are the two objects there with you? Take another good look at them; have they changed? How did they manage the journey?

7 A wise person or presence may come to talk with you about the cup or chalice, and the sword or staff; also about their relationship to each other and with you. If no wise presence comes, communicate directly with the objects; let them answer and tell you about

---

43 Commentary on the Cup and Sword exploration, Appendix 2.

themselves. Ask why they appear as they do, and why they were found where they were. Is there anything you need to know or do in relation to them? Explore the deeper meaning – the transpersonal dimension – of these two objects, and their potential for your growth and development as a whole person.

4 Is there anything you need to do to or for the objects while on the top – any ceremony?

3 In a while you will be descending the mountain. When you have finished talking with the wise presence, it will be time to bring the journey to a close. Return to the meadow, bringing the cup and sword with you if it's appropriate. Is there anything you wish to do with them before you lay them down? If so, do it before returning to this room.

Anchoring in the body. It may be helpful now to involve the body. Take up a foetal position, but be in your body in this room. When you feel ready, and remaining in the spirit of the journey within, begin to come to your feet.

4 Stretch and feel yourself into your body; can it help you by taking the shape of the first object you found? Let your body become that. Now, if it's appropriate, let your body become the shape of the second object that you found.

Now take up the first posture or position again. Try to see how this posture may relate to your life. Now take up the second posture. How may this posture speak to you in your life?

For the third and final stage, see if you can get some posture that will represent the creative coming together of these two objects; if there were a small ceremony with them on the mountain, express it bodily now. If not, ask the body to try to find a posture that symbolises their relationship and its significance for you. Get the feeling of how it would be if this were a state more often achieved in your life.

Take time to record your experience.

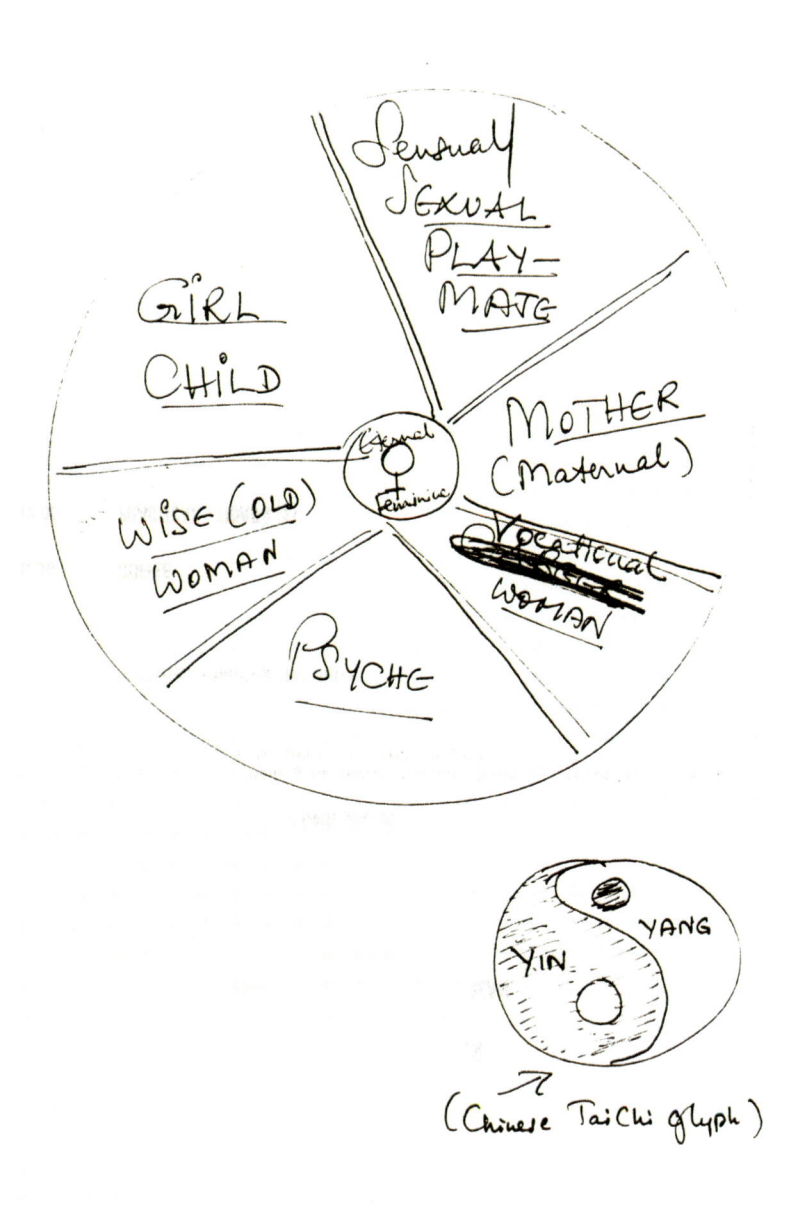

Facsimile of rough sketches: Barbara Somers

THE FEMININE PRINCIPLE

*Found in the spaces between the atoms,
the feminine is of the soul, of the poetry within prose.*

So the great Masculine and Feminine principles and energies, Father Sky and Mother Earth, are to be found in all life. *Yin* and *yang* flow in all of us. While the masculine is the exponent of spirit as air and fire, penetrating matter to make it fruitful, the feminine is the creative womb of life, the exponent of spirit in matter. *He* is to do with external reality, outer creativity. *She* is the subjective side of experience and inner creativity. Giving a form in which to embody the inner creation of ideas, he brings heaven down to earth. Giving body to new life, she raises earth to heaven.

Jung pointed out that, just as we have contra-sexual genes biologically, so there is a contra-sexual nature within each of us, man or woman. The masculine energies in woman he called her *animus* (spirit), and the feminine energies in man, his *anima* (soul) . The two principles are discrete. Correct rebalancing is the aim; retaining our own gender but allowing space for the *otherness* within. However, while Eastern psychology and alchemy acknowledge that we all have both, people in the West looked askance on Jung. Until the 1960's or '70's it was difficult to get books on the feminine; it was suppressed, seen as a deviation from the norm (does it not go with the left hand – both *gauche* and *sinister*?)

There is a crossover from the right brain to the left hand, the inner, subjective, non-rational; to the heart, the arts, the hearth. The feminine goes with the left side of the body and is about *being*, about earth and water. Conversely, from the left brain there is a crossover to the right hand, the outer, objective, rational; to the head, to mind and matter, science. This is the masculine. It is *right*. It is about *doing*, air and fire.

Receptive and yielding, the feminine has a diffuse rather than a focused awareness.[44] *Non*-rational rather than *ir*rational, qualitative, relatively un-map-able, it follows no outer laws and cannot be quantified, weighed or measured. But it has its own deep rationale and value. Receptive, nurturing and mothering as well as mystical, sensitive and alluring, this is the introverted, subjective side of us,

---
44 See *I Ching*, 'K'un, The Receptive', Wilhelm 1950, pp. 10-15.

Yin Right Brain Left Hand Feminine	Yang Left Brain Right Hand Masculine
Moon, Lunar	Sun, Solar
Being	Doing
Inner	Outer
Subjective	Objective
Non-rational, Heart	Rational, Head
Instinct, Feelings, Intuition	Mind, Matter, Will
Arts	Sciences
Earth and Water	Air and Fire

Chart 2:01 – Left and Right Brain

belonging in the depths of relationship and the truth of love. It flows in the arts, while the objective masculine is more about the sciences. It loves pageantry and display, colour and beauty. Its symbols include container shapes – this is the chalice-and-cup side. Though it does have to do with matter and material possessions, including money, yet images and stories of the journey of the feminine tend to hold the values of the heart rather than of mind or will, or matter. Inner rather than outer, they lead within and down, rather than up and away.

And *women* – not only men – are quite often unconscious of *yin* the Feminine.

The soul, the *anima*, in the myth and legend of all cultures has long been seen to have a feminine face. *Intuition* (perception, inner awareness, instant identification) belongs to men as well as women in their search for the feminine soul. Non-linear, needing time and space in which to function, this intuition must not be crowded. With her quiet inward voice she speaks in winged symbolism of the higher heart values. She is the 'third eye' of insight, compassion and universal understanding, resonating with our inner aspiration and higher potential, with poetry, music, art, dance, imagination. She stands on the shoulders of artists saying 'leap

> Left hand   Right brain
>
> Roots
> Beginnings
>
> Earth / Water
>
> Being / ♥
>
> Inner / Subjective
>
> Instinct / Emotion / Intuition

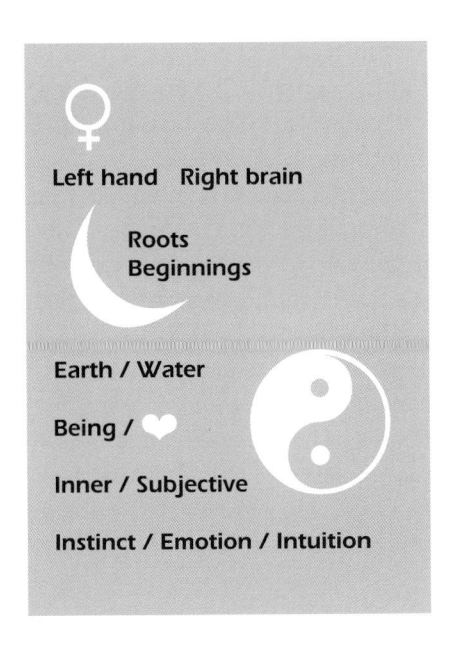

Chart 2:02 – The Feminine and the Chinese Tai Chi glyph

beyond'. Leonardo is said to have seen always the one face in many pictures. For Michelangelo, Psyche, the unconscious, was the veiled, intuitive feminine, taking the form of a butterfly on the shoulder or the flash of a white horse.

Looking at the elemental, archetypal differences from the masculine, we come to Earth, Moon, Water and Intuition. While Yang is solar, represented by air and fire, the intuitive journey of the feminine is via *earth* and *water* to the inner depths of meaning, 'the within of things'. It is also *lunar*, subtle, undefined; we are reminded of the Moon's cycles, waxing from half-full to full, waning back towards its rebirth in the new.

Instinctual Earth is stable, enduring, fixed. Mother Nature, the great creative feminine principle, is very strong in her steady seasons. She maintains the heartbeat of life, continuity within change, through the cycles of maturation, death, rebirth and growth. Every spring has brought sprouting; every summer the flower and autumn the fruit. In winter, Earth holds life in the pause of death, awaiting the new seeds of spring. The instinctual side of our nature is feminine. Symbols here may be of plants with their roots in the matrix of earth, of soil and seed-bedding, of small animals. If they are damaged or injured, the rhythms of our bodies may be disturbed and our Earth with her own autonomous rhythms hurt. In the urbanised, industrialised West we are pushed away from her. We need to be returned, re-routed – re-rooted – re-potted. Honouring tradition, in villages and towns the woman who was midwife also laid out the dead. Since the late 1960's people have increasingly honoured the earth – an important stage of re-awakening.

Moon Cycles. The goddess Luna is also under the aegis of the feminine principle, reflecting human cycles. Blood-flow, the menstrual cycle and its ceasing are tied in with the lunar rhythm of the tides, of the cycles and seasons of nature and human life. While the masculine principle sets the loom and gives the framework and the structure, the feminine, like the Fates, spins the thread, measures and cuts it. She weaves the patterns of creation. She is less focussed, more diffused, like moonlight.

The Water of Feeling. Water is unpredictable, mutable, always in flux, pulled by moon and earth. The flow, the movement in river or ocean, is feminine and of the emotions. Flowing into containers, it changes, taking their shape for a time and flowing out again; it cannot hold the shape of a broken container. Seeking always the most fundamental level, it is to do with the heart's valuation: neither this nor that, but both.

About *relationship*, Robert Frost wrote that the feminine principle moves by a totally abandoned zigzag – straight to the point.[45] While the masculine knows roughly how he'll be from day to day for weeks, months, even years, the feminine principle doesn't know from one moment to the next. In relationships she may be all fury, running the range of mood-swings. The head can rarely cope with the paradox. How can there be both love and hate, pain and ecstasy? But the heart can; at the same time both sad *and* joyful, high *and* low, it sustains the paradox where the mind can't:

'He only wants me for bed and board, he treats me like an idiot!'
'Don't you want to leave him, then?'
'Leave him? But *I love him* … !'

Both at once and both are true.

---

45 Robert Frost, in a letter.

Chart 2:03 – The Eternal Feminine

Girl Child
- relationships - if wounded, kicks against feminine
- trusts in femininity

Maiden
- aesthetic
- tender
- fun
- demanding
- seductress
- Siren

Wise Woman
- ageless

The Maternal
- protective
- nurturing
- releasing
- spider
- octopus
- Hecate

Psyche
- strange allure
- beloved muse
- inspirer of men
- serpent
- Lilith
- seduces and abandons

Vocational Woman
- co-worker with men
- the power of love fights for
- competes with men
- the love of power fights against

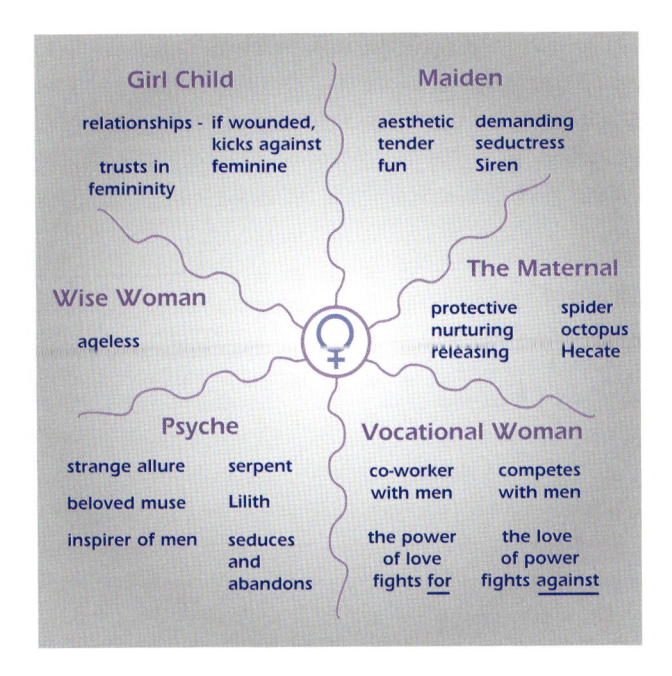

Chart 2:03 – The Eternal Feminine

These aspects arise in our dreams as symbols of the various colours of the feminine principle, flowing from one to another and back.[46] Our colour range may be limited: are we locked in with only two or three? As we become aware of the map, our spectrum may widen to the full palette. Each figure except the wise woman is described in terms of 'whole' and 'damaged', light and dark; the positive, and then what happens if that aspect has been hurt. They are not about 'women'; they are about the feminine in men as much as the feminine in women. They may appear among our images in any order.

The girl child

Bright-faced images. This is the divine, instinctual child, not yet trapped in time but carrying a sense of eternity. Full of potential, flowing with instinctual life, she is loving, joyful, happy, spontaneous and open. In touch with Nature's flow and the seeds and roots of life, the girl child models the feminine upon 'mother'; but she carries her own inner patterns of the feminine too.

---

46 This valuable map extends Chart 1:09, p. 23.

Dark-faced images. But she may be sad, traumatised, lost and abandoned. Dreams are of plants and flowers damaged, small animals wounded, nature hurt, roots torn up. Betraying our own potential, we lose touch with our instinctual nature. Or we are betrayed. Then appear crippled, dwarfed, cut-back, bonsai'd shapes and figures, sick and unrooted to remind us.

A child with a lot of feminine energy is early recognisable. Though pre-sexual, she plays differently from a boy, who is more attached to objects and things. Naturally interested in relationships and interactions, she experiments with ways of relating, behaving differently with different people. She is part of the chain of the feminine – the daughter, who becomes a mother, who has been a daughter – and needs to grow into her individuality without breaking it, becoming her own woman alongside her mother and other women. Where the boy learns to be most masculine by standing free of his mother, breaking away and relating to masculine figures in the world, the girl needs to stay in the feminine, not break from it. If her early relationships are positive she will trust in her femininity, taking its pattern from her mother, allowing it to grow from within. But should the mother give *too good* a pattern, or have none to give, the child will be wounded and kick against her own femininity, breaking the chain. Then she will have to attend to it later, re-mothering herself. However, given a good enough start, allowed to relate to the father and the otherness of the masculine, she will move on psychologically into adolescence.

The maiden

Bright-faced images. This delightful figure of late adolescence, playful, joyful and tender, is part child, part adult. Instinctual, full of feeling, fun-loving and fun-giving, she is hovering on the brink of life and womanhood. Sometimes shy, sometimes bold, she vanishes and reappears. Sensual with a promise of the sexual, she explores the languages of love and relatedness, lifting the human spirit. Images include doe and fawn, bud opening from white through rose-pink to red, mermaid, wood-sprite, water-nymph. She has a profound kinship with nature – here is the voice of ecology as well as of aesthetics. Loving beauty and the enrichment of the senses, she respects and values the earth, and is often passionate about trying to preserve and save it. She is the gipsy, the dancer and the tart, both nubile girl and prostitute.

Dark-faced images arise when sex, sensuality and play remain a muddled mystery – in men as well as in women. This is negative only if it lasts too long, leaving the sad person who goes on playing the little sex-kitten into later life. Never having learnt to live through a full palette, this *anima* still demands the presence of (and presents from) the male hero. Stuck here, she grows old. Demanding and seducing, she turns, twists and ties, using play to bind, showing her claws as soon as the masculine principle tries to go off on its journey. Thus Circe: Odysseus dallied for a long time, then tried to leave her island. But she had turned from the power of love to the love of power. She delayed him on the quest for his spiritual destiny, seducing and leading him astray through the senses. Thus the Sirens, Calypso, Delilah, the Lorelei, luring the hero from his task. Binding others and herself by sensuality and sex, the maiden has become frigid temptress, all body and no heart. Growth and movement are retarded, love is lust and possession, the sex-kitten is predatory cat.

Often the man's feminine principle will start here; his first sighting of the maiden reflects his *anima*, the first crescent of the new moon. The young person may be shocked by the sexual playmate within, as she establishes her femininity and otherness and extends her emotional range to men other than her father. With a positive start, however, she can meet males outside the personal family and experience this play-mating *on her own terms*. A profound gift is given us through the body, and she honours it. Even then she may need to explore her sensuality.

The maternal

Bright-faced images. Providing the nurturing soil from which new creation can spring, the maternal within us all guarantees creativity, growth and the future. This side of the feminine is not only about *physical* motherhood. Men have it too. Transformation images for the Mother are age-old: earth and the healing waters, the place of springs, the birthing cave, the fountainhead. The goddesses of mercy and the power of love – corn-goddess of fertility Ceres or Demeter, the queen of heaven, the Madonna, Kwan Yin, Tara – are full of dignity and respect for life. They are reflected in the woman who advises and helps, unites but does not bind, gives new inheritors to the life principle. The woman used to have her *only* power and identity in motherhood, with her children, cooking, home-making, nursing. As laundress, baker of new bread, the mother is seen to be like Mother Earth herself, a gentle tree providing shade from the sun, an arbour, a warm hearth, a cauldron of soup, a nest. And she loves the children and lets them go.

Dark-faced images. But on the negative side may be 'little me', powerfully holding her children against her. Up come images of the monster beneath earth or sea – the dragon, the octopus with its tentacles. She is Kali, the Gorgon, the Furies, a goddess intent on demanding. So she feeds on her children's young lives and potentials, keeping them infantile, snaking around them, demanding sacrifice and offerings of adoration and duty. She has become the old hag, Hecate. As dark spider-mother (in men too) she can at worst weave webs that render the daughters impotent; not wanting women around, she makes them unsure of their gender, if not frigid. And the sons are allowed no freedom to explore, uncertain about their masculinity, made eunuchs on her altar. The partner can be kept dependent and impotent, another child lest the 'mother' identity be lost. The threads of the spider are guilt, duty and love, all woven into a gossamer hawser that binds. And the person too is stuck and trapped in the role, having 'sacrificed' herself for 'love'. It's spooky. This is love as power. And she herself experiences the rage and anger of also being held under duress by that very hawser.

But when things are well, this is Mother Nature in her abundance, rich-breasted, generous-hipped, full of fertility, relatedness, caring and cherishing. Here are *full moon* images of setting free, loving and letting go. She knows about timing, about when to be there and when ruthlessly to say, 'Fly! You have your own wings!' So she pushes the fledglings out, knowing that whereas that which is possessed will leave, that which is left free will return.

The vocational woman

Bright images. This is one who begins to make relationships with her masculine principle. Here is Athene, a feminine figure in the law-courts, seeing mercy as justice. Love is for life, for clarity, for decision. Full of insight, judgment and discernment, she is benign empress, a mix of tender heart and clear mind. A co-operating, conjunct figure reminiscent of the whole *yin-yang* symbol, she combines heart with intellect, blending the *eros* levels of feeling and instinct with the sexuality, mind and spirit of *logos*. The feminine is here in a new relationship to the *animus* principle. She is the Amazon, brave and beautiful, carrying fire in her heart. She stands for the rights of the individual within the collective, and for all living things. In her career, called to work with ideas through inter-relationships, she is man's natural companion and helpmate in both doing and thinking. Equal co-worker towards the building of a new world, she also innovates in her own right. With humour and lightness of touch she speaks for the heart of the matter, for the individual within the collective institution, the microcosm within the macrocosm. Listen to her voice: 'That's good organisation, good planning,' she says, 'but don't lose sight of the people, the human factor, the individual.... '

Dark images. However, not only men but many women find this difficult to handle. Though her own vocational nature is innately feminine, how to use it without becoming too masculine? Go too far, and she opts away from the balancing spectrum, the range and palette of the feminine. And then the negative Valkyrie emerges, out for conquest and domination, helmeted and armoured in mail (male), aggressive, animus-ridden, damaging both male *and* female energies. (Likewise a man, if too heavily related to the feminine principle, may be 'anima-ridden', irrational and diffuse, the balancing masculine becoming tetchy, finicky and moody.) Rigid, aggressive and dogmatic, this person of steel is argumentative, overbearing, hypercritical, exacting, just missing the mark because out of touch with the feminine. She sits on committees, a harsh, metallic edge to her voice, overbearing but lacking true authority, sterile of ideas, opinionated, beside the point. Militant feminist, anti-man, anti-life, she (or he) uses the sword *against*, as she thinks males use it. Better keep it in its sheath and begin to honour consciously the difference between love *as* power, and the power of love.

But remember how the true feminine goes straight to the point – by a zigzag route and without knowing how she got there? Feminine earth and water here take on masculine air and fire. Called by an inner voice, responsible for her own self, she takes a stand, verbalising what she knows that she knows. She has her own *logos* principle. The world needs women with air and fire in heart and belly as well as water and earth – co-workers rather than competitors with men – people-loving instead of man-hating, fighting not against, but *for*.

Psyche

Bright images. This aspect of the feminine is classically represented with a female face. Possessed of a strange allure, she is beloved muse, inspirer and inner guide. Sophia, soul, Madonna, comforter and befriender in dark and unknown regions, such a person represents something mysterious. She opens up new thresholds and dimensions, leading from depths to heights. She is moon goddess – softly lunar, luminous, shedding a gentle, numinous light, a moonlit path on the sea. This is Helen for Paris, Beatrice for Dante, the beautiful beloved who draws a man beyond his mind, awakening creativity in both men and women. Ariadne holds a thread for Theseus in the dark labyrinth, leading the masculine principle (in the man, but also within herself and other women) beyond the known into the unknown. Comforter, sustainer; and she also knows how to swim.... Images for Psyche include the butterfly, deer, unicorn, the winged white horse. In folktales she is good witch, godmother, a transforming figure. She is the wise, veiled figure carrying a lantern who leads us on our quest, over the rainbow bridge towards the goal: the pearl of great price, the golden fleece, golden flower, Holy Grail.

Dark images. Psyche can be negative too, full of dark wisdom: Cassandra foretelling only disaster; Lilith the dark witch, full of magic and spooky intuitions – for intuition can be misused. Here is Hecate the withered, sterile hag (found in men as well as in women), destroying by dark powers and poisons and toxins. Keeper of shadowed mysteries, death-dealing, dismembering and devouring, she keeps the destructive, stinking cauldron bubbling. Psyche may become denizen of a fairy-world of illusion or a seducer into the underworld; indeed, the Queen of the Underworld may become the serpent who holds shut its door, or the Gorgon whose snake eyes can turn a man to stone. We recognise Rider Haggard's *She who must be obeyed*, or Keats' *belle dame sans merci*, the beautiful lady of no heart who enthrals and then abandons, promising all and delivering nothing. Choosing potentially creative victims, such a person evokes mystery in them, leads them three-quarters of the way to expressing their creativity; and then deserts them and moves on to another. She needs her own creativity, not a spiritual gigolo to live it out for her.

Even if positive, Psyche is of the *dark of the moon*. Yet she helps make a bridge between a man and his creator for, knowing how to see at night, she leads the artist beyond the reaches of his mind. Indeed, she will go herself as a light in the darkness, a thread in the maze, and evoke a different mode of seeing. And she herself needs help – to take a stand, take responsibility, know when to be silent and when to speak.

The wise woman

Androgynous, she has outstripped 'masculine and feminine' – she doesn't know which she is, and expresses both. She transcends 'dark and light'. She has been through the fire. Though ageless, she is often old, since wisdom requires experience of an inner marriage which it takes a lifetime to achieve (though the child is wise, it has no experience). Yet the wise woman is herself child-like and close to children. She is flexible to life's endless flows and changes. Quiet, she doesn't waste breath or words. She is wry and savoury: 'That's how it is'. Pragmatic, salty, witty, she can handle mud and blood as well as soul and spirit, pain and loss as well as joy and gain. She is juicy, neither dried up nor withered. She speaks *for* nature, growth, the child, helping link them with heaven, vision, the spirit.

In stories, the old lady gathering sticks often represents wisdom. She may appear in earthy or watery guise, at the source of the river perhaps, or as a tree, or in a cave or by a spring; living on the edge of the wood in a small hut or cottage, she keeps the hearth fires burning and the embers bright, often with a delicious-smelling cauldron. She knows the ways of nature and living things. Old yet young, she is pictured as good crone, wise grandmother, often cloaked or hooded, going with healing balms and animal skins to cover and warm, doing humble work as herb woman, gardener, beekeeper.

She comes in humble form because one who knows so much knows how little she knows. She listens to something greater, glimpsing a meaning beyond herself. She doesn't speak much, but near her in the forest animals grow, children play, trees bow down, plants flower. Midwife and layer-out of the dead, she is also midwife of the spirit; she brings to life with her intuitive perception the dormant forces in people. She loves the masculine in herself and expresses it. She also loves the feminine. Dancing creation's dance, she searches for ways to get the masculine and feminine in us all to dance together. She offers everyone a chance to live through stages which have been missed out – to let go, let be. As Sophia, divine wisdom, both solar *and* lunar, serving life as love, and love as life, she stands by the power of love, and unconscious and conscious are in creative interplay in the service of life.

Such images recur in both women and men, to heal and guide.

THE MASCULINE PRINCIPLE

*The masculine means to know one's goal
and do what is necessary to achieve it.*

This is the exponent of the will, in women and in men. As air and fire, it is of both spirit *and* matter, spirit penetrating matter to make it fruitful, make actual what is potential. While the feminine is of nature – of fields and meadows, rivers and streams, lakes, marshes and ponds – the masculine is about purpose, direction and goal. It is of the right, sword-bearing hand, which also wields the pen, the walking stick and the wand. Creative, light-giving, active and strong, its essence is power or energy and its image is heaven.[47] It points to where we are centred, the essential nature and quality of the archetype of the Self. It is about external reality; just as the feminine, dark and of the depths, gives a body to a new human being, so the masculine, light and of the heights,

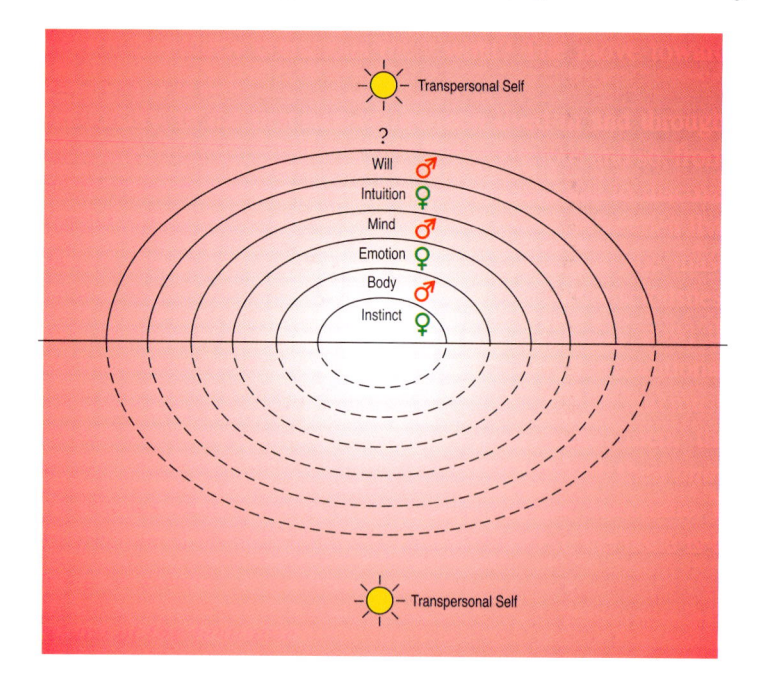

Chart 2:04 – Levels of Consciousness 2

---

47 See *I Ching*, 'Ch'ien, The Creative', Wilhelm 1950 ibid, pp. 3-10.

initiates outer creativity by lending form to ideas. And both bring heaven down to earth.

The masculine belongs with *logos*, the defining and separating *word* that lets us discover meaning through understanding. There is no creative consciousness without discrimination between the opposites. The paternal principle takes decisions and directs energy towards chosen goals, new structures, law and order. It can actualise. It has a sense of time. It involves willed effort, the power of duration, concentration and discipline to inquire, shape, form and lead. It relates to the collective in terms of principles rather than belief systems, valuing responsibility, self-control and the work ethic. It is lived out in vocation rather than relationship. Though not about identification, it concerns our physical and sexual identity, as well as our ego-identity and eventually our spiritual or Self-identity.

As with the feminine, the expression of the masculine may be positive or negative. Power is of value. Is it legitimate? Any focusing of energy, especially collective energy, can be democratic – or autocratic, through godfather figures. Will it achieve love? Do we manage through consensus and consultation – or by a bureaucracy, a multiplication of rules? Discipline is needed. Self-discipline is best.

The map opposite gives three out of the first five levels of consciousness to the feminine. It is interesting, as we saw, to map the sub-personalities from Workshop One onto it, noting their gender.

Some further polarities

Feminine	**Masculine**
depth	height
perception	judgment
soul	spirit
past	present
unconscious	conscious
being	doing
roots, beginnings	purposes, goals
diffuse awareness	focused awareness
mercy	justice
	(yet woman holds the scales!)
life ethic	work ethic
healing	medicine
caring	coping
homoeopath	allopath

sympathy	reason
religion	politics
Eastern religions	Western religions
Catholic	Protestant
	(a protestant Mother Church?)
concrete	abstract
kitchens	laboratories
imagery	visualisation
biology	chemistry, physics
consciousness research	behavioural psychology
mediumship	psychical research
spontaneity	calculation

While *opposites* are opposed, *polarities* are the two ends of a pole, or sides of a coin: both this *and* that, *yin* and *yang*, the eternity symbol of the horizontal figure 8. Working with and from both is what makes for psychological wholeness, the alchemic marriage. Yet, to be 'normal', we have usually neglected one in favour of the other. We are contradictory, at odds with each other, 'either this *or* that'. The battlefield of opposites is inside us too: our feeling and intuition are at war with our minds and wills. We are at war with ourselves.

The Masculine principle, going with the left brain and the right side of the body, is symbolised by sun and mountain, by air, fire and height. Its direction is upward. Its images include pointed, directional objects: swords, rockets, towers. It is conscious, active, extrovert and objective, looking to the outer world. Where the feminine aspect in all of us is about *being*, this is about *doing*. Aware mainly of mind and body, it is rational, to do with spirit and focus. Visualisation (seeing with the mind's eye and realising the intention) is masculine, where imagery (letting go and allowing images to surface) is more feminine.

A man (or woman) under its influence will use his inquiring mind, listening for his vocation to some life-task. He (or she) may be a leader, initiating change, aware of or concerned for his authority. He is positive, group-conscious and inclusive, thinking in wider terms than does the feminine. Loving truth and justice, he may bring them into being through law or politics. Orderly and self-controlled, he directs, organises and standardises. Perhaps he enters the sciences, or government, or management. He likes hierarchies. He may be caught up in theory, concept, intellectual analysis; but he also enjoys structures, fixing material things and making them actual. He learns the necessary technique – say, typing, or playing an instrument – before the flow can take place. He may be full of grandeur – authoritarian, aggressive, even war-mongering; but he also knows that failing organisations are those which have lost the feminine influence.

Unlike the feminine, which is always there and is in the round, the masculine develops upwards through stages. Like the development of an embryo it is linear, involving progression, growth and the journey towards a goal. While *the journey* of the hero is feminine, the masculine is *the hero* himself, the one who goes on the journey.

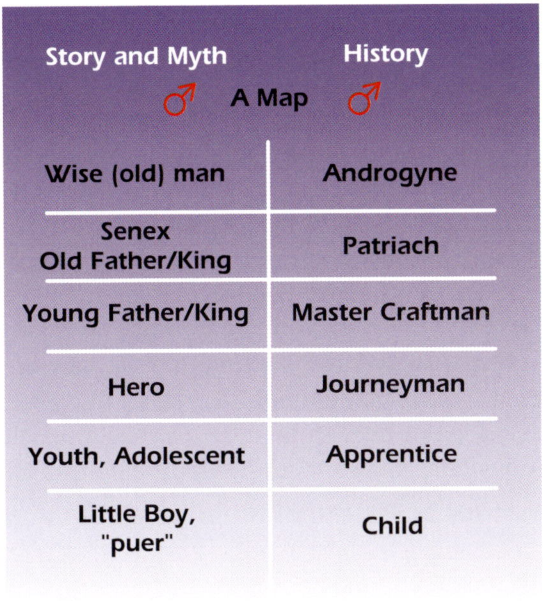

Story and Myth ♂	A Map	History ♂
Wise (old) man		Androgyne
Senex Old Father/King		Patriach
Young Father/King		Master Craftman
Hero		Journeyman
Youth, Adolescent		Apprentice
Little Boy, "puer"		Child

Chart 2:05 – Some Archetypal Masculine Figures

Again, each of these stages has its negative side. Those who fail to rise through any one of them remain stuck at the previous one.

The child

We begin with the boy or *puer* who, if free and happy, will be spontaneous and playful, open and fearless. From about three years old, he must back away from his mother; full of wonder, he has a real need to join in the excitement of what men do. This aspect in us all never dies. He needs help with his first lessons in doing a masculine job; this may well fail if his father is too far away or too authoritarian. If the child can't experiment with being a man, he will return to the feminine.

Soon, realising that the world does not revolve around him, the happy child is replaced by the wounded child. He withdraws and freezes in time, remaining unhappy and frightened. Many an adult is stuck here, lost, angry and manipulative, still searching for unconditional love, refusing to come out and play till he gets it. He has become the eternal boy. It's worth remembering that in Peter Pan (the archetypal *puer aeternus*) the children had lost their mother.

The apprentice

So the youth becomes apprentice – to the masculine principle.

However, struggling to be male, with father as model for better or worse, the young person just out of childhood doesn't usually have practical apprenticeship ahead of him. At school he learns, if he didn't already know it, that he must be competitive in pursuit of excellence. This is a period of powerful polarities: will he conform, or not? Be obedient to his family, or leave the nest early? He may picture the adult world as dull, arid, sensible, boring, practical, weighted down with responsibilities. Here's an end to fun, spontaneity, joy, laughter… freedom! No wonder he's reluctant to join in. Instead, he fantasises about his hidden genius without doing anything about it. Seeking total control and to be perfectly understood without having to explain himself, he will grow up only if life is just as he wants it to be. Otherwise, no deal! Many people stick here, refusing to grow up, allowing no room for debate, complexity or the possibility of being wrong. Though they play to the crowd, underneath they are lonely, miserable and frightened.

The journeyman

Historically, the apprentice became the journeyman,[48] trusted and sent out by his master. He began to discover his kingdom, his authority, his responsibility. He had something of the hero about him at this interface between adolescence and youth – the inner hero on a journey into consciousness, becoming lover, glimpsing his beloved at the start

---

48   Journeyman: qualified, reliable artisan working for another. OED.

of the journey. He was not breaking from the feminine but cutting the mother tie so that, at a later stage of the journey, he might seek the higher feminine. He would not find his true princess until he was ready to enter into his kingdom.

But, alas, there are few journeys left. This stage goes wrong because of the lack of any personal goal. The feather-bedding of the welfare state may have done damage to the masculine principle in us all. The hero is projected onto his peers, onto sportsmen and pop stars. His sexuality develops, with an emphasis on contrast. Violence erupts. Those stuck at this level may in fact hide their rage and be calm and patronising in the face of opposition. Black-and-white, simplistic, evasive, this young person 'knows' and will turn into someone who doesn't change his views in twenty years. Never swayed by the ideas of others, he stands firm and ignores them. Women too, of course: 'The lady's not for turning'.

The master craftsman

This is the stage of responsibility. No man is a hero to his own family. If all is well, the journeyman becomes young father who becomes master craftsman. As with the hero, the personal need may be in conflict with changes in society. But this is a real adult, full of honesty and integrity, who wholeheartedly takes responsibility for his own life and family.

If it goes wrong, this is when men, jealous of the shining of the young, turn to repressing them, preventing the hero from achieving anything. Detachment may mask lack of caring. The kind of schoolteacher, policeman or prison warder who abuses his power over the youth, or the nervous parent who plants self-doubt in the son, all may be stuck here.

The old father

So to the patriarch – the elder of the tribe, teller of tales, keeper of the myth. In the business world, he may be kicked upstairs from executive action to a more paternal role. Flexible and fluid, he has clarified his own values, principles, ideals and goals; they are open to scrutiny and change and never imposed on others.

If this stage goes wrong, you have the poor old *senex*. Grumbling, he dodders about, his age the most obvious thing about him.

Hypochondriac, backward-looking, complaining about the young and the world in general, he is an irascible petty tyrant, not wanting to go anywhere or do anything and scornful of those who do.

The wise man

Like the wise woman, this conjunct figure is in balance, a psychological androgyne. If there is a negative side, it is the wicked wizard. The positive is Gandalf, or the Laughing Buddha, or the Zen master, funny, tricky and loving. Immensely wise, he enjoys life, has fun, is completely spontaneous. He loves children and animals and simple things. Ageless, he focuses not upon the ills of body or society but on life itself. He eats when he eats, sleeps when he sleeps, laughs when he laughs. In him the masculine and the feminine have come together in glorious interplay, the marriage of heaven and earth.[49]

It can be interesting to explore among public figures: are they *fathers* old or young – or *wise men*? Are the different psychologies and psychologists informed by feminine or by masculine energy? What kind of exemplar does each great religion make?

Personal wholeness

For us all, wholeness lies in the uniting of the masculine and feminine within. Our goal may well be psychological androgyny. Then we move into relationships with less demand, less projection; the more fully and deeply because our need for a rebalancing 'other' can also be met from within. We saw the *anima-ridden* man, too heavily related to the feminine principle without the balancing masculine – irritable and spiteful, moody and diffuse, finicky and fussy, leaning emotionally on others around him. And we saw how, if a woman is too heavily related to the masculine principle without the balancing feminine – if she is *animus-ridden* – she will be overbearing and hypercritical, dogmatic and argumentative, with a harsh, metallic edge in her voice. Each just misses the mark.

When a woman is very much a woman, related to life wherever she finds it in herself and others, she will understand not only the rhythms and cycles of growth and the need for continuity, but also be open to changes. When she brings to her natural perception the ability for clear thought, the light of reason will give clarity to her insight and she will

---

[49] See the Oxherd, Picture 10, in Somers 1994, *The Fires of Alchemy*, pp. 228-231.

think things through, steadying the vagrant tendencies of the non-rational approach. She will focus rather than being diffuse, externalising her awareness, adding fire, direction, purpose and a new creativity to her own life and that of others.

And a man is most truly a man when he adds intuition and feeling to his analytical and rational nature, thinking more in terms of the individual and of human relatedness. Giving heart values to his judgments and mercy to his decisions, he internalises his awareness and awakens to the soul within. So new dimensions of creativity open up in beauty and the arts – whole realms of inner experience and outer expression.

THE COMING TOGETHER OF MASCULINE AND FEMININE

*Images and symbols may include anthropomorphic figures:
the hero, the wanderer, the persecuted one, the lovers united in death,
the warring twins, the dying and reviving god,
the sacred fool touched by the divine.* Joan Swallow

Masculine Symbols	for the woman ♂	Individual	for the man ♀	Feminine Symbols
	Man out there	Individual	Woman out there	
	Father	Parent	Mother	
	Inner Masculine	♂ & ♀ principle	Inner Feminine	
	Height	The Myths	Depth	
	Air/Fire	The Archetypes	Earth/Water	
	Spirit/Mind/Will	The Cosmic	Creative womb of life	
	?	- and beyond -	?	
	Spirals up and to the right		Spirals down and to the left	

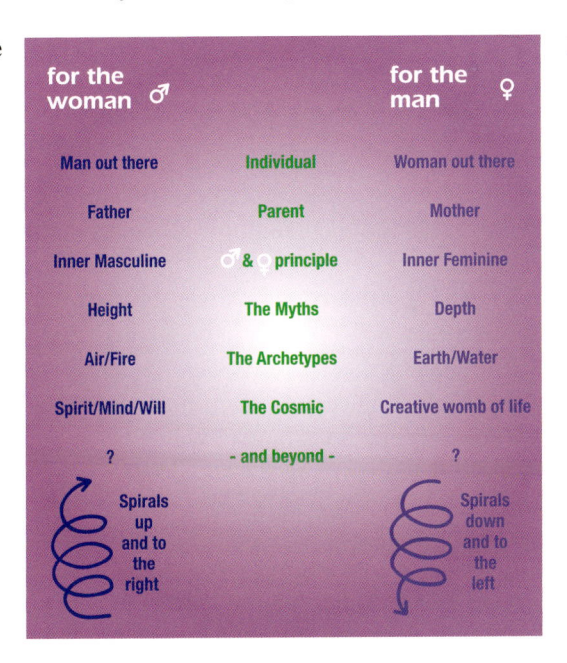

Chart 2:06 – Symbols of the Masculine and Feminine

Masculine symbols spiral with focused awareness in towards the mountain top, the flight to the sun, light and the heights. Tuned to the unconscious, feminine symbols are diffuse, left-handed, spiralling in and down.

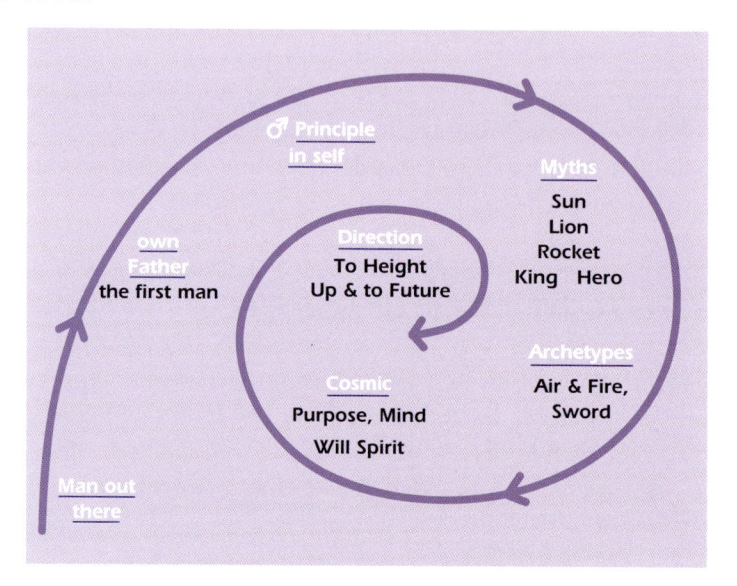

Chart 2:07 – Symbols of the Masculine

These arise in the dreams and imaginings of anyone – let's say a woman – having trouble with a man in her life. Universal, they merge in a spiral pattern leading up and in to the right, towards the hub of meaning. Concerned about husband or lover, brother, son or friend, at first this particular *man out there* will be in her dreams. Then the images broaden to encompass her environment and culture, her past, her childhood, her first contact with men in this lifetime. She realises the problem is not only, or not chiefly, with this man, but with her parents, particularly her own *father*. And behind Father lies her own masculine principle, her inner man, her *animus*. Dream symbols include pointed directional objects – the walking-stick and the pen, as well as spears and arrows, swords, towers, trains, cars and planes. (It's worth noting that while spaceships are masculine, their launching pads are feminine – just as a waterspout is masculine and a whirlpool feminine.) As the work deepens, male animals appear – bulls and stags, lions, wolves, stallions. Next, she becomes deeply aware of male characters in the *stories and myths* she has known, if she's lucky, since she was tiny. Fairy-tale people emerge: the prince, hero, king, wizard, sorcerer, court jester; also the gnome, the elf, the man-eating giant. Out of myths come the fool, the satyr, the trickster, the tempter, the centaur, the one-eyed monster. Beyond them are the archetypes of *air and fire*; no longer personal, the masculine is contained in these powerful energy-forms. Now for the mountain and the *flight to the sun*. On the perilous journey upward, she is lifted by mystical animals, often winged: the dragon, the phoenix, Pegasus, the unicorn. Yet further lies the *cosmic* level: spirit, mind, will, purpose, direction to the future. And beyond them, may there not be a seventh realm, and on beyond that? Hers is a height-oriented journey of dynamism, fire, purpose, clarity, thought, direction; spiralling up and to the right, it reaches upward and onward towards creative mind and will.

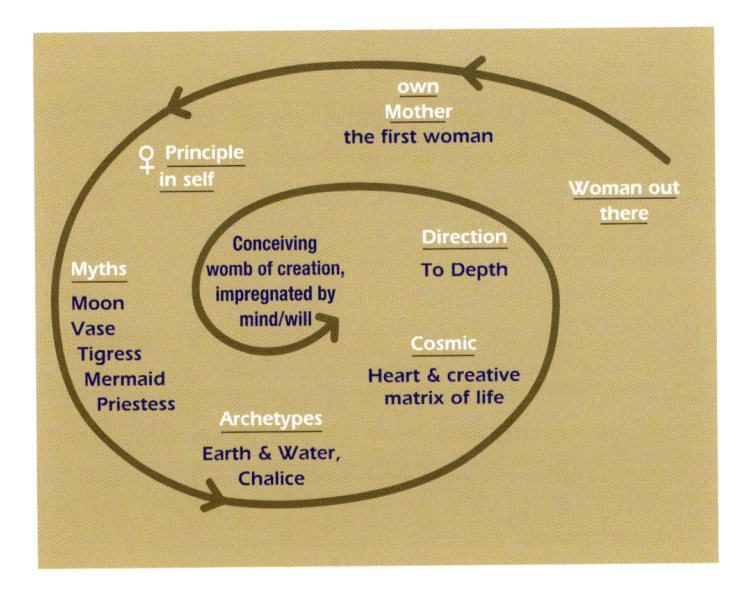

Chart 2:08 – Symbols of the Feminine

Conversely someone, let's say a man, with a problem relating to a woman in his life, will begin to delve. His journey will spiral to the left and down, exploring the depths. It's to be hoped this spiral will eventually meet the other one coming up.

At first, images bear on the present situation. He dreams of the individual *woman out there*: the wife or lover, the daughter, sister, friend. Symbols of the feminine follow, till he realises that, beyond the immediate relationship, his environment, culture and parents are involved. He must come to terms with his own *mother* or her equivalent, the first appearance of woman in this lifetime. Behind her lies his own inner feminine, his *anima*, his idea of womanhood. He goes further, breaking through the confines of the rational mind, and his images broaden to include containers – vases, baskets, boxes, shells, purses, cups – indicating the womb, the breast, the chalice. Now female animals appear: cats, cows, tigresses, rabbits, deer. It's in the *stories and myths* of the race: here are the princess, the queen, the fairy, the witch, the priestess; he meets not only mermaids and nymphs but sirens and gorgons and devouring sea-monsters, the virago, spider, octopus. At the archetypal level, he dreams of *earth*, of *water* in its many aspects, of ocean, cave, labyrinth, the underworld. He is spiralling down and in. Beneath all he encounters *the moon*, and constellations and galaxies of stars. He is approaching the *cosmic*, the heart and creative matrix of life, the conceiving womb of creation once penetrated and impregnated by mind and by will. Beyond this we do not know.

As we saw, learning to deal with the man or woman within us, we can better get on with the actual person outside. These symbols, coming in any order, help us to rebalance and understand our inner life. We relate it directly and practically to the outer till these universal symbols merge, their spiral patterns leading us in towards the hub of meaning. The true woman or man of no rank knows how to combine the two spirals, the two principles. And that is enlightenment.

EXPLORATION
THE MASCULINE AND FEMININE MET ON THE ROAD
(45 minutes)

Minutes

2 Leave behind this room, talking, words, the rush of the morning and the use of the left brain. Check round your body to see if you are relaxed. Go into story mode – a hovering awareness, an opening of the heart helping the flow of images. Your arms, hands,

shoulders have nothing to carry; your feet have nowhere to walk. Give them permission to rest.

Stage 1

4   Find yourself walking along a road, known to you or not. The sun is overhead, and water somewhere nearby. Have a sense of the sounds, scenery, scents, atmosphere. Note the time of day. Allow yourself a little while to enjoy it. Know that this journey is about the masculine and feminine principles.

9   First, on this road you'll meet someone (or it may be something) that most fully represents the *feminine* aspect of you. When you do, set up a dialogue with it, discover all you can about it, recognise why the feminine in you should take such a form at this point. If there are more than one, explore them too, seeking to discover why there are more than one at present.

3   Begin to bring this dialogue to a close. Before you move on, ask the feminine aspect to accompany you on the next stage of the journey.

Stage 2

9   Once more, find yourself walking the road. Now you meet someone (or it may be something) that most fully represents the *masculine* in you. Again, set up a dialogue, discover all you can about it, recognising why the masculine in you should take such a form now. Again, if you should meet more than one, explore this in the same way, discovering why, just now.

3   Bring the dialogue with the masculine towards its close. Moving on, invite both your feminine and masculine aspects to accompany you on the third stage of the journey…

Stage 3

8   Ahead is a place which you would naturally choose to commune inwardly, or to talk privately and intimately with close friends. Approaching this place, you become more and more in touch with your own *Self*, a listening Self who does not judge.

There in that place – together as you are with your non-judgmental, accepting, transpersonal Self – begin a conversation between this wise Self and the feminine and masculine aspects who have accompanied you. Explore in depth their relationship to each other and to you; the difficulties which any of you may experience; changes needed to rebalance the situation; and how to allow for the fuller development and creative expression of each in the future.

4 In just such a place of communion, with the feminine and masculine coming creatively together in the presence of the Self, a new potential of your wholeness, *a new synthesis*, may appear. Invite a *symbol or image* for that new potential of wholeness. What may be born from this?

3 Thank these aspects of your being; tell them you value them. Soon, begin to return to everyday consciousness; but bring with you the energy of that new potential of your wholeness.

We remember *Aesculapius*. That love is the greatest therapy was recognised in Epidaurus, a sanctuary for people in trouble. Sleep was induced, and the healing of the soul led to the healing of the body. Dreamers were put into a small place over running water. There, they were granted an image of the god and allowed to dream their dreams. Then when they emerged the priestess or the priest-healer was there, waiting for them. The speaking of the dream is what healed them, and the time and place to go into their inner landscape, meeting and dialoguing; and they came out to greater wholeness, there to seek of it in the world. So, come slowly out of your dream, and anchor in the present place.[50]

MARRIAGE AS A PSYCHOLOGICAL RELATIONSHIP

CONTAINER AND CONTAINED

One of the joys of Jung is that, rather than speculating or pontificating, he simply described what was experienced. He presented not theories but *observations* about relationships and interactions between feminine and masculine; his women friends took up his findings.[51]

In early twentieth-century Switzerland, the feminine principle was relatively disregarded. Marriage tended to be stereotyped. Polygamy was certainly not allowed out anywhere in Europe. The feminine side of the man was seen as a deviation from the norm and kept under wraps. And any idea that a woman had a masculine side was equally unacceptable.

---

50 Epidaurus, the sanctuary of Aesculapius, ancient Greek demigod of medicine, is to this day said to be richly endowed with springs and streams of healing water.
51 Jung 1909-10, *Marriage as a Psychological Relationship*, CW 17, para 331c-337.

Observing this, Jung came up with a model, mooting it in seminars from 1910 on. Stereotypically, the feminine was 'contained' *mentally* at that time, while the masculine was 'contained' at an *emotional* level. This can apply in any close relationship, hetero- or homosexual, or close but non-sexual – parent with child, friend with friend; one person tends to be Contained and the other the Container. The image is of a ball and socket joint, the one beautifully enclosed within the other. At first, they turn on each other in a very smooth and harmonious way.

The Contained person Jung observed as being relatively simple in their requirements; if these needs are met, they are content to be so held, living wholly confined within the relationship. Nothing new is sought. They give it their undivided attention, have no outside interests. A feeling of completeness is evident. They look to the other.

The requirements of the Container are far more complex (not better or worse, but different). These people are satisfied only for a short time. Diffuse, with more sensitivity, they seek variety and subtlety. Looking for possibilities, they do usually seek them first in their partners; but they may get irritated by the simplicity of the Contained one. Ironically, this simplicity may have been a big part of the original attraction.

Again, to change the image, the Contained person is like a small, neat flat or apartment with two armchairs by the same fire. The other needs to be there, and that's it. Meantime, the Container walks around in a larger space – a house with unknown rooms, attics, basements, a garden with a wall and a world beyond. The one longs to be together with the other in a small space; the other longs to be looking out, exploring.

However, Jung saw that all this varies even within one relationship. As the two people develop, change is required. Coming to feel exasperated, dissatisfied and resentful, the Container starts to disrupt the close fit. Yet she or he does need to come back, bringing their diffusion with them. The Contained one meantime, experiencing a sense of psychological absence, feels threatened and presses even harder to maintain the close fit. Yet this person does need to amplify and expand his or her awareness out.

So at least one partner has abdicated or abandoned their own needs, passively allowing the situation to continue. They are not coping. Possibilities for growth in the relationship fade. The ball and socket grinds to a halt and freezes. This is expressed psychosomatically, or in verbal conflict. The marital bed becomes a two-person institution – there is not necessarily a relationship at all.

If they are coping at least adequately, the roles can easily reverse: either can become Container or Contained in different areas. Having a young family may set up this coping situation. But it's a temporary strategy, no permanent solution. For real growth, they must both raise to consciousness the changing needs of the Container and the effects on the Contained. What was right for both five years ago may not now be right for either. How to be one's self in the relationship?

There may be a role change. If the Contained one recognises that there is a difference between their childlike side and their childish need for constant containment – or if the Container gets tired and needs to be contained in turn – then things may shift. It's to be hoped that they will begin positively-oriented negotiations, possibly with the help of a counsellor – it can be easier to talk to someone outside. Particular crisis points, rites of passage (or areas where such rites once operated), may mark the change from romantic love to a loving relationship.

Our requirements alter. We need both psychological and physical space and, often, more time to ourselves: one couple, living together, planned to marry and to live in two separate houses afterwards, not always to sleep in the same bed and each to have a front door key. A different couple met as each was divorcing from other people. She had a flat, he moved in. Then, his ex-wife sent him their seven-year-old son to live. Soon the three were frantic. With some trouble, he got his desk into her flat but – after the stereo – it was too much for her. In therapy, danger points were looked at: she didn't want the child, her two cats had left and ... the early evenings! For her, coming home after work was for de-rôling from her job; she wanted a gin and she wanted her cats. Instead, the men would assault her for their dinner. A solution: she wrote them both notes demanding ten minutes every day for herself. And they honoured it. The boy left, the cats returned, she became pregnant, she OK, he OK.

Elementary and simple things, breathing in and breathing out, are as important as practices such as yoga. We may go to the wall without them.

So the ball and socket pattern of Container *with* Contained is bound, with luck, to break. If *both* partners wish to be Contained you have two vines clinging. The aim is to have two Containers together. You may wish to reflect on a major relationship in your life, and how it was contained.

THE MASCULINE AND FEMININE WITHIN

THE FOUR PARTNERS

This model, too, applies not only to marriage but to any close partnership, sexual or not. It is a valuable map although, like all maps, it's not the whole answer.[52]

When a man and a woman come together and decide to marry, two go into the church, but *four* sign the register. This idea of Jung's, formulated by the nineteen-twenties, we now take almost for granted. Jung worked more and more on it: in every man, his internal *anima*, in every woman, her internal *animus*. The four are in continuous interplay, and the Self is greater than either. The couple *together with their internal opposites* constitute a four-way partnership.

1. First, the pair *meet* socially.

2. They *get acquainted* and, all unconsciously, the inner figures appear.

3. She carries with her, like a tail, her entire experience of the masculine: her relationships with father, brothers, grandfathers, uncles, teachers,

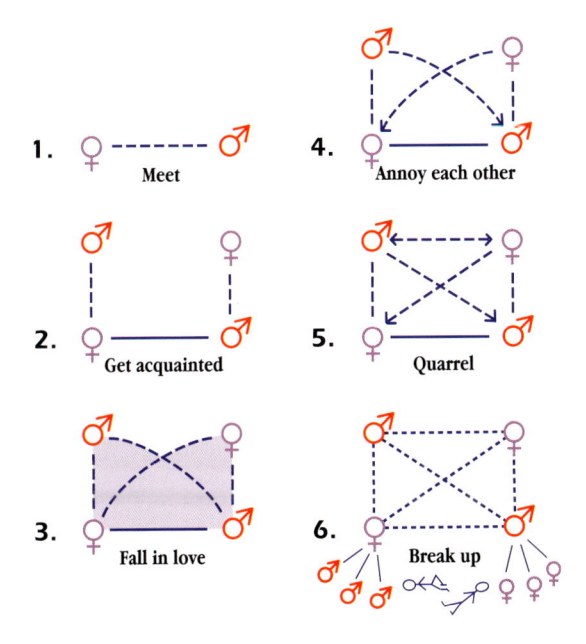

Chart 2:09 – The Four People at the Wedding 1

---

52 Jung 1909-10, ibid, para 338 ff.

heroes, archetypes; all she has seen through the media, through teaching, reading, scripting throughout her life. All of *that* is within her and she sees him as – all of it. He seems her own, unrecognised other self, her own unique masculine principle. And he, too brings to it all of the feminine principle: relationships with his mother, grandmothers, aunts, sisters, teachers, media, books, culture, his own unrecognised self, all his experience of the feminine. Between him and the reality of the woman, his partner, there is a veil drawn. She is the mysterious and bewitching other – she is all.

So, typically, they *fall in love*. Each is seeking the divine, the carrier of the archetype – and they've found it … The light changes; for a time the world is lit up by magic, delight, joy, perfection. They are in a state of complete harmony, one heart, one soul; it is like a return to childhood, to the mother's womb. This in-love stage is very beautiful, a genuine enchantment. As Jung said, it is an incontestable, genuine experience of the divine, a real communion with life. However, it is projection. They are seeing magical inner figures. Unconscious of that aspect in themselves, projecting it on the other, they will have chosen someone who seems to be like, or to complement, themselves. The back history of each person draws a veil between them and the real partner. This is the impersonal power of fate.

4. Now they begin to *annoy each other*. Enchantment is knocked, disenchantment takes its place. The negative, rather than the magical, is projected. Now this *she*, who had made his heart ache and reflected all his soul, is a shrew; and *he* doesn't change his socks for two weeks and is a bastard. Her inner masculine side thumps him. His inner feminine falls to sulking. The children, carrying the unresolved conflict at an unconscious level, become carriers of their parents' disappointment, grief and anger. Both partners are dimly aware, too, of *being* irritating. The earlier, magical force has gone; they scarcely remember the glory that has fled.

But they *did* see it. And arguably that glory was truer than the present disillusioned sparrings of the inner woman and the inner man. They are lucky if they fall into friendship and come actually to *like* each other – which doesn't necessarily go with being in love.

5. Times change, but in the late twentieth century children came to breathe in with their milk the belief that *men and women are not only*

equal, they're the same. But they aren't. They work from different aspects. That's what causes the trouble, *the quarrel*. The masculine shouts angrily, 'For god's sake, woman, be reasonable!' The feminine expects to be understood without explaining. The man says, 'It's now!' The woman, 'No it's not! Listen to me!' He goes moody, washes his car, vanishes into the garden shed, communes with the rhubarb in dumb-animal suffering. Big boys don't cry, or get hurt – or feel at all. 'It's that incomprehensible woman!' It's not; it's his own internal feminine. His partner, muttering, 'I'll get him! I'll wait for him!' closes her womb and her feeling-nature and has a headache. She's angry; her negative masculine side waits till she can hit him where it hurts: 'You spent a lot of time talking to Fred!' he remarks. 'Yes,' she replies, 'Fred's such a *man*!'

It is their mothers and grandmothers who have done this to men. For the feminine, having total command of the instinctual, feeling world, has all along said to them: 'You're no good at it!' On the other hand, the woman, mistrusting her own clear thinking, fears she'll lose the relationship if she says directly what she feels. Is there an edge in her tone of voice when she speaks the truth?

6. So, developing wandering eyes, they *break up*. He finds tenderness elsewhere, an actual 'other woman' at the same level, to whom he says, 'My woman's crazy, she doesn't understand me, she isn't intelligent.' The new woman says, 'I don't know how anyone could not understand *you*!' Soon, she in turn sees this new man as inhibiting her personal identity; so she goes to night school and does philosophy or car maintenance, till yet another man appears who praises and flatters her. She tells him, 'My partner only values my body, he rapes my mind!' Again, they swap.

This happens all the time. And those who choose *celibacy* are also stuck with relationships. To try and avoid them, saying, 'They're not in my nature,' just doesn't work. The trouble derives from the belief that the two of them are the same, coming from the same moment. But the masculine lives in the present, the feminine in the past and the future as well. And though religions say that life is about enhancement and understanding, they really believe that happiness is their goal. Wanting to be made complete, they feel sad. The children suffer. What's to be done?

7. Wisdom implies the marriage of masculine and feminine within us all. The road to joy leads inevitably through pain and disenchantment as, taking our projections back, we come through to a deeper relationship with the contra-sexual side of ourselves. To change, each one of us needs to *connect with our own inner partner*. Embracing the Buddhists' *all-encompassing warmth and friendliness towards our own experiencing*,[53] we are more in touch with the relationship within ourselves. For this is also about the marriage of Self and ego.

7. Connect with own inner partners

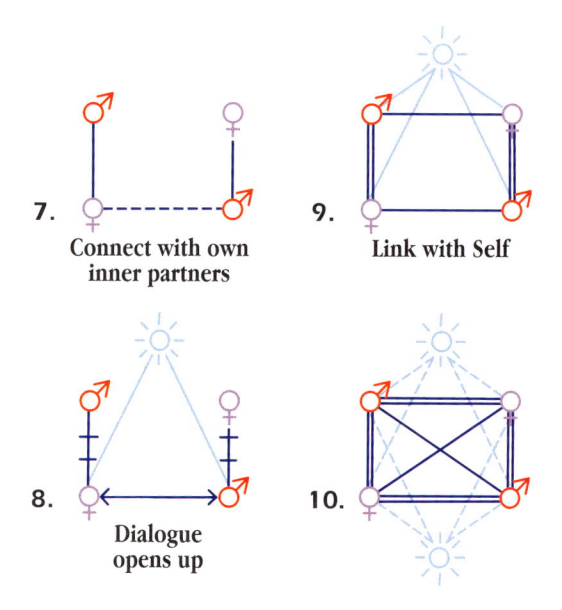

8. Dialogue opens up

9. Link with Self

10.

Chart 2:10 – The Four People at the Wedding 2

Derby and Joan apportion territory, staying at the bottom level, each using the other to prevent development: 'If it weren't for Henry/etta then I would be able to…' But when one of them becomes wedded to their own inner side, things change. An inner releasing of the other can have an instantaneous effect. A couple told of how one of them had decided to stop clinging to their son, who was abroad. In the same moment, thousands of miles away, he sent them a message saying that he was feeling newly free and would come home.

---
53 Maitri or metta.

8. So a *dialogue opens up* between the two people. The feminine part of him says to the woman out there, as to a sister: 'Go on, say it, I'm listening.' And her masculine side replies, 'Maybe he's got a point,' and listens in turn. He tries using the heart's pause to honour the feeling, intuitive, instinctual part of him. Attending with both heart and head to his partner out there, he approaches his own inner woman. The relationship becomes a place to use his heart as a sounding board, and be fully masculine too. And she, looking at her scripts and at him as a person, stops putting the earlier edge into her voice. No longer ruled by the negative *animus*, she can begin to be feminine again, and relate to her own masculinity. They begin to like themselves and each other. Many partners don't reach that, projecting onto the children instead.

   Stay together, or leave? The decision is clarified when each can say, 'Look for the inner *with me*, not with someone else.' This leads them from duress to choice. Now another dimension is constellated: the relationship itself begins to relate to something *other*. They have fallen out of the 'in love' state – into love.

9. At last, *a link is forged* between all four; the inner as well as the outer partners are relating with the Self. Real relationship is organic; it breathes in and dances, breathes out and parts. There is space; and boundaries too are honoured.

10. The Self is drawn below the bottom line of the map as well, constellated in the unconscious, creating a dance that's wider than the masculine and the feminine, beyond the personal. It is transpersonal.

Therapy helps set up the dialogue with the person's own contra-sexual, other side. The aim is not just to find wonderful images, but that inner and outer come to be experienced as one reality: Otherwise, the client is simply playing into the split and it is not integration. 'What does this mean on Monday morning?' For inner and outer are one.

DISCUSSION AND SHARING IN SMALL GROUPS

Again, we recall that evaluation of the material from someone else's imagery session is not helpful. Interpretations must come from the person themselves. See p. 40 above, and fuller commentary is given in Appendix 1.

DEVELOPING INTUITION

The prior condition for all intuition is love

Intuition is global. It is to do with life and growth and the long perspective.[54] According to Jung, it is perception of realities unknown to consciousness. Assagioli had it as a cognitive function which apprehends reality as a whole. Intuition is general rather than specific, subjective rather than objective, meaningful rather than random. Needing no intermediary, it is subtle, involving a special sensitivity, an evocation. It is the feminine principle in action. The masculine leads us to prepare the way; then we wait, receptive and expectant, listening for its voice. It is like a dish telescope, a feminine symbol with the masculine in the middle. We're not powerless to develop it, despite its mysterious character. We can prepare our minds by quieting, though not emptying them, and setting them gently aside. We can prepare our emotions by calming the heart's strong feelings; in a rage you can't be intuitive. We can prepare our bodies by a state of relaxed attention, without tension.

Intuition is rooted in work, doing the task and preparing the way. Then may follow those illuminated hunches in science, the business world, in art-dealing, in gambling. Thus, writers must first *write*; only then can it take over and write through them. They give up trying and it happens. Thus painting, even idly doodling, can lead to the truth more readily than brainstorming (which rarely works). Acknowledge the flow, catch the end of the thread; write it down perhaps, since it is not always easily recaptured, but without striving. Record with the recording angel. Intellectual discrimination knows whether it is reality or imagination; paradoxically, imagination, which helps, must also be transcended. We need a positive expectation that intuition will work in and for us, and a loving element of self-worth and acceptance, a suspension of judgment, a non-analytic, empathetic understanding. Our creativity is being engaged. Then – let go.

Assagioli distinguished between *personal* and *spiritual intuition*. To activate spiritual intuition we listen, still the mind and wait quietly. Reaching for the reality we wish to contact, we love what we reach for. With telepathy, for example, a bond of personal affection is necessary. Two people may deliberately try it, the first sympathetic and in love

---

54 See Chapter 9, pp. 339-342.

with the subject; but if the second hates it and is out to show the other is a crook then, as when a car goes under a bridge, the radio signal is smudged by static.

Incubating intuition

This receptive listening usually happens *after* the work has been done. How has it worked for people? Remember Archimedes in the bath crying 'Eureka!' Einstein is said to have first written down the theory of relativity on a napkin in his breakfast café. Those half-waking, half-sleeping visions arising from hypnogogic and hypnopompic states allow a vision that's most acute on the periphery. The chemist Kekulé who, as we have seen, developed the important idea of the Benzene Ring, 'saw' the image when half asleep: 'It's a spiral!' After years of studying the nature of the carbon-carbon bond, he had had a reverie or daydream of a snake seizing its own tail – a common symbol known in many ancient cultures as the Ouroboros. 'Dancing atoms whirling in a ring,' as he put it, 'the larger ones forming a chain dragging the smaller ones'. This vision came to him *out of work time*, through an intuitive flash that followed a mass of hard graft.[55] So – put it aside. An incubation period may be necessary. Sit on it, leave it, allow it to rest. Breathe.... Wait without anxiety, with clarity of heart, knowing when not to push or expect things. Get on with something else – it's not ready to hatch yet. You don't know the answer now, but you will in the morning.

Creative intuition bypasses the mind. However, some would-be intuitives are really muddled thinkers. Intuition happens when it happens. Personal striving, the desire to be right, the overuse of critical faculties, strong scepticism, all interfere with intuition. It is unrepeatable, so the desire to prove it by experiment is counter-productive. Anxiety is a heavy energy; indeed, even worry about *being* intuitive can get in the way.

Intuition and the four functions

The Intuitive function manifests itself through the other three. It can come through the left brain and the Thinking function; using it in the context, say, of maths or science, we need first to *know* about the matter, and only then be receptive. However, it generally goes with the right brain; for intuition to work with the heart, our emotions need to be clear and uncluttered, without anxiety, so that our Feeling nature can receive it. Intuition also works with the body and instincts through the Sensation

---

55 In 1865 Kekulé had suggested the benzene molecule contained a six-membered ring of carbon atoms with alternating single and double bonds, thus explaining some curious facts. Twenty-five years later he spoke of how he had discovered its ring shape. He persisted in critically testing his dream by logical intelligence when wide awake.

function, establishing a telepathic link like that of the animals.

Intuition may work for us through the richness of the many-coloured palette of life. It is often apprehended through imagery, whether personal or transpersonal. Symbols always point beyond themselves, helping to bring intuition to consciousness. Some types of meditation encourage it. It may come through the mystical awareness of the heart; through religion; through relationships and the emotions. Yoga can lead to intuition, as we learn how to handle the energies of the chakras.[56]

Intuition is often evoked in therapy by a need in the client. Evocation doesn't happen if only one person is present. As therapists, we can tune in through the intuition of mind, emotions or body. Asking a question, note whether your client leans back, hand behind the head, which indicates the contacting of old material, sensing of past experience; or leans forward, hand on forehead, reaching for the new, the future as yet not experienced. Continuing to rub those places may bring illumination.

Is this flash genuinely intuitive, not some wish-fulfilment? How to test its validity, discriminate the intuitive knowledge of the spirit? It is not the psychic hunch (that solar plexus phenomenon), nor mental telepathy; nor is it to be confused with dowsing, or 'psychology in the fingers'. Which speaks true: Mind? Feeling? Body? Learning to differentiate specific clues, we will later be able to transcend them: for some, the rising of energy in the top of the head is a clear sign; for others, it's a back-of-the-head buzz,[57] or a near flash past the ear, or an urge to action. Intuition comes with expectancy, not with anxiety. And – *love is an essential condition*.

Psychic awareness is the intuition trusted. Take the risk, keep the channel open, trust the flashes. As long as they seem appropriate, test your trust by acting on them. Otherwise the great Intuition in the sky will say, 'This person is not ready yet – I'll save my breath.'

GESTALT EXPLORATION
(50 minutes)

By a conservative estimate, as we shall see, three-quarters of all illness has a psychosomatic component. When the natural interaction between the Body, the Emotions and the Mind breaks down, you can talk to the symptoms themselves, both listening and *hearing*. To this end, once again

---

56 Raising them from sacral to throat, solar plexus to heart, base of spine to head. See Chapter 8.
57 Intuition is thought to be seated in the brow chakra, the 'third eye'; also in the alta major chakra at the back of the head. See Chapter 8.

place four chairs or cushions, marked Body, Emotions, Mind and Observer, in a diamond pattern.[58] From the Observer place you will be asked to take a notebook to the position of each in turn, sense into each and consult it.[59]

Stage 1

Minutes

2   So, in the Observer position, facing the centre, *become* the wise, compassionate Observer. See yourself in a column of light, in touch with the transpersonal Self, the prime mover in your life. Reflect on your present lifestyle, but make no judgments.

8   First, move to the Body position. Spend a moment getting in touch with your body. Put to it the following questions, accept its answers and record them in Body's terms:
> What does your Body experience as its greatest strength or asset?
> What does it sense is its weakest point; where is it most vulnerable?
> What unmet nourishment needs does it have?
> What next step in development would your body both *like* and *feel able* to take?

2   Return to the Observer position, leaving things of the body behind you. Centring yourself in the column of light, experience once more the calm and clarity of the wise Observer.

8   When you are ready, move to the place of Emotions. Spend a moment getting in touch with your emotional nature. Tune in to your feelings, remind yourself of them, how they flow, their weight. Now, put the same questions as before, this time to your feeling nature, and record your answers in feeling terms:
> What does your Emotional nature experience as its greatest strength or asset?
> What does it feel is its weakest point – where is it most vulnerable?
> What nourishment needs do your feelings have that are not being met?

---

58 See Chapter 1, p. 46.
59 Commentary on this Gestalt exploration, Appendix 2.

> What next step in development would it *like* and *feel able* to take?

2 Return to the Observer position, leaving all emotional material behind you. Centre yourself in the column of light; experience again the clear, compassionate Observer.

8 When you are ready, move to the Mind's chair. Tune in to your thoughts and mental activity, and put the same four questions:
> What does your Mind think is its greatest strength or asset?
> What is its weakest point, its most vulnerable?
> What are its unmet nourishment needs?
> What next step in development would it both *like* and *think itself able* to take?
> Record its answers.

Leaving your Mind behind, please return to the Observer place and centre yourself in its wisdom and clarity.

Stage 2

2 From the chair of the Observer, and as your transpersonal Self, find yourself inwardly in the kind of quiet place where you would go for private conversation. In this sanctuary, be joined by your Body, Feelings and Mind. With your knowledge of what they have told you about themselves and their strengths and weaknesses, spend a moment in communication with them. Are any conflicts of interest or problems likely to arise if their different needs are met? How do their view-points coincide – or not? For example, one of the nourishment needs of your Body or Mind might disadvantage or cause problems for your Feelings. Don't try to *solve* the problems at this stage, just identify and note areas of potential difficulty.

9 Now, visit the positions in turn, without separate instructions, each time going via the Observer position. What next step in growth would each now like and feel able to take? Together, can you find ways of capitalising on their strengths? Can they suggest how to help strengthen each other or eliminate weak points, allowing them to take the next step in growth? Give plenty of time for negotiation or dialogue; see if possible conflicts of interest or areas of difficulty can be reconciled, or at least moderated. You may need to visit them several times to get a solution or *modus vivendi*.

Stage 3

6 Re-centred in the column of light; be in touch with the clarity and peace of your own wise Observer. Consider what has been proposed. Now is the time to decide. Convey your decisions to Body, Feelings and Mind, including decisions *not* to change at this time. Make some appropriate affirmation and statement to yourself about what you will do.

3 To conclude, bring each of them into your consciousness at the centre of your life. Thank them for their parts in these discussions. Be glad you have them. Experience the sense of unity and strength that will come from any future changes, and the flow of energy that will be released in you. Rest in the Observer position, reflecting on your whole life, and what the balance of masculine and feminine means for you now. Return to the room in your own time.

SYMPTOM AS SYMBOL

Mind, Feelings and Body are like a three-pin plug: all in together, and the light comes on.

Symptom as Symbol

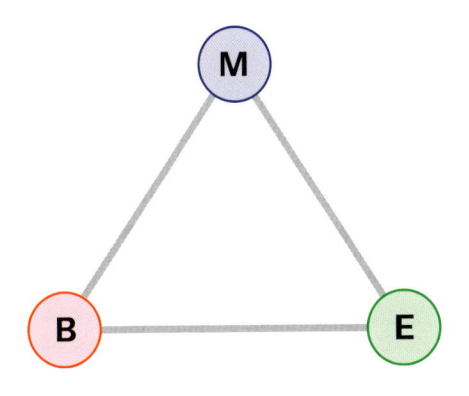

Chart 2:11 – Body, Emotions and Mind

The interaction of psyche and soma

We need to look at this beautiful trilogy on a regular basis – how are they getting on? The three of them act like a democracy of real entities. Their interaction overcomes a great deal, because of the natural homeostatic function of the unconscious. Naturally they thrive together and then our well-being is assured, whatever the situation. They have a vested interest in our health. When they are in good nick we can do just about anything; their well-being *is* preventive medicine. But is each getting nourishment? It's amazing how little they require; but are they real needs, like the need to love; or compensatory wants born of deficiency – hang-ups, feelings of inadequacy, desires for success and position arising from dependency?

Very often there's a battlefield both outside and inside us. Our wills, our Minds struggle against our Bodies and Emotions. We are at war with ourselves. Intuition feels trapped; it can't get through and, knowing things are out of true, will even help the Body become ill – to buy time, take a breather. It mobilises help by trying to die to impossible situations, reaching towards solutions, preparing for new ways of being. Our intuition realises that symptoms can be understood as a language of healing. Illness may be appropriate in our lives.

We are too easily split against ourselves, whether from inside or out. Then, one of the three becomes cut off. Very often the symptom will indicate this *left out* aspect. Dis-ease – loss of ease – is the system's effort to readjust itself, restore homeostasis and heal the splits (left from right, upper from lower; spirit, aspiration, purpose and will from instincts, roots, ground and earth). Symptoms offer graphic images: one man, a doctor, his Mind split from both Feelings and Body, found himself sawing his way out of the attic; another dreamed of his head as a closed box and his heart in a clamp; yet another heard her migraines saying, 'Don't hassle me!' – they were offering her blanket protection. We know more than appears on the surface.

Our Feelings quite frequently affect the Body via the Mind. Feeling gives energy. Mind gives direction and decides whether to act – or not. The Body often carries the can: it has to inform us about it. This can be extremely traumatic. Therefore it may be useful to ask your Body in the first place: 'What do *you* feel about the new job?' What do your Emotions have to say? And the intuitive Observer needs to ask us, 'How long since you last created something you love... worked for the joy of it?'

Be warned: the transpersonal Self in each of us has its tone-colour, its different field of work, way of being, of actualising, approaching the path. Looking at Mind, Emotions and Body in turn, we seek new energy, new quality, new direction. But these insights are for each one of us to apply *to ourselves*. To suggest there are psychosomatic aspects to *other people's* illnesses may stem from a cruel ignorance. As well as being ill, we put on them a burden of guilt for being ill in the first place. About others (as about their dreams), *never know first, and never know best*.

The mind

Energy follows thought. This esoteric statement begs the question, 'And who directs the thinker?' Yet where the Mind is focused, energy follows. The Mind is a marvellous muscle; its healing power of introspection, of both purposeful and spontaneous imagination, can actually undo disease. Mind as slayer, or Mind as healer? [60] Do we go in for hypochondria – or for something else? The mind is now being revalued: a new level is exemplified in the work of, for example, Brian McGee and the philosophers, the new scientists, Susan Greenfield.

Depression is the aching of an unused talent. However, the Mind has been taking some knocks of late. It will manage as best it can. But, poor old head – is it getting tired? Tired minds are often bored minds. They need *re-minding*, 'bodying', integrating. Then intelligence can grow, and the capacity to reason, to understand relationships. Both concrete and abstract Mind are developed by education and training – by active work rather than passive listening. The higher Mind needs to be exercised on problems. It learns by writing, reading, thinking through, by argument, disputation, questioning. It needs factors of interest. Given such appropriate nourishment, it is a searchlight putting in a great beam of light, not a blinkered carthorse stuck in one furrow. Its breadth is its usefulness. For refreshment, enlargement and diffusion it needs to breathe in – and breathe out. An instrument of exploration, its development involves mental exercise, differentiation, coordination. How is it used? What is learned and why? The Mind gives direction and co-ordination to the whole system, ideally by a gentle, meditative infusion of thought.

However, we may be in situations where Mind simply doesn't tally with Body and Feelings. If our jobs are not where our hearts are, it'll be

---

60 See Pelletier 1977, *Mind as Healer, Mind as Slayer*.

good old Mind that got us into them. A wonderful servant or lord chamberlain, even prime minister, it is a bad king; it can become a dictator, a terrible, rampant autocrat. Hence the need for the transpersonal Observer. (Even in the Gestalt exercise above, the Mind sometimes arranges that the Observer be thought of as just a side department of itself.)

Every image in our Minds has a motor element in the *Body*. Dwelling on the image produces a physical correspondence, and at times a willed, mental control of the Body may be called for. Conversely, every action of the Body produces a mental reaction or image, influencing the Mind. We learn by doing – practically, not theoretically – through ritual, sports, Aikido, T'ai chi and suchlike.

As we have seen, our Minds and our Emotions affect each other. Feeling directs the Mind, while Mind rationalises desire. Yet it's *emotional* energy that follows thought with a one-to-one correspondence. Mind intensifies feeling, mental images creating emotional whirlpools; and our Feelings give sensitivity to our response systems. When Mind is cut off, yet energised by Feeling, the danger is that an obsession may develop and run us, an *idée fixe*, a circular mental pattern. It is useful to consult our Feelings and our Minds separately, distinguishing one from the other.

The emotions

They do their best to stay around as part of the trilogy. When listened to, they don't play games. They need to be honoured. Telling about light and joy, love, laughter and play, they develop from the simple 'happy or unhappy' of our primitive selves to the wide range that goes with experience. They show in our interactions with people – our colour-spectrum, our range, a peacock's tail of anger, resentment, fear, amusement, disgust, guilt, pleasure, pain, affection, excitement. In relationships they run from love to hate, agony to bliss, joy to grief, rage to peace. They need coordination, to pull together rather than being in conflict. And they need integration with our Bodies and Minds. Since they give energy to the system they too need nourishment: companionship, nature, music, art, beauty. When Feelings are fed but rarely, we take on the environment, absorbing its depression and fear.

Feelings do try to contain themselves; but if not given a place, if always pushed back and pent up, then (reasonably) they are annoyed, and erupt. One man, with early signs of a pending heart attack, took his children and their friends to see the film 'ET'. To his embarrassment, he found himself racked with huge sobs in front of them all; the whole row of seats heaved. He was sobbing for the tender side of himself. Though his grief may have seemed disproportionate, he had no heart attack.

Emotions are not often dangerous, though we're sometimes afraid they will be disruptive. We may be unwittingly scripted to rein them in lest too much anger or joy bring disaster. Or they may be trapped and falsified so that we laugh when hurt, smile when angry. At the opposite extreme, we may let our feeling nature run the show with its excessive sensitivity, spilling over at some quite minor trigger, repeatedly 'catharting'. Demanding to be listened to, emotions are a nuisance if they get rampant. When cut off from the Mind and either over- or under-used, they can lead to symptoms – though much less likely to if *heard*.

Our Emotions may also be directly affected by the Body. Yoga, acupuncture, bio-energetics, many alternative therapies, feed back into and help release feelings. Certain physical disorders may be linked with the suppression of particular emotions. Thus, anger or resentment might, if suppressed, emerge as arthritis. 'A pain in the neck' is obvious. Love when thwarted could lead to heart disease; unshed tears to weeping sores, rhinitis or sinusitis; inner conflict to headache; clinging to the children or the past, to constipation; being much 'pissed off', to cystitis; a reluctance to look ahead, to short sight; failure to communicate, to sore throat. Even genetic illness may be precipitated by the emotional climate – or not. Falling in love, with a person or with life, can radically change things: like Elizabeth Barrett Browning, overcome negative feelings and physical symptoms may retreat.[61]

The body

Feelings do seem to have a direct effect on the Body with no mental image between. The rationale of the Body therapies is that *psyche* and *soma* are one and the same; when Feelings are repressed, psychosomatic problems can arise. Indeed, it is suggested that at least three-quarters of all illnesses have their origin also in the psyche.

But remember again that emphasising the psychosomatic aspects of illness may burden other people. We validly apply all this *only to ourselves*.

When Mind and Feelings are pulling together, the Body fits in easily. It is accommodating, a barometer and a good friend. Delicate, beautiful, like an artist's instrument, it will not lie, and rarely does it get itself into trouble

---

61 Elizabeth Barrett Browning had been an invalid until, falling in love with Robert Browning, she recovered.

(that's Mind and Feelings, not Body itself). The Body has its own language of Feelings. Given over- or under-nourishment, it can be heard speaking:

'My heart has gone out of it;
I have no stomach for it;
I am bone-weary, sick to death of it;
My fire speaks and I am burned up by it;
Water speaks and I am awash, inundated by it;
My earth, and I am bogged down, buried alive by it;
Air, and I can't breathe in it, daren't take a breather from it – must fly!'

The illness, the symptom, is thus seen less as a dire thing to be pushed out than as a creative language from which we learn. We rarely fail to get an early warning sign – the storm signals go up before the tornado hits. Symptoms in our right or left sides may indicate some lack. Our postures maintain our fears – notice how we use our hands when talking. Depression, that aching of an unused talent, may also be frozen anger. The Body affectionately sends a message – dragging exhaustion, perhaps? 'But surely, it's selfish to indulge, waste time!' We don't or can't take note – till it becomes a critical imperative.

The Body needs the nourishment of differentiation and coordination and the joy of movement. It needs food, exercise, affection, security, respect, challenge, interest. And its integration – first as a vehicle for the Feelings, then for the Mind – requires infusion, purification. This may be symbolised by abstinence of various kinds (vegetarianism, for example). Breathing is important; you can't get terribly angry if you're breathing properly. And what about the positive, joyous, creative use of the Body? What about sport, fun? And dying – 'to die daily'. Letting go is an odd kind of control; yet while we hold on we can neither die nor grow.

What may happen to make symptoms arise?

Suppose our Feelings are bored, full of malaise and depression, undernourished; typically, they signal with tears, resentment, fatigue. Given some sudden shock, they rage, fearful or grief-stricken. The Body tries to hold the system, sending a knot in the stomach. But we don't heed the knot; we have a drink, kick the cat, yell at the kids, run round the block. The Mind, having a vested interest in not being bothered, does nothing to help: 'Can't you see I'm busy!'

So Feelings ask Body to send Mind a clearer message. And it does: our teeth grit and grind in sleep, we get neck-ache, shoulder-ache, back-ache; our eyelids flicker with nervous tics. We go to the cupboard and take some tablets. But our heads still ache, being too much in authority; and now we're waking at two in the morning with nightmares. 'Those tablets are too weak – heavier artillery, please.' So off we go to the chemist for pills. More powerful, they quieten us for a bit, then cease to work.

Feelings are still not heard so Body, being friendly, sends another symptom: free-floating panic. At last, Mind wakes to the idea there is something wrong. We go to the doctor. Taking four minutes to deal with us (he also probably has tics, backache, panic attacks), he gives the Body proper pills, on prescription. So Mind gets its drugs. However, since we get no better, the specialist arranges for traction, physiotherapy, an operation, hospital – rest at last!

What's really wrong? Mind will do anything to avoid recognising Feelings, whose original statement, original shock, is still being suppressed. So feeling-energy has been driven into the wrong place and become rampant in the poor old Body. It can also be driven into the Mind channel. *Idées fixes* may follow, as we saw, and head tics, spinal lesions, neck-ache, migraine, compulsive or obsessive behaviour. Symptoms may include numbness, showing that the Body itself is split, with some bits ignorant of other bits. One woman, a very sharp-edged lawyer, visualised her masculine side as a chain-saw. Since her feminine came up as a great growing tree, she made it into logs, saying, 'Don't be ridiculous, stop making problems – I can't deal with you too!'

Integration of mind, body and emotions

Love is the only healer. Get people singing their own song. The internal artist who makes the symptom also makes the answer. Breathing both in *and out* can help us return to the order of the trilogy, not favouring the split. The Body will help. While true healers do discuss the nature of the symptom and its language, they also discuss the person. This is straightforward preventive medicine, and the earlier the better. We think there has to be a big adjustment. But it's usually small: the man who cried during 'ET' took to sailing a duck in the bath. Soon he was sailing a model boat, then a dinghy, and he was all right.

IDENTITY – 'WHO AM I?'

God respects me when I work, but loves me when I sing
Rabindranath Tagore

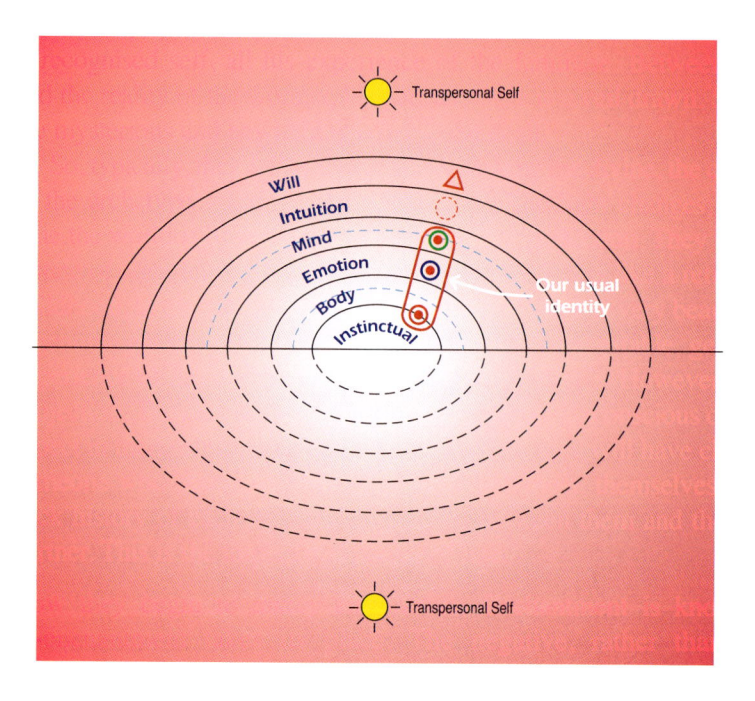

Chart 2:12 – Levels of Consciousness 3

As we have seen, these levels develop one after the other, Body, Emotions and Mind fusing into the everyday 'I', our individuality. It is then that the energy of the Self begins to disrupt things. We're blown apart. We become aware that we *are* not any of them – not our bodies, not our emotions, not our minds. We are parts of an infinitely greater whole of which the everyday 'I' is but a fragment. Our business is with none other than the Self.

Our journey begins. Many of us shop around for work – social, political, artistic, religious. We seek teachers, teachings. The arrows point upwards; the task is to reconnect with the Self in full consciousness. However, the Self is a powerful current. It shatters unprepared vehicles, so they need strengthening. We focus on changing the substance through diet, yoga and so on; and on changing the feelings to prepare the vehicles for the touch of the Self. 'At least I know who I'm *not*.' And the energy begins to flow from the Self. The Self is now using us.

How do we stay in good nick on the journey?

Here are three (somewhat platitudinous) ground rules:

> *Know yourself*. A special kind of listening – seeing, feeling, hearing – is required if we are to know what's going on. Our identity is delicate; it doesn't want to be 'helped' by being yanked up a bit – it will hate that. It has managed to keep clear so far, hiding. Won't it be clobbered if it's caught now? Remember Heisenberg's principle of indeterminacy: you can get the position, or the velocity, but not both at once. The microscope itself affects the particle. How do we listen to the parts of ourselves which have things to say? Our identity is to do with the masculine principle, yet if we look too violently, approach with too much energy, something runs for cover. So, attend with subtlety and delicacy, but don't project energy; don't be too heavy in your invitations. Cultivate attention – a particular listening, a form of dialogue neither too invasive nor too strong.

> *Love yourself*. It is quite difficult to give ourselves the *right* kind of nourishment and all too easy, on this journey, to give the compensatory kind. It is a common problem. Some people, realising for instance that they are rejected, might decide to go for power instead of love. 'At least I'll be top. If I can't be loved, I will beat them all!' How can we love ourselves?

> *Be yourself*. How do we know whether a thing is merely our own will, or the Self itself? The measure is joy – not love; that has a different quality. The old scripts repeat: 'If you enjoy it, it must be wrong – selfish!' So we deny ourselves what we really need. The test: '*Do* I enjoy it?' If not, I may need to look at it. Joy and fun are measures of whether we are truly in our being. People who 'help' without enjoying it are poison. Earn your living and only incidentally do good to people. Those having fun (obviously, not at other people's expense) are at any rate probably doing little harm. And the lazy? Arguably, they do the least damage.

EXPLORATION
THE GROUNDING EXERCISE
(10 minutes)

This exercise in earthing will take a few minutes. Based upon the ancient Japanese sword-fighting discipline of the Samurai, it is no stiff drill. It involves a triangle rising up through us and the sun shedding another triangle down, to meet in the heart.

Human beings are a connective bridge uniting earth and heaven. Children of earth, we are also children of heaven. Mediate that, now. Stand in your own space, claim your ground, take your stand, shoulder-width wide, balanced down. Your feet are flat on the earth, feeling the floor, the pavement responding, feeling the earth. Knees loose, body leaning on the earth, sagging towards the earth; held up as if by a rod, you claim the earth.

Bring attention to your feet; this is useful if you have head problems. Feel the response of the earth as pressure on the soles, the heels, the outsides of your feet, your toes stroking the earth. Take your consciousness down from your soles, into the ground. Close your eyes. Talk to the great Earth Mother. Endless events happen on earth – crises and chaos, agonies and wounds and conflict, joys and births and laughter.

Endlessly, aeon upon aeon, the Earth Mother springs out of the ground, stems pushing tendrils up and through, burgeoning with spring, covering the earth, out into the air. Summers increase growth, leaf and flower. Autumns bring fruit, harvest, the golden richness of earth. Autumns move towards the winter; leaves fall, the falling away of used patterns back on to the earth. Taken into and held in a quiet interim of darkness, it feels like death. But there is trust in the alchemy of the new spring, new growth, new seeds, new birth; confidence in the resurgence out of the very matter which has broken down.

And so, endlessly, century after century, the same pattern follows in our own lives and seasons. Feel now as if you were a plant with its roots deep in the earth, drawing energy up out of the earth. Draw up the green rising sap of life, renewal, hope, regeneration. This rising tide, from its birth deep down, comes in through the soles of your feet, rising as a triangle through ankles, legs, knees still relaxed and leaning, through till it energises the solar plexus.

When it reaches the solar plexus, feel the upper part of your body begin to lift; let your hands rise up. You're being drawn up from overhead; the upper part of your body is getting lighter, gently drawn up by a cord of light from overhead, rising towards the heart. This is the Father, Heaven, all light, drawing you up out of Mother Earth. But gently! Its golden strength draws you up towards your full heart, stature, potential. So, affirmation comes.

And now the benison of the returning sun, full of energy, lights as a great golden triangle down on you, through your brain, mind and eyes – purifying your vision, your throat, sanctifying your words – a descending triangle of pure gold, penetrating your heart.

Cup your hands around your heart, the alchemical flask. This is a marriage, a mating between Mother Earth and Father Heaven, a conjunction, giving birth to the moment, now. Drawing up the energy of earth, redeem the past. Everything that has been is redeemed in this moment. Drawing on the energy of heaven, draw the future in, the highest of your own potential; draw it into your human heart. In this moment of calm, of marriage between earth and heaven, you can be reborn. All that has been is here. All that will be, will spring out of this moment, now – now only.

And that's the Grounding Exercise, an exercise of action, not stillness but a movement. From this power point for the future, linking with power points of the past, move out to fight for, and to fight through, because you have come from your ground. Speaking words of peace, your voice comes from a place of peace. So, be rooted here.

If you do this once a day for nine days, nine years, nine decades, you will have acted in and from the moment, now. You will have gone out from this moment to be what you must, say what you must, do what you must – all that you can. So, go out now, out of this room – you need to move from it. Move with any movement you want. Let the energy flow. Lie down, or sit – and return.[62]

---

62 Commentary on the Grounding exercise, Appendix 2. Suggested programme and original reading list for the workshop, Appendices 5 and 6.

120   THE RAINCLOUD OF KNOWABLE THINGS

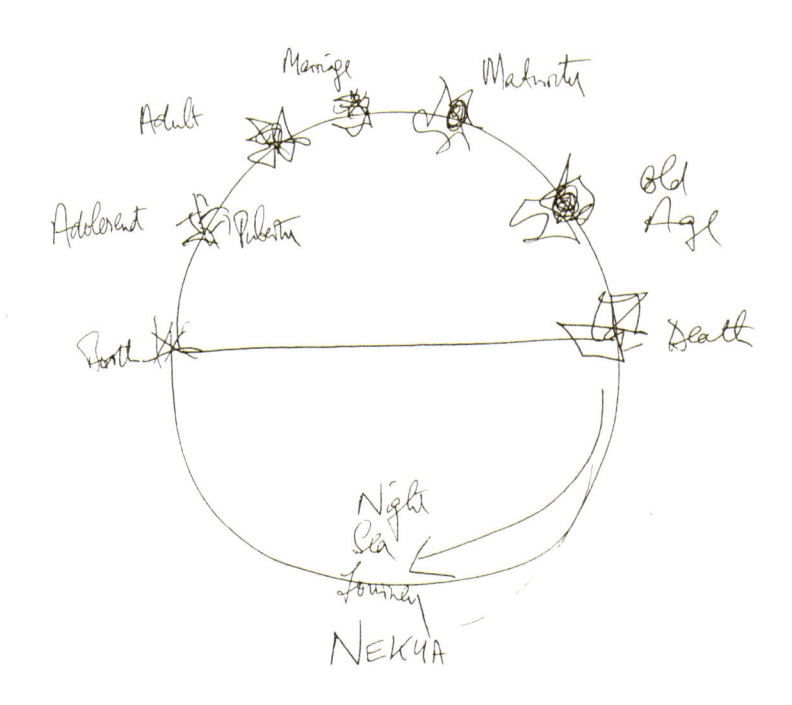

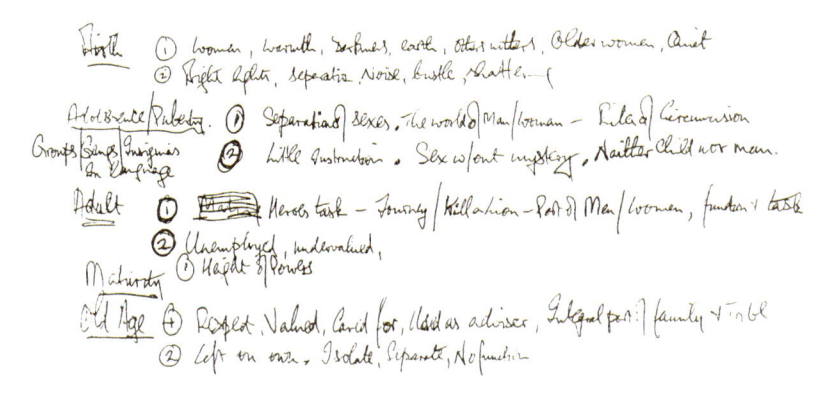

Facsimile of notes: Ian Gordon-Brown

CHAPTER THREE

Cycles and Stages

Workshop III

Ian Gordon-Brown and Barbara Somers

... we come from somewhere; we go to somewhere ...

INTRODUCING THE WORKSHOP [63]

Bridging

Workshop III presupposes a profound level of inner work. It's for the tried and tested, an initiatory experience which only happens when you're ready. Where the first two workshops dealt with persona, ego, shadow and the contra-sexual aspects, this one works towards an archetypal level, looking along time in both directions. In the Sub-Personality and Cup and Sword explorations, the imaging mostly had a strongly symbolic content, approached by the right brain. In this workshop it has an additional dimension: again, you are asked to use your symbol-creating, image-making side, but on the actual subject-matter of your life – the events, experiences, conflicts and joys of being who you are in this world. It's as if you are on the bridge between the left and right hemispheres of the brain and able to use the capacities and qualities of each together. This is a very creative way of exploring the psyche; but you may personally need to experiment.

PATTERNS and CYCLES OF GROWTH

We move towards the afternoon of life unconscious,
with experience and energy but only a morning programme

Our cyclic rhythms form, as it were, a trampoline for other themes. Although our individual pulse is masked by group rhythms from the

---

63 Some notes on the running of aspects of this workshop are given in Appendices 1 and 2.

collective unconscious, though exploration yields only a cut across today's emerging pattern, yet there is a fundamental drum-beat to our lives. The next cycle begins at the peak of each turning point. Changes are usually gradual, not sudden; only with hindsight do we realise that a new quality has entered.

THE SEVEN-YEAR CYCLE

The lower part of the chart (again based on Jung's map from Chapter 1) shows the Ocean of Dark Things, with the lighted Field of Consciousness above. Jung believed that we are not born as an unwritten sheet: there is an eternal factor. Appearing like the sun, rising out of the sea of unconsciousness, the small ego moves round and operates in the upper half, reaching its high noon at about thirty-five. But the transpersonal Self sits in the centre, with access to both depths and heights. *Individuation* is the ego's acknowledgement of the Self and the building of a bridge or channel between. This axis is crucial.

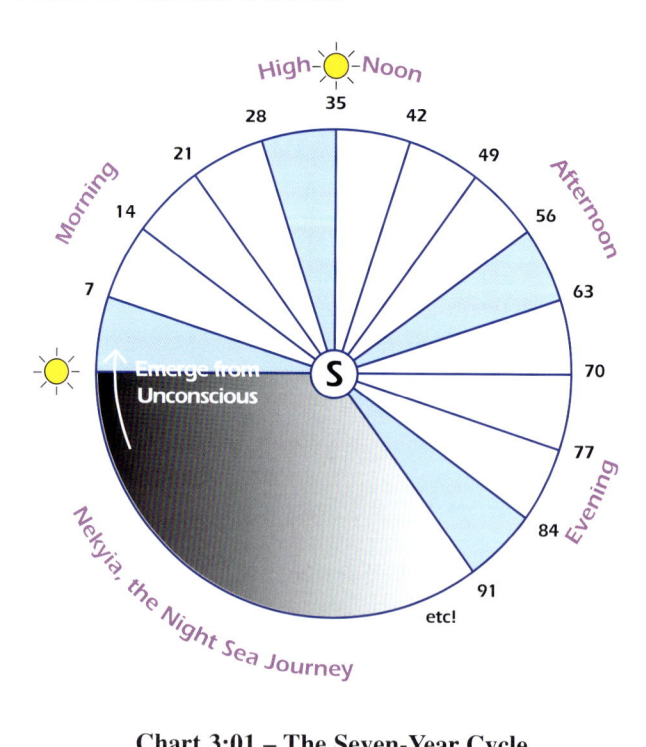

Chart 3:01 – The Seven-Year Cycle

Individual lives follow varying cycles: nine or eleven years perhaps, or five or eight. Here we look at the seven year cycle, since it resonates for many. Your own cycle doesn't have to start at birth but may be several years out. Work back from a major turning point – and remember the old esoteric law, 'suck it and see'.

First cycle, from birth to seven

Starting on the left, we are born out of the unconscious and enter the first segment. This is no friendly metaphor; it is to enter a more limited world, and thus a death. The unconscious is far greater than the conscious, and the idea we can control it is false. At this stage we are introverted, doing much unconscious absorbing.

> *The Body*. The child's learning is primarily physical; exploring and thinking, yes, but – obviously – childish. We double our weight in our first year. It's a crucial stage.
>
> *The Emotions*. Our parents are the sun and moon gods, wonderful, terrible, absent. The power of the child is projected on to them. If properly bonded now, it will always have confidence in people's goodness. But it picks up any underlying tension, ignoring smoke-screen levels of politeness. One child whose family was falling apart (though nobody spoke to her about it) kept tying up little bits of string, compulsively attempting to tie the family together. Guilt, fear and separation leave wounds that scar over, but ache when the wind is in the east. Accept them, make them positive; wounds that are loved can become enormously creative.
>
> *The Mind*. In these introverted nursery years the child is open to unconscious factors in the people around. It may be told it is loved – but it knows if it isn't. People who go into the caring professions often lacked this love as children. Ignatius Loyola: 'Give me a child till he is seven and I'll show you the man'. And Rudolf Steiner advised, 'Don't give them symbols till they are seven'.

The Turnover period from five to seven.[65] We've met our peers by now. Other gods enter; our teachers may contradict our parents. The quality of consciousness changes; we move out into a different way of thinking. This is easy or difficult according to our bonding, leaving us with a fundamental confidence – or the lack of it.

---

65 I am taking it that the transition phases are from 5–7, 12–14, 19–21 and so on.

Second cycle, from seven to fourteen

Now we usually become much more extraverted. There is a new recognition of the adult world.

> *The Body*. Physically, we develop competence, moving out and away into extraversion, exploring the external world. Rapid physical development continues.
>
> *The Emotions*. Still largely unconscious of them, we make links, share feelings. Friendships deepen; still without clear guidelines, we have 'best friends' instead. As emotional differentiation leads towards puberty, the peer group supports us in moving away from the parents.
>
> *The Mind*. We are still unconscious of it, as of the emotions; we think without being aware of it.

The Turnover period from twelve to fourteen. We go quiet. Crises are turned inwards. Consciousness of feeling begins to become dominant in our inner landscape. Ready now for spiritual as well as emotional development, we need the romantic and the heroic.

Third cycle, from fourteen to twenty-one

Another introverting phase, this. Bodies and feelings develop. Adolescents may turn against their parents. It may also be a mental phase; concepts and ideas become important. Have we laid claim to our own thinking function?

> *The Body* grows strange – exciting or fearful. Gender differences show up: girls clot together, boys form gangs.
>
> *The Emotions* at puberty self-evidently deepen again. Where in so-called 'primitive' societies marriage customarily took place at fourteen, with us confusion reigns, and insecurity about gender identity. Erikson pointed out the turmoil, the role confusion before identity is achieved. Who am I? Many young people at this stage have no certainty of themselves as masculine or as feminine. They may have a lot of the opposite gender in them, but that doesn't determine sexual preference. A lot of their homo-erotic yearning arises from fear of the other sex. Again, perhaps the body has one set of energies and qualities and the psyche another; sexuality is a search for their own nature.

Too many adolescents commit suicide. This peaks at sixteen. Overwhelmed, they see no way out. Emotional crises have to be controlled and pushed down, since their education has not allowed for feelings to be lived and understood. The school, since there is usually no proper listening, forces young people to go on turning outward till either they adopt the rules and live by regulation or, with an inward-turning thrust, explode in reaction. And *we never understood this ourselves*; we do the same to our own children, though our generation also had mystical and other stirrings. Yet young people generally become stable by the end of the period, managing to develop a sense of sexuality and gender identity. By twenty-one the alienated youth is settling, the tomboy becoming a woman.

The Mind. Developing the capacity to think, our minds are very sharp and our rational skills as good as they get. At sixteen, we can think faster than we can at forty. It's a time of critical appraisal, of re-active, passionate thought, full of values and outrage. Ideally, a university will teach people to think; but this is not the time for our *best* thinking, only for learning *how* to think. Anyway, we're often taught only how to digest stuff and take it on board, say 'Yes' and 'No', process the cultural rubbish of our age. And perhaps our own ideas should not be encouraged until we've thought through other people's. Detachment comes later. In any case, our own emerging ideas have not yet been tested in fire.

The Turnover period from nineteen to twenty-one. Now our emotional differentiation and range are increased. There is a powerful charge of feeling; the passionate gives way to exploration. If all goes well, we can claim our own identity, accept our gender. The mood changes. Is it safe to leave home? An unconscious decision is made. Our drive and aggression develop naturally; our tools are sharpened for the intimacy of the following phase.

Fourth cycle, from twenty-one to twenty-eight

This is a more extraverted stage. The body has completed its development. The emotions and the mind have their own proper place. Intimacy is appropriate. We may question our work choice: am I going the right way? Intuition comes in.

> *The Body.* Men diverge sharply from women, adopting different functions and roles. Men reach full size when they are about twenty-five, women stop physically growing at twenty-three. Once, woman's role was only to have children; now that is obviously fluid and changing.
>
> *The Emotions.* Deeper exploration of feelings with someone else is now possible. Knowing another, we learn about our own inner masculine and feminine, no longer using the other person but learning to *see* them.
>
> *The Mind.* Our own ideas emerge. Scientific and mathematical discoveries are made very young. We claim our own minds, not blindly adopting received thinking. Careers, once set for life at twenty, are delayed, chosen later if at all. The young take time to think, giving themselves some respite.

The Turnover period from twenty-six to twenty-eight. This is the 'first Saturn return'.[66] An intuitive inner voice starts to be heard. We track around the personality and find that the bounds have already been walked, the limits seen. Now we move round again, but differently, in a spiral, picking up issues from earlier phases, rediscovering what it's like to be in our world, claiming our ground. Crisis often hits.[67] We go for help, especially if we haven't dealt with the nursery phase.

Fifth cycle, from twenty-eight to thirty-five

This stage is first introverted, then extraverted.[68]

> *Body and Mind.* This is the light of high noon. In our thirties our functions are at their optimum, in full consciousness. We are at the peak of our capacities, furthest from the unconscious and from the moon. The sun casts no shadow, there is no sense of getting older, we are fully engaged in life and all seems fine.
>
> *The Emotions.* Any blocked, locked development from an earlier stage, any sub-personality that was warped and ignored, will be triggered at the crisis which may now follow – and the Chinese ideogram for crisis has a dragon for danger and a phoenix for opportunity. Crises aren't always bad; joy and success are also crises.

---

66 It is said that the astrological cycle of Saturn tends people towards outer crisis roughly every twenty-nine years.
67 Gail Sheehy 1974 writes of crisis at thirty years old. Sheehy 1974, *Passages*.
68 28–35 is the counterpoint to 0–7. (As 0–7 is the womb for 7–28, so 28–35 is the womb for 35–56; and maybe 56–63 is for 63 to the end of our lives.)

The Turnover period at thirty-five. So now we are adult, master of our thought processes, matured physically, with our emotional and intuitive development proceeding. However, we have not yet arrived. At the stroke of noon, the day changes. But so far we have known only the morning. We move towards the afternoon of life unconscious, with experience and energy but with no programme. We still want the heroic, the masculine; women too. Yet the need is for the numinous, the spiritual, the godhead.

Sixth cycle, from thirty-five to forty-two

In this midlife passage, the later part of our life calls us. Often we feel stuck, things lose their savour and crisis ensues. The unconscious has been growing too; the Ocean of Dark Things begins to stir, its messages forcing us to bring our attention towards the centre. There is a magnetic pull home towards the west. Light and dark are united more and more consciously.

What is the meaning? The ego must change to take on the colour of the Self. Erikson called this the adult phase, where the task is to be generative. We give back out of our abundance, or we stagnate.

The Turnover period at around forty or forty-two. Our children are now between fourteen and twenty-one. As parents, we see their adolescence from a different point of view. We can make friends with our own parents. Having run the gamut and seen them as divine, as diabolical, as human, they're now just OK. (Or awful?).

Seventh cycle, from forty-two to forty-nine

Our physical bodies may lose power or flexibility or immunity, but things go on being brought up from the unconscious. Since our growth needs are rarely being taken into account, a *midlife crisis* often follows, giving the opportunity to loop back and break assumptions. Input is from both outside and inside. Patterns spiral, offering again and again the chance to rethink whole sets of ideas. It's to be hoped we get younger, more playful, spontaneous, 'selfish', so that people say, 'Lucky you!' We learn to say NO, we stamp our feet. Otherwise, we become stiff and backward-looking, full of regrets.

The Turnover period at forty-seven or forty-nine. We make subjective decisions about our field of work, having a sense of how far we will go, or want to go. This is important: while coming to terms with a lesser success could depress us, yet it might be wrong to go further. We are conditioned to go on and on and on. Why?

Eighth cycle, from forty-nine to fifty-six

By now, body, emotion, mind and intuition are all asking, 'What's it *really* all about?' The menopause has passed – or not. The body changes. We *must* develop a programme for the afternoon of life, and it will be more about Self than ego. Intuitive decisions made now feel fine later. Strength is around, and also pain. Our parents are ageing; we no longer feel immortal. 'I am now an elder!' The children's deeper problems are emerging and we can only witness. There is nothing to be done. This testing period may shock and darken us. The light goes out – in part, though there are other lights. Having looked after others a lot, we may ask, 'What about *me*?' Rounding, deepening: 'What's it all about?' These are deeper and spiritually significant questions.

The Turnover period at fifty-five or fifty-six. What is the meaning? There is a change in awareness, to do with the journey of the Self. We want to leave old ways, do the things we haven't done. We can see it for ourselves. Things turn into their opposites. For instance, a very feminine person may develop their masculine side; a pattern where comfortable failure is repeatedly engineered may be reversed. Therapy, requiring slow maturing, begins broadly at midlife; like wine, we get better and wiser as we get older.

Ninth cycle, from fifty-six to sixty-three

By the 'second Saturn return' we have been round the bounds once more. 'Who am I *now*? What do I want to do with the rest of my life?' We may not be able to do it but, to survive and be any use, it's necessary to know. We use in practice themes garnered in earlier years. We make plans.

One plan is whether to live or to die. Chronic illnesses tend to begin here but, whether or not we go on physically for years, a decision is made at a deep level; shall we sink into old age, backward-looking, full of regret, lamenting the passing of time; or go on growing, learning, living? Do I become the poor old *senex*, familiarly grumbling as the age gap increases, repeating old reactions till I rigidify? Or do I become more flexible, growing in soul quality, getting younger and more open to the young – freer, less structured? If I am for life, understanding, freshness and spontaneity, I needn't sink towards second childhood but can become truly childlike. Someone inside me grows younger, reaches back to the child's sense of eternity – dreaming and remembering. Such people very often live longer, become quieter, have more energy and staying power, moving on to wisdom.

The Turnover period at sixty or sixty-three. From the afternoon of life we need to prepare an evening programme. The midlife crisis tested the metal; now we must think more individually. To die or to live? The decision will colour the rest of life with a quality of despair or of hope. Enough people have found the joy of old age, being flexible and unpredictable in their later years, for it to become normal. One woman, a seamstress, then became a comptometer operator. Re-trained in her fifties as a radionics practitioner, she did some O-levels which led her towards healing. At the age of sixty she found a job with the Society for Health Education and started to practise. At sixty-five, she became a full-time healer, setting up a training school. In her late sixties, she became a public speaker and was invited to Australia. At seventy-seven, she owned her first home. At eighty, she was running people off their feet.

Tenth cycle, from sixty-three to seventy

The task of evening is to gather and share the harvest. This is no frothy champagne but a rich, mature wine. Spontaneous, growing in wisdom, we are newborn each day. We've had it rough; pain and joy, life and death are all one thing. As we journey towards individuation, crises bring opportunity. Here are the wise people of our time.

The Turnover period at seventy. This is the end of the upper hemisphere of Jung's map; but nowadays we can go on beyond that, and very well indeed. Lots of people are going to make it into their late eighties and nineties; statesmen often do. The landscape was different for the elderly when 'threescore years and ten' was the most we could reasonably expect.[69]

Eleventh cycle, from seventy to seventy-seven

What does the Collective of the West *need* that requires thousands of old and leisured people? The question is crucial. Though only a tiny percentage are in residential homes, the statistics we hear are often based on them. Old people offer far more than psychopathology. They have

---

69 Psalm 90:10.

things to do. They are the elders of the tribe.

In the United States in 1970, an activist named Maggie Kuhn started a group as a response to her forced retirement at the age of sixty-five. She hired a church hall and advertised 'Freedom and Irresponsibility' for anyone over seventy-five. People flocked. They protested about war, Vietnam, social ills; they called meetings, got young people in tandem with them. With nothing to lose they would, as far as they could, take on the problems of the world. Nicknamed the Gray Panthers, in 1972 they were characterised as lively, quick-witted, controversial and action-oriented. Maggie Kuhn died in 1995, aged eighty-nine.

Twelfth cycle, from seventy-seven to eighty-four

The 'third Saturn return' at eighty-four marks the end of this period. It deepens meaning. *Inner* crisis has conditioned this latter third of life. We've been round the day-and-night cycle over and over again, opportunity following crisis as life, spiralling gloriously through the stages, has allowed us fresh looks. Those who have arrived here have had it rough. Pain and joy, life and death are for them all one thing as they 'become' towards individuation.

and on ...

Coming to the end of their public work, introversion follows and the wise often go out from this life. However, many continue. However old, there is at any moment the possibility of humour. One mother-in-law complained at ninety-one, 'I can't imagine why God isn't sending for me.' Then, considering: 'But perhaps *you* can?' In the final third, a person grown in wisdom is newborn each day. They used to get it wrong each time – now, they get the hang of it. In this time of creative fruition and re-birth, 'your young men shall see visions, and your old men shall dream dreams.'[70] Sharing their dreams, they are moving in towards home.

Coming home

The unconscious is at the bottom of the picture, the *nadir*, the Ocean of Dark Things, dark only because unknown. In Tibet, the moment of birth from this Ocean is taken to be our real death, as we saw. From the zenith of consciousness at about thirty-five we move till we are maybe eighty or ninety years old, following the magnetic pull home towards the west. The

---

70 Acts 2:17; and see Joel 2:28.

light and the dark unite more and more consciously. Then the sun sets. And perhaps we come round with it, to live again at its rising.[71]

SHORT EXPLORATION
THE PATTERN OF YOUR LIFE
(10 minutes)

You are invited to go within:
> Explore briefly your own pattern to date. Note what kind of thing is important for you in doing this – is it where you lived, who you lived with, who your friends were, what was going on in your inner world, what job you had? Is there any particular pattern or thread that emerges at this stage for you?

Share this with a partner if you wish.

SELF-IMAGE EXPLORATION
(45 minutes)

This invites you to lie down, but sit up to record. Relax, let your feelings be calm, your mind both quiet and alert.[72]

Stage 1

Minutes

3   Start by finding yourself in a theatre, in the auditorium; the curtain is down and hiding the stage. You know that on this stage are going to appear a number of characters, each representing an image or model which you hold about yourself. Spend a few minutes getting accustomed to the place. Are you alone or accompanied? What is the atmosphere? How do you feel as you wait for the curtain to go up, and for these aspects of yourself to appear as stage characters?

6   1. *Undervalued by self*. How do you feel when you are really *down*? All of us undervalue ourselves in some way; we have an image or model that's worse than the reality. Whether we believe it or not, we have it, and it may at times be valid. Think about this

---
71 Nekyia, the Night Sea Journey, see Chapter 4, pp. 204-206.
72 Commentary on the Self-image exploration, Appendix 2. There is an alternative Self-image exploration, Appendix 7.

undervalued self image for a while. Let an image of it come into your mind's eye, sense this image of being *down*. As the curtain rises, let this aspect of yourself appear on the stage. See it clearly; perhaps it has a name? Record it, draw it – the *undervalued self image*. Memories or feelings may be triggered – make a note to remind yourself later.

6 2. *Overvalued by self*. Relax, see that image go off stage and prepare to move on. How do you feel when you are really *uppish*? We also overvalue ourselves. I have an image perhaps better, more perfect, than I really am. Allow this now to appear on the stage; name it, draw it. Again, what memories and feelings are triggered by this euphoric, overvalued sense? Note them briefly.

6 3. *Ideal appearance of self*. Relax once again and see the stage clear. I also have a model of myself *as I'd like to be seen by others*, possibly contrasted with reality. Let this image appear – name – sense – draw it.

6 4. *How others do see me*. Once again, let the stage be clear. There are also in me models of how other people in general, or one person in particular, do see me, how they believe I am. I have images of what these are; some I *like* and some I *resent*. See two of these images appearing as characters on the stage – things that others project on to me, one I like and accept, and one I dislike. Choose one of each, and do two drawings. Name them if you can.

6 5. *How others want me to be*. Again, let that clear. Finally, there is in me an image of how one particular person, or other people, would *like me to be*, expect of me. It's what they want to change or mould me into; what they'd like me to become. Catch this image as it appears; name, sense and draw it.

Stage 2

6 When you are ready, slowly sit up and look in sequence at your notes or drawings so far. Get in touch again with each image; recall your feelings about it, consider the name you gave it: your undervalued self; overvalued self; ideal self; your images of how others do see you (one you accept, one you resent); and your image of what others want to make you into. Do they link together in any way? Next, set the drawings aside and spend a moment with these images

themselves; they are very powerful in life and in relationships. They interfere with authentic living. We need to *anchor in the body*: taking your time, rise to your feet and, with your eyes closed, get in touch with the weight of these images. Stand, sensing the heaviness and limitation of them, holding consciously the burden of all these characters. Feel how they limit and restrict you, how they hold you down. Let your body feel this; adopt your posture to represent how it feels to carry all this stuff.

Stage 3

3 6. *Free self*. As you stand, let your body move to *shake them away*. Shake off their weight; with an act of will, drop all these false, imposed models of yourself. Shed the old clothes. Put down the burden. *Let them go*. Begin to move into a body position that feels free; shake yourself free, shake out, shake off. Open all the doors and windows, free yourself of it. Sense the grace and power that may result. This is your *free self*. Then be still for a while, experiencing the lightness and release you feel.

3 7. *Realistic self*. Lie down again, close your eyes, recollect and centre yourself. Sense into what you really and realistically would like to be. Let an image of this *realistic* self come from within you. Examine it, feel into it; name it if you can, then draw it and any thoughts or feelings you may have about it. See if you can get some sense, some impression, of what the next step might be towards becoming that realistic self.

PROJECTION

My deeper aim may be to move towards seeing myself as a projection of the transpersonal Self

Our state of consciousness and unconsciousness determines how we perceive the world and behave to people and the environment; also, how we perceive and behave towards ourselves. We feel good – and unaccountably it's a rosy day and the world out there is pretty good too. But feel miserable and low, and we see a different world and a sad, grey day. We live in a hall of mirrors – often distorting mirrors. We see things out of true. We don't recognise the world as *mine*. It's *other*, foreign. We either yearn for it – it is beautiful, desirable, true; or we flee from it – it's terrifying.

My feelings towards other people often tell me about myself. And my images of myself and them control my behaviour. We are full of such images, seen through our own coloured spectacles. The more dominated by false images of ourselves (which we explored), the more we project what we don't like on to others.

Everything and everybody is a potential target for projection. We project on to a face, a word, an action, a belief, a race. As the parrot learns the swear-words before other things he hears because they're said so forcefully and with such feeling, so we project parts of ourselves with life and passion: our blocked energy, unresolved conflicts, unsatisfied drives to wholeness. Unconsciousness is at work, trying to control fear.[73] However, it never works perfectly. There is always a residue of anxiety. And since what we see mirrors the condition of the Self, to *internalise the projections* leads towards individuation.

Projection requires a hook

And there usually is one. Its level or size may bear little relation to the strength of the projection, but the hook is there. The person or object of our projection does contain some essence, however rudimentary, of what we project on to them. Projection without a hook is psychosis. And other people's projections onto us can hurt if we are offering a valid hook. Indeed, it takes time, first to stop feeling hurt, then to stop inviting the projecting. It's as if we are covered in velcro strips: the things people throw stick like burrs – because they are *true*.

At what *level of consciousness* is the projection occurring?[74] Not merely intellectual, it happens at bodily, emotional and intuitive levels too. The question is particularly important in conflicts between the masculine and the feminine. It opens up large areas in therapy.

Projection at the body level carries a high charge. It is about the body's prime, infantile need to be loved. Thus we seek parents in our partners, friends and colleagues, hoping they will take care of us unconditionally and perfectly – which is the unconscious function of relationships.

We may project mothering by taking care of others. We may project

---

73 Anxiety is infantile terror, projection one of our defence mechanisms. It has been suggested that Super-ego, Id and Ego may be likened respectively to a nervous spinster and a sex-crazed gorilla fighting in a dark cellar, refereed by a frightened bank-clerk. The vulnerable Ego-bank-clerk has to defend itself against both of the others; hence its defence mechanisms against overwhelming anxiety.
74 See Chart 2:12, Levels of Consciousness 3, above.

our power, our need to have control, by dominating, being in charge. Conversely we project our weakness by getting others to be in charge of us; perhaps we feel crazy or sick and it feels very safe. We create power structures – the Fatherland, the Welfare State, the Nanny State. They fail and we are left anxious; for when projection breaks down energy is released as abandonment, annihilation. As for our sexual urges, we betray ourselves by our stereotypes. Inhibited myself, I may have an urgent need to find people to despise – or to follow. So I let slip *all – none – never* statements: 'Mediterranean peoples – randy, the lot of them!' 'All men are beasts!' 'All women are devouring monsters!' 'British people – cold and buttoned up!'

Projection at the feeling level reduces unconscious material to make anxiety bearable. So we project negatively on to groups 'out there', fantasise our guilt into a group, which then carries it – the infidels, the heretics, the witches. More recent history has seen the Iron Curtain, South Africa, the Irish, the Jews and the Palestinians, Islam – scapegoats all. The world consists of 'them and us', or 'them and me', and it's loaded with projection, acknowledging but not owning something. Because, of course, what we think is *out there* may well also be *in here*. Though it's unconscious, we may catch it on the wing by noting any very powerful feelings that don't relate to our own accepted reality: hate, distrust, dislike, envy. We've seen how projection operates in relationships where, individually, a great deal of emotional heat is involved. We know about the family myth, the stereotype, the shadow, the 'identified patient' carrying the family burden. And we scapegoat individuals: child-molesters for instance – how powerfully do we detest them?

Projection at the mind level. This is about power: the most energetic projections are associated not only with sex and love, but with money, politics, religion. Many of us experience our most powerful feelings here. The Media constitute a massive collective projection, a world of false images on which we base our judgments, though true reports are pretty rare. Others project an idea of old age that leads to their becoming the *senex*, the Poor Old Fool who, far from being the Wise Fool, *wants* to be seen as a maundering twit, wants to avoid burdens. We may hope he'll at least develop a dry wit.

Projection at the intuitive level. Psychological literature is full of examples of negative projections. But *positive* ones can be just as powerful – and potentially just as damaging to both parties. Projections can all stifle growth. We project not only our false self-images, but our free and real Selves onto other people, and they onto us. Rather than being over-charged emotionally, we may be too under-charged to own our brightness, feeling ourselves somehow *inappropriate*: too meek, too stupid, too little. Unconsciously, we may value mediocrity; modestly stifling our unique creativity and projecting onto other people our potential and our outstanding qualities. In Bunyan's words, 'He that is down needs fear no fall.'

Projections between men and women

'Anima figures' catch the projections of men and *vice versa*. As we saw in Workshop II, falling in love is a beautiful example.[75] The image, the dream, the romantic idea falls at first onto a particular person: 'They are divine! And it's bliss.' But marry? Each thinks they can cope with the other, each has an investment in keeping the other happy. To maintain peace, neither shows their first irritation, thus reinforcing what they believe the other is like. So communication fails. Each time this happens, a hook for a projection is offered, till two images hide two angry people.

Collusion is an important ingredient. First, project onto the other a way of behaving, and then *make* them behave that way. 'Now look what you've made me do!' Thus sadists find masochists, doormats create aggressors, saviours are besieged by victims and the impotent marry the frigid. We need to hang in there, *see* the other, accept ourselves and them.

Transference and counter-transference are psychodynamic processes to do with seeing and being seen. They underlie *all* relationships of any depth. In our clients' eyes, as therapists we often carry the parents and are expected to behave that way. This can be a positive projection of charisma and authenticity, as with the worship of gurus, heroes, stars, ideals. Or not. But don't try to do therapy with your nearest and dearest – they are inside your focal length and you will see double.

Projection as a vital process

But projection is not always a bad thing. Jung also had a more positive view: it is a fundamental mechanism of the unconscious. Without it we cannot relate. It is a communication; less a defence than a means to see the unknown and explore reality. Unknown psychic content is recognised first *outside* ourselves, in a person or group. Eventually we must own it in ourselves; but needing, say, the heroic, we perceive glory in certain

---

75 See 'The Four People at the Wedding', Chapter 2, pp. 99-103.

individuals who mirror for us something we would not otherwise have found. And it is priceless. We choose someone authentic, on centre, with such a ring and resonance to them that they become for us the wise person. They project brightness along our paths and the radiant energy they give off is a hook for this very creative kind of projection. (Conversely, people may see the wise person in *me*. Dangerous, this.... Will I be sucked into believing the projection? 'Perhaps I *am* the one with the Message!' Alluring, but not true. It precedes a wonderful crash, deflating the illusion. Then I may be safe to get on with some small part of the work I *can* do.)

How to work with projections

Our deeper aim is to move towards seeing ourselves as a projection of the transpersonal Self. We are here to experience it as far as possible, in clarity and consciousness. James Hillman said of archetypal psychology that soul-making is where we take material back as soul-*substance*. First we encounter the shadow outside, studying what we see as inferior, unskilled, unacceptable, pathetic, looking at our dreams, at how we encounter new possibilities: 'This is ME! I am affecting this, generating this feeling, contributing, colluding'. Then we aim to act from Self rather than ego. Many of us know, for instance, that potentially we have a murderer in us; once we've recognised it, we need to begin to accept it. With a really ferocious projection, that's all we can do – we may not be able quite to befriend it. And, not act it out... Otherwise violence is done to protect us from violence. Instead, we lay down our stones and knives and guns. And since not only negative but positive projections are specifically valued in transpersonal work, we ask, 'What brought you through – what was the light within the darkness?'

How do we recognise projection? Listen to its language – inflated, exaggerated, superlative, full of sweeping generalisations: 'The young totally lack respect!' And the stuckness, the interminable complaint: 'In my young day.... ' 'Here we go again!' Note the familiar patterns: hero-worship, idolatry, absolutes, falling in love yet again with the wrong person. Let women ask themselves, 'What do you hate about women?' and men, conversely, 'What do you hate about men?' And both: 'Is the amount of emotional energy *appropriate*?' Are they enraged by trivialities, joyous over minutiae? *It is the abnormal over- or under-valuation of people that betrays the projection, the inappropriate emotional charge.*

How do we own our projections, positive and negative? Internalising them is a most powerful step towards individuation, one of the surest ways to know ourselves. But it takes courage; they hold back our anxiety. Recognising them is 'a moral achievement beyond the ordinary'.[76] But if anxiety is excitement without the oxygen, then to ease anxiety will release our energy. So we centre, gather, re-member, restore our sense of perspective, proportion and humour. Withdrawing projection does not make the other person disappear or change their behaviour – the bully still bullies, the guru is the guru, the wife still wife – but it's the crucial step before action. We see them differently, more clearly. So we begin to own our own archetypal energies, the deeper the stronger.

In a relationship, owning one's own contributions is easier if what is mine, what is not mine, and what is shared are all three owned. This often helps separate responsibility from over- or under-responsibility. Irene Claremont de Castillejo, in her lovely book 'Knowing Woman', said of projection that people carrying their own *dark* shadows, their undesirable qualities, instead of projecting them onto other people, become ever more integrated. Then, carrying their own *bright* shadows, they take up their dignity, strength and courage, and their imaginative insight refuses to be burdened by other people's unknowing projections onto them. So a tiny bit of the world's evil is transformed.[77]

EXPLORATION
THE SHAPE OF YOUR LIFE 1
(50 minutes)

This is a journey towards knowledge of your meaning and destiny. You will seek an image for the shape of your life; explore the myths and story-line; options offered and choices you couldn't or didn't make; intractable or impossible things that trip you up the most; moments of fulfilment or transcendence. And you will invite an image for the Self, your essence. Tuning into and observing the rhythms and cycles of your life till now, note when your energy has flowed strongly, and what you have then been drawn to. Also, note periods of ebb. Seek to contact the central drives of your life-force and how they have interacted with the world around.[78]

This inner journey has two main stages, with a break between. At the end of each, you are invited to make notes and draw key images and symbols.

---

76 Jung 1951, *The Shadow*, CW 9 ii, para 16.
77 See Castillejo 1973, *Knowing Woman*, pp. 30-31.
78 Again, it is as well to explain this at the end of the previous evening.

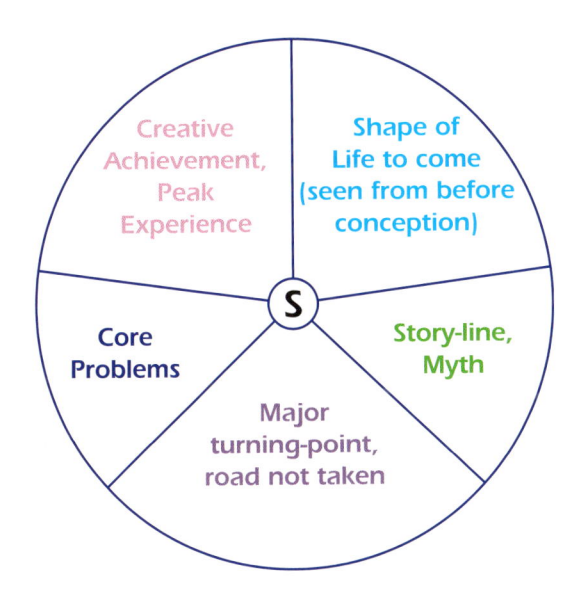

Chart 3:02 – The Shape of your Life Exploration 1

Minutes

5   Relax, let go of the day, enter your inner space and find yourself in a quiet sanctuary, a place of intimate conversation and quiet reflection. Familiarise yourself with it, connecting with your inner world and your essential Self. You may be joined by a wise person or presence; if not, seek for your own inner wisdom to help you. You are invited to look back from this place of sanctuary at five aspects of your life from conception till now. Between each, relax; be connected with the Self in your inner space.

8   1. *The Shape of your Life*. You are both conscious and adult, but not yet born nor even conceived into this present life – you do not yet have the body of a baby or child, but you have your present consciousness. Talk with the wise person or presence, or your own inner wisdom, about the life you are shortly to live – this life. Explore lessons to be learnt; tests to be undergone; qualities to be developed; and who your parents are to be, and why. Invite an image, symbol, impression, word or phrase for the *shape* of your life to come.

8   2. *Your story-line*. Every life has one or more themes or 'story-lines', conforming to some mythic or archetypal pattern; or each stage may have a different keynote or myth. Certain tales resonate, have a magnetic fascination. Particular characters and events capture our imagination. We identify with them: Persephone, Ariadne, Alice in Wonderland, an Ugly Sister, Florence Nightingale. Or the heroic – a Knight of the Round Table, Frodo Baggins, the Little Prince, the Green Man? We may identify with people's contemporary life-stories, or with stories from history or literature, fiction, television or film. Explore the myth or myths of your own life, seeking to discover the *story-lines* and the figures that appeal.

8   3. *The Road Not Taken*. For every choice we make we let something else go. There have been possibilities that we couldn't follow. Sometimes, what we didn't choose lives on in the psyche and calls to us. Opportunity knocks more than once. Return in memory and feeling to important turning-points, moments of choice, and the possibilities you didn't follow. Are they alive today? Can or should you do anything about them? Be in touch with their energy and explore any untaken opportunities. Invite images for one or two *roads not taken*.

8   4. *Core Problems*. We may be regularly torn apart by one, perhaps more, intractable and apparently insoluble problems or irreconcilable conflicts. Our Achilles heels, they keep testing us where we are most vulnerable – until we get it right. Their intransigence makes them a source of pain till, ancient enemies, they almost become old friends. Tune in to your own recurrent conflicts, your intractable difficulties, exploring the meaning of their presence. What are they trying to say? Sense an impression, image or symbol for the one or two *core problems* which may underlie any others.

8   5. *Creative Being and Achievement*. Likewise, we experience moments of expanded awareness, away from everyday consciousness, in a transpersonal state – spiritual, numinous, profound, mystical. Such times of fulfilment or transcendence may change our outlook on life, leading to a sense of creative achievement and creative being. Tune in to these profound times, when you have been most fully yourself. Explore peak experiences.

Contact their essence and their meaning. Seek to re-experience them, to understand how and why they happened and the effects in your life. Discover any common thread – of intuition, feeling, being. You may wish to invite an image for your *creative achievement and being*.

5 To conclude these first five journeys of exploration, *invite a symbol, image, impression, word or phrase* to represent the present stage of the unfolding of your *essential Self*, your Soul.

Returning to this time and place, note and draw these five aspects. The format in Chart 3:02 may be helpful. It is suggested you stay in the spirit of the exploration over the break.[79]

EXPLORATION
THE SHAPE OF YOUR LIFE 2
(35 minutes)

We move *forward* in time, looking from the place of sanctuary at four aspects of your life from now into the future.

Minutes

3 When you are ready, re-enter your inner space and relax once again. We have so far looked back at the stages of your life until now. Here, the psyche takes you quite rapidly forward in time. Images pass before your inner eye:

8 1. *Your own Funeral*. At some point in the future, the psyche halts and you find yourself at a funeral, with a body lying there. It's your own funeral that you're attending. Who are the people gathered? Here are your relationships, those you have connected with. Is there anyone you would like to speak to? What would you like to say? Is there something you wish you had done? Are there any gifts to be exchanged? Any feelings or emotions to share? Anything left that must be done, *unfinished business* you never had time for? So, be at the funeral which is yours.

8 2. *Review with the Wise Being – the Oncoming Light*. Passing the threshold of death, leave the funeral and move on. You are aware of

---
79 A coffee break; time here for a natural pause in the workshop's schedule.

a great light ahead of you; move towards the oncoming light. Aware of it as you are, find yourself in the sanctuary again, in another discussion with the wise person or presence. They *review your life* with you, telling you something of that life-episode from the angle of its deeper, higher meaning, and how its purpose has been met. A life which seems to have fulfilled its potential may well have contributed to the collective. Spend the next few minutes with this non-judgmental, compassionate, wise being, or with your own inner wisdom.

8 3. *The Cycle of Life and Death*. Now, being in a reflective, receptive, retentive state, contact the whole great circle of birth and life and death which you have reviewed. Sense it, feel into it, be closely in touch and involved with it, and invite an image or symbol, a word or phrase, that would express the sum and *essence of your whole life*.

① Your own Funeral

② Oncoming Light/Review with Wise Being

③ Symbol for Life/Death process

④ The Light and Warmth of the Sun

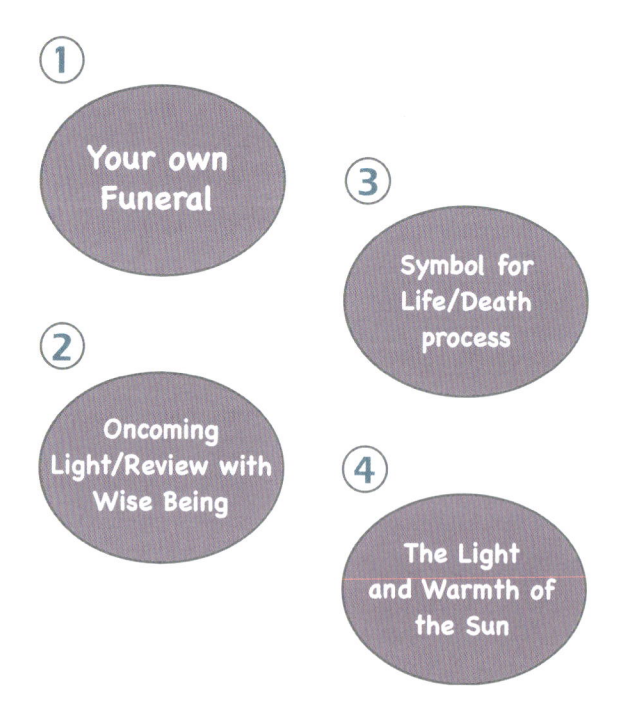

Chart 3:03 – The Shape of your Life Exploration 2

8   4. *Light and Warmth of the Sun*. Examine that symbol of your essence; note its size, shape, colour, whether there is any movement. Identify with that symbol, image, word or phrase. Become it. You are the image; imagine the sun to be shining warmly on you, filling you with its warmth and light.

Now, allow the *image to become smaller and smaller*, but continue to feel the light and warmth of the sun. Let the image become a dot, and disappear, until you're left with just the sun, and the light. Spend a few moments in that state of consciousness.

Returning to the present time and place, make final notes: your own funeral; the review with the wise being in the oncoming light; the symbol for the life and death process; the light and warmth of the sun.

CONTROL PATTERNS

Who or what runs my life?

Less deep than *unconscious* defence mechanisms such as projection, control patterns [80] are *semi-conscious* habits reactive to early triggers. Originally they kept us feeling safe. They are ways of coping, adjusting to the environment, controlling anxiety, controlling the future. They protect our inadequacies and sensitivities, enabling us to bury our fear and pain. And they're useful – they allow us to grow up behind them. However, like bathing-huts on earlier beaches, we go on using them when they're outdated. We can even *become* these control patterns, being controlled and blocked by them ourselves. Once-helpful habits, they've become destructive.

For example, a shy and introverted child may grow up always waiting for others to speak; or, conversely, talking so much no one can ask questions. One person may have to be top dog for fear of not being noticed, balancing shyness by becoming hail-fellow-well-met. Another has wobbly boundaries; feeling constantly invaded, this person is invisible in the kitchen at parties, hiding behind smokescreens.

Who or what runs my life? Have I chosen it, or has someone else chosen for me? How conditional is my life? We use control patterns for

---

[80] A concept of John Heron, Founder and Director of the Human Potential Research Project, University of Surrey, the oldest established centre for humanistic and transpersonal psychology and education in Europe.

many purposes:

To keep ourselves at bay, we always contact friends *first*; we fill our diaries, avoid being alone on holiday, live vicariously by being interested in others. 'I'm snowed under with demands!' Yet have I not given my address to scores of people?

To keep others at bay, we're always late – or always early. And busy, pressured: 'I'm so lonely and friendless – but, sorry, can't possibly come over in the next three months!' As children, we would do what we wanted only in secret, read only behind the curtain. Now, to keep feelings at bay, we talk only about either 'important' or 'trivial' matters.

In relationships. To pre-empt criticism, we criticise ourselves first. Not daring to allow that we might – just might – be all right as we are, we apologise in advance; saying 'sorry!' makes us almost invulnerable. Doing ourselves down so that others won't is still doing ourselves down. If that doesn't work, we develop wit, habitually knocking ourselves with humour (though it's important to keep the humour!) Avoiding endings, we get out of having to face new beginnings. Wanting to say 'No', we end up saying 'Yes'. And we let ourselves be controlled as a way of feeling needed; to avoid declaring, 'This is what I want!' we say, 'What do *you* want, dear?' We don't know what we want anyway.

The uses of control patterns. And they can be useful… For instance, if saying 'No' is difficult, why not deliberately develop a strategy to buy time: 'I never carry my diary with me; please ring again tomorrow,' thus telling a lie without compunction.

But control patterns often need updating or relinquishing. Go quietly inside yourself and consider your own past and present defensive control patterns. Have one or two served? Are they still needed? Could they be dropped? You may want to keep some for the time being – note them. Take your discoveries deeper; anchor them through the body, the five senses.

DISCUSSION AND SHARING IN SMALL GROUPS

Make sure once more that interpretations come only from the person themselves. Let no one try to evaluate the material from someone else's images. See p. 40, and fuller commentary is given in Appendix 1.

CHANGE

*The thrust of the psyche towards wholeness
throws up the extent to which we are lopsided*

Crisis points of stress, difficulty and uncertainty hit us at different stages. Growth rarely proceeds altogether evenly, but is characterised by crossroads of choice and decision, key points at intersections on the map of our lives.[81] Events prompt us to re-examine life in the light of hitherto unfamiliar impressions, thoughts and feelings. We are invited to consider *changing*.

What for you is change?

Character is destiny. Fate seems to act from the outside to make us conscious. So we have an accident, an illness, a bereavement, are made redundant in a job we expected to last for years (witness one lawyer, who only discovered when sacked that what he really wanted was music). When dramatic change occurs, ask: 'What has been happening in the unconscious?' Changes may *seem* sudden but – like spring bulbs growing underground all winter – are probably the visible evidence of forces that have been gradually building up. As the individual seed grows to its own unique nature, so inner change precedes outer. 'This is how I am and will always be' gives place to 'nothing is carved in stone'. We are often more aware of impending change than we realise; undercover work will have been going on continually. Take the 'sudden' fall of Communism; what seemed to happen all at once had required hard graft to set the scene. Outwardly we may be totally shocked, but inwardly we somehow *knew*; we felt it coming.

The only certainties are change and death. We resist both. If we believe there is but one life then, fearful, we struggle to survive, some more strongly than others. But if we see life as a continuum, death and change are natural, eventually to be welcomed. The death of what we value – of ourselves – is not mere loss but rebirth to a new phase or state. And change, like dragon or phoenix, is both danger and opportunity.

The urge to grow is often uncomfortable, so we collude to prevent change in values, emphases or dynamics and to maintain the *status quo*. But

---
81 Perhaps the nodal points suggested on Chart 3:01, The Seven-Year Cycle, above.

growth *requires* change. The Self creates it to wake us up. Knowing the time has come to upset the existing equilibrium, it nudges and disturbs us with its wisdom. Moods change, phases change, lost times call us, new things need to be born. *Opportunity knocks twice*, at least. Untravelled roads do remain: perhaps they need to be followed? We *can* go back and live again the time of some critical intersection; we *can* take up another option.

Or can we? At those crises or passages when all things lose their savour, though we may feel an impulse to change it can be hard indeed to do it. We are not free; we have family, children, are locked and trapped in outer circumstances. We *cannot* undertake what we want to do. Some may say there is no outer circumstance that we can't change. Yet what if we can't?

A real test is something we cannot prepare for. All our strength is called forth to deal with it. We have to draw on something else. We learn to go with change – to dance life more. We are then energised and the heart is brought back in. *Accepting*, not grudgingly but willingly, we become alert to changing patterns and movements. Many people live in the past or the future; but part of this change in awareness is learning to be more in the

Direction

Style

Building in parallel

Interludes

New beginnings

Patterns and Polarities

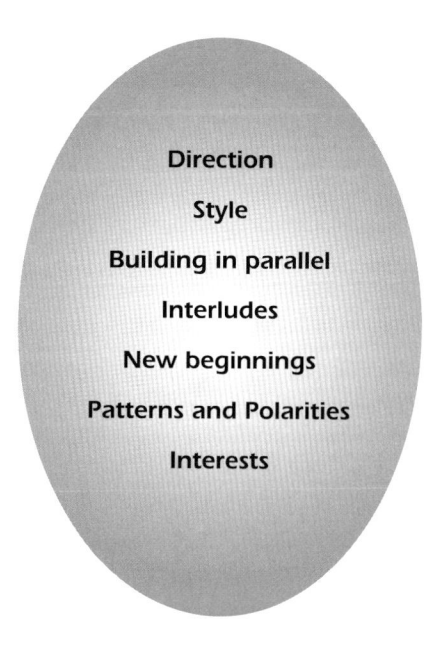

Interests

Chart 3:04 – Change

present, where the only true power lies. Listening, as in music, to the pulse and the changing rhythms, we celebrate the moment. The past is redeemed – now. The future grows from now. 'This is how it is – for the moment.' Unconscious of how the design of our lives is being worked out, we see the shape and reason only later. Prior unconscious work helps us to make a passage without total collapse.

Key turning points of change can be of a number of different kinds:

Changes of direction

Especially in our career may come a sense of danger, of crisis and transformation. 'Which life-cycle am I in? Where am I going? Is this a new beginning – a re-balancing of my life? Does this tell me anything about my direction, or is it about the demands of the time?' What goes before prepares for what comes after: those who've been on a 'height trip' may be stuck up the mountain and need to descend into the cave system below, and *vice versa*. Do I jump, or go over gradually? Do I need to do the same things, but differently? Do I need to move to a different area? Or, do I need to change, but within the same area? There is fear around: 'Who the hell am I? Do I *really* need to move on up the ladder? Or, perhaps, back down it? My confidence may not match my career success.' Some people deliberately choose undemanding work because it leaves their minds free for what they want to think about.

Changes of style

Changes needn't be big or dramatic. If life is controlling us, some small shift of perspective, rhythm or emphasis in the *manner* in which we do what we do may return control to us. For example, breaking the habit of a lifetime, we could wash up dinner *next morning* – or have breakfast last thing at night ... Why not learn calligraphy, writing hated necessary job reports as exercises? Or honour the decision to spend some time alone each day by putting a fire in the bedroom? We could throw away the old plastic mug and give ourselves tea in a really good cup. And for guilt and misery we could build in some worry-time each day.

Changes of relationship

A change in ourselves usually brings about a change in the other. Also, we sometimes have an inner knowledge which we deny. If someone is treating you badly – look within! For example, if your partner is threatening to leave the relationship, you may have no apparent knowledge of the difficulties or pain involved for them; unconscious projection or collusion is at work to protect you from an inner knowledge you don't want to face.

Especially around mid-life, the journey may lead us to find, or re-discover, our own chosen family, as well as our task. Bumping into people who ring our bells with an instant understanding, we are drawn towards them out of the accidental family of our birth. It's a great delight to develop close associations with these people; yet we may lose touch with them because of being caught up in our own family.

Building in parallel

This is a very creative way forward. We sense what we would really like to do, but we can't do it yet. Energy is running for it, but not enough to do it full-time. So – do it *as a hobby*. Do just a bit of it, without immediately changing other things. Simply make a little space, plant an initial seed, and experiment. Water it, nourish it, see where it goes, how it grows. Eventually you may become overloaded, and this will force a decision: by now the new seedling may be strong enough to be planted out.

We lose energy when our hearts are not in something. If you don't know what you really want to do, ask, *'What makes my heart sing?* What do I enjoy?' Not, 'What ought I to be able to want to do?' The doing of this new thing brings the heart back into the rest of life as well – whatever it is you do, let it make your heart sing.

Interludes

There are interludes when the life goes out of life. Everything is flat, stale, dead. The energy runs out and there is a feeling of emptiness, a vacuum, a sense of waiting. Nothing seems to be happening. Certainly, some of us have short low periods each day, even each hour; others may have longer cycles – every week or month, season or year – times when they feel below par. But this kind of interlude is different. It is *not depression*, though it may have that quality. Rather, something is breathing *in*, energy is being brought back. Dreams and imaging often reveal its nature.

Rather than defending against it, use it. Visualise it. What is its effect? If you fear this darkness, draw or write about it, listen to appropriate music. It may involve panic – but necessary panic, calling for less *doing* and more *being*. Panic attacks can be seen as active depression, blocked heart energy. The unconscious is pulling our libido away to a place where it is unavailable. Accept and honour the nature of the interlude, use it like a meditation, be alert for a break point in it. If it is treated too readily as medical, say with antidepressants, you may be dosing away whatever's seeking to come in – or back, or to the surface.[82] Drowning in dark waters, don't necessarily cry for help; rather, as Jung said, learn to be a diver and perhaps discover a pearl on the floor of the ocean.

Interludes may be necessary preludes to change, signalling a transition between two distinct phases. For the new to come in, the old has to fall away. Is something brewing in the unconscious? To give it energy and space, does something have to happen? Maybe the Self sees that, as things are, there is no room for change; only withdrawing energy from the ego gives change a chance. So it's the Self that takes the energy from the present task, drawing it back into itself, leaving a vacuum at ego level – a space for something new. When the energy goes out of a job or relationship, go with this loss of libido. Ask, 'What's below the surface?' We usually tend to rush the harder to make things interesting again: 'God grant me patience – but hurry up!' That's when it all goes wrong.

We do not need to change direction *during* these interludes. *Don't push the river*. The sabbatical principle is very important. Every seven years the field is left fallow – weeds draw up minerals from deep down, and sheep graze and manure it. The interlude, of its nature, will take time – accelerate it, and we may drop back into it. There is a feeling of dying. Wait with patience. Something has been grasped intuitively but not all through; only when it has finally been digested can the birth take place. With all depression, people need help to labour and go with the waves of pain until the interlude breaks and something new is born.

So, live an attenuated life – and do it thoroughly.... Hibernate, close down, so the seeds can grow.

New beginnings

It's as if we are in several incarnations in this one. One career in a lifetime is ridiculous; many people need at least two or three, including parallel careers. However, don't do anything new till there's so much energy rooting for it that *you can't not*. New beginnings need to be recognised and welcomed. Wait until it is impossible to refuse them and

---

82 However, medication is obviously sometimes appropriate; it can facilitate our working in a transpersonal way, rather than preventing it.

they will succeed without your trying.

Patterns and polarities

Polarities contain change. Our lives include introversion and extraversion, masculine and feminine, feeling and thinking; do we run more on sensation, or intuition? Are we process or product people, actualisers or transcenders?[83] Is this a time of *coagulatio* or of *solutio*, success or failure? Do we go in for caution or risk-taking; dominance or submission; play victim or saviour? On the one hand is *yin*, the solitary, heart values, feeling, sensing, contemplation and 'being'; on the other, *yang*, the gregarious, head values, thinking, intuition, the practical, 'doing'. Here are challenge and war; there, acceptance and peace. From time to time these need adjustment. Aiming towards wholeness, we see ourselves lopsided. It pushes us into balance as the other end of the pole forces itself into consciousness – macro or micro, orthodox or unorthodox, height or depth? – until, with creative self-understanding, we reconcile the opposing pulls.

Interests

A change here can indicate tides within the psyche. The profound ebbs and flows of interest in the mid-life period often herald a movement forward. Are we for art, science, religion, politics, social life, solitude? We explore what fascinates us. Where does the motivation lie, what gives us enjoyment, what turns us on? Something may cease to interest us, pointing to what is happening in the unconscious – professional reading may send us to sleep, while novels keep us awake for hours. Where our interests lie, there lies life.

Changes in dimension

And some important changes are not covered by the above, changes in depth, shifts into 'another dimension' – shifts of archetype. We are not made of the same stuff all through, but have within us several different energy-lines, as we shall see. An overview of these puts change into context. At what level do they operate?

---

[83] Transcenders and Actualisers, Appendix 8.

EXPLORATION
TRAVELLING THE ROAD OF YOUR LIFE
(40 minutes)

This exploration is a journey in three parts.[84] In the first, you travel the present road of your life. In the second, you continue along the present road, but this time into the future. The third stage takes you along a different road, route or track. Since you may find yourself travelling in a vehicle, at least for part of your journey, you may wish to sit up rather than lie out. Allow images to come to you; avoid interpreting or trying to think out meanings. Get thoroughly into the scene and let it develop as it will. Recording and drawing are at the end.

First journey

Minutes

10 Spend a moment relaxing and letting go. Find yourself in a vehicle travelling *the present road* of your life. As you travel, attend to a number of things: through what sort of environment are you travelling, and what is your direction? What kind of road, path or track are you on? What is your mode of travel? If you are in a vehicle, what kind is it; and if it is powered, what is the feel of the engine, the performance? Are you alone? How about the driver – are *you* driving? How about the driving style and pace? And, most particularly, how do you feel about this journey that you are on? So, travelling the present road of your life, note what you can about the journey.

3 Shortly you come to an *intersection* where the ways divide, some sort of fork. Note this intersection – you will be returning here. From it, you could travel along a different road, path or track.

Second journey

10 However, you do not at this point take that different route. Continue along the present road, but now into the future. As you do so, attend to the same things: the environment; the road or path; the style and mode of travel; the vehicle and its performance; your feelings on this second part of your journey, from the intersection into the future.

---

84 Commentary on the Road of Your Life exploration, Appendix 2

3 Find yourself back at the intersection where you started the second part of the journey. From here it is possible to take another route.

Third journey

10 Now, travel into the future, but this time take that other route, a different road, path or track from the intersection. Spend the next ten minutes travelling this *other* way into the future. Attend, as before, to anything significant: how you are travelling; the environment; your vehicle, if any. How do you feel about this other journey into the future?

4 And in a moment this third journey too comes to an end. Find yourself back where you started. From there, go to a quiet place together with a wise being, or with your own wisdom. In that wise presence, review the three journeys you have taken, recording them by writing and drawing.

ARCHETYPAL ENERGIES

Who or what is your God?

How to put the ineffable into words? We are in areas of which as yet we know little, although nuclear physicists are beginning to speak the language.[85] This is very tentative.

We are each moved by several fundamental core energies which will define how we travel in life. We tend to think others should be like us, and fall back in anger, even despair, when they are not. But we are of differing substance.[86]

Typology tries to map this. In whatever field, there are types: cat people, dog people, horse people; Rolls and old banger people; someone will have a Ford, someone else a VW, a third an Aston Martin. Children's nicknames are often accurate in pointing to profound differences in temperament. Always there have been mountains people and plains people. Pikemen were neither bowmen nor spearmen. Deep-sea sailors

---

85 An analogy can be drawn from high-energy physics: the creation and annihilation of particles, which are represented in potential form as mathematical functions. Certain mathematical or experimental operations serve either to bring the particle into existence or to destroy it.
86 The originality and creativity of the authors shone through again and again and was recognised. At a Workshop III in the 1980's IGB was asked, 'What books do these archetypes come from – what are your sources?' He responded: 'All this is not in Jung. Assagioli had it from Alice Bailey, but kept the esoteric connection hidden.' Joan Swallow came in: 'The way in which Ian says this is deeply original. It's not to be found in a book unless Ian writes it; he is an original. We are privileged to hear it from the original thinker.' (See n. 26 p. 41). Ed.

differ from those who love to mess around the coast in small boats; and they both differ from river people. Even out of uniform it is possible to distinguish Navy people from Army, and each from Air Force people. Sheep farmers are different from both cattle farmers and cereal farmers; market gardeners are different again. Some of us prefer a country cottage, others a flat in town.

So our core energies differ. How do we find them, since they are ineffable? At any given stage, which archetype is central to us, of the essence, and which are of the personality? If these conflict within us, we need to listen. If we grow and change, they overlap and interchange, leading to wholeness, the expression of the Self, the One. For these archetypes of the Self may be seen as the faces of God. To accept and come to one's true Self is to accept something greater than ourselves – to accept and come to God.

One way to become aware of all this is through images. Always, religions have embodied myths and legends, as attempts are made to interpret God, Fate, Destiny. The Sagas, the Bhagavad Gita, the Greek Pantheon, the Thousand and One Nights, Greek and Islamic stories, all

Chart 3:05 – Typical Archetypal Energies

indicate various *archetypes of the soul*,[87] as does the Jewish god of the Old Testament. And Wotan, god of Madness who heads the wild hunt across the heavens – Norse gods are warriors, warlike. So too the racial gods in the Arthurian myths of the Grail with their Celtic quality. The archetypes of native North Americans include 'all our relations; Grandfather Sun; Grandmother Moon; Father Sky; Mother Earth'. Around the Mediterranean, in Italy and France, is found the Dark Mother.[88] It pays not to neglect the roots from which one springs. Yet in the West there is neither place now for a warrior god nor any place for the dark mother.

Ruler	**Power**
Priest/Healer	**Love**
Consciousness-Teacher	**Fulfilment**
Devotee/Idealist	**Perfection**
Magician	**Manifestation**
Conciliator/Mediator	**Harmony**
Alchemist/Scientist	**Objective Truth**
Artist	**Creation/Ideas**
Manager	**Organisation**
Don Juan	**Conquest**
Hero/Explorer	**Venturing**
etc.	

Chart 3:06 – Some Archetypes of the Masculine Principle

There is a shadow to all of this: serving an archetype is very different from being overwhelmed by it – or thinking we are 'becoming' it. It is the *contents* of the archetypes that are experienced, not the forms themselves. Yet the face of God indicates the archetype of the Self. We may ask, 'What

---

[87] See Campbell 1968, *Creative Mythology*.
[88] The Major Arcana of the Tarot also point up some easily-recognised archetypes, such as the Fool, the Magician, the Empress, the Lovers, the High Priestess, the Hermit, Death, the Devil, the Star.

is my god?' Is it duty, love, creativity? Is it healing, teaching, justice, beauty? Any of these words go with archetypes. Asking, 'What is my real, basic energy?' can lead towards our thread, task, function, path – and then it's simpler. If we can hold to what is our god and follow that line – follow our bliss, as Joseph Campbell said – then we will begin to be true, not sidetracked into inappropriate tasks, secondary functions and outdated ways. This is when we may be drawn towards our own spiritual family – our chosen family, rather than the accidental family of our birth, as we saw above.

During the first half of life we discover what we're *not*. The energy of a sub-personality may have been running our lives for years before the core archetypal energy of the Self knocks on the door, often at a midlife crisis. And since archetypes of people's Selves differ, we shall look first at seven major archetypal energies which manifest respectively in the will towards Power, Love, Knowledge, Harmony, Truth, Perfection and Manifestation.[89]

The Ruler

The will to Power is the archetypal energy of the Ruler that motivates leader, king and emperor; and the great queen, the empress, the conquering heroine. The God of someone under this archetype is power. Under the influence of Shiva, full of energy and action, the urge is to *achieve*, overcome and conquer. Here are the general, the chairman, the statesman; most political figures have the electrically-charged aura of a monarch. Ideally, they are bent upon human rights and freedoms. As a force for justice, they value the power to accomplish – and use it well, as did, for example, William Wilberforce, Elizabeth Fry, President Gorbachev, Margaret Thatcher.

In the *shadow* of this archetype are violence and force. The drawbacks of Rulers include isolation – up on their own in pursuit of a task, they may cease to notice individuals at all. To achieve the goal is essential, even by grasping, by brute manipulation or violent imposition. Occultists may be found among them. To develop, they need to become *inclusive* and heart-based, and learn to be *less centred*.

The Priest-healer

The will to Love fills with its energy both Priest-healer and Teacher of Consciousness. Readers may find this more familiar. Bent upon health and

---

[89] For more detail, see Chapter 7, pp. 285 et seq.

wholeness, those under this archetype include doctor, nurse, healer, listener, scholar. For them, God is love. Here are found both the ambassador and the true psychic, each motivated by the urge to *fulfilment*, expansion and initiation and moved and absorbed by the desire for consciousness and wisdom. Influenced by Vishnu, they are full of love and caring. Attracting and radiating, they inspire others with their compassion. Almost in spite of themselves, healing power flows through them.

Their drawbacks centre mainly round invasion; these people include others too much. Relationships are what matter; their *shadow* may well involve floppy boundaries. They need to be *more centred*, less invaded and invading, developing and remembering their own space and boundaries. Also, in their longing for subjective truth, the therapists, spiritual teachers, group leaders among them may well be subject to inflation, mistaking themselves for the wisdom they seek to mediate.

The Thinker

The will to Knowledge characterises a different kind of teacher. Its energy motivates the Thinker, the Philosopher, to whom to know and to impart knowledge is all-important. For someone influenced by this archetype, God is thought and God is all-knowing. Here are the entrepreneur, the communicator, the educator, influenced by Brahma, skilled in planning and effective communication and full of the urge to *understand*. Characterised by the intelligent use of the mind, they are concerned with adaptation, development and evolution.

They generate ideas and conceptions, but in the *shadow* lies the manipulator. 'These are *my* ideas, not yours!' Their drawback is dogmatism. They need to stop trying to brainwash other people; and to cultivate *stillness and true reflection*, giving them an overview and letting them select and discriminate. Then, lost in deep thought, they will be true metaphysicians and philosophers.

The Mediator

The will to Harmony, the will to Create – this is the energy that motivates Mediators, whose God is harmony, as well as Artists and craftspeople for whom God is creator. They long for peace and beauty, for things to flow. Here too are Explorers, whose God is to venture and dare. Conciliators, artists and explorers, all keenly aware of the vibrations of things, seek expression for their ideas. Their energy is in *expression in form*, making visible the invisible. Subjective, they are in touch with what seems beyond the individual, in the collective unconscious, the wellsprings of creation. The conciliators and mediators are full of the urge to bring about relationship between others, 'at-one-ing', seeking conflict resolution. In the late 1950's, on a new impulse, institutes for Peace Research were set up by people under this archetype – though the name was later changed by those under a different archetype to 'The Centre for the Study of the Resolution of Conflict'.... They use game theory for negotiation, so that both sides are advantaged by decisions.

The *shadow* for explorer and harmoniser is the tendency to despair or fall into chaos. They need to develop *steadfastness*; Gurdjieff well understood this. The artists' drawback is that, full of vision, they may yet lack application – too low a ratio of perspiration to inspiration. The mediators may become stuck on fences, seeing both sides – 'both yes *and* no!' – to such an extent that decision becomes impossible. They need to decide and to act.

The Scientist

The will to Truth is the energy behind Researchers, Scientists and Alchemists, for whom God is objective knowledge. The archetype of truth informs not only the Rosicrucian and the alchemist but the academic and the engineer. It is practical truth they seek: the will to find out, discover, disprove, and only so to know. The energy of the archetype leads them to experiment and differentiate, seeking always objective truth and understanding.

The *shadow* of these seekers after truth may include overmuch detachment, leading them to forget the microcosm in the interest of the wider search for knowledge. They are likely to be head-types, out of touch with their feelings. The creation of the atom bomb exemplifies this, their drawbacks including a possible lack of ethics or humanity to match their knowledge. However, scientists themselves are beginning to *speak the language of consciousness*. The physicist Stephen Hawking said, 'For me, physics is about seeing better, further and deeper'. Where scientists used to be at variance with religious thinkers, now some may be at the very forefront of knowledge, at the place where physics meets mysticism.

The Devotee

The will to Make Perfect. This energy has led to the Idealists and Devotees of the Christian era. God is perfection, God is the ideal. Characterised by adoration, those under this archetype include the saint, the missionary, the martyr and the preacher. 'God is on my side!' Though sympathy and tolerance are ideally valued, the urge is to perfect devotion, idealism and abstraction. Here are followers, disciples, students, apprentices, devoted servants of a person, a cause, a family, responding with faith and prayer. Bent on perfection, the devotees of the Piscean era have clustered around central figures, favourite teachers: Christ, St. Francis, the Buddha, Milarepa – or Bhagwan, Sai Baba, the Moonies.

The *shadow* here is exclusivity. '*My* god says so, therefore I am right.' The drawbacks are bigotry and fanaticism, for devotees can readily be fundamentalists. The will to perfection of this era has caused much psychological damage in the Jewish and Islamic, as well as the Christian, worlds, 'Be ye therefore perfect' came to mean, 'Be ye therefore masculine, as woman is imperfect'. (Still today, some men thank God daily that they were not born women!) They need to develop both *tolerance* and *sympathy*. It is desirable that this archetypal energy should wane now, giving place to the energy of the Magician.

The Magician

The will to Wholeness. The God of those under the influence of the Magician is *manifestation*. They include business entrepreneurs, theatrical producers, choreographers – and again, some teachers. The wand of touch goes with the magician. Here are perfect form and effortless economy of movement, all energised by the urge to make manifest. If the purpose is humane, the energy is that of transformation: they shape and organise matter with elegant efficiency. Knowing about systematic organisation, co-ordination and bringing together, they also understand incubation, ritual and magic. (Managers, good at organisation, are subtly different from magicians; though, with a magician behind them to inspire, they will be excellent at it.) Certain individuals never seem to *do* much, yet things happen around them. Deftly, they make manifest; apparently not working hard, they unlock trouble by a subtle move. Combined with a priest-healer, a magician is the best healer of all. In this era the archetype of magician is coming into consciousness – into manifestation.

The *shadow* of the archetype is inflation. The magician's drawbacks include manipulation and deception, for they can misuse power to bring about dark ends and render other people, including family members, mad. They need to develop *humane purpose and pure motive*.

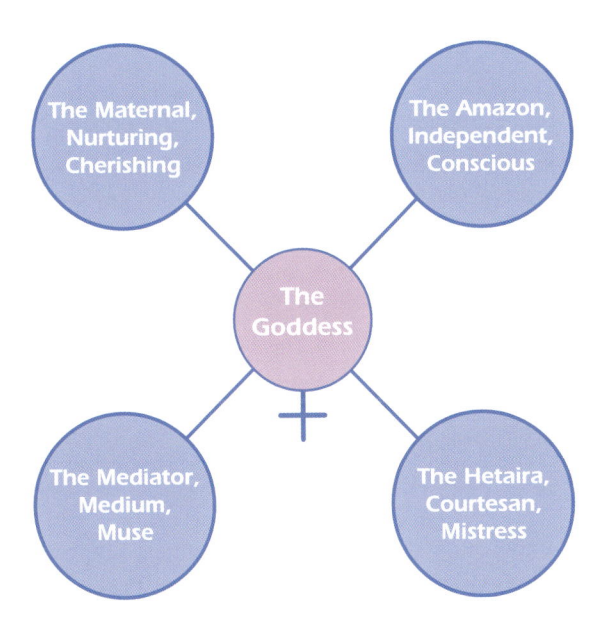

```
        The Maternal,           The Amazon,
        Nurturing,              Independent,
        Cherishing              Conscious


                    The
                    Goddess
                      ♀


        The Mediator,           The Hetaira,
        Medium,                 Courtesan,
        Muse                    Mistress
```

Chart 3:07 – Four Archetypes of the Feminine Principle

This limited list[90] is based upon Toni Wolff's[91] comment, that the *feminine* can be characterised by just four distinct ways in which it *relates to the masculine*. Again, this is not about men and women, but about these two great archetypal energies and how they relate within both women and men. Eventually, we need to assimilate the attitudes that go with all four, being able to see how we relate to the masculine principle Maternally, as Mistress, as Comrade and as Muse:[92]

The Maternal

This comes from the archetype of the mother. Someone with this energy is primarily a nurturer; she cherishes a man primarily as father and provider to her children. She sees him as the source of ideas – he is her intellect. A major drawback is that, in nurturing him as well, she can be smothering.

---

90 Limited because of time constraints in the workshop. See Chapter 2, pp. 73–83 above, for more feminine archetypal energies. Ed.
91 Toni Wolff, associate of Carl Jung (and now acknowledged as long-time mistress), in Castillejo 1973, *Knowing Woman*, p. 64.
92 Any attempt to make this scheme fit with Jung's Four Functions is doomed to failure. Getting a map of the psyche on to a flat bit of paper just won't work – it needs, rather, a sphere with no edges.

The Hetaira

This is the mistress, the courtesan. Someone influenced by this archetype is mapped opposite to the mother. Companion on many levels, she is courtesan on the sexual. The personal relationship with the masculine matters most; her partner, her children, are secondary to the lover. The 'other woman' in the triangle, she reflects his personal, unconscious *anima* back to him. She makes a mistake about herself if she tries to marry him by ousting his wife. She is *mistress*, not wife. Her drawback is that, getting this wrong, she makes herself and others miserable. Though herself perhaps married or in a career, she may turn her sons into secret lovers and her daughters into close girlfriends, thus hampering their own relationships.

The Amazon

Someone under this archetype is independent and self-contained. Having a vocation and a career, she may marry or have affairs but is not dependent on it. She loves like a man, has brother/sister relations with men. Conscious of man, she does not mediate him; rather, as comrade and workmate, she challenges him. The drawbacks are that she is often hated by men, who fear her rivalry and 'keep her in her place'. Hence, a familiar voice in her head, 'I am no good!' Picking up from others their inner disdain of her, her own negative *animus* may react by becoming aggressively feminist; she needs, rather, to put soft socks on his hobnails.

The Medium

Opposite to this on the chart is the Muse, permeated by the unconscious of another person. The archetypal inspirer, she relates to the other by making the unconscious visible for them, living it for them. She picks up what's going on and voices it. She dreams for them and for the group. She is a passive vessel, helping them to live, create and die. A drawback is that she needs a very strong ego herself to cope.

The way of integration

Someone may, for instance, start out with a lot of *maternal* energy, and, becoming more conscious, emerge with an independent *career*. Another, beginning as a powerful *ruler* in the home or at work, may only later become a *teacher of consciousness*. The dominant archetype has its opposite, and that opposite also expresses itself. So the mind which first resonated to the energy of *scientist* or *alchemist* might convert and go over to the *devotee* or to the *artist*. Another person might have started as a *disciple* bent upon following perfection and only later become a *healer* of body or soul.

So we are all influenced by several archetypes, and they are like the gods. The energies of the One, the Self, our essential core, irradiate our soul, touching and transforming our substance till we begin to awaken to something *other*, turning from ego-concentration to wider contexts, inner and outer. A considerable struggle may follow as the personality, confused in subtler ethers, tries to reclaim its autonomy. But at last we begin to attend, listen, respond to the resonance and follow the call of the One. And as we reach out to something greater and deeper, we are *met* and drawn home on our thread.

SHORT EXPLORATION
CORE ENERGY
(10 minutes)

To find your core energy, your archetype, take a few minutes to go within.
    Ask yourself:
        What is your highest value? Your energy? Method of work? Way of integrating?
        Which is the most resonating of the archetypal clusters? And add to them, too.
        Who is your god?

So, seek your own core energy, and the archetype that goes with it.[93]

---

93 And see the explorations in Chapter 7 below.

REVIEW OF THE THREE INTRODUCTORY WORKSHOPS

Have patience with everything unresolved in your heart …
try to love the questions themselves
as if they were locked rooms or books written in a very foreign language.
Don't search for the answers,
which could not be given to you now,
because you would not be able to live them….
Live everything. Live the questions now.
Perhaps then, someday far in the future, you will gradually,
without even noticing it,
live your way into the answer.
Rainer Maria Rilke [94]

How shall we proceed? 'Round things off nicely, now!' commands the ego. The Self states simply, 'There is a road.' For all we know, there may be nothing else at all. The journey, without offering any rules, invites us to consider choices. Here are a few suggested questions.

What is my style? Do I live things out or am I quiet? Am I open or closed? Receptive or proactive? Reality-testing or patient? How do I cope? What do I do and say today? The ego and the Self may have different answers. In practice, it *is* possible to give ourselves space and boundaries. We can feel the sense of being between earth and sky, as in the grounding exercise; it makes it less risky to fly. And it's easier to go into the sea knowing that land is there. We can notice projections – therein may lie the inner feminine or masculine – and control patterns, learning to use them consciously. We can develop new ways of imaging, working with dreams and symbols, being aware of archetypes; recording by writing, painting and making things; valuing our own records.

We *can* allow contact with the wise presence. We can build a sanctuary, a place to go for rest and reflection, and maybe meet the wise person there – it is possible, out in the Monday morning world. Home is where the heart is; or whichever organ for you is central. We often resist what we enjoy but, working with the body in yoga, dance, swimming, we become more aware of how the Self inhabits the body in a very intimate way. It is the vessel in which our energies are held. Love the body.

---

94 Rilke 1903, *Letters to a Young Poet*, No. 4.

The 'Onion Map' again

The onion, to be read from inside out, shows the link between the personality and the Self. The dotted line across represents the threshold of consciousness. We and *our outer lives* are mapped below this, near the bottom, down in the outside world – a small person, a reflection of the Self, shone upon by rays from the Self through all the layers of the unconscious. When bombardment comes from life, the *persona* is the first area to be explored, with its associated roles; then the *ego*. As we become aware of the *shadow*, in come the *inner masculine* and *inner feminine*, beautiful and conflicting. For most of us, wrestling with our images of *anima* and *animus*, the inner mother and father, as well as our symptoms and what they may symbolise, is a lifelong task. Approaching the *archetypal* layer, looking at levels of meaning, will and purpose, we are reaching up into the unconscious. The wise, transpersonal Self is overhead, with its link down to the centre. Charted again at the bottom, it sends its rays streaming from above and below to the threshold to form a diamond over the map. All begin to come together as we draw nearer to *becoming* the Self, living consciously and fully in the outside world.

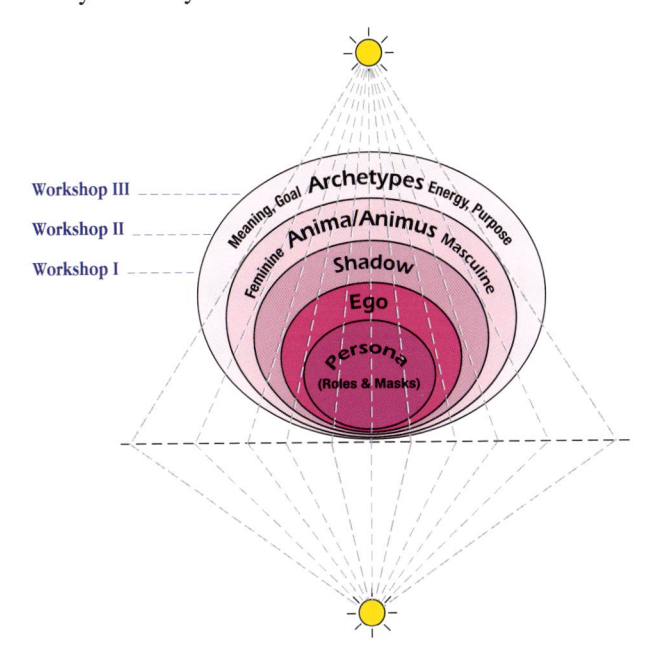

Chart 3:08 – The Onion Map 2

What draws people to Transpersonal workshops? Perhaps they are in trouble, have a yearning, are in some way dissatisfied; or have simply been brought by the Self. So they come and see. And what they most gain (as from a good Jungian analysis) is a sense of *richness*. How to handle this without being overwhelmed? Ignore it – put it to one side? How many dimensions to life do they want? If two were enough, they would not have come in the first place. The workshops offer some dimensions.

Workshop One – Approaching the Self

The workshop dealt mainly with the past and the present. We became the Traveller on life's journey; and we began to own and accept our Sub-personalities, those lesser-known parts of ourselves. Sub-personalities are fairly quickly identified, showing us the *persona* (how we sound, as through a mask, the roles that we play; necessary at times, but dangerous if we get stuck and think we *are* the masks); and behind the persona, the *ego*, the self with a small s, the wearer of the masks, the personality; and the Self with the capital S, the wise person or presence evoked by asking 'Who am I? Who am I as I feel myself to be, the real and valid me?' Behind the ego hides the dark figure of the *shadow*, that which is not yet in the light. The greater the light the deeper the shadow. Jung, seeing the shadow of love, said that it's not safe to be about without your shadow. It's not all bad; it's a compost heap from which come the first intimations of the Self. (Yet still, if life is dark, we might try switching on the light.) Symbols, dreams and fantasies come from the lower unconscious as well as the higher and we sought to map them. Some sub-personalities are themselves shadow figures carrying dormant potential. It is never too late to own undeveloped facets, unlived life, lost parts of ourselves which may be in the dark. How do we survive great joy? We used a Gestalt method of consulting within; reaching towards the transpersonal is a lifelong task, and this more lengthy process can help. Such a dialogue among body, mind, feelings and wise observer can be used for any situation. What do they *say*? And we may trust the *body*: it doesn't lie. However, the first three 'dimensions' or layers of the onion are not alone enough.

Workshop Two – The Masculine and Feminine Within

The whole range of *anima* and *animus* in each of us may have been evoked by our search for the Cup and the Sword; and we journeyed again to meet them on the road. We examined polarities – especially those between head and heart – learning to recognise our place on the axis in different situations. We look at images of mother and father, using maps of the masculine and feminine: the Four Partners at the Marriage, and Jung's image of the Container and the Contained. We explored Symptom as Symbol, acknowledging the body as carrier of other dysfunction, seeking its needs for nourishment in the Gestalt exploration. In the Grounding Exercise we drew strength from the earth, feeling down through our feet, drawing sap up through our body to our heart; then, we drew energy from above down, on to our face and into the inner marriage in our hearts, mother with father, earth with heaven.

Workshop Three – Cycles and Stages

In crisis, again, lie opportunity and danger. In this chapter we have explored meaning or its lack; choice, direction, purpose, the energy of who we *really* are. The Shape of Your Life exploration has involved imaging both time past and time future; the cyclic rhythms in the psyche are stepping stones, inviting us to own and release ourselves, flaws and all. *It is wholeness we seek, not perfection.* We've examined the Projection of our self-images, our 'ideal model' and, feeling the weight of these unconscious contents, shaken off their images and won free, ending by earthing the real and realistic self – always we bring in the body. We've looked at Control Patterns, asking how, semi-consciously, we cope and protect ourselves. What do we do with our experience? The Road of Your Life exercise explored where we are going *now* and in what sort of vehicle, taking two alternative ways into the future, exploring 'the road not taken'. We have examined some Archetypal energies, the god or the gods. These are different from sub-personalities. We've asked what kind of teachers do we resonate to: hero, wise woman, magician, scientist, priest-healer, muse. Not 'why?' but 'what does it mean?' Then the Inner Sanctuary is revisited, deepening and anchoring the experience.

And so we move towards:

Workshop Four – Initiation and beyond it to *The Other Self* ... and on.

EXPLORATION
THE SANCTUARY
(10 minutes)

Now we may begin to approach the Centre of Transformation, the sacred place where the temporal walls can dissolve to reveal a wonder. To have a sacred place is an absolute necessity: a room, a certain time each day, where you don't know what's in the papers this morning, or who your friends are, what anybody owes you, what you owe anybody. Just experience and bring forth who you are and who you might be. Having and using such a sacred place of incubation, at last something will happen.[95]

> So now, revisit your own sanctuary. It may be a newly discovered sanctuary, it may be one you have known a very long time.

> From it, cloaked in its strength, protected by it, bringing its energy with you, see yourself coming out, to *meet*. First, to meet the world immediately around you now – then this world later today. Feel your embracing and healing energy going out towards the earth – today. Now, tomorrow's world – your own outer world in its widest sense – all the people you know – all those you will get to know – all the world.

> And in that place of widest contact, know yourself once again within your own sanctuary; and know that your sanctuary is the world and is your own place. You and your sanctuary and the world are one.

> So, taking the energy and love of your own place out with you, wrapped in its wisdom and compassion, go forth into the world.[96]

---
95 See Campbell & Moyers 1988, *The Power of Myth*, p. 92. New York: Doubleday.
96 A suggested programme and original reading list for the workshop, Appendices 5 and 6.

CHAPTER FOUR

Initiation and the Myth of the Journey

Workshop IV

Ian Gordon-Brown and Barbara Somers

An initiate is ultimately one who initiates

INTRODUCING THE WORKSHOP [97]

Individuation

From time immemorial there have been mystery schools and centres of spiritual training (ashrams, religious orders and their more modern counterparts: the club, the fraternity, the lodge) offering seekers a path of accelerated development, a progressive initiation into new, expanded states of consciousness. The modern counterpart of initiation is *individuation*. Seen from the perspective of Transpersonal psychology, the path of initiation, both inner and outer, is the journey between the individual's first conscious response to the transpersonal Self, and full Self-realisation. Our whole nature is involved, our substance transmuted, the quality of our consciousness transformed. The locus of self-identity shifts. Inner symbols, rituals and keynotes relate the would-be initiate to changes in the energy patterns within the psyche. Each major stage is aimed at helping people to understand where they are. At each, the groundwork of the past is tried and a vision of the future seen. And it is emphasised that each phase of the *individual* journey is paralleled by similar processes in the *collective* psyche.

Such progressive initiation into new and expanded states of consciousness is often experienced as crisis. The Self operates unperceived until, with some disruption, the person becomes aware of it. Then the link between personality and Self grows stronger; the traffic

---

[97] Some notes on the running of aspects of this workshop are given in Appendices 1 and 2.

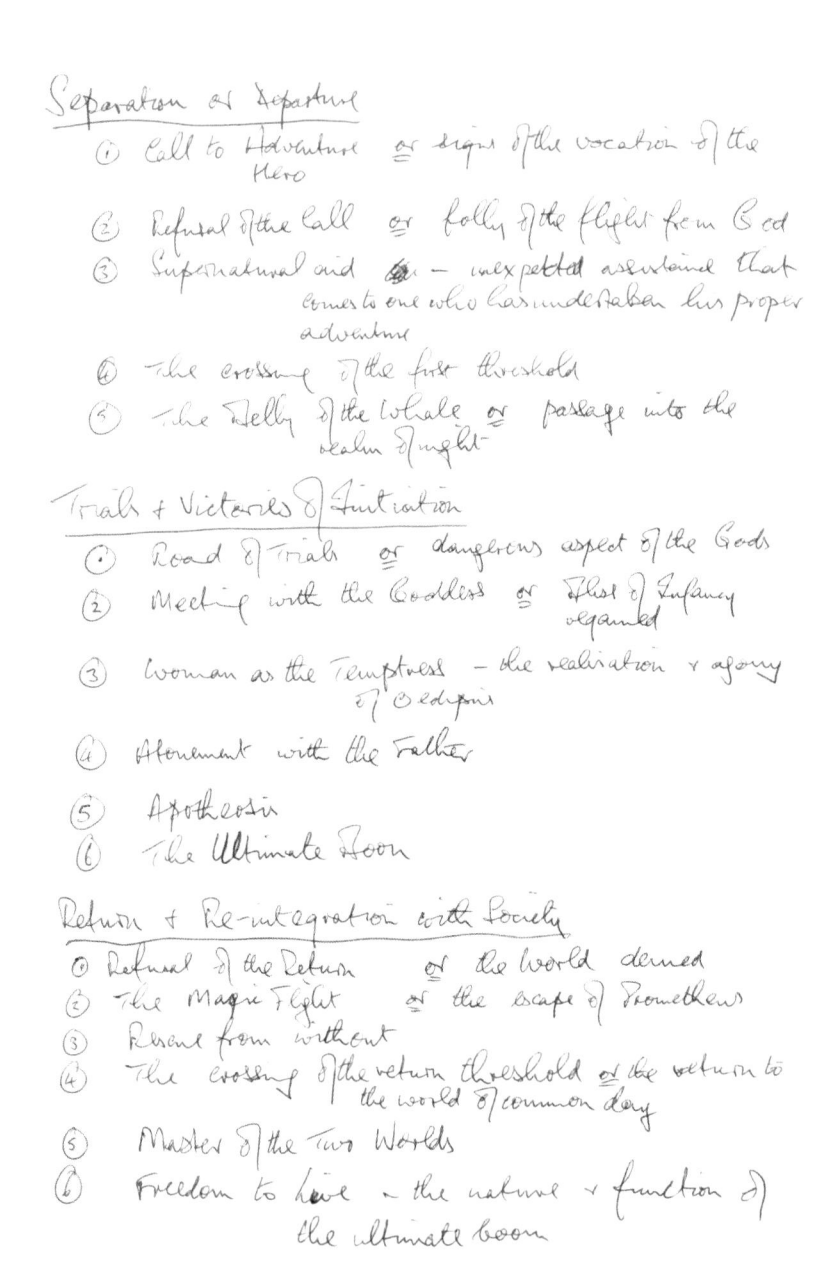

Separation or Departure
1. Call to Adventure or signs of the vocation of the Hero
2. Refusal of the Call or folly of the flight from God
3. Supernatural aid — unexpected assistance that comes to one who has undertaken his proper adventure
4. The crossing of the first threshold
5. The Belly of the Whale or passage into the realm of night

Trials & Victories of Initiation
1. Road of Trials or dangerous aspect of the Gods
2. Meeting with the Goddess or Bliss of Infancy regained
3. Woman as the Temptress — the realisation & agony of Oedipus
4. Atonement with the Father
5. Apotheosis
6. The Ultimate Boon

Return & Re-integration with Society
1. Refusal of the Return or the world denied
2. The Magic Flight or the escape of Prometheus
3. Rescue from without
4. The crossing of the return threshold or the return to the world of common day
5. Master of the Two Worlds
6. Freedom to Live — the nature & function of the ultimate boon

Facsimile of notes: Ian Gordon-Brown

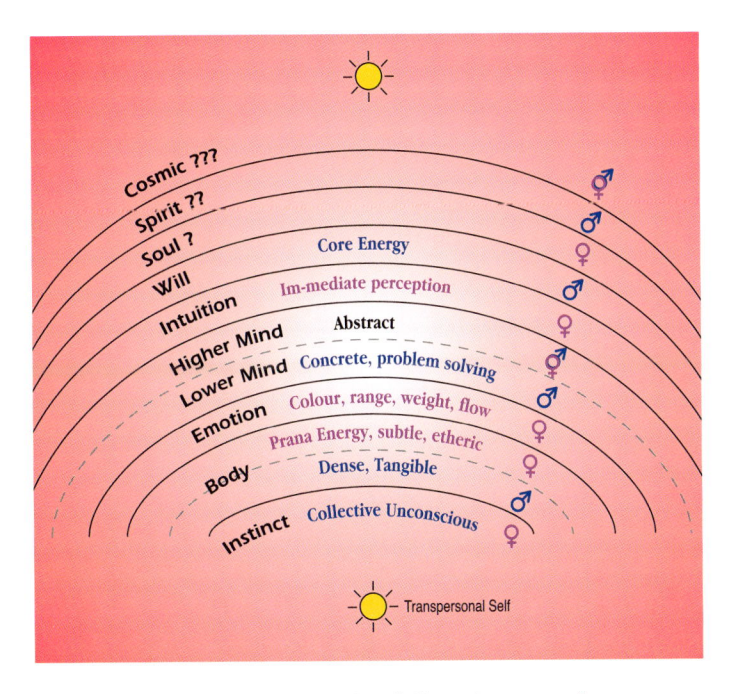

Chart 4:01 – Levels of Consciousness 4

becomes two-way, the field of awareness expands and centres in it and they learn to be in touch with it consciously and at will.

On the path to individuation there are major stopping or transition *points of initiation*. Each is the culmination of all that has gone before. It marks a death and rebirth, a passage from one state of being to another, an awakening till they function mostly within the Self. We develop from the body level to the emotional at adolescence and by our twenties our minds have also developed. We *have* a body, we have emotions and we have a mind; together they make up our personality, a centre of identity which 'has' all three. Yet *we* are distinct from them – they are not the Self, which has a unique resonance.

So in this workshop we look at initiation as a growth process on through the levels. Fire, destructive and transmuting, is the key signature. Tests are involved. None can escape. We cannot prepare for the confrontation with the shadow and we are bound to fail, at least the first time. Light and dark constantly alternate, symbolically blinding us like St. Paul. As the scales fall away, we start to attend to the Collective: we listen for words – in the air, on the web, in the pub – that are losing or gaining potency. They carry energy. The planet is undergoing a transformation, an initiation of its own involving all the kingdoms of nature – mineral, vegetable, animal, man.[98]

Myth. The nature of both journey and goal is shaped by our own personal myth and its tone, quality and colour. We resonate to different stories. We need to know our own, for it will shape us unconsciously whether we know it or not. We are in service to the race; the myth has us as much, or more, than we have it. Like a surfer, we ride its energies to become creative and effective. Myth is the secret opening to the energies of the cosmos. Not everyone knows or can find that opening, especially now that we have largely stopped telling stories to children – indeed, we may be losing touch with myths, though we are also creating marvellous new ones. Yet myths bring out the Magical Child and validate his experience that the world is glorious. 'Turn but a stone and start a wing.'[99] And Aristotle, of all people, said that a lover of myths, which are 'a compact of wonders', is a lover of wisdom.

Exploring one story in depth, we may come to recognise our own more clearly. We shall take the life of Christ, the never-ending story of emergence, experience and return, as our medium. It is a very good map, leading us to an inner temple where we may discover our own myth from deep within. But here is a different story to start us off.

THE STORY OF BUDDHA

*Be a lamp unto yourself
and work out your own salvation with diligence.*[100]

Prince Gautama Sakyamuni, protected by his father from knowledge of the world, was kept in ignorance of old age, sickness and death; and also of monk-hood, in case he decided to renounce the world. It had been prophesied that he would become either a world emperor or a Buddha so, to keep him attached to worldly things, his father gave him three palaces and forty thousand dancing girls.

By sixteen, Prince Gautama, well satiated, was ready for other experiences. Out one day in his magnificent chariot drawn by four horses

---

98 Mineral, involving the transformation of materials and atomic energy; vegetable, relating to trees and to fire; animal, about domestication; then come humans with their etheric energy. Perhaps there is a line, a hierarchy of devas, beyond this?
99 Francis Thompson, 'In No Strange Land'.
100 And see St. Paul too, Phillipians 2:12.

'as white as the petals of the lotus', he saw a sign from the gods – a decrepit old man, crooked, bent and trembling. Horrified, he turned to the charioteer: 'Who is this man?' Hearing for the first time about old age, Gautama declared: 'Shame on birth, since to everyone that is born old age must come!' Distressed, he returned to the palace. His father extended the guard and, to distract him, had his son most lavishly entertained.

Again, the gods fashioned a diseased man. 'Shame on birth that brings disease!' cried the Prince, making another agitated return to the palace. His father laid on every seduction and distraction and further extended the guard.

A third time, the gods intervened: they fashioned a dead man. 'Shame on birth that brings death!' exclaimed Gautama; and the palace guard was stretched a whole league around.

At last the gods fashioned a monk, decently clad, whom Gautama's friend the charioteer praised for his retirement from the world. Thrilled, the prince sensed his own destiny in the shape of the monk. Called to be the hero, he must transfer his centre of gravity from the known and familiar to the unknown, fateful region.

Gautama's father is the ruling principle, 'tradition'. He *is* this world, holding back the young man. The four beautiful horses, plus their chariot, are the five senses. The charioteer is friend and guide to the prince.

So Prince Gautama secretly said farewell to his wife and child; on his steed Kanthaka he made his way miraculously through the guarded gate, leaping the vastly wide river beyond. Assuming monkish clothes, he moved as a beggar through the world for many years, transcending the eight stages of meditation. Retiring to a hermitage, he spent six more years in struggle and extreme austerity. The trials of the hero always include the theme of near-failure. Like Parsifal, Gautama collapsed to near-death. But it is indispensable to the circulation of spiritual energy in the world that we return at last. Recovering, he returned to an ascetic, wandering life.

Soon afterwards passers-by noticed that the very tree he was sitting under was made radiant by his presence. Seeing this, a young girl called Sujata gave him milk and rice in a golden bowl. Remember Ariadne, the maiden who saved Theseus? Gautama accepted it. When he tossed the empty bowl into the river it floated *up*-stream, signifying the reversed wheel – the *ars contra naturam*. His triumph was at hand. It is said that birds, animals, plants and gods paid homage as he walked, heavenly choirs made music and the perfume of garlands of celestial glory led him to the Great Tree of Enlightenment, under which he would redeem the universe.

Under the Bo-tree he sat down, fixed in the Immovable Spot. As Christ was approached by Satan, so the future Buddha now faced Kama-Mara, the tempter, the god of love and death. On an elephant, surrounded by his army, weapons in his thousand hands, Mara assailed him to break his concentration. Whirlwinds, rocks, thunder, flame, burning coals, blistering sands and four-fold darkness were hurled. But, by the power of Gautama's ten perfections, the missiles were transformed into celestial flowers and unguents. Mara then sent his three daughters, Desire, Pining, and Lust, to distract him, but he stayed in contemplation. Challenging his right to sit on the Immovable Spot, Mara's army flung mountain crags at him. Gautama simply touched the earth with his fingertips and, to bear witness for him, the Earth goddess roared a hundred thousand times. And so Mara fell in obeisance to the future Buddha, who sat in meditation for the next forty days.[101]

Then the greatest temptation came: filled with doubt that he could communicate his message, he thought to retain the wisdom for himself. But Brahma Himself descended from the zenith, the vertical, imploring him to return and teach gods and men.

And so the Buddha went back to the cities, bestowing knowledge of the Way, giving men the Eightfold Path to enlightenment. His supreme injunction: *Be a lamp unto yourself and work out your own salvation with diligence*. And so, as Pontifex, bridge-builder, he became Bodhisattva, the Returning One.[102]

STAGES IN THE LIFE OF CHRIST

Is the figure whose coming is awaited in the age of Aquarius already here?

The life of Christ is an endless story of emergence, teaching and return. Born in the stable, appearing in the Temple, did Jesus feel how vocation can, as it were, pull us from in front? At his Baptism, *Jesus* took on the role of *Christ*. The Desert followed, tempting his new power. At his Trans-

---

[101] It is said of the next forty days that Gautama – now the Enlightened Buddha – sat for seven days motionless in bliss; for seven days stood apart and gazed at the Bo-tree; for seven days, paced between places of sitting and standing; for seven days lived in the pavilion of the gods and reviewed the whole doctrine of causality and release, bondage and freedom; for seven days sat under the tree where Sujata had given him milk and rice in the golden bowl, and meditated in the sweetness of Nirvana; and for the remaining days the Buddha enjoyed the sweetness of liberation.

[102] Noble Eightfold Path, and Bodhisattva vows, see Appendix 9.

> 1 BIRTH   Cave, incarnation
>   Heaven/Earth - Bridgemaker
>   THE TEMPLE
>
> 2 BAPTISM   "My beloved Son"
>   Waters of Emotion.
> 3 TEMPTATIONS IN DESERT
>   Use or mis-use of powers.
>   Labyrinth, doubts, uncertainties.
> 4 TRANSFIGURATION   Integration of
>   Self and Soul.   Kundalini Work.
> 5 CRUCIFIXION   Dismemberment.
>   Crucified between opposites:
>   time/eternity;   matter/spirit.
> 6 RESURRECTION
>
> 7 ASCENSION

Chart 4:02 – Stages in the Life of Christ

figuration he was recognised by God and men. Then, the Crucifixion; hung between opposites – humanity and spirit, time and eternity – repeating the story that we are both human and divine. And the Resurrection.[103]

Christ's birth

The second birth takes place and we are born into the cave of our own hearts

The tale is heavy with symbolism: Christ the Son, born to the Mother in a stable or cave in Bethlehem, the House of Bread. Bread for economic reality; the cave for the place of initiation; the gifts of the Wise Men symbolising the three aspects of the personality: gold for the physical and material, frankincense for emotion and the incense of purification, myrrh for the mind, the source of bitterness and suffering. And the little child, whose sign is a star.

For us, birth, *the first stage of initiation*, reflects the life of the *body*. The

---

103 See Bailey 1960, *The Rays and the Initiations* Vol. 5, 'A Treatise on the Seven Rays', p. 340.

story starts with *re*-birth, perhaps many rebirths, each following an initiation after a time of relatively unconscious living. Then comes the *touch of the Self*, through some early awareness or teaching. Like birth, rebirth can be a terrific crisis, apparently intended to let the energy of the Self break through. Inner symbols, rituals and keynotes relate the would-be initiate to the energy changes within. By such crises our substance is transformed and development takes place. This seems to be what crises are for. The key stages of initiation overlap; we seem to spiral through several incarnations in this one lifetime before reaching new interests, new aspirations, new values. Afterwards we feel whole – differently whole. It doesn't last. But it remains a memory: something came through – something is forever different. The seed did spring and has begun to grow.

Humanity together seems to be experiencing a second birth; it's happening to enough individuals to be significant. The mass of people, unconscious but affected by the Collective, are at a stage just *before* rebirth, a time of darkness and unconscious growth. The world may be a long time, even years, in this dark space; but some second births do take place into higher consciousness.

What happens to individuals ready for the touch? *Except a man be born again, he cannot see the kingdom of God.*[104] Already effective in the *outer* world, they are still largely unaware of the *inner*. They don't know the Self. When crisis ensues, new energy pours in as disruption and testing. It is like the stage from conception to birth but less pleasant – in fact, it may be very difficult. In this womb there is no light. Change comes upon them, the worst ever in their lives. Lost in a tunnel with nothing at the end, not knowing what's going on, they sweat it out in the dark, going through hell: not yet reborn, with no new values, nothing to hold on to, no hope.

Those of us struggling with addictions, schizophrenia, perhaps living in institutions, may be among those going through this for the first time. It's to be hoped we find something – something happens – that makes us realise all is well. We shall be reborn. Mastering the associated crisis, we for ever remember how, tested to destruction, we did see a light – we did come through. All was in preparation for the second birth.

For others, the Self awakens overnight. They may feel the long waiting period occurred in a previous life; now, it's only recapitulation. Some children are born knowing their purpose, their mission in life. Consciously aware of their destiny at three or four or five, they recognise they came

---

104 St. John 3:3.

from a special source with a special task. Again, this knowledge fades; but later they wake again to the vision of the path ahead.

At the *second birth* we are born into the cave of our own hearts, as was Christ in the stable-cave with the animals. Millions experience this, (including just about all who are reading this book): the prelude in the womb, the birth itself, finding our new relationship to the Self, becoming a new person. These are the *twice born*. As the newborn child is nurtured and cared for so, immediately after the second birth, we too may be given a longish period of relatively unconscious living with no special testing, simply growing naturally, resting while the leaven works. As children are named after the first birth, as novices receive a new name on profession, so people often change their names: a new note is sounding from within.

In the Temple

An inner note sounds

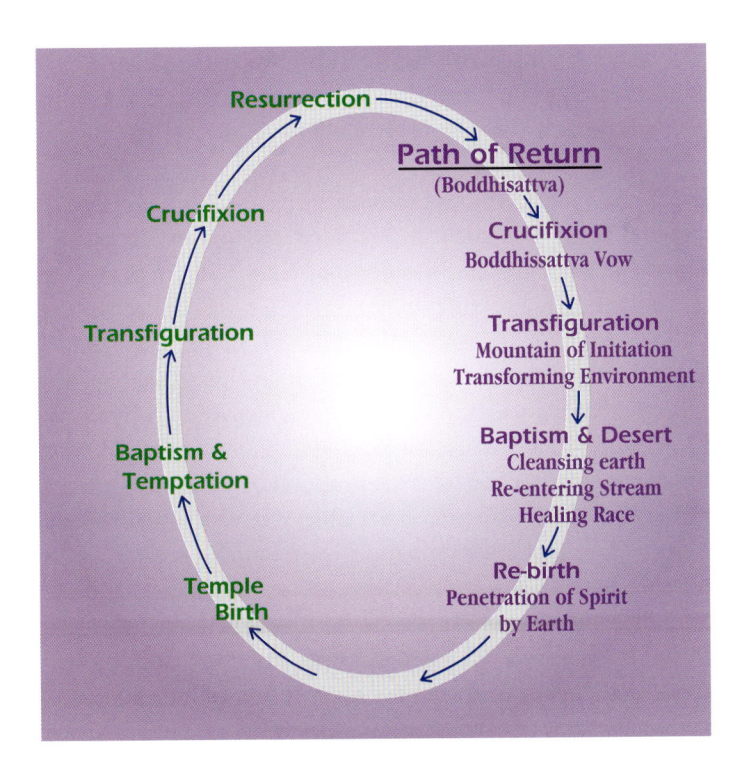

Chart 4:03 – Life-Stages

To Jesus at twelve years old there came a conscious awakening: a call, in the Temple where he was debating with the doctors of the church. Hearing it, he responded to his parents, *Wist ye not that I must be about my Father's business?* A long time of 'unconscious' growth followed – hidden years. Where did he go? Training as a carpenter, learning the trade, moving from apprentice to journeyman, aiming towards becoming master craftsman, did he also find a vocation in the mystery schools of the day, perhaps among the Essenes or in India? His life from twelve until thirty was a conscious journey towards Baptism, the climax of the process. How is it paralleled in our lives?

Christ's life cycles out – and returns. On the path of return, opposite the birth and the temple experience, is *rebirth*. His call in the temple parallels our mid-life peak at around thirty-five. Still unconscious of the transpersonal Self yet, we hope, of sound conventional morality with a personality well formed, integrated, capable and effective, we are in our spiritual adolescence. At adolescence we become aware of a new series of impulses, responsibilities and needs. Recognising the need to search for the task of his life, the kid has first to grow up. Even children of genius, those recognised as prodigies, very much need anchoring in and relating to the world.

Collectively, the economic difficulties of the larger community represent this stage. We understand ecology, recognising that what we are polluting is the environment, the *body* of Earth. So we try to make the United Nations effective in our struggles for the collective soul, the surrounding environment and the health of the planet. Each nation wrestles with matters of welfare, health, education, social security. The trans-national movements, welfare agencies and NGO's arise as instruments of collective consciousness, grappling with world population, pollution, basic human needs and the irruption of 'evil', the shadow of war and terrorism which mirrors the battle between the Self and the personality.[105] Extraverted personalities still actually control the mass of the people.

The map opposite, read from the bottom up, shows life before and leading up to Baptism as consciousness rises. We are born to our accidental, *given family* and lead the average life of an 'ordinary' person in an 'ordinary' world. Then something stirs, pricks at our hard shell. Ideas creep in, break through. 'Who am I?' We feel alien, lonely and isolated.

---

[105] As Freud, Reich and others have pointed out

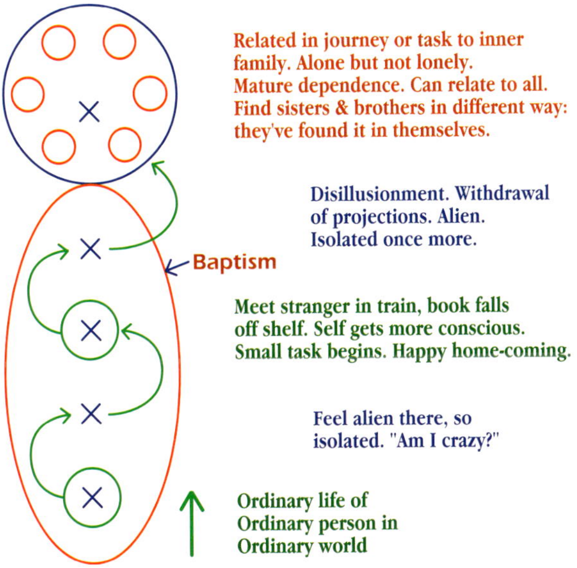
Related in journey or task to inner family. Alone but not lonely. Mature dependence. Can relate to all. Find sisters & brothers in different way: they've found it in themselves.
Disillusionment. Withdrawal of projections. Alien. Isolated once more.
Baptism
Meet stranger in train, book falls off shelf. Self gets more conscious. Small task begins. Happy home-coming.
Feel alien there, so isolated. "Am I crazy?"
Ordinary life of Ordinary person in Ordinary world

Chart 4:04 – Finding your Chosen Family

Our fantasies scare us – 'Am I going crazy?'

Then – something happens. We meet a stranger in the train, a book jumps out at us, we sense a world of meaning. For the first time, we have come home. And it's a very happy homecoming. The joy of finding our fellows.... At last we can talk about what 'really matters'. We often start at a *physical* level, adopting disciplines – dietary changes, exercise, vegetarianism, nature therapy, sexual exploration, creativity, physical yoga. We give things up – 'alcohol's out now!' We may be beset by anorexia or addiction. It is a time of great crisis, disruption, testing, change.

So it is that, for the first time round, we become followers, maybe of art, of music, of science; or of a person, someone who's an ecologist, a poet, a Tory; or we find an 'ism' that becomes our god: Catholicism, Socialism, Feminism. We embrace new values, new aspirations, new interests. We shop around. We go in for politics, or help refugees, or join an ashram. Individually we embrace personal growth, idealistic service; we study the humanistic psychologies, we meditate, work with myths and symbols and dreams. Collectively, many thousands of us experiment, founding and joining communities. And we go beyond, into depth psychology, Psychosynthesis ... Transpersonal psychology.

This conscious stepping-out on to a particular path can last a long time. We start full of certainty, trying to convert people: 'I've got the message! I'm on my Path; now I must tell everybody, teach others!' Each new thing seems better than the last. This early search is full of enthusiasm – and perhaps of spiritual selfishness. It's not too dangerous, as it is not yet *directed*; but it's a sign neither of great spiritual advancement nor of deep understanding. There is clear – and there is pre-clear. This is still *before clarity*. Many people are at this pre-baptism stage today. Much needs to clear.

Disillusion necessarily follows. To our horror, this new lot is very similar to the original 'given family' from whom it was so hard to break. The teaching is dogmatic, inadequate; the idols break, the gods fail. And they have to. The projected god out there is bound to disappoint. Failure sets in as the 'ism' falls. 'We've tried to make the transit, cross the river – and we've nearly drowned....' Even if, in the end, we manage to withdraw our projections and get across, won't we just feel alien and isolated all over again? Some people spend their whole lives searching for teachers and groups, always ending dissatisfied, never quite getting to the core of their spiritual impulses. 'What's it all been *for*?'

It does have a purpose. It serves our calling. At least we know who we are *not*. The path of conscious evolution requires training, hard work, self-discipline and the anchoring of new insights. The temple was once the convent or monastery, where long periods of retreat alternated with short bouts of intense work. Nowadays the temple is within us. Then, it was all about self-sacrifice, doing what you're told – seven years in the kitchen, and you learn to contribute. Now our inner work is in the jungles of the Western world, not in retreat but all day long. Then, the habit was worn as a symbol of the church. Nowadays, wearing peculiar things is largely out and we search in 'the disguise of ordinary secular dress'. Then, there were passwords and rituals and secrets. Some still carry that on, but today many people are past this stage. We become our own guides, take personal responsibility.

So, coming to terms with disappointment, we are drawn to some particular small task. We *have* to do it; it's the call of our soul. And in the doing of it we start finding certain other people. These are our *chosen family*, our inner group; truly our brothers and sisters, but this time in a different way, with a different sense of reality. Though scattered all over the world, we know them years later. We are related in terms of the journey or task. It is a mature dependence; what we find in them we also begin to find in ourselves. The Self takes over more consciously as we are led towards the emotional testing of the Baptism. The inner note is sounding.

The Baptism
The energy descends

Jesus was baptised in the Jordan, the river winding through the plain of the everyday world – plain, for all to see. His ministry didn't start until after it: teaching, training disciples, making a public impact in consciously chosen, directed service. Before baptism, Jesus of Nazareth, local teacher; after baptism, Jesus Christ. Now more in charge, the Self comes to meet the ego.

Jesus when he was baptised went up straightway out of the water: and, lo, the heavens were opened unto him, and he saw the Spirit of God descending like a dove, and lighting upon him: And lo a voice from heaven saying, 'This is my beloved son, in whom I am well pleased.[106]

Baptism by water, *the second stage of initiation*, symbolises the *emotional* plane. Baptism means moving into and flowing with the river of life, the stream of the transpersonal Self. *It*, the creative centre, provides whatever central experience washes us clean. Entering the stream cleanses our feeling nature (for most of us the core problem). No one can escape the Baptism – washed through, dragged out, cleared. What is it all about? It means lifting energy into the heart, lest we become solar-plexus-dominated individuals; recognising both our own and others' feelings; in touch not only with our emotions but also with our shadows and contra-sexual sides. Until we move from emotional hunches towards clear, mystical intuition, we cannot take any real load. Many thousands are at this stage: the waters of life settle from muddy to pure, from turbulent to peaceful, polluted to crystal clear. A magnetic channel is made, granting unclouded vision and freedom from alloy. Energy descends.

Individuals going through the Baptism, clarifying their own nature in this way, often fall for the *second* time under the grip of some ideology outside themselves. Needing still to project the Self by asking the parents, they seek a guru. Realising the failure of the first passion, they now find the *real* one. 'At last! This is it! *That* was all juvenile rubbish, but now I've

---
106 St. Matthew 3:16.

seen the light!' So they become devoted for the second time – but now to a cause. Real devotees need to be kept at arm's length. 'Helpful' people, full of the impulse to serve, worship and love, they overvalue their place on the path, their very important message. Too devoted, even fanatical, they distort reality.

The gurus (who can't always carry the stress) are a statement about the followers. *By their fruits ye shall know them*:[107] inner work, study, service, review, quality control and the growth of consciousness – are they practised here? *Don't push the river*. Pseudo-gurus, ideological and perfectionist, run off-centre movements following many paths, proselytising, competing for followers, promising 'Enlightenment – In One Week!' They adopt pseudo-techniques (relaxation and a little self-suggestion will readily dress up as meditation). They can be recognised by how they handle dissent, by their inflation and the egocentricity that comes from identification with the divine. Focussed on their organisation and the money it raises, they put on sensational events designed to draw people, but fail to know the difference between spiritual and personal growth. Aiming towards *kundalini*, they reach burnout.[108] Many followers are unconscious of the false claims being made.

So, once again, *disillusion* with the spiritual leader must come. 'He's all right with the broad plan,' we protest, 'there's no inherent conflict. It's just the application – in practice it simply doesn't work!' Or the supervising disciple advises, and we disagree. 'Whatever I do is wrong!' Scepticism grows. This really is painful. 'Surely, these were the *real* gods, weren't they? I've devoted myself to them – and now they too have feet of clay!' The shadow dominates. I am in danger of joining the ranks of the cynical disillusioned.

It's to be hoped I realise I'm human, notwithstanding my great illuminations, and can begin to see reality. Run more by the Self than the ego, sitting lightly, I am shedding my intense seriousness. 'It's all very important!' has given way to the chuckle of the Laughing Buddha. Some sort of marriage will have taken place within. My devotion will be to inner growth, not to outer causes and teachers. Only now may I go on to a truly spiritual line in the world, at a Collective level. Soon now I may become fit to be let out.

The Way of Intelligence leads to Light
The Way of Consciousness leads to the Gate

---

107 St. Matthew 7:16 and 20.
108 Kundalini, see Chapter 8, pp. 311-312 and 322.

The Way of Presence leads to the Innermost Centre
The Way of Introspection leads to Revelation
The Way of Discipleship leads to the Master
The Way of Service leads to Liberation [109]

Humanistic Psychology takes devotees and clears and disillusions them. Not spiritual but personal, it deals with illusion, disillusion and shadow. It is about growth, projection, emotional consciousness, about being yourself and encountering others. At a relatively early stage, feeling-oriented encounter can be an emotionally forcing and clarifying process.[110] Freudian work takes us back a little further. At the Collective level, Jung brings us to Psychosynthesis and Transpersonal psychology. The Transpersonal also has its share of devotees, but the feeling content has changed. Devotion is to inner growth, not to outer causes and teachers.

When devotees turn to the task, the task grows out of them. With the Prodigal, they say, *Make me as one of thine hired servants*. They sit at home – and they sit differently. Some theme (healing, alchemy, yoga) draws them: the focus is on the Baptism and the desert and the preparation experiences that follow. And then – initiation: people flock to them and they don't know how many they touch.

So they become human again, relate to *all* people quite easily, drink with the lads, enjoy the market place. After what may have been an intense period of loss and loneliness, they discover who else is on the path: their own spiritual family – or at any rate their inner friends. They resonate to the same note. They are alone but no longer lonely.

The Temptation in the desert

Then was Jesus led up of the spirit into the wilderness to be tempted of the devil.[111]

How was Christ tempted? The three suggestions made to him by Satan could be seen as referring to the life of the body, emotions and mind

---

109 See Alice Bailey, very slightly different: 'The Way of Intelligence leads to light. The Way of Meditation leads to the gate. The Way of the Presence leads to the innermost centre. The Way of Introspection leads to revelation. The Way of Service leads to liberation. The Way of Discipleship leads to the Master.' Bailey 1944, *Discipleship in the New Age* Vol.1. p. 639. Also: 'The Way of Sacrifice is eternally the Way of Joy. The way of Joy leads to the Place of Peace....' Bailey 1944, ibid. p. 365.
110 There are groups which touch on, and may become schools of, initiatory training. At least at one stage, Findhorn in the North of Scotland did attract devotees; and so too did the Wrekin Trust, embracing an idealism that somewhat ignored the shadow. But those who stayed at the core of these groups have worked through the devotional stage and gone out changed, to work in the world.
111 Matthew 4:1

respectively:

> First, the devil said to him, 'If you are the Son of God, command that these stones be made bread.' He replied: *Man shall not live by bread alone but by every word that proceedeth out of the mouth of God.*
>
> Then the devil took him up to a pinnacle of the temple at Jerusalem. 'If you are the Son of God, cast yourself down; angels will stop you dashing your foot against a stone.' *Thou shalt not tempt the Lord thy God,'* was his response.
>
> Thirdly, the devil took him to the top of a high mountain and showed him all the kingdoms of the world and their glory. 'I'll give them to you if you fall down and worship me.' *Get thee hence, Satan; thou shalt worship the Lord thy God and Him only shalt thou serve.* [112]

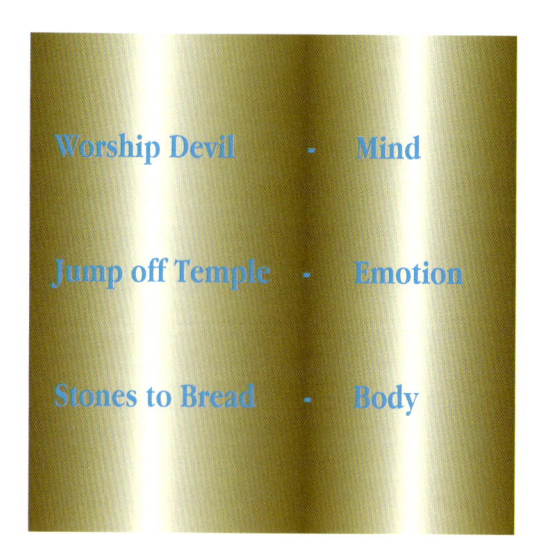

Worship Devil - Mind

Jump off Temple - Emotion

Stones to Bread - Body

Chart 4:05 – Tempted in the Desert

It was after Christ's baptism that he was led to spend forty days and nights in the desert. Because of the new relationship with the Self, he was beginning to have power. Jesus the personality was overshadowed by Christ – the Self. The purity of Christ became a magnetic purity.

---

112 Ibid, 2-11.

We also are taken by the Self from the stream into the desert, the solitary place, to meet the devil. By definition no water here – and after the Baptism we may be glad about that. However, our emotional nature, clarified in the river, may yet try to swamp us. The wilderness, the mountain, are *astringent* places of contemplation, spiritual retreat.[113] Here the personality's feelings, moods and desires are stilled and the heart's full range is widened from tears to joy.

And here we experience failure and hubris, light and dark, undergoing our own tests of power. Our motivation is tried. As we begin to re-own our projections, the Self charges us with its energy. *It* has found *us*. Its new power is awakening, stirring us up, putting on the heat and the pressure, enabling 'shadow stuff' to emerge into consciousness. We come to terms with the shadow, where our power lies. Christ's temptations were to do with *how* to use his new power, *how* to wield the sword. We once feared that power was 'bad'; we dreaded it, loved it, hated it, and when it came we didn't know what to do with it. Now we become much freer with it. Before Baptism we needed an outer teacher. Now we must manage on our own – be able to say 'No' to God – tell him, 'I don't think You quite understand life down here!' Unilaterally, many individuals are on the way to this; energy *is* coming in, a genuine spiritual potency of the Self.

So we've had our trial runs; but the symbol of the Self has still been 'out there' – we haven't really known it within ourselves. We've kept going back to school, having mini-baptisms, reverting. And now at last the devotee is settled and comes up smiling. Only now are we given jobs to do. We may become outer teachers – and they are needed – wanting others to join us. Earlier, we would have been starting premature movements. Now, with authority, we speak words of power and authenticity.

But this is *much* more dangerous. This is the desert experience: at the moment of breakthrough, new tests of power. All too easily we revert into Messianic complexes. *Inflation*! What we want to happen, begins to happen. We must be careful what we want.... Do we manipulate, demand power and misuse it? Do we go in for 'kill the leader', in youthful rebellion against the ruling order? Knocking it down, do we become totalitarian rulers ourselves, crushing the meek underfoot? 'I am the Lord of the World!' Carried away by the inflationary glamour of 'me and my message,' even a well-developed personality may be unable to hold the centre, may break down into psychosis and irruption from the unconscious.

---

113 In some North American initiation rituals, the belief is that the tutelary spirit can be won by ascetic effort in the wilderness – withdrawal into solitude and immersion in the life of the cosmos. See Campbell 1959, *Primitive Mythology*, p. 319.

Now we must contain the power so that it resonates and causes something to happen; but *in* the other person. Now, what we decide to be and do will actually help and transform the group, the Collective, as well as our own lives. Remember: *an initiated person is one who initiates*.

Look back to Chart 4: 04, Finding your Chosen Family. Baptism was about loneliness – we're all on a lonely journey, and we usually project our longing for the 'other' onto a person or a teacher. But after the desert's solitude, we travel with other people. Then, as we saw, we are alone but not lonely. We have found our *spiritual* family, friends whom we've known for ever, it seems, with a sameness of core and identity of spirit. And, ultimately, the inner marriage takes place; as well as feeling ourselves part of a spiritual group, we sense that we have an inner teacher.[114]

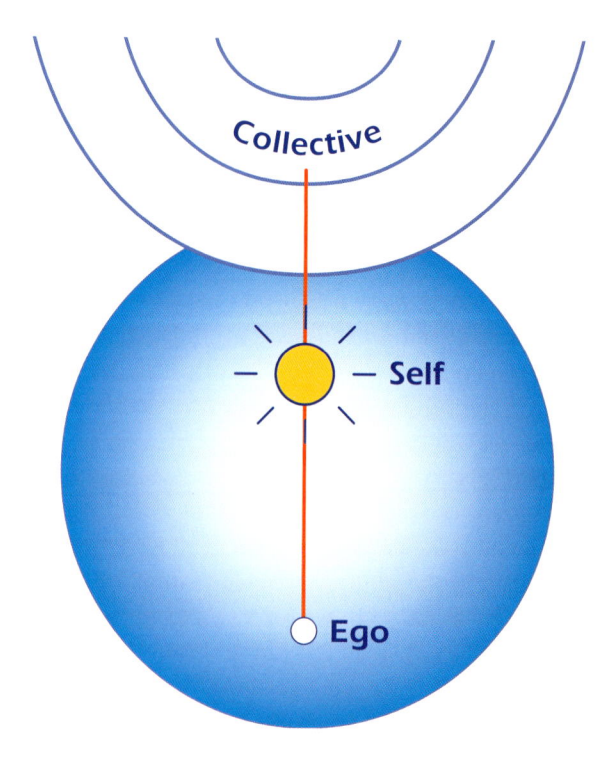

Chart 4:06 – The Transfiguration

---

114 Six Stages of Discipleship, Appendix 10.

After the temptations, Christ's ministry began in increased and dependable service. He took up his task, chose and trained his disciples. Now his vision was clear: future achievement, triumph, death – and resurrection. Spiritual maturity had been achieved. Then, once again, the dove of God descended.

The Transfiguration on the Mountain of Initiation

Jesus took Peter and John and James and went up into a mountain to pray.
And as he prayed, he was transfigured before them:
and the fashion of his countenance was altered, and his face did shine as the sun.
His raiment was white and glistering, as white as the light.
The disciples were asleep all this time, but they woke up and *saw his glory.*
There came a bright cloud and overshadowed them, and they feared as they entered into the cloud. And there came a voice out of the cloud, saying,
'This is my beloved Son, in whom I am well pleased; hear ye him.' [115]

The Transfiguration, *the third stage of initiation*, is about *mind* and *will*, the will of the soul.[116] *Hear ye him*. This initiation brings a new message from the Collective to the human family, a new perspective, a new cycle of expression, of reality-testing. Energy flows through the chakra system, Crown and Base centres meet, spiritual and mental intuition are integrated and the personality is fused with the Self. Father Spirit meets with Mother Matter and matter is lifted up and glorified. And that's true *kundalini*.[117]

The road rises with us, out of the mass towards the mountain. Secrets once revealed are now discovered. We may no longer over-indulge our introversion, for we too are becoming initiators. And with success: we have some power and impact, and the right to speak. Initiated people initiate things. Divinity is manifested in service. We can take on small tasks and break new ground, perhaps becoming central figures in some creative group or enterprise that gathers people together. Although as agents of the Collective our impulse is transpersonal and our will and motivation to do with the human family, yet handling worldly success can still be a problem.

Christ went up the mountain with three loved disciples; again, they may symbolise the physical, emotional and mental aspects of us. The *personal* psycho-synthesis becomes a *trans*personal synthesis. Transfigured, the Self, partly in the psyche and partly in touch with the

---
115 Matthew 17:1-5. See also Luke 9:28–35 and Mark 9:2–7.
116 Reminiscent of the 'little hut' initiation. Somers 2004, *The Fires of Alchemy*, pp. 221 and 227.
117 Kundalini, see Chapter 8, pp. 311–312 and 322.

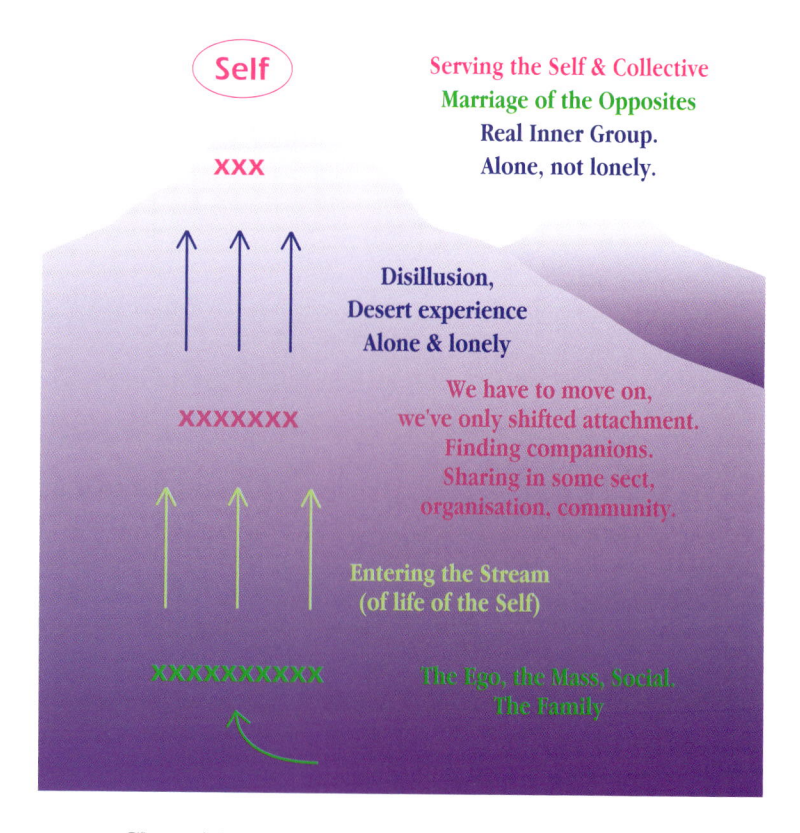

Chart 4:07 – The Mountain of the Transfiguration

Self

xxx

Serving the Self & Collective
Marriage of the Opposites
Real Inner Group.
Alone, not lonely.

xxxxxxx

Disillusion,
Desert experience
Alone & lonely

We have to move on,
we've only shifted attachment.
Finding companions.
Sharing in some sect,
organisation, community.

Entering the Stream
(of life of the Self)

xxxxxxxxxx

The Ego, the Mass, Social.
The Family

Collective, begins to function in the world. The spirit is now of participation: the initiate's relation to the Collective must change. This is important. Can we pursue a spiritual path in the midst of life, with only short periods of withdrawal? To be in therapy is to do a transfiguring job on ourselves; and our dreams can take us out of the personal centre towards enlargement and expansion, even if only as fragments or flashes.

Looking for someone to carry out a task, one would seek emotional maturity in a person not perfect, but able to stick out traumas and keep on with the job, dealing with issues as they arise. And a few such people do become agents of the Collective. It has very little to do with their personal life, decisions, growth, *dharma*, or whatever; it involves the total personality. These pioneers of transformation and individuation have been to the mountain top. After the Baptism they were still learning to let *It* do it; with the Transfiguration, energy comes through with no barrier or block.

A number, perhaps a growing number, of figures have been fully here, though few are well-known and even they at a relatively junior stage. (Leonardo da Vinci, I suggest, is somewhere beyond the Transfiguration, more profound yet. Also Shakespeare; and Socrates – he took the poison voluntarily and his note sounds over millennia.) They, and others like them, are the spiritual pioneers of the race.[118]

The Crucifixion
Even the transpersonal centre disappears

This is *the fourth stage of initiation*. I can say very little. While the person who is transfigured isn't yet perfect, to be a disinterested channel for the Collective you have to give up *all* that is of most value to you. Till now, tracking towards the mountain top, you've wanted what you're doing to be useful. You've wanted to be *right* and in touch with the Self – doing what the Self wants. Now, that's relatively unimportant. Public recognition has to go. Everything you've won so hard has to be offered up, embalmed. It must be a stage where you *don't care* what happens to your work. You are a pure channel for the Self, doing the will of Mother Earth and Father Heaven. For instance, de Chardin accepted the Church's ruling not to publish his works in his lifetime. It was enough to be and to do.

This is the depth perspective – you go down to the god empty-handed. The transpersonal centre disappears too. Your notions are turned upside down: this is not 'self-sacrifice' but rather, a making holy, whole, sacred. Crucifixion? Death – of what? What is it? Pain and agony? Dismemberment of all that has been, as the ego dies to the Self?

Christ's Resurrection and Ascension
These are the non-returners

And so a person might be born again – yet again – to *Resurrection*, a new form of life, *the fifth stage of initiation*. From the cave of the tomb, they are reborn to a new kingdom, to re-memberment, at-one-ment, atonement. Here are Christ, Buddha, Krishna. As Buddha developed detachment, dispassion, discrimination, so Christ showed us the way to individuality, initiation, identification with a new revelation, new tasks,

---

118 As well as historical figures such as Joan of Arc and Paracelsus, we might remember, for example: Abraham Lincoln, Rudolf Steiner, Sri Aurobindo, Maynard Keynes in economics, Albert Schweitzer, Mahatma Gandhi, Teilhard de Chardin. Then, some slightly more recent and accessible figures – Pope John XXIII, Martin Luther King, Mother Theresa, the present Dalai Lama, Nelson Mandela. Also musicians: Bach, Mozart, Beethoven. And several of the modern physicists as a group, including Marie Curie and Max Planck. Albert Einstein and Carl Jung each brought in a new illumination and anchored it.

new capacities. These are the non-returners, going to another state, a different level of being. They have learned all the lessons of the human lot. They are no longer bound to the wheel.

Of the rest I have nothing to say.

EXPLORATION
THE DOOR AND THE CAVE
(40 minutes)

So to the life of the *body*. This is the Door of second birth and initiation in the Cave. You will meet both Doorkeeper and Initiator. You may hear an initiatory word of power, find a magical wand or Talisman[119] or discover a jewel in the heart of the lotus. It is about the preparation of the body to receive a new influx of energy. Bear in mind your own myth and, if it differs, follow your own path, interpreting in your own way.

Minutes

8   Move deeply into your inner space. In a few moments, find yourself travelling across a plain towards a sheer, high rock face. As you get closer, you see a door set into the face of the rock, with a figure standing by: a *Doorkeeper*. Spend some time there with this Doorkeeper, who will help you do whatever may be necessary before you pass through the door and enter the cave within the heart.

3   Standing before the door, centre yourself. It opens; you pass within. Find yourself in the cave of the heart, a sacred, holy place, a temple or sanctuary. Stand before the Initiator, perhaps with one or more friends of long standing to help you carry the energy of the initiation. Wait quietly for a few moments.

8   You are taken to the place where the Initiator waits with a rod of initiation. When you are ready, the Initiator touches your heart centre, and you experience the opening of the heart lotus. Your being fills with the love, the core energy of the Self. Your aura radiates. Search within your heart, and find the jewel which is your Talisman, and a symbol or symbols to represent where you are at present. Let the jewel show you what you need to know.

---

119 The talisman, see Chapter 6, p. 270.

8 Take your Talisman, the jewel within the lotus, as your guide, mentor and friend. Become very small and enter your body. Spend some time experiencing your body and its energy from within. Discover from this journey what it needs in order to become a better instrument for the energy of the soul, and for creative living. If for any reason you cannot enter the body in this way, use the jewel as a means to explore its spiritual needs from without, a way of seeing into and through it – perhaps like an X-ray – nourishing, cleansing and healing it. Find out what your body needs, and what specific qualities are ready to be developed in the world just now.

8 The journey into the body ends. Find yourself before the Initiator again, in the cave of the heart, and tune once more to the experience of the opening of the heart lotus. The Initiator will communicate with you, whether in words, images, symbols or in other ways, some of the things you need to be or do when you re-enter the everyday world. The Initiator may give you a gift, or show a symbol or symbols for any latent spiritual qualities you should now develop.

5 The ceremony ends. When you are ready, move forward; another door opens. Pass through into a familiar world and soon find yourself in a quiet and much loved place, where you rest awhile.[120]

RITES OF PASSAGE 1 & 2

Better light one small taper than lament the darkness[121]

Fascinated by the Self, by initiation and the initiatory process which appears to be constantly at work in dream images, symptoms, spontaneous happenings and the hammering of life itself, we link our personal experience to that of the Collective. Rites of passage are outer expressions of this inner process. All cultures have developed their own mysteries and ritual practices, each designed to help initiate an individual across a threshold and ensure that the previous stage is fully left behind. The past was about childhood, the present concerns the individual and the future is about responsibility and collective participation in the world. With each stage we widen our context, our world view.

---

120 Commentary on the Door and the Cave exploration, Appendix 2
121 Barbara Somers's version of a saying of the Buddha: 'It's better to light a small candle than curse the darkness.'

Keepers of the mysteries

They have been appointed in all cultures. Hierophants, priests and priestesses, mistresses and masters, shamans and witch-doctors, they spoke for the god of that tribe. Performing the rites of passage, they helped the people to pass in safety through the stages. Only a few individuals could form these bridges for others, could connect the person to the Collective, the human experience to its divine meaning, the outer form to the inner spirit. They made conscious what already belonged to the tribe and the nation – to humanity, not just to the individual.[122]

Where are they now? Where are the *modern* keepers of the mysteries, initiators into new dimensions of consciousness? They are rare. People claim to 'initiate' each other, but few can support the claim. Shaman – or frenzied berserker? Initiatory heating, burning, magic sweat, mastery over fire? There are many false gurus, as we have seen. Individuals still feel lost. Who to turn to? The wise woman, wise priest, wise doctor or healer, are too busy. No one is there in the fundamental moments of our development, so we pass alone through these passages, in great pain and in full consciousness. This is new. Therapists and counsellors may hold the bridges, but the secular state often pours scorn. Some scientists (by no means all) still say God is dead. So the scientists themselves become the gods, leaving many individuals adrift in the face of a vast, mindless universe, confronted by a great computer, a huge Moloch feeding on their life-force but giving back nothing in terms of deeper meaning.

Other times in history have certainly also had their darkness. But this lack of initiation is our modern challenge and opportunity, not only in childhood but also in puberty, in marriage and mid-life, at the climacteric and in the hour of death. All those stages in life were formerly numinous points at which the Collective intervened with its rites: today they are frequently points of anxiety for the individual. Who grieves with us? In fact, where collective rites no longer exist and the problems relating to these transitions devolve upon the individual, his or her responsibility and understanding are so overburdened that psychic disorders are frequent.[123]

---

122 The shaman is essentially an ecstatic. He is reduced to bare bones so that he can journey to heaven, to hell or about the earth. He undertakes the journey for four reasons: to meet the god face to face and bring him an offering from the community; to seek the soul of a sick man who has wandered away or been carried off by demons; to guide the soul of a dead man to its new abode; to add to his knowledge by frequenting higher things. In order to journey, the shaman leaves his body, symbolically dies. 'I must know how to go and return. I must know the inner territory.' His own Shamanic initiation involves the insertion of magical substances, torture, dismemberment – scraping away of the flesh until just the skeleton is left. There follows a period in hell, where more teaching is undergone before the ascent to heaven for consecration.

123 As Erich Neumann pointed out in the 1960s

Modern initiation

So we provide our own threshholds. Lacking initiating figures, we are our own initiators. The Self (through dreams, symptoms, therapy, awareness) continues to initiate us into life's deeper mysteries, evoking inner guides, initiatory priests, hierophants. Our images now act as bridges from the personality toward the Self – inner bridges where once there were outer rites of passage. Indeed, our images *become* the rites of passage, helping us to be self-responsible and keep tapers alight in the surrounding dark. They help *us* to redeem history; and only the individual can do that.

Jung pointed out that, in the last analysis, the essential thing is the life of the individual, for individuals make up the nations. He went on to say that they alone have supreme value – they alone make history. Only here do the great transformations first take place. Great events are, at bottom,

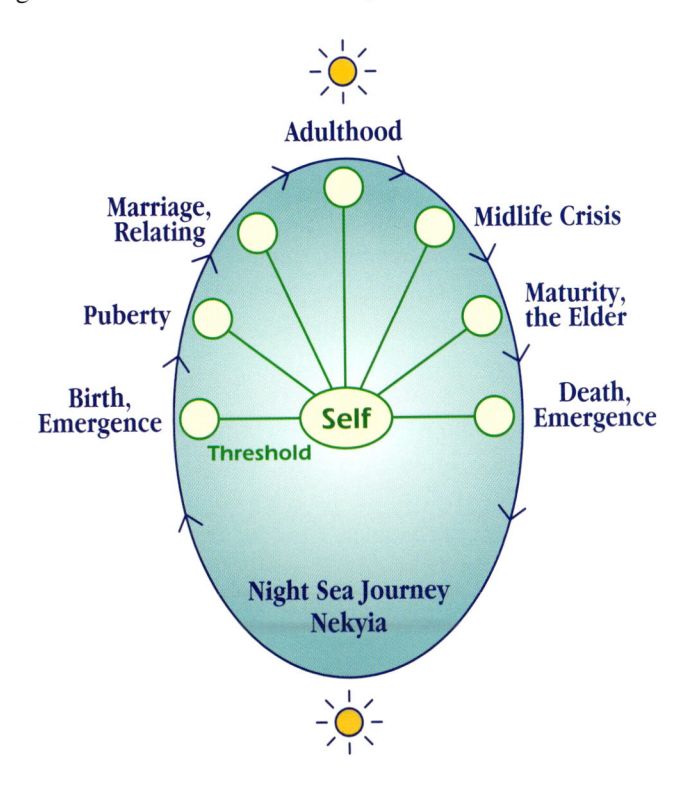

Chart 4:08 – The Seven Stages of Life

profoundly unimportant. The whole future, the whole history of the world, will ultimately spring as a gigantic summation from these hidden sources – within individuals. In our most private and most subjective lives, we are not only the passive witnesses of our age, and its sufferers, but also its makers.[124]

Here, the Self also represents the god, the hierophant, initiator, mystagogue. Based on Jung's map, it shows both the individual and all humanity. Above the threshold there is a passage or rite of entrance at each of the stages of life. The stages cycle through with a rhythmic pulse-beat, marked by anniversaries – the coronation or death of the leader, some massacre or disaster, some miracle of healing – bringing completion, attachment, meaning, fulfilment. As noted, it was *expected* that people would come to these markers, dying to the previous stage before crossing the threshold to the next. The ending, the change, was allowed each birth also a death to that which, if nicely safe, had become suffocating.

Rites of entrance

We too walk over these thresholds. Goaded, sparked awake, we say, 'No one else will do it, so I had better'. A new, life-giving wine of consciousness is fizzing through and the old skins have split. If we miss a stage, life initiates us, often through pain, crisis as ever bringing both danger of holding back, retrenched, unable to face the inexorable challenge, and opportunity to make the passage appropriately. Forced by life and circumstance, we move into the new and unknown.

Birth – emergence

In early cultures children were born with primitive rites. Usually attended, within a small place, in dimmed light, with breath and warm bodies close by, birth was celebrated under the aegis not of men, unless a priest, but of the feminine, the Earth Mother. The child emerged into the touch of women, to be laid straight away on the mother's breast or on the earth – child of earth, and child of God. Birth should be known to be painful. It is followed by intake of breath and the cry of renewed life. The rites of birth are close to those of death; we die to the womb and are born to life.

Music and festivity followed the birth, marking joy and celebration of life. The child, ritually dedicated to the totem by the priest or witch-doctor, stood for the security of the future. It was the richness of the family, the

---

124 See Jung 1918, 'The Role of the Unconscious', CW10, para 45.

guarantee, the measure of wealth, the promise of the continuation of life; and also an addition to the Collective. Lamentation would follow if it was a girl. Joy was greatest for a boy who could protect and fight for the tribe, his strength seen as ensuring the future of the culture.

The modern equivalent offers a clinical approach, safer physically, yet impersonal. Since the 1930's the child has been quite likely to be rushed into the world, often induced, arriving into the shattering experience of strong lights, loud noise, bustle and separation. The mother has been largely unsupported in her natural fears, perhaps left for longish periods, perhaps drugged, attended for any length of time only if it has been a premature or difficult birth. There are many virtues in modern intervention, but we need to be aware of the losses. 'Who celebrates my baby?' Very blessed is the woman who has someone close to her through that passage. Often after the birth she is left by the attendants and neglected again. The child's arrival may be followed by its forcible parting from her. Impersonally handled, smacked, drugged, it may be said to have 'bonding problems'. It is born out of paradise.[125]

In the last few decades there has been a change, a swing-back, a rebalancing. Once again, birth may be companioned – at home, underwater, squatting, with fathers present – yet also with all the advantages of modern intervention available; and again to a large extent handled by nurses.[126] Hope lies in how many people realise and help to make this more generally available.

History is alive within the modern psyche; inner images support us in outer crisis. How? It's a great mystery. But before the birth the mother still dreams of muscular passages and tunnels, of bridges across.[127] As birthing once took place in ritually dimmed, small, dark places, so modern imagery too is often of a small alembic, a tiny place for this major process to occur. As women were once known to be the background matrix out of which the man emerges – as the midwife was the same woman who laid out the dead and was also herb-lady for the tribe – so the Earth Mother is still present in our symbols. Modern mothers dream of being attended by

---

125 And the Baptism of children today, if it happens, is often cursory and meaningless, more a dedication to a secular god, a totem of the material tribe, than to God.

126 See Leboyer 1974, *Birth without Violence*, inter alia.

127 'Rebirthing' is the exploration of birth traumas in adults by those such as Frank Lake, Arthur Janov, R. D. Laing and others. Stanislav Grof was led back to profound belief in God by observation of people in adult rebirthing sessions. Dying to the womb, in pain, they are born to joy. Before 'birth', he says, their imagery is Greek, Christian, Western. Afterwards, it changes, now seeming to derive from an obscure Oriental source. And there is a 'flabbergasting' resemblance to Indian accounts of a second, 'spiritual', birth. See Grof, quoted in Campbell 1972 *Myths to Live By*, Pp.262-3. See also Grof 1975, *Realms of the Human Unconscious*.

a woman who holds in her hands the mystery of birth. And in the modern psyche, inner birthing draws out the same motifs: the precious ore mined from the Mother lode, the river-source or mouth, the labyrinth, grotto, stable, cavern – Christ in the cave.

> *Pause to reflect*:
> Consider your experiences of birth and of being a very small child. There is also the second birth, when the Self is born into consciousness and we wake out of sleep.

Childhood and puberty

For native Americans – Sioux, Inuit – as for Africans, Australians, the tribe was contained in a cantonment (a containment), and outside was the Other World, the enemy. 'Over there' were demons, nightmares, ghosts, the ancient ancestors; in here, the child was held, touched, carried on its mother's back, contained by the tribe around the camp-fire. All were there together. Life went on around – men as well as women, work as well as love. The elders were available. Totems were there, the insignia of the god; the god was visible to the child.

At evening, as the sun god rolled into bed in ecstasy, hero myths and collective dreams would have been told round the fires and the children would have listened. Now, too, fairy stories told to children must be in order; the children demand it and won't be content unless the tale is complete. The rhythmic beat of the stories makes a continuum with life in the womb. There is a 'correct order of going to bed'; all must happen according to the ritual. Toys impose order on an unknown world: loving their teddy-bears, they move towards relationships with people. Failing to make the transition, they may be left in adulthood with obsessive patterns set up to placate the gods.

Sexual exploration and play were probably allowed in the tribe until children were between seven and eleven years old. Both boys and girls were left to learn skills by imitation and observation till, at the onset of puberty, the sexes were suddenly parted.[128] Work and play were necessary for what was to follow, each an offering to the Collective. Boys were separated from their mothers and sisters and put with the men. The rites of puberty were designed to cut the umbilical cord. They had been aware of the (often frightening) inner rites undertaken by their elders as they were prepared to be men and warriors. Now, dying to childhood, leaving

---

128 See Eliade 1949, *The Myth of the Eternal Return*; and Eliade 1963, *Myth and Reality*, on rites and symbols of initiation.

the women and the profane world, the boy was to go from dependency to responsibility. He was to become aware of the lives of the men, tilling, hunting, harvesting, preparing for war. He began to know of the work-plan of the tribe.

Boys now had their own birthing-place. They underwent initiatory ordeals in hut or cabin, alembic for facing the incubus. Sometimes lasting months, sometimes involving a constant increase in severity, these warrior or priestly ordeals were the first preparation for life. In withstanding the prescribed trials of strength, their sexual manhood was attained. A boy might be buried up to his neck, hung by the heels or covered in honey and ants. Such secret and dramatic rituals went from circumcision to the skinning of the penis, hardening the muscles of his manhood, making him confront his own fear. Suffering, supposed to be inflicted by superhuman beings, had a ritual value, and extreme suffering was an expression of initiatory death (indeed, certain serious illnesses, especially psycho-mental disorders, were regarded as a sign that superhuman beings had chosen the sick person for initiation). The young man never went back to his mother. Given a new name and a new mode of being, his sexual adulthood was confirmed. The inner rite is not known, but he had had his first link with the *tremendum* of life, sexuality, fear and death. Now he knew of the god, the sacred totem, the circle with its centre and the cycles of the sun.

Female initiation was less widespread and less dramatic than male. At first menstruation, girls were set apart, isolated in a small place and led as a group into the female arts. Before, the girls had prepared the yarn, though they'd done no actual weaving. Now, watching the women, they learnt spinning and weaving, how each individual is a thread, essential within the woven fabric, in the hands of the magical Fates who spin, measure and cut.[129] A girl, too, would learn the work-plan. More, she was led and initiated into the dark lunar mysteries, cycles of magic. Darkness was emphasised; in some tribes she was allowed to see the moon, though not the sun. No longer a girl but a daughter of the moon, a full-bodied woman to be impregnated, she learned about giving birth, weaving the fabric of creation on the vast loom of birth, death and rebirth. At the end of the process came exhibition to the entire community, the ritual bath, the procession symbolising her acceptance as a woman.

In learning the cycles of life, death and rebirth, both boys and girls were placed in the continuum of the ancestors – that which has been, is

---

129   Somers 2004, *The Fires of Alchemy*, p. 133.

now and must be in the future. In dances, rites and heroic myths, they undertook responsibility to the god. Taken up into apprenticeship for the tribe, each established his or her present place within the larger family. Some were prepared for war; others for responsibility to the totem, the visible symbol of God. The hierophant, the priest, the shaman were also visible. Standing at the centre as initiator, they held the rites through: the young were helped by the midwifery of one that stood for God.

Does it sound idyllic? It's very doubtful *indeed* that it was....[130]

And the impulse is as alive as ever. The Bar Mitzvah is an obvious example, and still there are many degrees and levels of initiation into secret societies and confraternities. However, in this secular age we have largely lost the rituals. Lacking other provision, the young respond with outer worship in temples to Mammon. Their emergent energies, fuelled by the strength of their emotions and no longer channelled by apprenticeship, run higher than at any later stage. Unheld by rites of passage, they are rarely trained to work for the group. And the modern tribal totem in the shape of the gadget presides over all.

It is fascinating how, lacking outer ritual, young people set up their own rites, their own anti-heroes, their own insignia, codes, music, dress, style. Moon, sun – and now, stars! Pop stars, media stars, sports stars, heroes and anti-heroes of all kinds. It is not people *known* to the young who stand in these places. Their gangs, sects and freakish ways tend towards the Collective; their peers, not the adults, become their leaders now.[131] Gang wars follow as, risking their own and others' lives, they experiment violently with life and fear and death.

Yet, we must have heroines, heroes and anti-heroes: so it has been attested in myth and legend from time immemorial. Responding to this need is an emerging modern folk history. The young seek something to give them a sense of belonging. Their dreams and imaging still speak of the need to fight monsters as they struggle to leave the nursery; to catch a first glimpse of the beloved 'other' to set them on their quest with a sense of purpose; to model themselves on their chosen stars; to find causes, anti- or pro-, until their own heroic qualities can emerge. And so, tackling the dragons of the parents and of their own fear, they prove their mettle and their guts.

---

130 It is certainly not to be supposed that the author believed that at some time or place in history there was a Golden Age, now lost to us. Life in the past was often, as Thomas Hobbes pointed out, 'nasty, brutish, and short'. Barbara Somers held that the Golden Age exists rather in the Collective unconscious of humanity, and may be manifest in any place and at any time, past, resent and future. Ed.

131 Teddy Boys, Flower People, Skinheads, Punks.

Adolescence needs to be re-established as a major threshold of emergence, rather than as something to be got through as rapidly as possible. Old, and also deeply, passionately new, this great rite of passage has to erupt into consciousness. We ourselves may never have passed it. Our hope is that it does happen. Recognising and benignly guiding it to creative rather than destructive ends, the good-enough parent says, 'Go beyond me.' The Collective still needs the individual. As we need God, so *God needs us* to help him create. Helping adolescents, and our own adolescent within, means giving them something to fight *for*.

> *Pause to reflect:*
> Who and what was my image of the heroic when I was aged twelve to sixteen?
> Who or what is my present image of the heroic?

Courtship, and perhaps marriage

By the age of twelve – certainly sixteen – the young person was relating to the *otherness* outside the immediate family, village and tribe. Marriage has always been for the awakening, widening, domesticating and re-channelling of sexual impulses and to ensure the continuation of the people; later, for the development of romantic and chivalric love. Arranged to legitimise children, marriage linked the name with those of other families, tribes and nations, and so prevented incest.

Outer marriage, ancient and modern, has changed remarkably little down the millennia. It is still celebrated with ritual – festivities, flowers, vows, exchange of gifts and rings and tokens. People are around, friends and family, with candles, music, wine, gaiety, joy and laughter. In Chinese, Egyptian and Greek myths, the officiating dignitary acknowledges it also as an *inner* marriage to God or the gods. Frequently today too this is the priest's role. Until the Romantic era, love-matches were rare in the West: marriage was arranged, assuring the tribe's continuance. However, now it is expected to be about mutual love as well. Modern people struggle with body image, gender identity, *id* urges, guilt, duty and laws imposed from the super-ego. They may rebel, waiting with teenage groups and gangs for a new idealism to arise. Living closely with someone is a huge test – how far have they grown beyond the nursery? It's difficult to express feeling. Can they face life away from the parents? And – becoming a parent themselves – the responsibility?

Inner marriage ran from ritual prostitution to extreme celibacy, similarly marked with exchange of tokens and vows, changes of name, celebration, candles, flowers, wine. But now the monks, nuns and ascetics who carried this celibacy are leaving their orders; out in the world, they are often bewildered, guilty at breaking their commitment, lost without their faith and meaning.

Plato's creation myth is relatively recent: humankind was split into two halves once and for all by Apollo, at the order of Zeus, who felt that happy, complete humans were dangerous. Each person's life is a search for an 'other half', for rounding, completion and wholeness. This wrenching apart and coming together of the conjunct masculine and feminine is still alive in modern dreams, images and stories: a coin is broken, shared and later sought and found once more. The dark face seeks the light and *vice versa*. There is a once-remembered completeness, unity – a mysterious marriage within. Seeking the inner union of self with Self, our souls need completion within ourselves as well as with another.

The pressure is on. Not only marriage but the family are going for the knock today. In villages the grandmother and midwife, the doctor and priest, young and old, wise man and wise woman, all lived together. Romantic love itself has led to the break-up of extended families, as has love outside marriage. Though women are generally no longer seen as chattels, though there is in the West no *droit de seigneur*,[132] yet very small units (our nuclear or single parent families) do require a lot of psychological energy. And longevity raises a different stress. *Till death us do part* is one thing if it's until we are forty-five, but – eighties, nineties?

Can we live any longer with the split of inner from outer, of spirit from matter, of God transcendent from God immanent? Do we not have to raise hell and bring heaven to earth? The meaning is here, pointed to in secret by the alchemists.[133] We can't do it by *either this or that*, as others have done it. It is *both this and that*. Each of us has to find not only the other person outside us, but completion, symbolised by the *yin-yang* symbol, within ourselves. Married within, we can relate to another outside. Perfect joy is both inside and outside us, the orgasm of spiritual ecstasy that brings into being the young Christ, Buddha, Krishna floating on a lotus – the jewel of a new birth to something different. Struggling towards that, many of us become more conscious.

---

132 Droit de seigneur – alleged right of a feudal lord to copulate with a vassal's bride on her wedding-night. OED.
133 See Somers 2004, *The Fires of Alchemy*, pp. 8, 37, 98

Pause to reflect: If life is the search for the *other* – the other half – go inside yourself, and consider:
>   What are the qualities of my other half, inner or outer?
>   What are my experiences of the outer and the inner marriage?
>   Can we – can heaven and earth – any longer be split apart?

Adulthood

From thirty-five to about fifty-six is Jung's 'high noon'. Standing in consciousness at the zenith, thinking through, taking responsibility, our challenge is to *go on* both outwardly and inwardly to psychological adulthood. Development doesn't end with physical maturity. Therapy (for we may well need the help of another person) tweaks bits up through the carpet and shows the pattern. Adulthood means looping up those bits.

In traditional societies the adult male was both householder and warrior. Little has been written about this. Fighting and working for his tribe, emerging as master craftsman, he guaranteed the future by becoming a parent in his own right, responsible for patterning the new generation. Individuals making application for greater consciousness were set apart and initiated further into the deeper mysteries of the tribe, becoming hierophant, initiator, master. A woman might become priestess, sybil or oracle, supported by the inner energies of the god or totem. Through ritual, a direct link with the gods was established and confirmed.

Now, the man and the woman are each fully responsible. Finding our way and direction without help, at full stance, in consciousness, *we do not work because we know; we know because we work*. True initiation takes place in the heat of the kitchen. The right to apply for initiation is what makes a person an initiate – not the initiation itself, not the seamless white robe. The ceremony only confirms the reality of what has happened: direct recognition by the god. Those earlier rites of passage had to do with the refining process, just as gold and silver are proved and cleansed of their dross by fire.[134] This was the Zen of Now. Acting from the moment, learning that they were carriers of the spirit of the gods, vessels of the divine, they could walk in the world.

Pause to reflect:
>   What for you is adulthood?
>   Reflect upon the high noon of your life.

---

134 We recall Paracelsus: Thine is not a wedding garment. Magic has opened thy heart and made thee known; therefore even as gold and silver must thou be refined from blemish, and tested. Seven times more severely than gold and silver is cleansed of its dross by fire, must thou be tried. This is demanded of thee; Thy transient wealth belongeth to another. In Somers 2004, *The Fires of Alchemy*, p. 117.

Midlife crisis

However, between thirty-five and forty-nine – or at any age from seven to ninety – if our adulthood is precarious, if we remain inwardly immature, too rigid or insecure for its challenges, we may begin to crack. As Jung said: 'Wholly unprepared we embark on the second half of life'. It is as though, at the height of noon, a resonance goes right the way through, as from a tuning fork. A note sounds from the Self, resonating from the centre down to the very Ocean of Dark Things. Old values don't stand; psychosomatic illnesses follow, danger and opportunity.

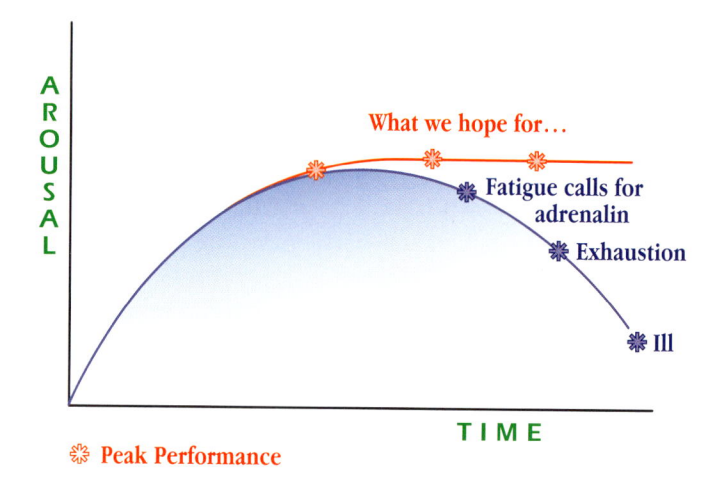

Chart 4:09 –The Human Function Curve [135]

Today, we go over the top of this stress curve. Performance is mapped on the vertical axis, arousal (too much of which is stress) on the horizontal. Starting at zero, healthy tension rises diagonally to the right, and should fall back naturally to the left, to zero again, with rest and a good night's sleep. However, we aim and intend to continue up and to the right indefinitely. So, reaching a crest, a point of fatigue, instead of falling gently back to the left we begin to topple over to the right. Fatigue leads to exhaustion, performance falls off. Beyond this, down and to the right,

---

135   With acknowledgements to Peter Nixon.

is a point at which even minimal arousal is the last straw and leads to breakdown. Thus we reach zero performance again on the vertical level, and on the horizontal, are far over into stress. *What to do?* Ask the affected part of the body – ask the symptom. Listen to what it says.

Western society earlier afforded a work-style inherited from the parents. Religious and spiritual organisations held us from the centre; we saw them as parental, relied on them. Now we are expected to parent ourselves, to earn, pay our way, be an example to the young, all with no inherited structure and a broken tradition. How far, inwardly, do we remain rebellious children? Hitting trouble, we feel lost in an alien world with only our own bootstraps. We carry on, dependent, assuming old programmes and truths will last, fearing the break-up, preferring not to grow. But the morning's truth will not hold in the afternoon.

The Titan Procrustes tested people. A demigod, he had a hostel by the roadside offering a meal and hospitality. Travellers seduced into lying on his bed were lopped off short if too long for it, stretched to fit if too short. Society is a Procrustes bed. Have we the courage to stay on our true path – or do we creep squeaking under the duvet? The rack is something like the loom: on it, we break – or we grow.

We need *colleges for forty-year-olds*. Adulthood requires new patterns of thought, feeling and behaviour to lead towards the richness and roundness of maturity. The structure of society, economics and education can't handle such deep need for change and development, new interests and the resurgence of growth in individuals. Modern men and women search for someone to point to the *inner* wise person, the inner hierophant, one who knows. Our hope lies in self-integrity in the face of new situations, a conscious pursuit of the Self. When we stop and are quiet, we hear the voice within calling for a change of life, a deepening of meaning, a change of direction. As the Polish proverb has it,

The forties are the old age of immaturity.
The fifties are the youth of maturity.

Pause to reflect:
   What has emerged from the crises you've known, at whatever age?

Maturity

The Apollo journey up towards the sun – the Pluto journey down towards darkness and the luminosity within it – are they not one and the same? Full light and depth at once would be too much. The initiator takes it stage by stage. We need fewer priests now; our voices are our own. At least we know who we're *not*, where we're not going. There's resurgence of a new kind of energy. Tai Chi, for instance, was created by the mature for the mature. Coming together with the children, these people throw down their skills and begin to dance.

Maturity was an acknowledged time of privilege, with leisure to mellow and use energy creatively. There was an innate wisdom, a maturity of soul, encapsulated in those who held the treasures of the tribe, garnered the harvest of the past and initiated the others. Advising on politics, they became carriers of the myths of the ancestors, re-linking the people with their folklore and legends. Allowing for dream-time, responsible for the speaking of dreams, they themselves could dream for the tribe, be soothsayers and oracles. They taught how suffering needs meaning, how pain is the great teaching on this 'planet of pain'; how rightly to let go, since holding on to pain increases it and perhaps letting go means it doesn't hurt too much. If someone's suffering was loss and sorrow, they taught them to imagine how the dead must feel: 'So you are grieving, when I am released!'

'I'll start living *now*!' Though much goes on that should not, it's only *im*maturity, rigid and insecure, that says, 'It wasn't like that in my young day!' The test of maturity is *humour*, which adolescents lack. In our sixties, seventies, eighties we can begin to act as if we were mature people. A chuckle emerges. 'Tell God I'd like another chassis for this marvellous engine.'

> *Pause to reflect:*
> Who am I now?
> Who am I not?
> What is wisdom?

The time of the elder

The bird of wisdom perches only on snow-covered thatch. So they were listened to, these keepers of the mysteries. Their spiritual flowering was allowed for, they were turned to as guides and advisers, taking the established place they had earned, giving their experience back to the people, known to all. To be an elder was about being rather than doing, preparing for death and for rebirth, perhaps going walkabout – in some tribes the old voluntarily went out and were left in the snow, returning to God and the ancestors.

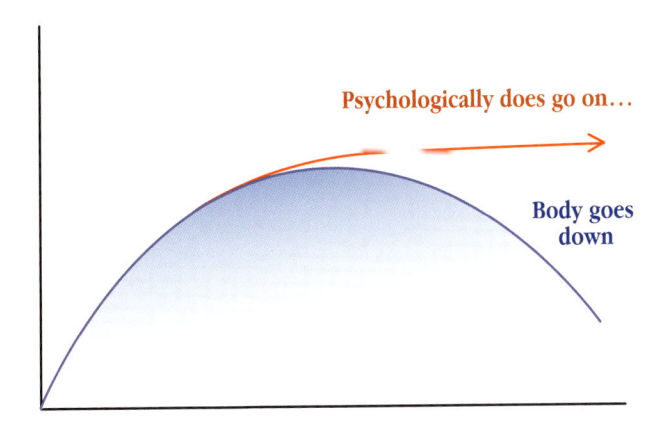

Chart 4:10 – The Time of the Elder

Wisdom in an elder shows in increased radiation in their aura; not up and over and down, as with the stress-curve of the mid-life crisis, but up and steadily rising into eternity. We live longer now, have more time than the tribal people, yet we often embark unprepared towards the wholly marvellous threshold of dying. We hope for a richness, a roundness, a coming together of inner and outer as we approach the deep mystery of death. The late evening of life is for retirement and re-evaluation. Physically we do go down but, whatever happens to the body, inwardly we can rise, not taking on the psychology of our chronological age but preparing to become participant in this greatest of all mysteries. The form loses energy but life gains vitality. Though conserving our strength somewhat, we may be more physically active, mentally aware and spiritually alive than ever.

Pause to reflect:
What is it for me to become an elder?
Is there time in my life for play, humour, relaxation, fun?

The Night Sea Journey – the Nekyia

Jung brought the *nekyia* out of the Greek myths.[136] It is said that no one can become an enlightened one except by consciously undertaking the Night Sea Journey. Death, the great threshold, is the only certainty. Nothing can be reborn unless it has died. Our image is that we come from somewhere, we go to somewhere. At death, we re-enter the unconscious, shed the vehicles. This is the dark night of the soul, the descent into hell, the crossing of the Styx. We remember the story of Osiris and Seth and Isis – the dismemberment, scattering, so-called deadness, the stillness before rebirth.

Christianity has brought about the horror of death which has followed the splitting of body from soul. Can we tolerate that split any more? Eternal damnation and hellfire are relatively new ideas, out of the Puritan ethic of the Western world, where heaven and hell are viewed as reward for this life. The old man with the scythe is a modern-ish invention, as is any idea of punishment, Dante had no such concept.[137] The earlier Angel of Death was gentle, a relief, a friend and guide, coming as Ferryman with his boat to fetch you for the Crossing. The soul went into the underworld, not for hell but for a period of *purgation* prior to the homecoming, the awakening, the rebirth, being re-gathered to the gods, to God. *In my Father's house are many mansions.*[138] Some Eastern religions hold that we enter a state of excess (though we don't stay in it long!) And there are the different heavens – seven, nine or sixteen of them? In Babylon (as in Dante) there were said to be seven planetary heavens. While Valhalla was a kind of gory male paradise ruled over by Odin or Wotan,[139] yet also there is Shambhala, the Overworld, Bliss, Nirvana. Tibetans enter the Bardo state; it's birth that is seen as sadness, and death as joy. Both the Tibetan and the Egyptian Books of the Dead are really books of *life*, because what is seen at the time of death is – life.

But, though we may sense that we have a right to choose to die, if it's not our time we may not go.

The old rituals – oral, not written texts – say little. *Those who know don't speak.* But death was seen as an *awakening*, a passage ahead. We know death was prepared for, discussed. It was an honour, a privilege to come to this, to rejoin the ancestors, take but temporary leave. People die

---

136 Nekyia: a descent into Hades and a quest for the 'treasure hard to attain'. See Jung 1951, *The Psychological Aspects of the Kore*, para 311.
137 Dante 1300-1320, The Divine Comedy. The soul chooses its own state.
138 John 14:2.
139 Valhalla, where the souls of slaughtered warriors feasted on wild boar and fought each other to the death just for fun (though miraculously the consumed boar was always reconstituted and ready to be cooked again, and the killed warriors also returned to life).

gently if they've lived a full life and are tired and ready to sleep. Old elephants go to a place of dying; old people were in that same small, dim place in the village, in their own bed, surrounded by family and friends, priestess or priest. If they died alone it was by voluntary choice. The same woman officiated before and at death as before and at birth – dying was held to be valuable. The family mourned the hero fallen on the field of battle only because he had been cut down too soon for the rituals of the culture. Warriors would be brought home to complete their business.

So the wise elders re-gathered the gods into themselves, with no split between heaven and hell, accepting both this and that; and meaning was everywhere. That death was also seen as *rebirth* is amply shown in the marked similarity of burial rites to birth motifs. There was a laying of the body in the ground, in a cave, a small dark place, swaddled and folded to the foetal position before being put into earth or fire for the mystical return to the Earth Mother. Even the humblest dead had wine, food and materials provided, for it was a passage *to* something. The person had always known death not as an end but as a journey, often in a sacrificial barge or boat or raft for the crossing of the river (to this day our coffins are somewhat boat-shaped). They would be accompanied by priest, family and friends for the embarking on the ritual ship.

Traditionally, rejection and rage were allowed for, and attachment. You grieved for someone you loved during six weeks of mourning, with wailing, lamentation and sorrow. The celebration-after-mourning followed, the transition marked with singing, incense, music, wine and feasting; for those who die well have lived fully and death is reward for a life well lived. After the necessary time of limbo came the awakening; new-born within the ancestors, they became part of the myth of the tribe. 'Return quickly, return soon!' So the dead awoke and were returned as a gift, entering a new state of being. Dreams and images still show that the psyche rarely sees death in terms of corpses and burials, but rather as threshold, journey, continuation, rebirth, a passage *to* somewhere. If grief is allowed, then celebration and joy and hope still ensue, as testified by the Irish wake.

So now, the time has come. We face our worst fears, our dread of extinction. No previous experience helps. Most of us are unprepared and unfamiliar with the process of dying. How many of us have been with a dying person? The dying are not allowed to *talk* about it – the last great taboo.... They may long to but they can't, they still don't mention it, don't admit they are dying for fear of hurting those who remain. For the sake of family, friends and medical people, they are often left to die alone, in a perhaps impersonal hospital where people may be embarrassed to have them dying at all, perhaps on a life-support machine ensuring quantity of life without regard to quality. Occasionally they may be efficiently shoved over to clear the bed. Clinically prolonged, or hurried on, they cross the threshold isolated, dying among strangers.

For those of us left behind there are few rituals to support our natural sense of outrage, our sense of betrayal and guilt (and our relief) when death intervenes in life. Time is not allowed for our human grief. Around the will the vultures gather. And the anniversary is a time-clock in the psyche.

In Socratic thinking, a whole culture can be judged by the way in which it values its ageing people. How does our present culture stand up to such a measure?

Reappraisal is needed, passionately; as is the importance of dying at home with people to talk to. With the setting up of the hospices, Dr. Elisabeth Kübler-Ross, Dame Cicely Saunders and many others have renewed people's interest all round. Near-death research and exploration into past lives also give much hope, for there seems to be a universal belief in reincarnation.[140]

During the course of their lives, many ordinary people personally experience a number of *nekyias*. Collectively too: some hold that there is a group incarnation in which our individual destiny finds place. Organisations of all kinds spiral through consecutive trials by earth, water, air and fire, dying to old patterns and being reborn to new, until all life is a continuum of rites of passage. In what form shall we emerge? In the dark, our dreams give hints of light and life – a bird, a baby, an egg, a shoot breaking through. If enough individuals change, we shall awaken. Those who come through, keeping that flame alight, are worth turning to. They are our salvation.

Pause to reflect:
The *nekyia*: the seventh and greatest ritual, the deepest, the still point of consciousness, prelude to rebirth. Who is attached:
    Is it the one who identifies?
    Is it the child?
    Is it the loving heart?

---

140 Consider St. Joseph's and St. Christopher's Hospices; Dr. Thelma Bates who helped develop hospital support teams for the sick, and pioneered work on death, dying and bereavement; Raymond Moody 1975 with *Life after Life*; Stanislav Grof 1977, on *The Human Encounter with Death* and transformation. And Peter and Elizabeth Fenwick and their Near Death Studies; Sogyal Rinpoche with his *Tibetan Book of Living and Dying*; the Dalai Lama.

EXPLORATION
THE WATER OF EMOTIONS
(40 minutes)

Reconnect with your Jewel, your Talisman. If you didn't have one, be prepared to find one now, as we journey through the *emotions*.

Stage 1

Minutes

4   Find yourself by water – whether the sea, a lake, pool, river, stream, waterfall or pond. Recognise that you are looking at a symbol of your present emotional life, your feeling nature. Do not enter the water yet; spend some time observing what happens above, around, on and in the water, as it mirrors the shifting states of your feelings and emotional consciousness.

4   Let the image change. Again you are by water, which now becomes a symbol of how you would really like your feeling nature to be – an *ideal model* of your emotional self. Again, do not enter this water but observe it closely, getting the feeling of it and of your surroundings.

7   Return to the first image, the water of your present emotional life and feeling nature. Taking your Talisman as guide, mentor and support, when you are ready, enter that water if it's appropriate, and let the images of your emotional life tell you about this aspect of your being. Experience its nature and its problems, and discover perhaps what may be done to bring it closer to its ideal state. If the water is polluted and impure, discover the cause. If it is muddy and dirty, why? If the surface is rarely calm, let the water itself show you the reason.

2   You leave the water. Let go the feelings of the last few minutes. Spend the next little time clearing and centring yourself.

7   Return now to the *ideal water*. Enter the water, experience it, exploring now *under* the water if you wish. Discover how you may experience this more often in everyday life. Consider ways in which the first could be turned into the second in practical living.

Stage 2

7 Now, let the image of your ideal emotional nature appear again, how you would actually wish the water to be. This time, you find the Initiator standing with you. You realise that you are about to experience, or to re-experience, a baptism. Enter the water, again exploring *under* if appropriate, to experience the ideal state of your feeling nature. Expect images to come which will show you what to do in order to experience this state more often in future living. Stay in the experience for the next few minutes.

2 Find yourself once again now with the Initiator, and any inner friends who may have been with you in the Cave. If there were none, allow them to make themselves known to you now if that's appropriate. The Initiator is standing by the water to baptise you.

7 You are baptised and initiated in the water of your new, true, ideal emotions. Leave the water and return to land. Face the Initiator and spend a while discovering as much as you can about your essential relationship to this figure.

Prepare to take your leave of the Initiator, and of any other figures. In your own time, make your farewells; return to a quiet and peaceful place before recording.

DISCUSSION AND SHARING IN SMALL GROUPS

Remember, any interpretations must come only from the person. See p. 40, and fuller commentary in Appendix 1.

INITIATION AND THERAPY

Initiation means to awaken, to remember where we came from.

Carl Jung saw psychological problems as the suffering of a soul that has not yet discovered its meaning. Abraham Maslow showed how, once our basic needs are met for security, love and self-esteem, we begin to be motivated by altruism and the desire to be of service. Aiming for self-transcendence, 'self-actualising', we make a creative contribution. We've dealt somewhat with personal issues and the integration of the shadow. What next? Recognising Plato's famous myth of the cave,[141] we start to 're-member' the soul. First we search outwardly; some undertake shamanic journeys or vision quests, for example. We are learning *about* something. This is not yet *direct* experience.

As personality and soul start to fuse, the stresses increase. Through dreams, physical symptoms and the happenings of life, we may have direct experience of the numinous, developing a sense of the abyss, the void. It is *awe-full*. Coming to the gap, we must make the initiate's leap. The loss of ego feels like death, annihilation, hell. Both Jung and Maslow held that the ego is a problem only when alienated from the values of the soul. Therapy is a *necessary* bridge to those values. It is the *soul* that is being initiated. We need support.

Therapy helps us encounter life and death equally, making conscious our issues of sex, power, love and death. We need someone who will offer us midwifery to awaken Soul, helping us stay with the downs as well as the ups. The *therapist* stands in as initiator, supporter, the soul's companion and encourager, attending upon, midwifing a new identity. Healing by the loving atmosphere she engenders, the therapist witnesses psychological deaths and rebirths; and she is also attendant upon the soul preparing for physical death.

As Lord Buddha said, *At the end of the way there is freedom; till then, there is patience*. We need patience, and we need practice. Chop wood, carry water. We return to the known and familiar, but with new insights, 'seeing the place for the first time', in Eliot's phrase – living in two worlds at once, aware like the tree of both ground *and* sky, roots *and* fruits, ego *and* soul.

Matter itself leads to the subtle, the causal, the absolute. As human beings we have a double nature: the phenomenal *ego* linked with body and mind; and the eternal *Self* linked with spirit. *Spirit* is the indestructible, creative ground of existence and being, the divine ground against which all partial realities have their being. The *soul* is in a third position, witness of both, the invisible bridge connecting body and mind with spirit and the heaven above with matter, with the ego, the earth beneath. The soul is the divine spark lighting the flame of the spirit.

What happens in those moments when the client breaks out from the

---

141 Plato, Myth of the Cave, Appendix 11.

fragile shell of the ego to glimpse the wider context, the divine ground of their being that underlies reality, beyond ego-sense? The dreamer starts to awaken; the perspective shifts from the periphery to the centre. For a moment, ego-concerns drop away. The therapist needs to be alert, ready to shift levels and come alongside. Equally, the therapist must be able to change priorities and perspectives in the work, encouraging the soul to speak.

And there is a danger here: the *invalid* awakening of love and spiritual values, of creativity, of spiritual vision, of spirit, may lead to stress, emptiness, depression, yearning and despair. Sought as ends in themselves, they form 'entangling golden chains'. That is why midwifery is required. Initiation needs helping at every level. Having glimpsed oneness, expecting to work it back into life, a person may find not transformation but flat desolation and aridity – like Plato's escaped prisoner, back to dualism again. The journey may well lead through despair, till the therapist muses: 'I wonder why your soul chose *this* particular passage?'

Therapy aims not to *avoid* a person's problems, but to *hear* when the soul speaks from behind them. Together we work to release the writers' blocks in their life-story, the sticking points in the narrative, laying out the pieces of their personal jigsaw to ponder together. So the contexts are deepened, locked viewpoints changed, narrow outlooks and concepts broadened. And the initiate finds a greater sense of accompaniment, responsibility, purpose and meaning.

In therapy, initiation involves awakening and remembering. *St. Teresa of Avila* offered a bold metaphor: the silkworm seems to die, yet becomes a beautiful moth. First the caterpillar, greedy for teachings, experiences and visions, searches externally. Then in its cocoon it turns inward, to silence, contemplation and solitude in the 'interior castle'. God does the work, transforming it. Nothing seems to be happening. Finally it emerges into the sacred marriage, the mystical union, the death of the separate ego. Now the little self is free from its limitations in the boundless ocean of life. No death this, but a victory over death, a rising and a resurrection. Deep ecology and true service, this leads to the fruitfulness of the soul, which means serving the *whole*.[142]

The metaphor of the *oxherd*, unlike St. Teresa's, starts externally. First, the ox of our true nature is lost. Seeking him, we find and follow his

---

[142] Teresa of Avila, *The Interior Castle*, pp.126 ff.

tracks, the spiritual teachings. Glimpsing him, we realise that only direct experience will do, so we have to discipline ourselves. Catching the ox, we begin to integrate the shadow, quieting the desires of the mind. Then we master the released energies as we learn to herd this great beast, till we can befriend him and ride him home. Now we belong in the universe, alone, recreated moment by moment; until all phenomena, like the ox himself, vanish. The oxherd becomes one with the Source. At last he returns to the market place to awaken others; he goes beyond in order to return. He follows no path. He is invisible to those who cannot discern.[143]

> *Pause to reflect*: Look now at your own life and ask:
> What does my soul see?
> What needs to be healed, reconnected, linked, remembered?
> Looking at your practical life as if it were a tree, ask:
> What is it rooted in?
> What are its fruits? The nature of its trunk?
> What are its needs for nourishment?

The *Upanishads* offer an image of two birds, inseparable companions, perching on the same tree. One eats the fruit while the other looks on. The first bird is the individual self feeding on the pleasures and pains of the world. The other, the universal Self, is silently witnessing.

> *I am thou and thou art I: and wheresoever thou mayest be I am there. In all am I scattered, and whensoever thou willest thou gatherest Me: and gathering Me, thou gatherest thyself.*
> Apocryphal Gospel of Eve

INITIATION IN MYTH AND LEGEND

Myth and folk tale [144]

Myths are distinct from fairy stories. Where popular folk stories and fairy tales portray the perilous journey as *physical*, mythology and the higher religions see it as a journey of the *spirit*. Typically, the *fairy story* or *folk tale* is microcosmic, the journey of the ego. A personal or domestic triumph is made. Usually the hero or heroine – youngest, poorest, most despised – emerges, overcomes a personal oppressor and becomes royal.

---

143 The Oxherd, see Somers 2004, *The Fires of Alchemy*, pp. 204 ff.
144 This section, pp. 211-221, was in part contributed to the workshop by Barbara Somers, and in part by her colleague and friend Joan Swallow, to whom grateful acknowledgement is made; see n. 26, p. 41. Ed.

The hero is mortal; it is he who achieves.[145] Rescue is from without. The helpers come from the realms of instinct – animals, good fairies, gnomes, elves, fairy godmothers and fathers, genies in bottles. The hero is granted *things* – three wishes, gold and silver – and the highest goal is to live happily ever after. Jack and the Beanstalk, Cinderella, Snow White, the Little Goose Girl, Aladdin – they are such microcosmic tales, involving the regeneration of home and hearth.

Myths and legends, on the other hand, are macrocosmic, epic tales. The hero or heroine is part mortal, part divine: maiden goddess, divine boy, child of a god, royal soul in straightened circumstances. Helped not by fairies but by royal beings (angels, ancestral heroes, winged creatures), by gods and goddesses themselves (Athene, Hermes the mystagogue, guide of souls) he is granted not wishes but talismans and words of power. Indeed, in myth the hero often becomes Pontifex the Bridge-maker, becomes even an incarnation of God. Scaling the mountain, plumbing the depths, he himself becomes the navel of the world, the umbilical point where eternity and time intersect. The highest goal is to bring back the fruits of his experience – the Holy Grail, the Fleece,[146] the Golden Apple,[147] the Elixir of Life, the means of wider regeneration for the Self and for society at large.

In our time there is a revival of interest in myth, reflecting our deep need for ritual, mystery and magic. Whether the hero is our friend Dummling of the fairytale,[148] or the demigod of myth, the journey is much the same. Tolkien marvellously *combines* fairy tale with myth. His Hobbits Bilbo and Frodo are instinctual, from the Shires, home-loving yet adventuring, with their Ring of Destiny and their Crack of Doom. It's epic, it's mythic – a deft mix of the ridiculous and the sublime, and very true to life. Whether in these great profound tales or in our well-loved folk stories, our hearth stories – whether in languages of folktale, myth, legend or dream – certain themes of individuation and initiation are constant.

> *Pause to reflect*:
> Contemplate the themes of your own life which emerge in dreams, in your favourite myths and legends, films and stories.
> How do they relate to the themes of emergence, initiatory experience and return?

---

145 Or heroine. I shall refer to both hero and heroine as male, because it is the role of the masculine in both men and women to make the journey. While the feminine is the journey, the masculine goes on the journey.
146 Jason and the Argonauts, see Graves 1955, Vol.2, Section 148 ff.
147 The Golden Apples of the Hesperides. See the *Eleventh Labour of Hercules*, Graves 1955, Vol.2, Section 133.
148 Chapter 1, p. 56.

THE HERO'S JOURNEY

Starting with the call to adventure, he passes through separation and forgetting, experience and scattering, to the ultimate return, the homecoming to a remembered place.

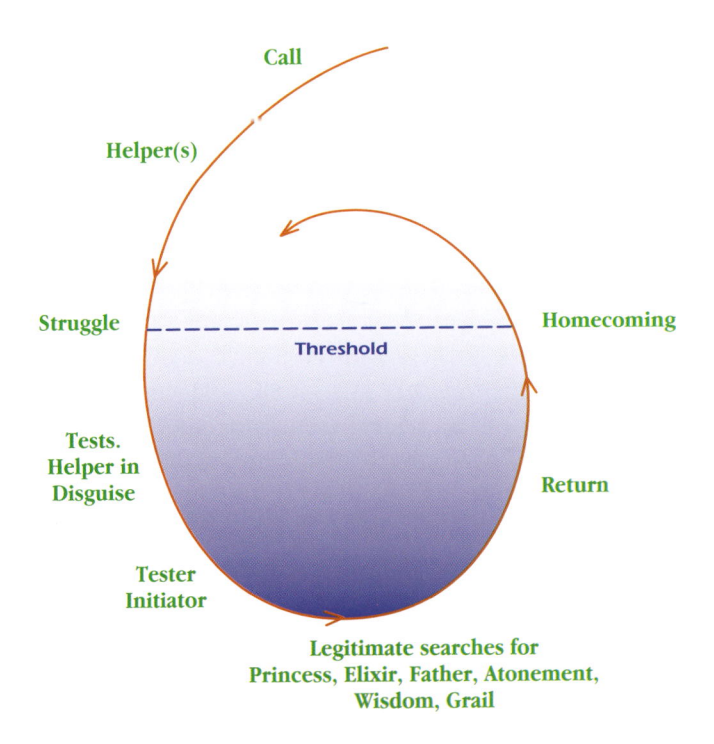

Chart 4:11 – The Hero's Journey

First, he is *separated*. The call comes in many ways, luring him from his beginnings in the common-day hut or castle. It may be interior, or he may be pushed from without, but it brooks no refusal, for flight from the god is folly. He is sent – or carried – from the known and familiar, out and away to adventure, whether voluntarily or accidentally, whether by malign or benign agents. And so he journeys through enchanted forests to a far country, the great unknown: the magical island, the kingdom underground, below the waves, above the sky. And here, he *forgets*.

In both folk lore and myth, the hero must cross the first threshold of adventure, passing between the Clashing Rocks into the belly of the whale, the dentated womb, the crevasse of Mother Earth, the realm of night. Taking the perilous descent to the underworld, the road to death, he encounters the dangerous aspect of the gods – serpents, demons, witches, wizards, monsters – and Cerberus, the many-headed dog, keeper of the threshold to the underworld. These are the guardians, to be placated, outwitted or overcome. Unexpected and supernatural aid comes to him who has undertaken his proper adventure. Led only by his helpers and his own vision, again and again the hero passes barriers and slays dragons.

Will he stand? With all its false starts and dead ends, this road leads him through *dismemberment* to expansion of consciousness, illumination, the victories of initiation. For this is also the road to immortality. On it he meets the goddess – perhaps encountering woman as temptress, as did Odysseus, perhaps regaining the bliss of infancy – and finds atonement, oneness with the father, apotheosis, the ultimate boon. Ultimately, he *returns* through the oft-remembered gate, *re-membered* from dismemberment. To refuse to return to society is to deny the world, take the magic flight, the escape of Prometheus. But if he crosses the return threshold to the world of common day and is integrated again with society, he brings gifts to the Collective and becomes master of the two worlds. So, through birth, initiation and resurrection from the tomb, he brings the freedom to live. And that is the nature and function of the ultimate boon.

Two myths illustrate the journey of the hero. While Odysseus was *in*voluntarily driven about the Mediterranean by the winds of the angry god Poseidon, Theseus, hearing in Athens about the Minotaur in the Labyrinth in Crete, *voluntarily* chose adventure.

Theseus

Theseus volunteered; and Ariadne, daughter of King Minos, seeing him disembark with the Athenian youths and maidens to be sacrificed to the Minotaur, fell in love with him. She agreed to help him if he would take her with him from Crete and marry her, and he gave her his pledge. Daedalus, who had created the labyrinth, gave her a skein, a 'clew' of golden thread – a simple thing, but without it all would have been lost. The golden thread is of Zeus, the chain of gold linking heaven and earth, the world-centre. The great Mother goddess, the cosmic spider, spins the thread from her own substance and weaves the web, binding everything together on the loom of life and destiny. They cannot be separated – spinner from spun nor creator from created.

So Theseus, hero-saviour and adventurer, journeyed consciously into the Labyrinth at Knossos. Out of the masculine principle he travelled on the feminine thread of intuition, the wisdom given him by Ariadne who is soul, psyche. The two in co-operation brought about the death of the beast, the savage Minotaur, the dark unconscious *id*, the force of sub-human nature. Led once more into the light, Theseus eloped with Ariadne but then betrayed her, leaving her on the Isle of Naxos. We note that, while he then continued to struggle, Ariadne herself moved on; she turned from Theseus, the mortal hero who had abandoned her, to a god, Dionysus. Honouring the thread, she became an immortal.

Odysseus

However, in our second myth, Odysseus, King of Ithaca, made the dangerous voyage *in*voluntarily. Returning from the Trojan wars, he was helped by the nymph Calypso to prepare for departure to his wife Penelope in Ithaca. But Poseidon wrecked his ship and he had many adventures, by mistake. When his men ate the drugged fruits of the Island of the Lotus-Eaters, he dragged them, nearly asleep, to the ship, tied them there and was tied himself. When the Cyclops, the giant Polyphemus, ate some of his men and kept Odysseus and others prisoner, they burned out the single eye of the giant with a tree-trunk and escaped by tying themselves beneath the bellies of the sheep which Polyphemus let out of the cave to pasture. When King Aeolus sent Odysseus off with all the Winds in a bag, his men opened the bag and his ship was blown back to Aeolia, delaying the journey once more. Circe turned his men to swine. But Hermes helped Odysseus, in his realisation and agony, to bed her and persuade her to restore them to human form. And he visited Hades, where the blind seer Teiresias told him how to reach Ithaca again. And so at last he returned home.

The Return

As we've seen, the hero's journey starts and finishes in the home. The heart of the home is the flame in the hearth. This is the focus, the foyer, with the chimney rising to heaven and the smoke ascending. The hearth is a symbol of the centre of life, the special place to come home to. Hearth, heart, earth – though we use the term 'central heating', modern homes often lack any focal point, any connection between earth and heaven. In story, the opening in the roof is vital (and so is the chimney – how else could Santa Claus arrive?) Prayer, incense, the light of the candle flame, the sacrificial smoke, the *mantra* and the intercession, all rise up. Thus, burned in the fire of life and struggle, our aspiration leads to experience.

Flung out via the spokes of the earthly wheel, scattered towards the rim we, like the hero, are whirled around it, into and beyond satiation. But at last we move down a spoke towards the hub, returning by another path and to a different centre, as the knights returned to Arthur's Round Table. And the hub of the wheel, the *still point*, is marked by altar, lantern, spire, the pinnacle of the dome of the temple.

However, first the spokes of the wheel dissolve to become a labyrinth trodden by the hero. This is a common theme; by individual effort he must follow the feminine thread of wisdom along the labyrinthine way. At first it's easy; the centre still belongs to the personality. The path seems to go there at once, before spiralling away into an uncertain middle area. We too

Chart 4:12 – The Labyrinth in Chartres Cathedral

Initiation and the Myth of the Journey

are full of doubt – often for ages – lost again and far from home. But at last the labyrinth draws us back by another path – and to a *different* centre.

Sometimes it is not a labyrinth but a maze, full of blind alleys and mistakes, false starts, dead ends, *culs-de-sac* – a knotted way of perplexities and difficulties. Turf mazes are still found in our villages, webs once walked, sometimes on their knees, by pilgrims who couldn't get to the Crusades or the holy places, the ancient churches or cathedrals, to signify the journey of the spirit. Eliot wrote of life as labyrinth, as experience, as initiation:

In order to arrive there,
To arrive where you are, to get from where you are not,
You must go by a way wherein there is no ecstasy…
In order to possess what you do not possess
You must go by the way of dispossession…[149]

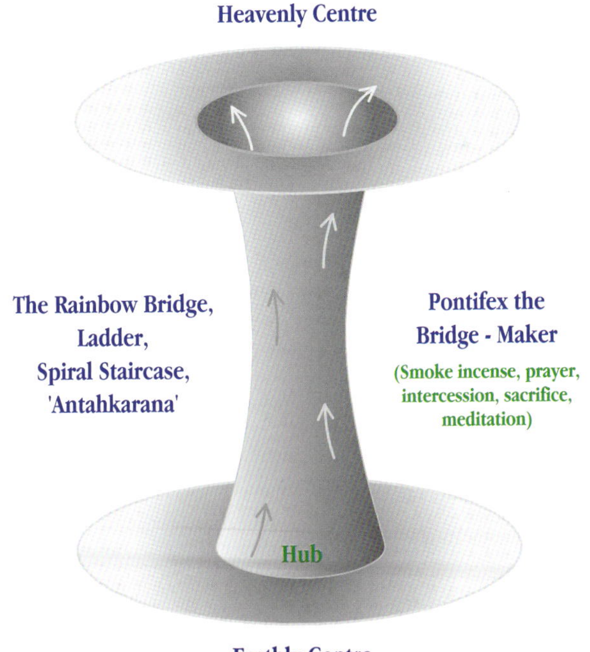

Heavenly Centre

The Rainbow Bridge, Ladder, Spiral Staircase, 'Antahkarana'

Pontifex the Bridge - Maker
(Smoke incense, prayer, intercession, sacrifice, meditation)

Hub

Earthly Centre

Chart 4:13 – The Bridge and the Ladder (Antahkarana)

---

149 Eliot, *Four Quartets*, 'East Coker', lines 135-141 (by kind permission of Faber & Faber).

This central ladder is the core where eternity and time intersect. The ladder rises from a point on the earthly wheel to meet the heavenly wheel. This is *umbilicus orbis*, the world navel, 'the still point of the turning world'.[150] It is Buddha's immovable spot. The legend tells how the Tree of Life grows at this point: Yggdrasil, rooted in darkness, green-golden and sun-filled at its crest, an inexhaustible spring at its foot; the Bo-tree of the Buddha; the sacrificial cross of Christ; the World Tree of Attis, Wotan and Osiris. Sometimes the earthly hub is marked by a sacred city of the gods. It may be a hall – Valhalla – or a cosmic mountain with, in Eastern legend, a lotus of light at its peak and in its hollows the cities or caves of demons. Here is the impregnation by divine energy of the womb of the world, the solar ray igniting hearth and heart, the axis joining and turning the two wheels. It is the nipple of the Universal Mother. It is the Rainbow Bridge of light, the *antahkarana*.[151] The midpoint of the sky is a sun-door through which souls pass back and forth from time to eternity.

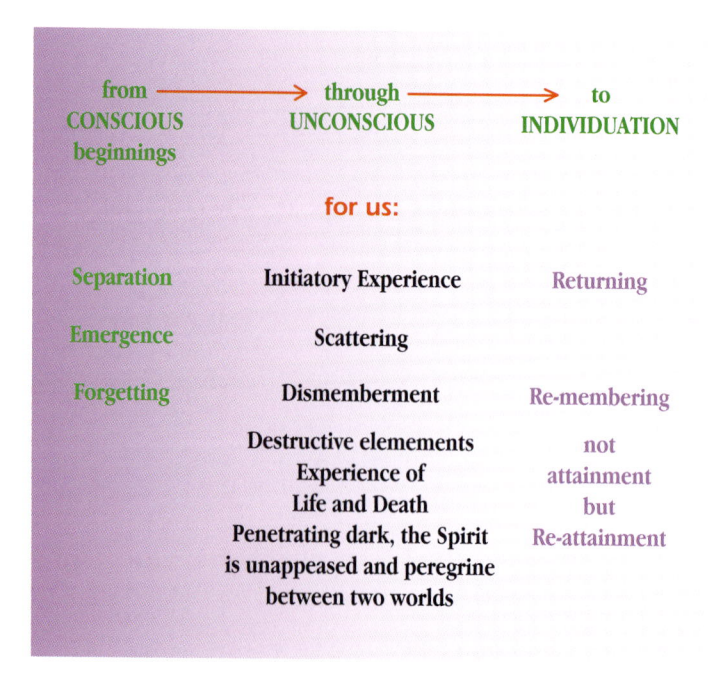

from	through	to
CONSCIOUS beginnings	**UNCONSCIOUS**	**INDIVIDUATION**
	for us:	
Separation	**Initiatory Experience**	Returning
Emergence	**Scattering**	
Forgetting	**Dismemberment**	Re-membering
	Destructive elements	not
	Experience of	attainment
	Life and Death	but
	Penetrating dark, the Spirit	Re-attainment
	is unappeased and peregrine	
	between two worlds	

Chart 4:14 – The Myth of the Journey

---

150 See Eliot, *Four Quartets*, 'Burnt Norton', line 62.
151 Antahkarana: a term much used by Bailey 1960, *The Rays and The Initiations*. See Chapters 9 and 10 below.

Through it the god descends into incarnation and man ascends, lifted on an axis of ascending smoke from the hub of the earthly to that of the celestial wheel.

It is a symbol of continuous creation, the maintenance of the cosmos, a lit force ever renewed. And who finds it? Who is the hero who ascends the ladder? Is the ego prepared to die?

Reading the map across (opposite), we are reminded of two worldwide mythical stories about returning. First, the Prodigal Son left the father's house, went out on the wheel of experience, and was at last drawn back, no longer the person who set out, but different, tempered by life. He had lost a lot of his value in favour of something infinitely more beautiful. Secondly, once the choice had been made and they had eaten from the *tree of the knowledge of good and evil*, Adam and Eve were turned out of the Garden; angels were set to prevent their return. Perforce they emerged from Eden, moving out into experience and individual choice, peregrine[152] between two worlds, belonging in neither. Would any of us ever leave the Paradise Garden unless made to set out on the journey? However, in the Garden there was another tree, the *tree of everlasting life*.[153] Eventually they came home after all for, in the end, the tree of knowledge leads to the tree of life. Ultimate return to the One brings us back to the Paradise Garden by a different gate, to eat of that tree.

What is our own experience of the call? Always, the hero moves beyond established bounds, defying the ruling principle, leaving the tomb of the womb. Seeking the higher womb, we risk that it also may be our tomb. We choose to live. The great and wide may have to become the small and narrow. In the process, resistances are broken and pride, virtue, beauty, life itself are put aside as heroine or hero bows and submits to the intolerable. Swallow or be swallowed. *Yoga* means yoke, binding; *religio* is to re-bind: we are for ever bound by the past, the present, the future.

The quest is to discover, challenge and assimilate our own opposites: danger and opportunity, punishment and freedom, dependency and responsibility, childhood and adulthood, dragon and treasure, poison and healing – can we withstand the recognition that they are not out there, but in here, of the same flesh? Can the ego put itself to death?

We think of Inanna, or Ishtar, hung on a hook in Hell by Ereshkigal; of Persephone ravished into the underworld; Prometheus chained to a rock, his liver pecked out by an eagle. Again, Oedipus, limping to his

---

152 Peregrine: foreign, outlandish, from abroad. OED.
153 Genesis 2:9; 2:17; 3:3; 3:22-24.

'Father, Heaven'

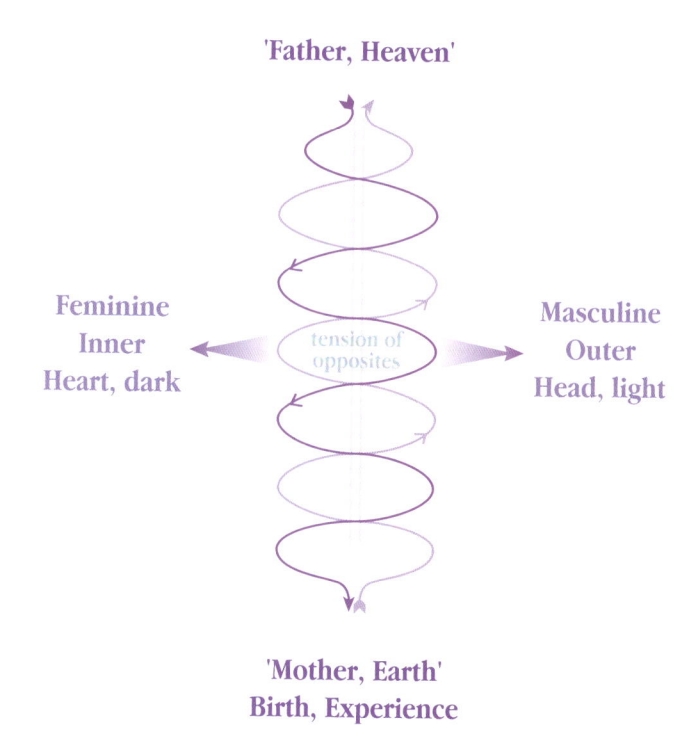

Feminine ← tension of opposites → **Masculine**
Inner **Outer**
Heart, dark **Head, light**

'Mother, Earth'
Birth, Experience

Chart 4:15 – The World Axis

inexorable destiny; and one Ophoros who became Christopher, patron saint of travellers, though he didn't do much travelling himself. With an arrogant pride in his great strength, Ophoros would serve only the greatest. First he served the king, but then he saw how the king feared the devil. So he left the king and served the devil, until one day he discovered that the devil feared the crucifix. So he decided to serve Christ – if he could find him. A priest advised him to *wait*. For many years he stayed by a ford and carried people over the river. One stormy night, a small child came. Ophoros lifted him with ease but the burden grew heavier and heavier so that he barely made it to the opposite shore. He asked the little child why it was so heavy. 'Because I carry the sins of the world,' came the answer. Realising that he had taken Christ, the Self, on his back, he forged on. Giving him remission of sins and eternal life, Christ re-named him Christophoros, carrier of Christ. The whole story is here at one ford, one bridge.

Who is the hero? Symbolic of the divine, creative spark within us all, the hero waits to be known and re-membered into life. To be illumined is to recognise that dismembering is in order to remember. God and hero are together the seeker, together are the goal, the outside and the inside of a single mystery. The heroic task is to come to knowledge of this unity in multiplicity and make it known.

Christ said, *I and my Father are one. I am the door: by me, if any man enter in, he shall be saved, and shall go in and out, and find pasture.*[154] Such symbolic passages take on new sense. In our greatest bondage lies our release, realisation and freedom. The pattern is universal. Attainment leads to re-attainment, discovery to re-discovery, godly powers won lead to the realisation that they were always inside us – we were always there. We arrive, to find we never left the circle.

> *And the end of all our exploring*
> *Will be to arrive where we started*
> *And know the place for the first time.*
> *Through the unknown, remembered gate*
> *When the last of earth left to discover*
> *Is that which was the beginning.*[155]

EXPLORATION
THE DESERT AND THE MOUNTAIN
(45 minutes)

This exploration is the journey of both *mind* and *intuition*; but it is no head trip. The character of the mind has had to be reconstituted into an organ or instrument clear, limpid and simple enough for divine knowledge and guiding intuition to be found and used in service of the soul.

Minutes
6   For this journey, it will be appropriate to recall your earlier sensing into the life of Christ. Start by finding yourself in a desert. Coming towards you are two figures, one dark, one light. You recognise one as your shadow, the dark unconscious side; and the other as the

---
154   John 10: 30 and 10: 9.
155   Eliot, Four Quartets, 'Little Gidding', lines 240-245.

light side. They are, perhaps, the 'tempter' and the one who helps you to resist temptation. Your consciousness has been changed by the Baptism: what temptations are represented by the dark figure? Spend a little time exploring how you may be tempted now, in your new state of consciousness. What is the relation between the dark and the light in your nature?

4   The desert scene fades. Leaving those two figures behind, find yourself moving along a highway. You are alone, but others are travelling the same path. Ahead is your goal, a distant mountain. Spend a few minutes experiencing the journey.

6   As you move on you are joined by several companions with whom you feel a special affinity. They may be known to you, or not. It is as if you have known them for ever. Sense the comradeship you feel with these friends. What are their characteristics? Aim to understand more deeply the quality or energy that links you to them. You are alone but not lonely.

9   You now realise that if you are to reach the mountain you need some training. Nearby you see a *university of light*, where there is a *school of consciousness and wisdom*. You enter, perhaps leaving your companions for the time being. You may find a wise and friendly adviser to help you. Go deep within yourself and, if need be with the help of this adviser, seek what your mind and your intuition need to learn at this stage of the way. Dwell on these symbols or recognitions, and explore their meanings for you.

5   You leave the university of light, perhaps with your companions. The once-distant mountain now seems very close. Soon you reach the foothills and begin to ascend it. Climb almost to the top, *wait*, and look back.

7   Now move to stand on the mountain top itself. There the Initiator, who may have changed or not and is of great wisdom, waits for you and touches your soul with the rod. You experience the integration of all the forces of your nature – body, feelings, mind and intuition – in the energy-field of your soul. Stay in the energy of that integration. Expect some sense of your way ahead, some vision of your true vocation.

4   The Initiator gives you a gift, as token and reminder of this

experience; it is yours to possess for yourself, for others and for the world. Listen to the voice of the silence. Sense into your relation with the Collective. Expect an image or symbol for the next stage of your life, your future task.

4 The experience on the mountain top ends. Find yourself descending into the world and anchoring in the body. When you feel ready, return in consciousness to this present time and place, bringing your gift with you.[156]

THE INITIATES

You can't cross a chasm in two leaps

The initiation on the mountain is the *personal* initiation. In the next, personal and Collective are joined. We saw how each major stage of initiation has common features: the groundwork of the past is tested, the present consolidated, and the future glimpsed or seen in vision. The whole of our nature is involved: intuition, mind, feelings, body. *Karma* is substance transfigured: to change it we must change our substance. Between Baptism and Transfiguration our substance is gradually transmuted, the nature of *karma* changes, our energy-patterns are altered and the quality of our consciousness transformed. Inner and outer symbols coincide and the locus of self-identity shifts from the personality towards the Self. And though the journey of each individual is unique, it is paralleled by similar processes in the Collective.

Before initiation – as, so to say, the *once-born* – we are on the hero's quest, moving out from the cosmic womb towards the circumference of the labyrinth, the world of manifestation and increasing fragmentation – partial, off-centre, labyrinthine, full of disharmony and disorder. Disunited, we miss the mark. This is the *fall*. Falling into error, people and animals no longer speak the same language.

After the second birth we are *twice-born*. On the spiritual quest, returning we find once more the sacred centre within. It is whole, it is one, it is Paradise regained. We have met the Initiator, who is there both at the beginning and at the end, and been touched with the initiatory rod.

---

156 Commentary on the Desert and the Mountain exploration, Appendix 2

Inducted into a new way of being, our perspective and values re-oriented, we have crossed the threshold of the door, been through the testing trial, encountered the polarities, 'the devil', the shadow. Before breakthrough we will have had a period of blindness or blindfolding. Thus 'dying', we have passed from time, been born again into eternity and given into the Father's hands. The wise, the twice-born, realise, even in the womb of time, that they have come from and are returning to eternity and the Father.

The very wise, the *thrice-born*, know that *she*, time, and *he*, eternity, are one and the same substance. The world of time is the womb of the Great Mother. Begotten of the Father, who is beyond time, we are conceived into the womb of time, where life is compounded of *his* light and *her* dark. Here we dwell, removed from the Father. So, in Hindu, Tibetan and other Eastern traditions, Buddhas and Boddhisattvas copulate with their own feminine aspects; Shiva with Shakti. When did we ever leave home?

Who are the initiates? We know who died; but who has been reborn? Such a person has authority, yes. They have withdrawn projections. Their god is the god within. They know how to say No. By the time they reach the mountain top they are neither perfect nor tidy, still subject to error, still sometimes run by the personality. The aim is to serve the whole and they don't do that if they are trying to 'be good'; for the unconscious (Collective and individual) erupts, and conflict, ego with Self, personal with transpersonal. But they listen to God. Where do they find God? It's not about their personal life, decisions, growth, dharma. It is, rather, about their working relationship to the Collective. Where is God but in the conflict?

Initiates, as we've seen, are those *who initiate*. They know because they work, not work because they know (remember Thomas Edison: 'Genius is one per cent inspiration and ninety-nine per cent perspiration'.) They are twice-born to *be* the place, to *be* the work, answerable only to that, not to mother or father, daughter, brother or anyone else. No longer is it a conscious struggle, endless questioning or questing. Sacrifice – making sacred – is not required, because all is already sacred. Now there is less introversion, less self-absorption, less needing to *know*. They can make great efforts, write books, do their life-work, their real research. Total commitment is required and given, a quiet determination to *walk on*, whatever. Though they will have been 'tired to death', though their bodies are tough as old boots to have survived, yet they can walk on because of the strength beyond. Here is the patience of eternity, all impatience gone in the face of death – and why rush further along *his* road? The body of an initiate is now becoming the body of immortality, of resurrection.

> *From wrong to wrong the exasperated spirit*
> *Proceeds, unless restored by that refining fire*
> *Where you must move in measure, like a dancer.*[157]

EXPLORATION
CONTEMPLATION
(10 minutes)

In this workshop, you have been to a door in a rock face, and found the jewel in your heart. You have explored the water of your feeling life, and been baptised. You have been to the university of light, and travelled to the mountain. You have met your true friends and companions on the way; explored your own myth. You have met the initiator – been initiated.

> Go to a quiet place and contemplate your life, now that you are initiated into a new energy, the energy-field of your soul.

> And, bringing your gifts with you, return into the world, in your turn to help to enrich and enlighten the Collective.[158]

---

157 Eliot, *Four Quartets*, 'Little Gidding', lines 144-146.
158 Suggested programme and original reading list for the workshop, Appendices 5 and 6.

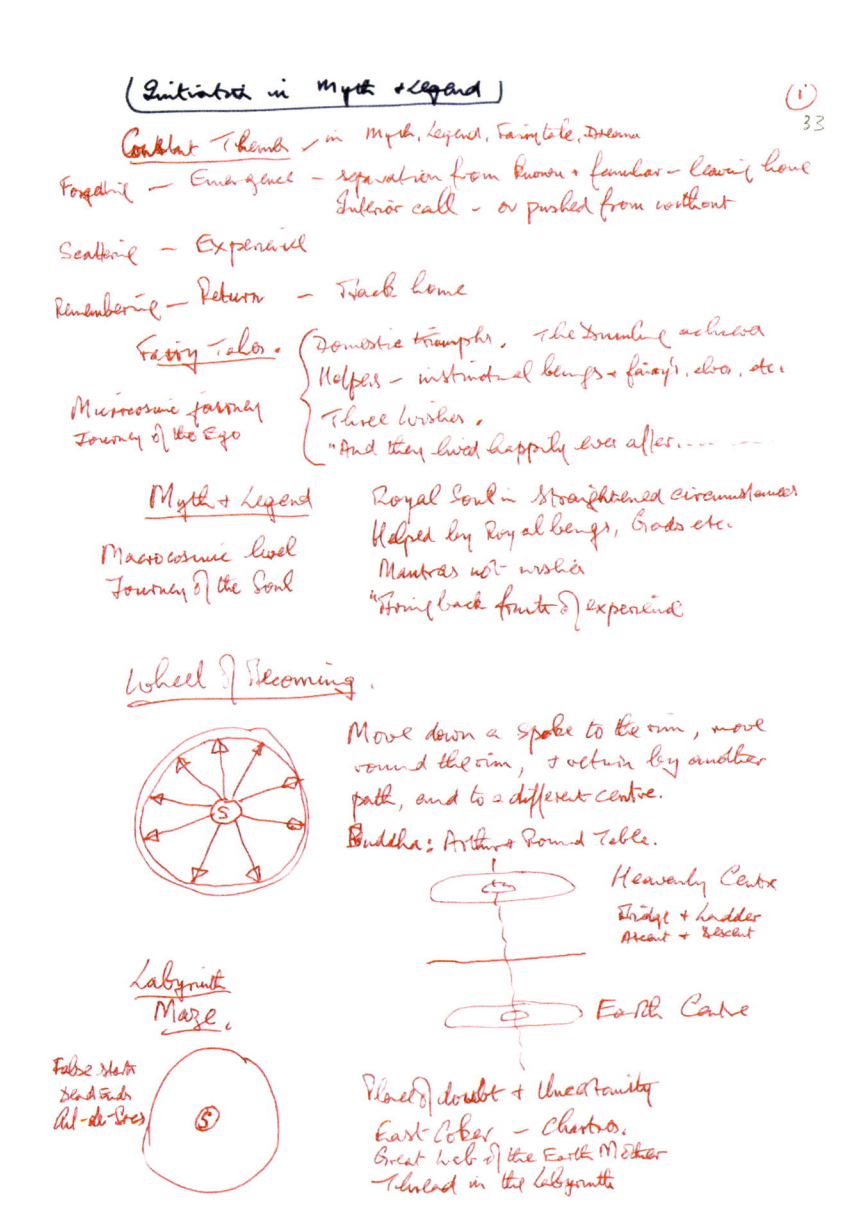

Facsimile of notes: Ian Gordon-Brown

CHAPTER FIVE

The Other Self

Workshop V

Barbara Somers and Ian Gordon-Brown

The jewel is lost in the mud, and all are seeking for it;
some look for it in the east, and some in the west;
some in the water and some amongst stones.
But the servant Kabîr has appraised it at its true value,
and has wrapped it with care in the end of the mantle of his heart.

Kabir[159]

INTRODUCING THE WORKSHOP [160]

Singing Stone

Once upon a time there was a young warrior among the Sioux.[161] He went North, East, South, West, searching all the way, experiencing the many different aspects of himself. His journey home was round and round.

When a member of the Sioux 'took the pipe', he would hold it up stem to the sky so that the Sun could take the first puff, then address the Four Directions. Joseph Campbell pointed out how, in that frame of mind, addressing ourselves to the horizon – to the world – we are in our place.[162]

He knew that he had been named after the most sacred object: Singing Stone. His task was to find the true Singing Stone. Though difficult, this quest probably wouldn't take very long, since he was brave and had a good horse. The Elders told him to set out towards the North.

With his horse he travelled for months Northward and had many adventures, finally reaching the far and frozen lands towards the Pole. He sought the wise men of this rough, rocky, barren place of ice-caves and snow. Could they help him find the Singing Stone? 'No', they said, 'you must search to the East.'

---

159 Kabir, 15th Century Hindu/Sufi mystic. *Songs of Kabîr*, No. LXXII.
160 Some notes on the running of an aspect of this workshop are given in Appendices 1 and 2. No programmes are suggested for this or subsequent workshops.
161 This Native American story is also told in Somers & Gordon-Brown 2002, *Journey in Depth*, pp. 250-252.
162 The Faiths of the Cheyenne People, Appendix 12.

Remembering his home and his own people, he continued his journey in a wide sweep towards the Rising Sun. After many further adventures he reached the Mountains of the Morning. Here at last in this beautiful land – these wide spaces, windswept hills – must be the Singing Stone. 'The North was not the way for me!' However, the Singing Stone was not here either. The wise men of the East told him: 'You must go South'.

By now the young brave was not so young. He was growing tired. His horse died: sorrowfully, he left it buried among the people of the East. Thinking with longing of home, he summoned his strength and set out Southwards, alone and on foot, to fulfil his quest. He crossed many huge rivers in spate, traversed or went round great lakes. After narrowly avoiding drowning he reached the South; but the Singing Stone was not there.

The journey to the West was the hardest yet. Long and weary was this lonely push into the heat of the desert sun. He travelled by night, sometimes with fellow travellers, usually all alone. Heat and thirst befuddled his brain. He longed for the cool lands of home, for his own people. He longed just to *stop*. But, compelled by the Singing Stone, he travelled on. Many a time, exhausted and in despair. he thought that he would die before he reached the lands of the Western tribes. And they too told him: 'No, you won't find the Singing Stone here!' He had travelled to all the four quarters of the earth seeking the Singing Stone, and it didn't exist...

Disappointed, disillusioned, old and tired, he began the long journey home. He came over the hill. There was the circle of the tepees and the totem of his people. It looked the same, and yet different. But what was this? The children were pouring out from the settlement to greet him. They were expecting him. They *knew* him, they called to him from afar with welcome in their voices, they led him into his own place to be refreshed and rested. The Council of Elders, in full panoply, welcomed him. They had a great feast ready for him; they brought him to the centre and called him by his name: 'Singing Stone! We greet you, returned from your search. You have faithfully followed the call. You have found your true name, your sacred treasure. Welcome home, Singing Stone! Know now that *you* are your own Quest; you *are* Singing Stone.'

EXPLORATION
THE JOURNEY THROUGH THE FOUR ELEMENTS
(45 minutes)

Singing Stone's story is found among tribes and peoples everywhere because, though first we seek to *discover* the goal – questing and searching for the stone, the *lapis* – at last we *become* it.

This four-stage exploration invites you to experience the tension of opposites, as well as the *third position* which may come in. In each of the four quarters there will be ten minutes or more, to explore the elements (Earth, Water, Air, Fire) in whatever order you wish, allowing the most significant life-experiences in that element to be evoked and noted. Feedback, discussion and comment in small groups will follow.

Minutes

2 So, begin by becoming quiet. Be in touch with your intuition, dynamic and always able to open to potential, to change. When you're ready, find an inward place to serve as the Centre from which to go out and return at each stage. Be at this central starting point of your life. Let the present fall away. Be at the beginning of things.

8 Now for the *first element* of your choice, Water or Fire, Air or Earth. Experience it, get accustomed to its energy, quality, feeling, possibilities and sensations. How have you experienced this element in your life – in places, in work, in relationships both inner and outer? What are your feelings about it in terms of the past, the present and the future? When you're ready, begin to return to your Centre. Has its energy changed? Record in pictures or writing, noting keywords, making simple headline notes to remind you.

2 Centre yourself again, quieten and be in touch with your intuition. Be very much in your own space. Begin to be led towards the second quarter.

8 And when you are ready, journey into the *second element*. Explore it thoroughly, sensing it, noting your feelings and thoughts. Be aware of the body. Note the quality, the energy and the possibilities of it.

2 Rest back and return to your centre. Again, quieten and allow yourself to be in your intuition.

8   Be led to the third quarter, moving towards the *third element* of your choice, exploring and experiencing it. Where and how does it play a part in your actual life, past, present and future? Be aware of places, activities, work, play, relationships; note yourself and your reactions.

2   Once again, be inwardly still.

8   Let your intuition lead you to the *fourth element*, and do the same things.

2   Finally, what is the meaning of the order of your journey?

3   At the end, gather them all together at the centre.

DIRECTIONS, ELEMENTS AND FUNCTIONS [163]

The only thing I know is that I do not know.

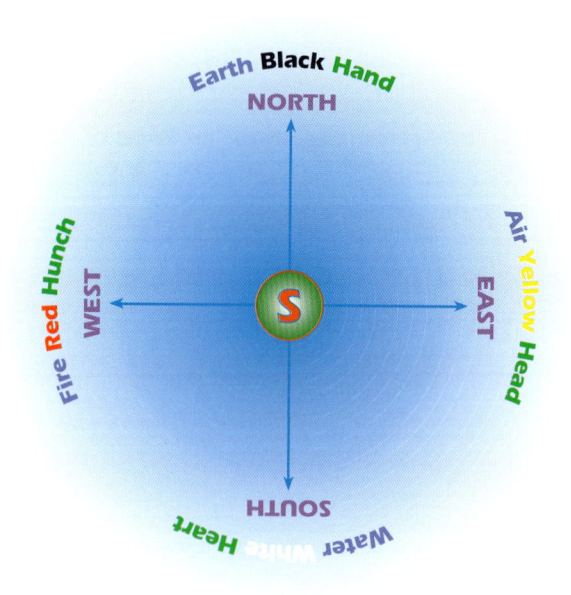

Chart 5:01 – The Four Directions

---

163   The Four Functions: developed from Chapter 1, pp. 48 et seq.

THE OTHER SELF   231

Our fundamental journey through the *four directions*, which also involve the *four elements*, Earth, Air, Water and Fire, is linked with individuation and usually involves testing. It is often shown in mandala form to represent the ego with the Self at the centre.[164] We have seen how our spiral circumambulation bears in from the periphery towards the hub, sometimes through a labyrinth, sometimes a spiral centred on the cross of the Self. The directions are the arms, with gateways both external and internal for exploring the elements. Singing Stone moved out from the centre, up the arm of the cross, to circumambulate the four directions and four elements in a circle or square or spiral, bearing in at last from the periphery to rediscover the centre.

The four functions typology

In Workshop One we saw how Jung recognised Sensation, Feeling, Thinking and Intuition as the four ways by which we interact with the

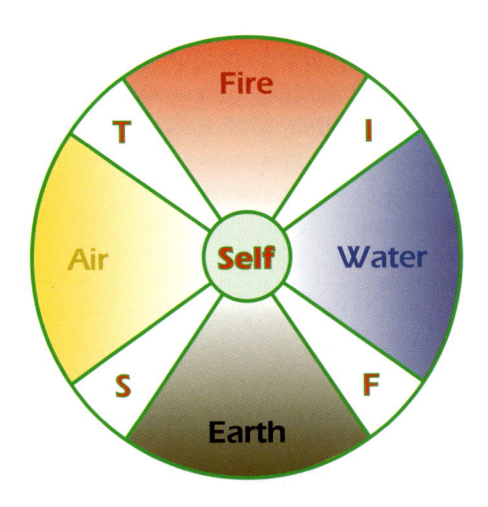

1.	**Fire;**	intuitive,	speculative thinking;	**Red**
2.	**Air;**	empirical,	practical thinking;	**Yellow**
3.	**Water;**	intuitive,	diffuse feeling;	**Blue**
4.	**Earth;**	grounded,	sensory feeling;	**Black**

Chart 5:02 – Elements and Functions

---

164 Mandala: often a circle containing a square containing a triangle in which is a dot. The triangle is the nature of the Self; the square's fourfold, directional shape is for wholeness. The circling of the square in a *circumambulatio* represents the understanding of the fourfold nature of the universe. Sometimes God is the dot in the triangle in the square in the circle. Argüelles 1972, *Mandala*.

world: Hand, Heart, Head and Hunch.[165] Though we draw them as a cross, we tend to forget the Self in the middle. While the Functions offer four gateways in and out of the mandala,[166] *they are not* the part of us that is seeking to become whole. Ideally, all four would contribute equally in our lives and we would live in total awareness. However, they don't; one usually leads and the other three are in the background. Although the map is flexible and we try to alter it to fit ourselves, it's difficult to change it altogether. So *sensation* types may be aware only of what they see and do; those over-caught into *thinking* become narrow-minded pedants; heart-based people majoring in *feeling* come to see all as either good or bad; while the highly *intuitive*, relying on hunch alone, may simply be out of touch. Each thinks nothing else counts. The Self is lost.

The Way of the Snake. Do we remain so polarised, fixed into our natural and inherent way of being in the world? Is only Head *or* Heart *or* Hand *or* Hunch familiar? Do the unfamiliar functions calcinate and die? It is said that Jung argued that it's *not* so fixed. It is a dynamic wheel. Certainly we can't usually go from the most differentiated straight to the least, and many people will be scarcely conscious even of their auxiliary second and third functions. Yet we can develop 'by way of the snake'. A naturally *feeling* person, for instance, may not readily develop the polar opposite, *thinking*, but the mature self can eventually encompass it if *sensation* and *intuition* first become conscious. Like threads that show only on the back of the tapestry, out of sight, the colours need to be brought through into the pattern on the front. So we draw forth extra healing from within, making towards wholeness.

The Turn-type. Our fixed maps may evolve less by the slow way of the snake than by the dynamic, moving pattern of Chart 1:20, The Dynamic Turn-type. Instead of projecting our failures onto people around, we get on the move. We don't turn the wheel; *it turns us*. The Other Self, our pole star, takes the centre of the compass. We are oriented to our own lode-star, the true Self. Forced as it were towards the hub of the Wheel of Fortune and away from the rim, we grow by pressure on our being to action. Even the hurts, difficulties and appalling things that happen are useful. For instance, one of the four functions, say *intuition*, will be driven right down through 180° by some trauma – perhaps most cruelly. But then the wheel turns and up it comes, carrying its own light with it. We now have experience of its being both up and down; we've

---

165   Chart 1:19, The Way of the Snake, p. 55.
166   Argüelles 1972, ibid, p. 62, inter alia.

been moved away from *fixatio* to *coagulatio*: adamant, hard diamond, clear and reflective. This is the stone both tender and strong, the gentle strength and power of Singing Stone.

Each of us has our own myth, as did Singing Stone, but we get stuck. We wait for permission – for even one other person to say, 'It's all right; go ahead and be you!' *In therapy*, we aim to create and hold for the client the *temenos*, the precinct of the temple sacred to the ritual, the place of safeguarding, of respect for the person and what is about to happen. Moving towards wholeness means rediscovering their myth, fulfilling their unique potential, figures stepping in from the unconscious to parent the hurt child, reconnecting with the roots. The killing wound heals. The ugly duckling raised by the hen is terrified to go in the water, but he's also driven mad by the hen-nature of his mother (remembering that *too perfect* a mother, not only a terrible one, may leave him beautiful but with no life). Now their inner imagery reaches and joins past, present and future. The ugly duckling goes at last into the water and swims.

As counsellors, our practice makes legitimate parts of *ourselves* with which we have difficulty. We're drawn to heal others' wounds to heal our own. And that is all right. However, it's well to remember: *gain a counsellor, lose a friend*.

THE 'INFERIOR FUNCTION'

Myths show how the voice of salvation is at the bottom of the abyss, how the darkest time heralds the light, the real message of transformation.
Joseph Campbell[167]

Where do you *suffer*? What is your Achilles heel? Where do you habitually feel put down? Or cock it up? Or fail to respond as you should? This is the least differentiated function: 'inferior', to stay with Jung's original term. However developed we may be, it remains a burden we carry around. And it's not just the *feeling* function; ours may be *intuition*, *sensation* or *thinking*. Whichever – slow, weak and crippled – it is hypersensitive, barbaric, primitive and inappropriate.

---

167 See Campbell 1988, *The Power of Myth*, p. 37.

Yet it's central to us; it's what we value most, the door to new life, the Redeemer. It mediates the shadow, or God, or the way in for the Self. Here, the polarities of the ego (love or hate, good or bad, right or wrong, light or dark) give way to a more fundamental, positive pull to the centre. The inferior function brings the numinous, for peak experiences don't come by the easiest route. It may be the fourth that has been missing from the Trinity. Indeed, it's the very devil.... We project it, our own Incredible Hulk. It triggers a high emotional charge or affect; we fall in love through it. And are we touchy in this area! Someone's heavy boots are on our eggshells. Our reactions are dead slow: we don't know what we feel till later; even then we respond inappropriately. Our inferior function is quite infantile; it hasn't grown up yet. It gets the timing all wrong. It absolutely cannot take criticism, thus betraying which one it is.

> *Inferior feeling* is both childish and explosive. There may be a silent and powerful attachment to people, or sudden conversions to whole systems of ideas and beliefs.
>
> *Inferior sensation* makes the world of *things* seem inimical; Sod's Law predominates. We do things clumsily, at snail's pace; changing a light bulb is a big deal. Out of touch with the body, yet we may be passionately in love with nature.
>
> *Inferior thinking* means getting the wrong end of the stick. Unable to organise our thoughts, full of second-hand opinions, we can't think a thing through. We may be cynical, even tyrannical or, conversely, too gullible, accepting other people's ideas without a backward glance.
>
> *Inferior intuition.* When *sensation* runs out of steam, up comes Cassandra, a dark light from behind, apocalyptic and intuitively filled with catastrophic superstition. She grabs us. Hypochondriac and fearful, we suffer a primitive dread, childish and hopeless.[168]

If all four functions come out as inferior, then a great deal of work has gone before....

As counsellors, we may deal with various crises without having experienced those *particular* things ourselves. We can help with relationships, for instance, even though we're not in one now, because we have ourselves been in the land of crisis and gained experience and awareness there. From our own recoil into inevitable reaction, our own

---

168 Keirsey & Bates 1984, *Please Understand Me*.

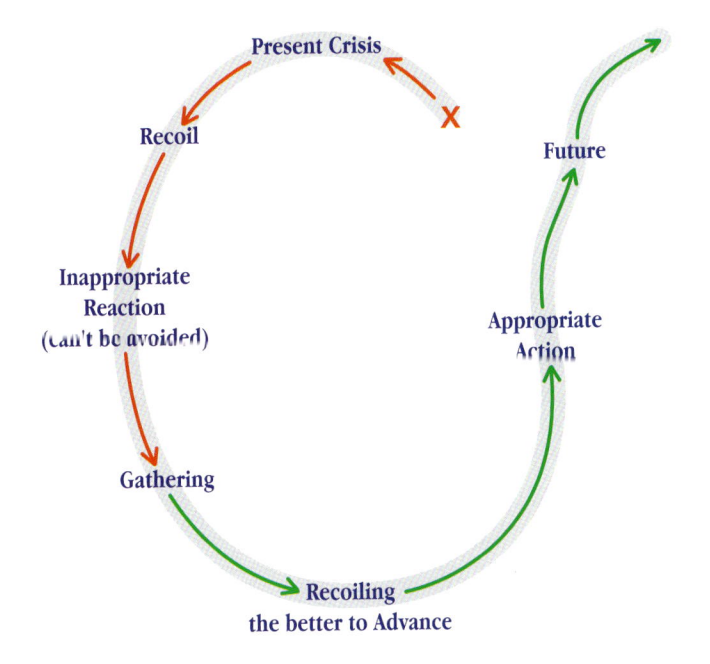

Chart 5:03 – Crisis and Nourishment

gathering of nourishment in the depths, we know how the recoil may become the drawn bow that moves us into the future. So our personal difficulties may meet the client's different ones and each enrich the other. In fact, we may be better at handling traumas *not* our own; less drawn in emotionally, we can stand more firmly on the rock.

Therapeutic people who attract stories of others' problems are still bleeding, still struggling themselves. The difference between counsellor and client is that, as counsellors, we have an underlying trust: there is a bridge.[169] If the client's ego-identity is shaken, we take a stand beside them, holding the bridge at their personality's end of it, however inadequately; and our own end may shake with doubt and effort. We help them hold their inadequacy, their dreams, the masculine and feminine, the parents. We are beside them when archetypal images appear, helping them face these irruptions from the unconscious. We stand up for their identity in this world. We are *with* them – but not *in* their trouble. We see their world as if it were our own, but only *as if*; remembering always that if

---

[169] Yet psychotherapists, as well as doctors, dentists and analysts, have a high suicide rate. If, as can be, they lose this trust, may they not hand on their despair?

they haven't the ego structure to be responsible, then as counsellors we haven't the skill to deal with them.

About *transference*: strictly speaking, neither counsellor nor psychotherapist is supposed to work with it – only the analyst. But transference is in all human relations. Taking someone's hand when they are in a dark place, helping them hold it till they can stand on their own – this *is* transference.

EXPLORATION
THE DOOR AND THE MIRROR
(35 minutes)

This exploration is about the soul's quest for wholeness through the functions, particularly the 'inferior' function. We go through the mirror of the ego in pursuit of the Other Self, looking for the crossing of a threshold and initiation into new life. Slowly *by way of the snake*, (see the *yin yang* symbol) or as *turn-types*, to navigate through life we do need all four. At least we work out who we're *not*, what we're most *un*conscious of, what is inaccessible. If the most differentiated, 'superior' function gets tired, the least differentiated comes to the rescue and sees us home. Befriend it.

Rather explore than make declarations. Here is a journey into your own map.

Minutes

2   Begin by finding yourself in a place that is home. From here you will be going on a short journey towards unfamiliar territory. As you set out, know that you are moving towards the house or place of the *wise being*; or it may be the house or place where wisdom can be found. Here you will receive something you need to know. When you arrive, knock and wait quietly.

4   A *wise being* or *wise presence* will come and take you to a special room where there are a *door*, and a *mirror*. The wise being explains that you will need a Talisman[170] for the journey, to accompany you on the next stage. Take a little time with the wise being, getting to know the room, the door and the mirror, and finding your Talisman.

8   The wise being explains that you are to make two journeys to the

---

170   The talisman, see Chapter 6, p. 270.

other side of life: one via the mirror, the other via the door. On the other side, on each journey, you will meet an aspect of yourself. You may choose to take the first journey through either the door or the mirror, and the second through the other. When you are ready, choose one of them, and go through it. There you will find an aspect (or it may be, aspects) of yourself, who lives *only just* on the other side of your life. This aspect will tell you about themselves and their world; and of how it is when they interact with you, or appear back on your personality's side of life.

You may wish to ask questions: What was I at first? What am I today? How has the compass turned, and how often? As a child? Today? Which functions have turned up? Which have turned down?

8   After a while, return to the room of the wise being, who explains you will now, secondly, go through the other (the mirror or the door). You will meet another aspect of your nature, one who lives almost *exclusively* on the other side of your life. When you meet that second aspect or aspects, let it, or them, show you where they may have influenced your life without your knowing. Again, you may wish to ask questions.

8   Finally, take your Talisman and go even deeper to where these two aspects dwell. When it is appropriate, ask them if they will come with you to talk under the guidance of the wise being. So, asking those you have met to come with you, return to the special room. They can go back to their world whenever they wish. Take a few minutes to explore any issues with them.

5   See the inhabitants of the other side of your life return whence they came. Thank the wise being for guidance and hospitality, and ask for an image or symbol to represent what you need to know from these meetings. As they all return to their own world, come back yourself to a place of safety.

Make notes and pictures. You may wish to draw a map of your own *inferior function*, perhaps putting an X in a circle, with the Self in the centre and the functions spiralling out from it.[171]

---

171   Commentary on the Door and the Mirror exploration, Appendix 2.

ALCHEMY AND THE ELEMENTS

*We are continuously taken where we are not,
in order to become who we are*

In his confrontation with the unconscious, Jung was looking for a scientific language for what he was observing and experiencing, both with his patients and with himself. He described how a dream in which he got stuck in the 17th century led him to study Alchemy.[172] He acquired an old Latin tome on the subject but didn't read it, thinking 'Good Lord, what nonsense! This stuff is impossible to understand'. But it persistently intrigued him; he followed it up and soon found it provocative and exciting. He realised that, though almost completely incomprehensible, it spoke the language of symbols, his old acquaintances. He knew he must learn from the very beginning to decipher it, crack the code. And he did, and it took him ten years.[173]

He soon found that alchemy coincided curiously with his own analytical psychology, and that the experiences of the old alchemists were parallel with his own. Without history, there can be no psychology of the unconscious; to explain the secret of the personality, which was his declared idea and goal, we need to go deeper than our own personal lives.

Alchemy goes in stages; so too does our inner development. The process can no more be hurried in aiming for Self-realisation than in trying to turn base metal to gold. And the true alchemists, the *adepts*, were aiming for the one as much as, or more than, the other. The false alchemists, the *puffers*, were those who used the bellows too much; but it is chemistry, or internal process, that does the work.

First the old alchemists took the *prima materia*. They put it in the flask, sealed the cap hermetically and set it to the fire till it was cooking – in 'a nice cooking heat'.[174] Inherent within this basic raw material lay gold – lay divinity. It had to be discovered, retrieved and put in a flask, or *alembic*, which must be created externally and was very difficult to make. It had to be crystal or glass, hermetically sealed at a special heat in a special oven.

The mystery is, what was the basic material – what is it for us? In the dark, the shit, lies the adamant and unchanging gold. So too for the

---

172 Jung 1963, *Memories, Dreams, Reflections*, pp. 228 ff.
173 The four stages of Western Alchemy: Somers 2004, in *The Fires of Alchemy*, deals with the subject in detail.
174 See von Franz 1979, her wonderful Lecture 1, 'Origins of Alchemy', in *Alchemical Active Imagination*, pp. 1-20.

Alchemists. Their life-experience, and ours, is the mess, the mass, the clay, the *massa confusa*. First we gather this *prima materia*, all we have been and are, the thing wherein is the treasure, and then the four transmutation processes will turn it to eternal gold. Or that's the idea.

The stages of alchemy

We recall that, in the individuation process, there is a sense of journey, a circumambulation bearing in on the centre, the Self. Jung had explored, both externally and internally, the mandala shape of the four elements and of his four functions.[175] Finding that the circle (of the circumambulation) and the square (the fourfold, directional shape) are fundamental motifs within the psyche, he studied recondite texts, his vast reading revealing that alchemy also offered *four* basic stages, all with several names. They go roughly with the four directions, *nigredo* with North, *solutio* East, *coagulatio* South and *sublimatio* with the West. They involve trials by fire, water, earth and air.

He saw how we need not remain one-sided – the wheel can turn. Together with the old alchemists, we come to the first stage: the *massa confusa*, the stuff of our lives to date, is submitted to heat in the flask which is the body. (I would emphasise that these stages vary with individuals; we may go through them many times and in any order, and they overlap. We can map onto them experiences both tiny and huge. We are squaring the circle.)

Nigredo – the first heat

This is the blackening stage, also known as the *calcinatio* or *mortificatio*, where the 'death of the old king' takes place and the ruling principle of the ego dies. We leave home; and the path often leads *down*. Our parents' scripts, our outgrown authoritarian principles, assumptions, stereotypes – all lose their power as, reduced to black ash, we descend below earth into heaviness, loss, confusion, depression, thwarted rage. 'Let me out!' we yell, as the ego-light dims into darkness and hell-fire. This *putrefactio*, this darkness of the pits where we can't look back, is marked often by questioning, re-valuing and the need to *surrender*.

It is described as a time of unbearable tension, of infinite trickery. 'I'm in a pressure-cooker,' someone said. 'Trapped in an ivory tower!' from another. We learn to remain there, trusting, despite the dread that if we let

---

175 From the simplicity of the dot (which is God) in the triangle of the Self in the square of the elements in the circle of the ego, we move to the equal-armed cross of Earth which may be formed of functions within the circle and square. An eye, a flower, a fountain may represent the dot, the triangle may become a six-pointed star in the square in the circle in another triangle in another circle – which is God. See Argüelles 1972, *Mandala*.

go – what will we be? With nothing to hold on to, alienated as in Munch's 'The Scream', will we fall into the pit? People tell of confusion, being not themselves, out of control and out of focus, often in deep depression. Death is around, and an envying of the dead: 'I was in complete loneliness and despair – life just wasn't worth it.' Weighted by rage and anger, one wrote: 'I'm in a dark hall. The snake is rising from within!' Another: 'I don't fit in, I want to break out!' 'I can hardly breathe.' 'I'm like a bat out of hell!'

The *calcinatio* involves complete dryness. 'I'm just a husk of me – isolated in a desert.' It's a relentless stripping with no way back. Disorientated and 'mashed down', we are forced to go on through an arid landscape. Highest inflation is the danger: we certainly need to be companioned in this deepest *Trial by Fire*.

Albedo – the second heat

Neptune, Moon, Mercury. More heat is applied to the mass until the black begins to turn grey. It vaporises, dissolving in the *solutio*, the watery, lunar, feminine stage of dissolution, and the steam of the soul rises. The corpse of the old king is shown, with cherubs ascending in the steam. What was hard, rigid, fixed has to become fluid, mutable, 'drowned in moon-fluid'. Grief, loss, bereavement are washed through by tears, the necessary libation of the heart. This internal weeping affords an exquisite sensitivity. We fear we'll never stop. The solar light of the ego is fragmented into a spectrum and gathered again into a pale light, a whitening. We are drowned in the lunar light of a new kind of consciousness. The masculine and feminine, which had been projected out, are internalised. We become open and vulnerable, no longer closed and untouched.

The *solutio* is about feelings: love, attachment and letting go. This second heat signifies willingness to continue the process. Volition comes into play, the gutsy ability to go on and keep walking. The ego has to be overcome and drowned in vapour. Physically, water-retention may indicate a fear of letting go. Within the flask, two dragons fight and kill each other with their own poison. We fall into a different death. As the ash begins to turn grey, *water* comes from it. We can't be substantial, everything's awash, unfixed, melting. 'I am humiliated by my weeping.' Ice and snow turn back to water. 'For me, it's sitting in the bath and my heart's breaking,' said someone. 'I'm holding back a tidal wave,' said another. 'Down in my boots and waterlogged!'

Might they experience the water as, though wet, yet warm and comfortable? Images are often oceanic: 'I'm adrift in a boat – in the sea – breathing under water – pearl diving – sitting at the bottom of the ocean'. The counsellor might suggest they build an ark, or hope a dinghy will come alongside. 'It's healing after the struggle.' At last, the *solutio* may be felt as having no boundaries, pending freedom. 'The teeming waters are a relief – the relief of rain – no more splits!' Separateness, merging and confusion become indistinguishable and new perception is gained; what had been projected onto outer men and women is internalised. It is *Trial by Water*.

The old alchemists had to carry out many washings. Let's hope for us there may be a Washerwoman, washed herself by the oceanic experience of love and joy, helping us through this *batismo* or *ablutio* stage to a different understanding of love. We are purified by this washing. It turns eventually into the Peacock's Tail, *cauda pavonis*, where the white light breaks for a moment into the spectrum of seven colours; then they too vanish, and all turns to silver-white. *Aurora*, the new dawn of understanding and perception, has risen, silver out of the white.

This baptism too is dangerous. We're pure, we're lily white, we think we're twice-born – not a once-born washerwoman. It's at this stage that we set up religions.

Citrinitas – the third heat

Jupiter, Saturn. At this lovely stage, we lift out of water on to dry land. The fire is lessened to 'a gentle, lenient heat' and we come back to *earth*, our own ground. All has been flexible, fluid; now, moisture gathers, soft and pliable, cohering in a new way. The ruling principle has been dissolved; this-or-that has given way to both this-and-that. A vapour of the soul is raised, forming white-gold which becomes the yellow-gold of a new dawn, *citrinitas*. We are beginning to cohere. Also called the *coagulatio*, this stage is about endurance, holding, standing, keeping clear. So we are made coherent, hardening yet flexible, coming together and uniting in a bond of earth.

This yellowing of the gold is the ultimate stage for many Western alchemists, a time of great danger and great opportunity bringing new understanding, new perception. Where our soul had previously been opposed to earth, now it comes back into the body, embodying us, uniting the opposites – feminine and masculine, head and heart. We begin to understand the third that rises out of dualism in the mysterious mystical marriage. All that has been gives birth to the divine child, *Mercurius*, the philosopher's son.

Towards the end of this stage comes on the final heat, the highest yet, raising the spirit out of the flask. The alchemist is tired. And now he has to commit even more to hold the fire at top heat. We, too, really do need to stay with it now. Increased tension – aeonic tiredness – the weariness of many lifetimes – we're walking up hill through treacle. 'So much to work on! Will it hold?' We steady the pace, learn to let go. *Trial by Earth* or *Trial by Air*, this. We're making a soufflé: 'This is it! Now I can let go!' But the oven door may yet slam. So we start again.

If not, we may become cosmic boy-scouts, setting out to save the world with fairy-gold. Feet off the ground, a bubble of hot air lifts us off. Inflation! How to tell if we're inflated? We listen to ourselves for the messianic urge to salvage souls. If people vanish when we approach them with the panacea.... Usually, we need to get on and salvage our own. People who claim to be high teachers are really in the foothills. It's a phase; but one where we can be dangerous to our fellows. The kingdom is almost under our feet – and what do we do with it? We must withhold assumptions and wait for the coagulation. Is this indeed our ground. If so, 'On this I stand, by this only can I live'. Parsifal (like the alchemist – like us) misses it, being too quick. Believing we have the philosopher's stone, we drop it. The *citrinitas* is as dangerous as the others.

And then, though it needn't come in classical order:

Rubedo – the inner fire [176]

Jupiter, Sun. This is the reddening, the pure red gold. All is raised to heaven, sublimated to the Other Self. The alchemists' aim was to 'raise spirit' in the highest offering, highest fire of this *sublimatio*. This is *Fire beyond Fire, Fire of Air*, the tincture of the gold of the pure essence of the Self, the supreme attention with no tension. On Jupiter's altar of sacrifice, all we were, are and shall be has been placed as an offering. Soul and body are burned by the light of this fire. It goes out in the light of common day, and it needs recharging all the time.

The Christian cross, made of the vertical of the spirit and the crosspiece of personhood, is about sacrifice; it is where the ego tried to block the Self with a flood of shame, a sense of failure, a discounting. But

---

176 Somers 2004, *The Fires of Alchemy*, Chapters 4-7, 'Calcinatio', 'Albedo', 'Coagulatio', 'Sublimatio' respectively.

'sacrifice' means to make sacred, not to give up. Now the cross-bar moves down to make the equal-armed cross of resurrection, of wholeness. This is Easter to all the Good Fridays before. From Gethsemane, Christ is off the cross. It is accomplished. The two selves begin to coincide and become as one, a golden link in the Hermetic chain of the alchemists.

This stage belongs with the second half of life; the warriors recognised Singing Stone on his *return*. But remember – there is still the passage to hell before the resurrection. 'Embrace doubt as you would your concubine', moving through doubt towards certainty.

For us, this reddening is often the red-gold of *humour*. Consider the different forms taken by the element carbon: a piece of coal – a diamond. Raised to heaven, our consciousness is transformed. Fixed and solid, it doesn't fluctuate, yet is flexible. The sun is rising through the heavens and won't be dimmed. The stone is made adamant; this is the quintessence, the elixir, the precious fluid, the divine pill. It is the lapis, the simple stone, foursquare and grey. Singing Stone.

> *Here lies the mean uncomely stone,*
> *'Tis very cheap in price.*
> *The more it is despised by fools,*
> *The more loved by the wise.*

EXPLORATION
JOURNEY TO THE OTHER SELF
(35 minutes)

The ego has accomplished much, rounding out consciousness. The second exploration – a deeper and more profound search for the Self, the essence – needs preparation. Every important journey calls for wise decision: how to travel, what posture or dress for the persona, what to take, what to leave behind, what to offer up to the Self.

Minutes
- 4 So find yourself in some quiet centre, perhaps one from which you previously journeyed. Spend the next few minutes preparing to travel to the place of the Self.
- 5 You may be joined by two companions: firstly, a Talisman, as mentor and support to help you overcome obstacles. Secondly an

inner or outer *friend*. This friend knows the way to the Self. Expect your friend to appear, and choose your Talisman.

8 Now, with your companions, you set out on the journey. Spend time travelling towards the place of the Self. On the way you may face difficulties or challenges or tasks, each of which is a necessary preparation for the approach to the Self. When you meet these trials or obstacles, do what you have to do, with the help of both Talisman and friend.

6 You attain a vision of the central mandala where the Self is to be found, an inner place set in a sacred precinct. You journey to the outer court of this sacred precinct, the Temple of the Self. Wait in the outer court – you do not yet enter the place where the Self resides. Now your friend and your Talisman can go no further. You leave them behind: you have to move to the mystery of the Self alone. Prepare yourself.

3 When you are ready, move from the outer court towards the sacred interior space. Spend a little time outside but near this inner precinct where the Self is to be found; experience its energy.

6 And then, when you are ready, search for some way of entry – perhaps a secret door leads to the inner sanctum, the holy of holies, where the mystery of the Self resides. For the next ten minutes, approach if you can the Self; and be with whatever part of the Self you are ready to receive at this stage of your life.

3 When you are ready, make your way back to this world. Those who return slowly, come slowly. Those who return quickly, come, then rest and record. There is plenty of time.

THE OTHER SELF

If you play hide and seek with God, take care you don't hide so effectively that He can't discover you.
From 'The Cloud of Unknowing'[177]

Just as astronomy before Copernicus and Galileo was earth-centred, with the sun and planets revolving around our world, so we tend to have

---
[177] By an English Mystic of the 14th Century..

the *ego* in the middle of our own maps, the centre of our universe. The pre-Copernican world view was like that of the child; and to the childish mind, the small self *is* in the centre. Any idea that the sun was in the middle was strongly resisted as a blasphemy by the stuffier of the old philosophers, who really did think man was the centre of the Universe; a pre-Galilean treatise stated: 'Horses' excrement is sweetly scented because God knew Man would spend a lot of time with horses'.

Set the four functions at the four ends of a cross. Typically, our journeys have been through two of the functions and included only positive aspects of the third – we have lived quite well with *thinking* and *sensation*, allowing only positive *feeling*, backing off and avoiding any deeper awareness; *intuition* is unconscious, down at six o'clock. After all, we don't really *have* to develop the fourth, or even the third. However, remember Singing Stone – the *four* directions; the *four* stages of alchemy; the Trinity with the Devil, or the Mother, as the inferior function. Awareness of the four-fold, rather than three-fold, nature of the psyche is essential.

Every new discovery is also a loss. The ego resists coming off the centre. The Self has to reassert. Jung saw it as a pattern, the ego moving spiral-wise around the centred Self.[178] And the true Self grows closer and more distinct, a magnet for disparate members of our nature, our personality. As it draws nearer, the little ego runs round and round the central point like a frightened animal, terrified, always in flight, yet steadily drawn in.

For many, when the outer world runs dry and ceases to appease the hero's appetite for life, hunger and emptiness follow. The salt and savour are lost to deadness, flatness, yearning and longing. Outer experience fails us; we recoil, retire hurt, turn in on ourselves, seek another to sub-stand our sense of defeat. Often there is internal wondering and questioning: 'There may be, there must be something else?' Alan Watts told how a park keeper asked Schopenhauer, whose small dog wandered on to the flowerbeds: 'Who do you think you are?!' 'Ah, if only I knew!' replied the philosopher. We may despair; many go in for alcohol as an attempt to seek the spirit – or drugs, or routine, or pills from doctor or psychiatrist. And so we die.

---

178 See Chapter 1, p. 12. Jung 1944, *CW 12*, para 325-6.

> *In order to arrive at what you are not,*
> *You must go through the way in which you are not.*
> *And what you do not know is the only thing you know*
> *And what you own is what you do not own*
> *And where you are is where you are not.*[179]

If we're to awaken and become alive, we need to search for the lost aspects – find another ruling principle. Fairy story, myth and legend are all about this. Some of the mythical heroes, the prodigal sons, first spend time *outside* in the ego's world, gaining treasure they can cash in on. But at last even the materialistic ones (Jason, Hercules, Odysseus) come to see the sun as the centre of the universe. The hero needs to find an *inner* kingdom. The Prodigal Son becomes homesick at last, realising he has to get off the rim of the wheel of life and down a spoke to the hub. The wandering tribes of Israel seek their homeland, the New Jerusalem; the questing knights return to Arthur's table; Singing Stone comes home.

The Self comes searching

Though in a collective *nigredo*, we are being drawn home. The Other Self, the Self of the helio-centred Universe, draws in the disparate bits of us. The Self comes searching and the iron filings must be shaped to a new magnetic field. So through the labyrinth we go, starting from the outer world, passing *temenos*, the sacred place, wandering towards the centre. Slowly we re-orientate, realising the sun *is* the centre of the Solar System after all. We equalise the four-armed cross, putting the Self in the centre, giving a different viewpoint. Then the cross becomes a square encircled by the Self. And the Self is also in the centre of the cross in the circle. We begin to find God in the Self and the Self in God.

The mandala

What are the shapes of God, or of the Self? As the fourth function is incorporated, Jung found the square and the circle repeated in dreams and visions as images of God. Divided with a cross into four segments, they symbolise the Self's striving to achieve wholeness and total unity. They involve the enclosure of sacred space and penetration to the Centre. So, again, the *mandala*, also a picture of the deity, in Sanskrit a magic circle, focussing the ego, re-centring our consciousness. The Buddha is the *jewel in the lotus*. Ego-consciousness is focussed and centred down to a point,

---
179 Eliot, *Four Quartets*, 'East Coker', lines 142-146.

broadening into a wide world of true contemplation. In the West, we are familiar with the *wheel of rebirth* with its rim, spokes and hub; with the *spiral*, the *mystical rose*, the *sunflower*. Images include a temple in a grove, a pool in a forest glade, islands in lakes, a fountain in a square, a walled garden, a tree in a round bed in a square garden or vice versa, a round table in a French square, a labyrinth such as the one at Chartres, a plateau in a ring of mountains, the lotus and the water lily.

> *The Self is below. The Self is above. The Self is to the West, to the East, to the South, to the North. Truly the Self is this whole universe. The man who sees and thinks and understands in this way has pleasure in the Self, plays with the Self, copulates with the Self and has his joy with that Self. He becomes an independent sovereign. In every state of being, freedom of movement is his.*[180]

This is new. The esoteric teachings describe the adept as one who 'copulates with the Self'. Not even in the presence of – with…. There is no desecration of one by the other; and within the Temenos, the sacred precinct, the place of power incorporating the inside and the outside worlds, somewhere between sacred and profane. There's a story of the very pure man who cleaned Krishna's temple. One day – horrors, what blasphemy! – he heard music in the courtyard and rushed out to purge it away. And it was Krishna Himself, dancing.

It's to be expected that the Self will come for us. Light is circulating. Is it expanding – or inflating? The ego is all unconscious of the *shadow*, which appears as an attacking apparition, cushioning the curious polarity between ego and Self, tempering us by fire. The Self will take control – unless we resist it; and there is a very natural resistance of the ego to the sublime. (Arjuna fought to the last ditch.) It tries to block it with a flood of shame, a discounting, a sense of failure. It's easier to have the sublime out there in the world; for the price to be paid is loss, and the ego is more aware of that than of gain. And this is a right and proper reaction, guarding against inflation.

But then, the ego doesn't know much anyway. For the Self to take the lead we need to allow, to let go, till the circulation becomes a spiral. We can even take the odd short-cut. The aim is nothing less than the transformation of consciousness as we move toward the philosopher's stone:[181] the diamond body, the heavenly heart, the 'purple hall in the city of jade'.

And there is loneliness. Some bits we do with friends, other bits we

---

180 Chandogya Upanishad, 800 BC, drawing on earlier tradition
181 As the old alchemists described it: 'Out of man/woman (pairs of opposites), make a round circle whole, extract the quadrangle (square of the four elements) from this and from the square the triangle of Body/Soul/Spirit. Make a round circle and you have the philosopher's stone'. (From the *Rosarium philosophorum*.)

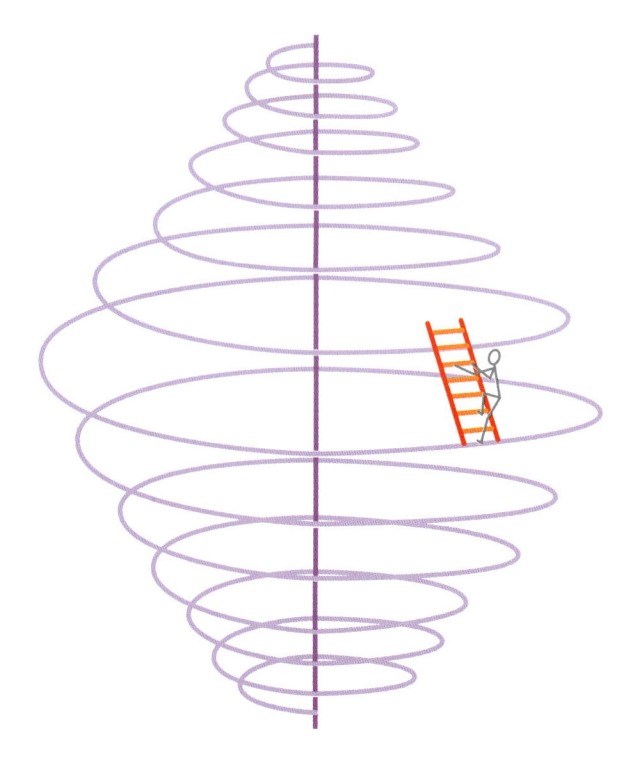

Chart 5:04 – The Spiral Way

have to do on our own. Often, it alternates. There is a saying among Sherpas: 'If you can't do the next pitch without me, I have no right to lead you there. And if you can, you don't need me.' There's no Wise Old Person at the top of the mountain. Now we stop projecting on to inner figures: 'My guide says.... ' Instead, we take responsibility ourselves for what we say. The idea of the *threshhold* is important here. There is a story:

> One went to the Beloved's door and knocked. A voice asked, 'Who is there?' He answered, 'I am.' The voice said: 'There is no room for you and me.' The door was shut. After a year of lonely deprivation he returned, and knocked once more. The voice from within asked, 'Who is there?' The man said, 'You are.' The door was opened for him.

So we end up with an eight-spoked wheel, a compass to steer by. This is preventive not only of lopsidedness but of crisis: the more conscious we are, the less likely to hit crises. We become more open to experience, to people, to life – more able to work with *time* and with rhythms. And with change. From midlife on, many of us are lost, a long way from home. The tension reflects our anxiety and guilt about being who we are *not*, either voluntarily or because the wheel was forced round. However, *we are continuously taken where we are not, in order to become who we are*. One woman much blocked inwardly told how, in London's Oxford Street, darkly she saw a reflection in a shop window. All at once: 'Aha... an Other!'

On our pilgrimage to find the Self, *the Self comes searching for us*. The lineaments of the Other Self come through experience of the little self: there is a baby Buddha at the heart of the lotus, the Philosopher's Child, eternal youth, eternal life. The wise say of it that its fruits are quiet, and work, and joy – the missing elements of the gods. Confucius described it as the *way of knowing*, a knowing which is everything, without which life is not worth living. For Lao-tzu it was *homecoming*. The Taoists knew it as *the golden flower*. The Buddha said it was the *view of the heart*, and Plotinus, *the way of inward vision*. As we know, Jung called it *the way of individuation*. These are the patterns of God. The pattern comes out 'in small', the little eye of God. One old lady at a workshop: 'A lotus? No, dear. But I might manage a daisy.'

It may be appropriate to end the workshop with the Universal Blessing of Buddhism.[182]

---

182 The Universal Blessing of Buddhism, see Chapter 10, p. 365. Original reading list for the workshop, Appendix 6.

250 THE RAINCLOUD OF KNOWABLE THINGS

Hand-rendered drawing of the Spiral Way: Alison Gaffney

PART II
Intermezzo
Emphasising the Practical

252 THE RAINCLOUD OF KNOWABLE THINGS

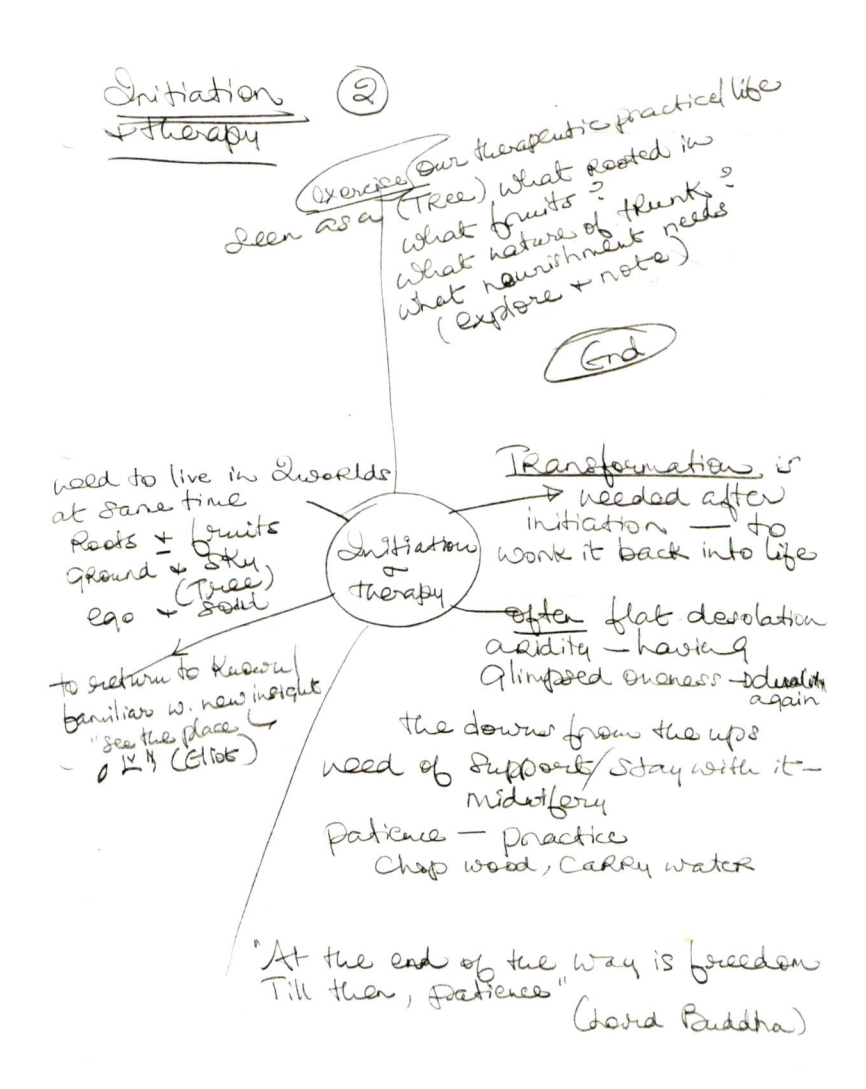

Initiation ②
+ Therapy

Seen as a (exercise) Our therapeutic practical life
(Tree) What rooted in
What fruits?
What nature of trunk?
What nourishment needs
(explore + note)

End

need to live in 2 worlds
at same time
Roots + fruits
Ground + Sky (Tree)
ego + Soul

to return to known/
familiar w. new insight
"see the place"
0 M" (Eliot)

Initiation
&
therapy

Transformation is
needed after
initiation — to
work it back into life

often flat desolation
aridity — having
glimpsed oneness — duality
again

the downs from the ups
need of support/stay with it —
midwifery
patience — practice
Chop wood, carry water

"At the end of the way is freedom
Till then, patience"
(Lord Buddha)

Facsimile of notes: Barbara Somers

CHAPTER SIX

Imaging and the Transpersonal

Ian Gordon-Brown [183]

*Transpersonal psychology is a perspective based on the reality of ...
a higher or deeper or inner Self*

INTRODUCTION [184]

Transpersonal psychology

As a force, Transpersonal psychology emerged through a group of men and women interested in ultimate states and their empirical, scientific study. Its pioneers include Carl Jung, Roberto Assagioli (Italy), Abraham Maslow and Viktor Frankl. Among the original board members and editorial staff of the brand new Journal of Transpersonal Psychology (founded in 1969) were some other familiar names: James Fadiman, Stanislav Grof, Arthur Koestler (England), Michael Murphy, Ira Progoff, Anthony Sutich (editor), Miles Vich, Alan Watts. In 1968 the name 'Transpersonal' was agreed upon.[185]

As a model of the human psyche, transpersonal psychology is a perspective based on the reality of a spiritual Centre or Self within every individual, a higher or deeper or inner Self that is the director, controller and monitor of our lives. This Centre, to which we can each make reference – this Self, Soul, Atman, this wise core of us – is the chief motivating and co-coordinating energy within us. It tends towards the finding of new meaning in life. The task of the transpersonal psychologist is to facilitate the release of this energy in individuals and in groups. One of the faculties it employs to this end is the imagination.[186]

---

183 This chapter is based on a workshop IGB ran several times, entitled 'Running Transpersonal Workshops'. It includes the Transpersonal Training Manual he offered to students.
184 No reading lists are suggested for this or subsequent chapters.
185 Anthony Sutich wrote in the first Journal of Transpersonal Psychology: 'Early in 1968 during a discussion in which Dr. Abraham Maslow, Dr. Viktor Frankl, Dr. Stanislav Grof and Dr James Fadiman participated, the general dissatisfaction that had rapidly developed with regard to the choice of "Transhumanistic" for the journal was thoroughly explored. The outcome was a recommendation that "Transpersonal" would be a much better title for the new journal. The recommended substitution was such an obvious improvement that it was immediately accepted.'
Sutich 1969, *Some considerations regarding Transpersonal Psychology* p. 14.
186 Some roots of Transpersonal psychology, Appendix 4.

ACTIVE IMAGINATION AND PSYCHOLOGY

The guided daydream was designed to lead, to contain and to cure

A brief historical background [187]

By the 1850's the doctors had entered the field of mental health and taken over. Via *Frederic Myers* and *Theodore Flournoy*, via *Mesmer*'s work and mediumship, in came 'trances', crystal ball-gazing, automatic writing, hypnosis. *William James* held that this was a 'means of access to the unconscious'. *Pierre Janet* saw that split-off parts of the personality (sub-personalities, ideas) would take on an autonomous reality and enact inner dramas as replays of the experiences and traumas of the ego; and the doctor could enter into and alter such dramas to 'heal' the patient. This was a precursor to later *guided imagery*.

Sigmund Freud encouraged his patients, *via* hypnosis, to visualise and re-live repressed traumatic experiences. In 1892 he dispensed with the hypnosis; sitting behind them in a darkened room, he moved to the obtaining of verbal and visual images by free association, the patient freely expressing as one idea triggered another.[188] He realised that the mind, by associating ideas, will bring together significant material from the unconscious, which he regarded as a repository for forgotten and repressed experiences. He saw fantasy as a defensive, censoring language for infantile sexuality; the ego creates the unconscious, the brain creates the mind and the image is but a symptom of something else. However, we must also note that Freud said that, before the creativity of the artist, 'analysis must, alas, lay down its arms'.

To many psychologists from the 1920's on, the source of images was no longer seen as divine but as subconscious: not above, but below. They observed not mystics or holy men or shamans, but hysterics: not visions but hallucinations. No longer bringing the inner to the outer to enrich and inform everyday life, they went into heroic mode, annexing the inner *from* the outer, taking the outer towards the inner to impose order. By splitting man into various systems – perception, cognition, memory, sensation – they lost touch with spontaneous imagery in its own right. They developed methods of therapy other than verbal in order to lessen the need for interpretation and to bypass 'transference issues'. Jung

---

187 Details of the pioneers and others referred to in this chapter, Appendix 13.
188 Anna O. was the first reported case of directed mental imagery. Breuer & Freud 1895, Appendix 13.

commented: 'The gods have become our diseases.'

However, this was not the whole story. Certain European psychotherapists were aware of 'the meditative zone' in which 'creations ripened in the unconscious appear to the mind's eye'. *Carl Happich* attempted to stimulate this by suggestion, inviting images of sitting by water, a landscape, a mountain, a chapel. *Wolfgang Kretschmer* also sought to develop *meditative* psychotherapeutic techniques. Projection tests, such as TAT (the Thematic Apperception Test) and *Rorschach's* experiments are in the same general line, as is much of Freud's work on dreams, and *Melanie Klein*'s view of infantile imaging. Indeed, Freud wrote that thinking in pictures is older than thinking in words, and closer to the unconscious.

In 1932, *J.H. Schultz* presented his Autogenic Training Techniques, involving a self-induced hypnotic state reached *via* the relaxing of the body and the noting of its responses to concepts such as 'warm', 'heavy', 'light' and so on. *Marc Guillery* in Switzerland took this further. The value of Autogenics lay in the connecting of imagination to the body; its disadvantage was its over-concentration on the neuro-muscular and somatic control of the autonomic responses. Where in that is the divine?

The guided daydream

Robert Desoille,[189] with his 1938 technique of the *directed daydream* or waking dream (rêve éveillé), developed archetypal imaging, devising a set of motifs (mountain, cave, meadow, for instance) which he asked the patient to explore via mental imagery. He particularly noted 'up' versus 'down': 'up' means warmth, light, euphoria, more 'positive' images – up the mountain, taking the chariot up towards the sun; whereas 'down' into the ocean or cave (there meeting, perhaps, a dragon or sea-monster) means anxiety, fear, cold, rapid breathing and increased heart rate. Moving to the left indicates the past, to the right, the future. Aiming to address pains and anxieties in the depths of the personality, he introduced motifs from myth and fairy tale: wicked witches, helpful magicians. Proffering, say, the Sleeping Beauty, the tasks of Hercules, the journeying of Odysseus, he would invite the patient to take a magic wand or meet an inner guide to help transform any difficulties. This kind of *guided daydream* was a method of suggestion and intervention by the therapist, and was designed to lead, to contain and to *cure*.

---

[189] Desoille: Appendix 13, and his Directed Daydream, Appendix 14.

In Germany in 1948, *Hans-Carl Leuner* [190] started a long-range experimental study, attempting to enlarge Desoille's method. His technique of Guided Affective Imagery uses ten symbolic motifs to encourage images to develop freely and spontaneously. The patient lies on a couch and one such 'standard situation' is suggested, the aim being to release and transform any negative energies locked up in the symbols. He observed and sought to evoke an 'inner psychic pacemaker', an aspect of a person's consciousness which knows the real nature of their problem and what to do about it. In his report on the outcome, published in English in 1975, Leuner provided data apparently demonstrating that symptoms abate significantly faster with imagery than with other techniques that do not incorporate it.

Carl Jung and active imagination

Jung also saw behind the material a hidden continuity and meaning; in paying attention, the ego established a connecting line to the psyche itself. Not only were the complexes revealed, but *that which they were attempting to make known from the unconscious*; not only personal knots but the non-personal realm, where lies the source of myth, fairy tale, religious belief and ritual, the basic blocks on which consciousness rests. Where Freud's free association induced a flow of *memories, the ego using the image* to express itself, Jung's active imagination encouraged a flow of *imagery, the image using the ego* to express itself. He saw painting, modelling, writing, poetry, dancing, ritual all as means of channelling the inner towards the outer; the ego, relaxed from the usual controls, acts as a bridge out, externalising and giving form to inner experience, whether personal or of the soul.

Following his split from Freud in 1912, Jung had lost his equilibrium and was deeply off-centre. To regain his balance he mobilised his 'inferior function'.[191] As an intuitive, in his case this was the Sensation function. With stones and pebbles, he began to build miniature cities and towns by Lake Zurich, irrigating them with water channelled from the stream. Being again at play as he had been as a child brought him a sense of peace and security. He wrote that the imagination is author of all human creation, of all that is greatest in our lives, and that *play* is its dynamic principle. Thus, serious work needs the imagination of the child, an insight for which we owe him an incalculable debt.[192]

---

190 Leuner: Appendix 13, and his Standard Situations, Appendix 14.
191 The Four Functions, see pp. 233-234.
192 See Jung 1921, 'Psychological Types', *CW 6*, para 93.

In this spirit of 'serious play', he began to explore the unconscious, playing with the imagination by stilling his mind, approaching the interface and letting whatever came take on a life of its own. Mythical landscapes unfolded; he went on journeys into imaginal realms, his ego becoming a screen onto which universal, external images could be projected and play. He recognised parallels from myth, legend, story, folklore, anthropology, alchemy and art. Figures appeared: a blind old man whom he knew as Elijah; a young woman, Salome; a serpent; a horned figure he called Philemon, with kingfisher wings. In this way was laid down the basis of his therapeutic work.

At the end of his life, Jung wrote that all his subsequent creativity and accomplishment were already contained, as images and emotions, in these initial experiences, fantasies and dreams.[193] He wrote them down and painted them in his Black and Red Books, continuously checking their relevance to his life, his family and his professional experience and so anchoring the unconscious into consciousness. Although it had taken him forty-five years to distil, in the alchemical vessel of his work, the stream of lava he had then hit upon, his life had been reshaped by the heat of its fires, compelling him to incorporate its incandescent matter into his scientific world view. Everything essential was decided in those most important years, the primal stuff of a lifetime's work.[194]

Figures arising spontaneously in his patients' dreams and visions came with personal meaning beyond their conscious understanding. Through active imagination, he encouraged them to visualise mental images. Asked to hold such dream figures in contemplation, and to 'complete' dreams broken off or interrupted by their waking up, their imagination would stir and their unconscious start to unfold. With the ego as onlooker, asking questions and moving with the drama, the spotlight of genuine enquiry was turned on and the dialogue began. And their imagination would lead beyond, from the inner world of nature to the very basis of their psychic life, the roots of their ethical and cultural development. The outwardly-turned ego 'forgets' the unconscious and needs help to 'remember' what it already knows. Jung saw active imagination as a prime help to such remembering, preferring it even to spontaneous dreaming as a direct link, inner with outer. For him, this use of transpersonal imaging meant a return to the divine.

Jung called us back to respecting the sacred. How may we attend

---

[193] See Jung 1963, Chapter 6, 'Confrontation with the Unconscious', *Memories, Dreams, Reflections*, p. 217.
[194] Jung 1963 ibid, p. 225.

appropriately, listening, integrating and anchoring it into our lives? Awareness can be trained. We can teach the ego to surrender its usual vigilance and control, freeing the observer from attachment to the object of awareness till ability to reflect on that object is regained. We can gradually dis-identify from daily preoccupations and daydreams, transfer our usual attachments, coalesce around the chosen meditative form. So 'reality' changes and we are faced with new phenomena. Jung wrote that Meister Eckhart's art of *letting things happen* was for him a key to the Way. We must curb the tendency of consciousness to correct, help, negate and interfere in the psyche, and leave space for simple, peaceful growth. And simplicity is difficult.[195]

MORE RECENT HISTORY

Dreams come unbidden,
but in the waking dream we dream while awake

In Italy, *Roberto Assagioli* (1965)[196] offered a use of dream analysis that departed from and extended the formulations of Freud. In developing *pychosynthesis* he researched and embodied various imaging techniques to obtain associations from dream elements. Like Desoille, he developed the *guided daydream,* and Psychosynthesis practitioners continue to use it extensively. He would have the patient undergo extended imagery sessions, beginning with any unresolved or conflicted incident from the dream.[197] The set-piece scenario might involve confrontation, or at least dialogue, with bear, dragon, monster, giant; he would have them carry on a conversation with it. 'Stand and watch it, talk with it. See the octopus change into a shark – into a dolphin – into a mother, a child, a wise woman. Shall we feed the threat? Come to a reconciliation with it? Make friends with it? Shall we exhaust the image? Sprinkle it with an essence? Place it in a magic fluid? Even, shall we kill it?' (However, we have found that attempting to 'kill' images is not useful.[198]) Assagioli was using imagery for therapeutic ends: 'What it means is this.... '

Except when it doesn't. More and more, this was helping the ego to *overcome*. But, may active imagination not have other intentions?

---

195 Jung 1931, Commentary on *The Secret of the Golden Flower*, para 20.
196 Assagioli, Appendix 13. His symbols of transpersonal experience, Appendix 14.
197 See Epstein 1992, *Waking Dream Therapy*.
198 'Killing' imaginary figures, p. 234.

An American influence came in with *Penfield, Dement* and *Kleitman*.[199] They acknowledged dreams, but still the ego predominated and set the pattern. They found that stimulating the temporal cortex with electrodes brings visual imagery, so they concentrated on physiology, using hallucinogenic drugs, experimenting with sense deprivation, noting rapid eye movements and brain rhythms. And they reduced the unconscious contents to 'nothing but....'

From 1965 on there was a movement back towards our origins. *J. L. Moreno*, watching children play in the parks of Vienna, was led to introduce Psychodrama: a person starts from a life-situation or a memory or a dream and moves to act it out, using themselves and others in the group. This brought a return to spontaneity, releasing fantasies and images, and demonstrated the cathartic value of play and drama. *Ira Progoff* brought *twilight imagery*, working freely with fantasy imaging and introducing the 'Intensive Journal'. *Fritz Perls* founded Gestalt. *Piero Ferrucci*, developing the work of Roberto Assagioli, introduced the *guide* and the *talisman*. Arnold Mindell with his Dreambody, *James Hillman, Stanislav Grof*, have generally taken a more transpersonal approach, freer than those who had gone before.

MENTAL IMAGERY TECHNIQUES IN ANALYSIS AND PSYCHOTHERAPY

Imagination is a major psychological function,
both conscious and unconscious

Jung's rich and fruitful exploration of myths and symbols in relation to psychological processes, as well as his particular concept of archetypes, gave the use of visual imagery new depth and perspective. Imagination, the evoking and creating of images, is a major psychological function of both conscious and unconscious. All these techniques — *guided daydream, imaging* or *fantasy*, and also *visualisation* — are based on and make use of this fact. Imaging has great relevance to therapists and to all who love artistry in life. So long as the client is able to receive and anchor what comes up, Jung recommended active imagination.

---

199 Details of the pioneers and others referred to in this chapter, Appendix 13.

That being said, it has risks. It is suitable only where the ego is strong enough to hold an equal balance with the unconscious; it is plainly not for anyone likely to be inundated by the unconscious – anyone with schizophrenia or a fringe psychotic personality. Dangers include taking it for granted as a method, making it stereotypical rather than unique; also of being hooked, addicted to the imaginal world, and so becoming un-footed. Imaging must be grounded, anchored, worked on, made conscious and lived with.

Guided imagery moves with freedom, like a dream, through past, present and future. It helps us remember who we are, what we are about and why we are here. It is very useful in helping a person move from idle fantasy into more constructive, purposive, definite channels. To enter a dialogue prepared to let something happen, to hear the 'otherness' of the psyche, giving it free rein and loving attention, will enable the fantasies to flow and take form. Then the ego may actively experience a drama before, beyond and transcending itself. Barbara Hannah gave six reasons to include active imagination:

1. When the unconscious is overflowing with images.
2. To reduce the number of dreams when there are too many.
3. When not enough dreams are remembered.
4. When someone feels particularly stuck, inwardly or outwardly.
5. When the adaptation to life has been injured.
6. If someone falls into the same hole again and again, when it can break the repetitive pattern.[200]

To be submerged in a mood means to be in a primitive state of possession, with the ego identical with the raw emotion and unable to reason. But reason is an attribute of our conscious *logos*. When emotionally disturbed, or making irrational outbursts, it helps to become as conscious as possible of the feeling. Focus and concentrate on the mood, sink into it without reserve. Then, separate deliberately from it, stand back and look squarely at it. At the interface, the intersection between the two worlds, symbols appear – numinous, 'living' figures. As they arrive on the bridge across, they are recorded, remembered and interacted with. Wise persons (archetypal and collective, knowing more than the participating ego) speak with the age-old wisdom of the world. Dark, threatening figures can equally be objectified and conversed with.

---

[200] From lecture notes, Hannah 1967. See also Hannah 1981, *Encounters with the Soul*, on Jung's Active Imagination.

The ego is needed to hold the bridge, to re-translate, externalise – though *not* to attempt to direct things. Dialogue can strengthen the ego, assuring it that it will not be overwhelmed; a stronger, more flexible, more spontaneous ego results, responsive to but not controlled by the unconscious. Thus creative energy can be freed.

USING GUIDED IMAGERY

*Guided imagery places our personal journey alongside
the journey of our soul*

In our own work we have returned particularly to Jung, moving away (except with groups at workshops) from any set formulae and developing his method of *serious play* with the psyche, the play of imagination. With their own 'talisman' to guide them,[201] clients require little intervention from the therapist and are left relatively free. The aim is for them to be played upon (or with) in that spirit of serious play. As counsellors, we hope to approach with openness, patience and willingness to learn, letting go of labelling and assumptions, respecting the client's image as unique (and certainly not to be disposed of by books on symbolism). The image invents itself. It is not dependent on the conscious ego; indeed, the ego foregoes its 'power over' and is prepared to be taught something new.

The vital point is not what happens *in* the imaging; it's what goes on *afterwards*. Frequently, something is released to flow into further creative expression. Jung's patients themselves quite often felt that certain material needed to be made visible. 'That dream was so impressive,' they'd say. 'If only I could paint – express its atmosphere!' They might feel an idea should have symbolic rather than rational expression; or they'd be gripped by an emotion which they could explain only by giving it form. And so they would draw, or model their images in clay, or do sculpting or weaving. Sometimes they would dance their unconscious figures or express them in singing or poetry.[202] One mode moves into and out of another; the flow can include visions, or take the form of words, sounds, dialogue, sand-play, ritual enactment. It can lead to meditation, perhaps using the *mantra*, the *koan*, the *mudra*. It dis-identifies people from their usual attachments, requiring the ego's full participation.

So, to reiterate: active imagination gives insight into 'how we happen

---
201 The talisman, see p. 270.
202 See Jung 1935, 'The Tavistock Lectures', *CW 18*, para 400.

to ourselves'. It helps us remember what is already known intuitively; not only *our* personal experience, good and bad, but the collective experience of the soul. Our ego-life is a screen on to which the Self projects universal images and symbols, the creation myths of life, death and eternity. The symbols of great art are neither private nor subjective but a common language, enabling us to communicate with the past and the future as well as with our contemporaries. When *It* speaks, all artists, storytellers and mythmakers experience that 'otherness'. Although we see 'through a glass, darkly', we are drawn to the symbols that arise because *we already know them.*

Psychologically, yes, guided imagery will contact our complexes and our personal, repressed, unconscious history. But what is the unconscious trying to reveal via our life and history? Not the image but the psychic reality *underlying* the image, a continuity of meaning beyond the merely personal. Conscious and unconscious are interdependent, the unconscious giving the content, the conscious helping to mould the form. The one could not speak without the other. Guided imagery leads to the *trans*personal dimension, pointing to creation itself. A way is offered for modern people once again to become at home with their imagination and their souls.

Some important questions

Is the imagery authentic? Obviously it relates to the present level of the person doing it. If it is ego-inflating – no; images arising from pure ego-selection have a different quality. However, if it is balancing, enhancing, healing – yes; it breaks any humiliating dependence, affording liberation by our own efforts as we find courage to be ourselves. As pacemaker and guide, the transpersonal Self helps to free us: *the transference is to inner images rather than to the therapist.*

What is the relevance to my daily living? Active imagination strengthens the bridge between inner and outer. A reductive, analytic mode often renders life flat, while working with the interface brings enrichment, meaning, new energy and a sense of adventure. Michael Fordham commented that the ability to use active imagination is a sign that we have developed the capacity to be alone, creatively and positively, neither isolated and absorbed into a fantasy world, nor retreating from outer life and relationship.[203] By this touchstone we know whether we are genuinely

---

203 See Fordham 1980, *Analytical Psychology*.

aiming at psychological independence and individuation, or, like satellites, remaining content to push responsibility out to someone else.

What makes my heart sing? Ask yourself, what carries you through? Get behind the didactic to your own associations: 'What does that remind you of? How does that feel – at the level of body, emotion, atmosphere? Is that an old feeling or a new – when did you feel like that before? How did you handle it – how would you *like* to handle it – your stance, attitude, voice?' Isolate old patterns, scripts and attitudes – are they still alive today? How relevant are your present adaptations, defences, control patterns, viewpoints? Outmoded – up for review? Work to your images of strength. Find the light and carry it into the darkness.

Who am I? I stand with the creative artist, between the inner and outer worlds, potentially raising material far beyond the capacity of the conscious ego. I have *initiated* the unconscious by participation and intervention. Neither arbitrary nor ritualistic, I need, rather, to acknowledge both certainty and uncertainty, the known and the unknown; to submit, and yet know *who* submits and *why*; to make a conscious submission in order to enlarge consciousness and understanding. The participation of the unconscious increases with involvement in the drama.

A TRANSPERSONAL USE OF SPOT IMAGING AND THE GUIDED DAYDREAM WITH INDIVIDUALS [204]

The true therapist is the Self of the client; the skilful counsellor facilitates the work

Active imagination is not the same as *visualisation*

Visualisation is an active procedure where the person is asked to picture some specific scene or object; the image is deliberately and consciously constructed in inner space or, if it appear spontaneously, its change and development are under the conscious guidance and control of the Centre, or Self.

Imaging, however, aims to clear the consciousness of all preconceptions and ideas, and let the unconscious speak to the conscious by means of images which it – the unconscious – then projects on the clear

---

204   This section largely comprises the Transpersonal Training Manual offered to students by IGB.

and waiting screen of the conscious mind. As images are received, questions are fed back to the unconscious, requesting elaboration or clarification. Thus *imaging* lets the unconscious do it, where *visualisation* is a more deliberate activity. Both visualisation and imaging serve four main purposes:

> *Growth towards wholeness.* The individual can build in desired qualities, strengthen faculties that may be weak, construct bridges of communication between the component parts of the inner world, and create a greater synthesis and wholeness where before there may have been division and fragmentation.
> *Building mental models.* In all forms of creative work – artistic, technical, with people – it is possible to explore possibilities by constructing inner models to be tested in outer action.
> *Diagnostically.* A dialogue is set up with the psyche; images and symbols are evoked which provide statements about the nature of the client's difficulties.
> *Psychotherapeutically*, to release, transform and redirect energies previously blocked by, or locked up in, the problem.

Requirements of the client. These techniques are not to be used with drug-takers, those on tranquillisers, pre-psychotic or very schizoid people.[205]

Requirements of the therapist. Those who stomp with heavy boots should keep out of the sensitive garden of the psyche. Take care: imaging techniques are deceptively powerful and can be disruptive in clumsy hands. Without first-hand experience of the inward life, a counsellor can give little help to those for whom it is an important, or indeed primary reality. Therapists with no transpersonal awareness may, at worst, classify a deeply spiritual experience as a 'psychotic episode' or, at best, as 'neurotic unrealism'. The difficulty is compounded by the fact that seriously disturbed people who do need hospitalisation and long-term orthodox treatment may also experience the peaks.

However, an intuitive understanding can be developed. It is vital for the counsellor or therapist to have some basic understanding of symbols and images, whether from art, literature, religion (including liturgy and ceremonial), pictures in the media, pictures in the mind, dreams or meditation. First 'read the person'. Read the symbols in that light, not the other way

---

[205] Dr. Anthony Thorley, who worked for many years with drugtakers and later ran workshops on addiction under the auspices of the authors, comments that IGB was rather draconian here. 'It is now considered that these techniques can be used with drug-takers and those on tranquillisers – where it is thought suitable.' He also observes how difficult it is to judge who is 'pre-psychotic'. Ed.

round; and from the inside, with the heart as well as the head. Does the image correspond with the reality, making a realistic statement about the person's situation, or merely reflecting how they *think* things are?

SPOT IMAGING

What lies behind the client's words?

We derived this technique directly from active imagination.[206] It is a prime way to help people remember what they already *know* at a deep level, not only from their own personal experience, good and bad, but of potential as yet unrealised.

First, *on the spot*, the therapist catches a gesture, phrase or image which has put the client in touch with some potent past event; or it may be a recent experience which for them carries a charged atmosphere. Then, *on the spot*, gently encourage them to dialogue inwardly, allowing memories brought up by the experience to flow back and pick up other similar feeling states. Helping them stay true to the quality of the experience requires a soft voice and a slow pace, avoiding interpretation.

Imaging techniques have an uncanny ability, in skilled hands, to cut through to the heart of the matter. Work with any image that comes up; it may point to the time and place when the difficulty originated, throwing quite new and different light on its nature. *Feelings* rise towards the surface unrecognised by the client; but the counsellor will sense them, realising that talking needs augmenting by imaging. A highly structured, partially structured, or largely undirected situation employing free association may be used. It is what lies *behind* the client's words that needs to be heard; the inward note and motivation that the unconscious is seeking to reveal. The same general approach can be used to relate imaging material to the *body*. Afterwards, use whatever emerged as a basis for further discussion, constantly referring to the present life of the client, creating in the session a blend of the non-rational with more rational therapeutic work. The past is irredeemable except in the present moment, and the future grows out of the present.

Spot imaging may last for a longer or shorter time. Adopted for short periods as part of a normal counselling or therapy session, it can be used

---

[206] See Gordon-Brown & Somers on spot imaging, Chapter 11, 'Transpersonal Psychotherapy', in Rowan & Dryden 1988, *Innovative Therapy in Britain*, p. 238.

for diagnosis as well as for therapy; also, to familiarise people with, and train them in, the technique. The counsellor's first task is to spot what is important; then to get the client to stay with it. It is all too easy to fantasise on a key image, sliding past or pushing away painful material; the normal, and very human, reaction to pain, to fearful objects, unpleasant feelings, threats, is to resist or suppress them. Once the person can hold an image and its associated emotion, they can explore it to find out whence it came and, in the case of negative feelings and frightening images, discover any positive, creative energy locked up behind it.

Next, it may be appropriate to move to a longer guided daydream.

THE FULL GUIDED DAYDREAM

Silence at your end does the work

Guided imagery is when, as client, someone else comes with us on our journey. It allows our imagination full play around the orbit of feeling, noting all fantasies and associations. Before such a longer individual guided daydream – and indeed before all work with active imagination – the therapist first relaxes and prepares themselves and us, familiarising us with some of the possibilities and ways in. It is a deepening process involving personification: we become the observer. An image or scene from a dream, a vision, a fantasy might arise; perhaps a life situation or activity, a waking dream or a body symptom: perhaps a thought, a feeling, a voice, a story. We might concentrate on a striking picture or photo until, through our spiritual eye, it becomes pregnant and alive, filled with living power – not simply the image but the underlying energy, the *source*. It suggests making pregnant by giving attention to. Here is an example:

> First, as the one who sees with a single eye, I am separate, *watching* the scene or action: for instance, I see a horse....
>
> Secondly, there are two egos; I see myself *interacting* with the scene – I watch myself going through the gate – standing on the hill looking down on the horse....
>
> Then thirdly, I as observer am interacting *within the action*: I see myself talking to the horse, stroking it....
>
> Next, I become *involved* – I am *on* the horse experiencing the feeling

of the wind in my hair, seeing the landscape. At this stage, I still feel I am *me*....

At the fifth stage, I enter the imaginal world, not through the will of my ego, but by *being moved* within that world, being within the imaginal body, what Mindell called the 'dreambody'....

Sixth, I *become* something different; for instance, I become the horse crossing a stream – become a rock on the hillside....

Finally I am *moved by* the imaginal; I experience changes in the way I perceive, different from my usual ego-ways. My gender, age, even my species may be totally other....

Preparation

From the therapist's side, a long guided daydream is not something to embark upon lightly. Though it can be very valuable both diagnostically and therapeutically, it is not usually appropriate in short-term work. It needs preparing for before time: in a prior session, decide together what aspect of the client's life-situation is to be explored. Discuss the focus of the dream: any problems, patterns, chronic illnesses, sub-personalities to be looked at. You might prepare those who don't visualise easily by talking about the hero's journey – Pilgrim's Progress or the Odyssey, Lord of the Rings or Narnia. Tell them that, without preliminaries or discussion afterwards, a long guided daydream can last an hour or more, so the best part of two hours must normally be allowed. A quiet consulting room with couch and cushions is desirable.

Sitting or lying?

The *sitting position*, in contrast to the use of a couch, facilitates ego control over imaginative processes; so for talking augmented by short periods of spot imaging, counsellor and client need to be on an equal footing, adult speaking with adult, focussing on the present time and how it relates to the future. For this, a similar pair of comfortable, fairly upright chairs are best. However, the exploration of long-repressed material and early memories comes most easily in the *lying position*. So for the long guided daydream, which may involve regression to early childhood, the spontaneity of symbol formation is facilitated by relaxation on a couch.

As guide

The sensitive attention called for involves your feeling nature, mind and intuition. Before accompanying a daydream, spend a few minutes quietly tuning in to your client's consciousness and need, centring and grounding yourself for a moment or two before they arrive. Relax. Attune yourself to them. You will be making steady observation of their expression, body movements or tensions, so place your chair where you can see their face; check that it is far enough for their comfort, but near enough that your suggestions and their responses can be made in soft, quiet tones. Have writing materials, including torn-off pages, and access to a clock. Make notes (which you can later offer to them). You may need tissues. Do they wish to tape-record the session? Lighting should be muted, to facilitate imaging. They may experience a drop in temperature, so have a rug close at hand.

Beginnings

Ask the person to lie preferably on their back, with eyes closed, and allow them to relax and settle down before starting. Remind them about the nature of the journey and the length and structure of the session. Explain that you will take notes for them – they needn't struggle to remember details. You will note the key words and images they tell you as they go; and they will preferably write up the whole experience at home, for discussion in a subsequent session. If it suits your style, tell them in advance that at the end you'll go and make a drink.

Pace and time

The pace of a guided daydream is slow, gentle, easy, non-directive. A soft voice, a measured speed will not disturb the state of relaxed and deep inner quiet. As well as living through their world of images, the client reports to the guide on how things are going, and so has a dual focus. Anything too much in the style of everyday life will take them out of the inner world. But keep aware of the passage of time, gently reminding them towards the end.

Style of intervention

Remember that the client's material is always valid; don't insist on sticking to your own script. Intervene only if necessary, by *making helpful suggestions*, such as to feed, cleanse, miniaturise or enlarge the image; and by *asking helpful questions*:

'How old are you?'
'How are you feeling now?'
'How old is this figure?'
'Has this figure got a name?'

Avoid leading questions, or anything that implies a judgment or interpretation. Discussion and comment come after, if at all. The more open-ended the question, the more neutral the tone and the more non-directive the style, the better. Speak quietly. Don't bully. Imply no judgments; stay neutral. Try to experience their images with them. Carefully watch facial expression, body movements, postures, sounds such as sighs or gasps; keep careful note of them. Don't seek explanations; ask for clarification only if necessary – avoid curiosity. If you think you missed a vital word or image, it is all right to say, 'I couldn't quite hear that....'

Touching

Think twice before making physical contact with clients. Use caution in deciding whether it will be helpful to hold their hand, rest your hand on their arm, even at times to hold them in your arms while they weep. Have a soft cushion at hand which they can take and hold; it can for the moment become the person or object which has evoked the feelings.

The journey

Start by asking them to imagine they are in a safe place, probably in the open, known or not. They may choose their own home or, if that is a place of pain and tension, some place where they have known quiet, peace and joy – the *meadow* is an appropriate starting point for almost everyone. If they seem at a loss, ask them to imagine that they are in an unknown part of their home town, where lives the person who is to tell them about the journey they are to undertake; or before a mirror – go through this looking-glass to the world of meaning on the inner side of life. Alternatively, you might suggest that they start by finding themselves:

> by a lake, on which is an island, where meaning is to be found;
> by or on a river, travelling towards a special place;
> in a garden, where something of importance awaits them;
> in a forest glade, where a treasure is hidden;
> visiting a house that is special for them in some way; exploring it outside and in;
> by the seashore; something is coming in from the sea towards them;
> following a stream, towards either the source or the mouth;
> climbing a hill or mountain, discovering something of significance at the top;

in a meadow, where there is a specially significant place;
in an old library where there are archives that need to be discovered.[207]

Height and depth

Some early ways of imaging tended to go for therapeutic *height*, taking people 'up the mountain' too much and too soon, risking their being caught into high places and neglecting real life.[208] Generally, in imaging, going *up* indicates light; going *down* is dark and shadowed. It's all too easy to give the impression: 'You could change your unconscious if you would only relate properly with the image!' However, the Transpersonal is equally about therapeutic *depth*: the dream has us, rather than our having the dream.

The talisman

It is well for clients to invite a figure to accompany them on the journey, a mediator of wisdom and compassion. This non-judgmental *talisman* often takes the form of a small object that can be carried in the hand, or an animal, or a human or mythic being. Its understanding and knowledge exceed that of the ego. Once it is invoked, attention is paid to moods and feelings and autonomous fantasy fragments. Acceptance is given to any image from the unconscious; the ego co-operates in formulating it, feeling and suffering it. The talisman stands in for the Self and can at any point be turned to for advice and support.

So invite the client, when relaxed and in their inner space, to choose possibly an animal, or something they can carry in the hand, to accompany them on the journey. If it's a large object, let them miniaturise it for the period of the daydream. Allow time to establish rapport with this talisman, holding it, entering into the feel of it. If there is no talisman, say, 'Your own wisdom is coming with you.' It is even quite possible to say, 'Would you like to ask *my* talisman what to do?' It is best never to undertake a long guided journey without a talisman. Do not over-use it (remember that it is the dreamer who is going on the journey), but check with it at critical moments. Remind them of its significance as a symbol of the Higher Self, its magical properties in guiding and protecting them in difficult situations. Consult it before taking any step that appears hazardous. It is a source of confidence and strength, corresponding to Leuner's 'inner psychic pacemaker',[209] standing in, as does the Observer chair in Gestalt, for the client's deep centre. The talisman may change. If

---

207 More symbolic situations, Appendix 15.
208 See Desoille, p. 255.
209 See Leuner, p. 256.

it gets lost, ask: 'Could you have outgrown the need for that particular image?' Just occasionally it may not tell the truth: then, let *another light* shine on the client (or on the talisman), or invite them to get in touch with a deeper wisdom.

Sensations of the daydream

Monitor them for particular images; for example:

'What is the atmosphere of this place you are in?'
'What does the water feel like?'
'See if you can take ... in your hands and say how it feels?'
'Can you touch ... with your hand? What do you experience?'

The client should be encouraged to tune in to the *body*, reporting particularly what part or parts are most affected, and perhaps inviting another image which may remind them where they first experienced that feeling. This can point to the source and origins of deep-seated and lifelong problems and difficulties, helping them not only to understand the meaning of the pain, but also the possibilities for a positive transformation of the energies. Explore the body's reactions:

'Is your body reacting to this?'
'Can you tell me what sensations your body is feeling?'
'Does this feeling have a bodily location, and where is it?'
'Where do you sense physical tension at this moment?'
'Allow an image to come up to express this tension?'
'How is your body feeling now?'

Feeling tone

Deep and long-locked-up emotions may most valuably be discharged here. Ask:

'What are you feeling now as you talk about . . .?
'Can you stay with those emotions for a moment?'
'What do they represent?'
'Call up an image to express that feeling.'
'When did you first have that feeling?'
'How did you feel inside when I asked you that?'

Confronting

Don't try to avoid their challenging an inner figure during the dream. As guide, the talisman may advise the path to confrontation, rather than offering a way out. This is often exactly right. Something in each person knows what the problem is, and what needs to be done about it. The talisman does not absolve the counsellor from the responsibility of guiding the daydream, but it does allow the client's transpersonal Self to play a direct and important part.

'Losing the client'

Occasionally someone enters an area of inner darkness, perhaps despair, from which they do not seem able to return. The talisman does not 'work', nor do the gentle, non-directive methods of the normal procedure. It may then be necessary for the counsellor to speak with authority. Call the person by name. In order to bring them back to a position of security and comfort, you may assert that they are moving towards a light, or that a light is moving towards them. If necessary, say that you are with them in the darkness, leading them out by the hand. And it may now be appropriate to take their hand in yours; the reinforcement of the voice by physical contact can be an important support and reassurance.

Sleep

'Allow' them to fall asleep during the dream if that seems appropriate – they *will* wake up. Don't let your own concentration wander.[210]

Moving on

Daydreams tend to be divided into chapters. Sometimes people move themselves on to the next section of the inner journey without prompting. More often the counsellor suggests moving on when they have exhausted the potentialities of the present stage.

RUNNING TRANSPERSONAL WORKSHOPS

...as when dancing, soon the dance dances the dancer...

What is people's motivation in coming to the workshops? What are their unconscious wants and compensatory drives, what nourishment do they need, how can they have a better balance between masculine and feminine?

Transpersonal psychologists work with the Self; most others don't. The Transpersonal, as we have seen, transcends the strictly personal, and also

---

210   More on the structure of the journey, Assagioli, Appendix 14, and IGB Appendix 16.

includes it, leading towards wholeness and meaning. These workshops come from both sides of the Atlantic. Transpersonal psychology owes much to the twentieth-century wave in the USA; here in the UK there is as yet very little. My hope, certainly for the three introductory workshops, is that they will be run all over the country, maybe in the evenings, maybe at weekends, by small numbers of people doing them because they love to; it's a way of making honest money and it's to be hoped it's helpful. If they stopped enjoying it, they would need to stop doing it.

Group leaders

Who shall run these workshops? The key requirement is that you be the right sort of person. Having your own spiritual path behind you is the best ingredient; it gives another dimension – more than the mere thing. Mine is the work of Alice Bailey, Barbara Somers' the way of Zen and the Buddhism of Tibet, with the work of Carl Jung. The principle is, *the Transpersonal knows best*. Assume there is something *guiding* to which, ultimately, you work. Facilitate that, give it time and space to work its magic – keep out of the way enough to let it happen. Don't talk too much. You must be authentically yourself, doing the workshop your way, with integrity and sincerity, in a style that fits you, that you're happy with. Let it happen.

For a weekend with say twenty people, two leaders are desirable, or a leader and a helper; ideally, a man who represents the masculine and is in touch with the feminine, and a woman who represents the feminine and is in touch with the masculine. For success, the mix needs to be right.

Participants

And who will join these workshops? Those who come – are those who come. Some may have been over-persuaded, finding on arrival that it's not their scene. Some may feel they *ought* to come. These have the worst trip. Such pressure may be actually harmful and certainly does no good; the task is to let the Transpersonal apply the pressure. Though the workshops seem gentle, they are at times very, very powerful. This is archetypal stuff.

Who should *not* participate? Even after a workshop has begun, you can turn people away. As a general rule, no one with a psychosis does any imaging. Nor anyone with notable bi-polar disorder (though after a workshop, people often do have mildish high or low spells, which then turn). Nor people with even mild depressions, for they may be triggered into lengthy phases. If in doubt, admit someone after telling them it's only if you talk first to their GP or psychiatrist. Be very careful with people who have been or are on non-prescribed drugs, especially hard drugs. Be particularly cautious about imaging, as their ego-strength may have deteriorated. It usually takes at least seven years to get over hallucinogens. And what effect does imaging have on people on anti-depressants?

Twelve to sixteen participants is ideal. Smaller groups can be heavier. Up to a point, the newer people are to the work the bigger the ideal group, though above eighteen it can become uncomfortable. But we often book twenty or twenty-two, perforce.[211]

Advertising

Have no marketing techniques and *do not advertise*, though literature should be available. People hear about the workshops by word of mouth. In a sense they are already self-selected. A 'magnetic' radiation is inherent, a sense of the archetype to which the work is linked; without that, no amount of advertising avails – it can seem positively offensive. Magnetism draws the right people and those for whom the message is too elementary will go elsewhere. Let the magnetism do it. (Industry, where it *doesn't* do it, works in a different way.) Organisations that do advertise may even prevent some fundamental energy reaching out to the right people. Enjoy yourselves, and everything else is secondary. Come from the *heart*. Be true to the central energy and just being there and doing what you do reaches and touches those who need it.

The workshops

When to hold them. Friday evening to Sunday midday is better than the whole of Saturday and Sunday; the curve of energy and attention is enhanced by three fresh starts. An alternative is an evening a week for several weeks. Residential weekends are tiring since, by demand, you have to give Saturday afternoon off.

The room. Before the workshop, lay out *chairs in a circle*, obviously checking temperature, lighting and comfort. A carpet is desirable. Have everyone's name to hand. Make notes during the personal introductions, and learn the names while your partner is talking. Provide good enough art materials.[212]

Diagrams and visual aids. These are essential, indeed, critical. An old-

---

[211] Who comes to subsequent workshops? In our experience, of those who attend Workshop 1, 55 % come to the second and 45 % to the third workshop; once a person has come to Workshop 2, they are 85 % likely to come to the third; and those who attend all three are 90 % likely to continue with further workshops and training.

[212] Large paper, boards to rest on, and wax pastels are satisfactory.

fashioned and excellent way is to use flip charts inter-leaved with blanks, drawing long-winded charts in advance and building up simple ones as you go. Appropriate models and maps provide structures for the explorations, helping people understand, giving them an image and an insight into what you are together exploring; but remind them always that *the map is not the country*. The theory is useful as a kind of hat-rack for what follows. The clearer you are, the fewer the questions. However, the passive-receptive kind of group is the most difficult; so if you want a discussion it may be better not to be too lucid – which is comforting.

Trust the process. In your own consciousness as you lead the journeys there may be a feeling that the group leader shouldn't let people evade, escape, con themselves. But you *never* need to pressurise. Do not impose. Let the Self and the situation provide any pressure. If the sword must be applied, let it be to asserting the fact, not to the person. Again, *silence at our end does the work*.

Tell people that this is an encounter with the Self; motivation is the key. All psychological energies have a positive original value. For instance, as we saw at the beginning, anger can hold the energy of frustrated creativity; jealousy indicate the sensitivity of love; fear involve caution and heightened perception; doubt spell objectivity and the need to see and accept things as they are. Therefore there need be no self-criticism, but rather an understanding of themselves and a new consciousness of their lifestyles. The aim is to abandon 'should' and 'ought' and move toward wholeness, with the Self as the centre. Seeing themselves as they are, they can accept themselves, disengage from judgment and transform the energy. They need not censor – accept the first flash of an image.

If someone is in a difficult space. Encourage them to sit up for the imaging with their eyes open; lying out takes them deeper. Tell them that *sharing* afterwards is always voluntary; indeed there are times when they positively shouldn't, when the material is too new, too fragile, for the light of day. There is no compulsion. This is true, and also lets out people who are scared, or who have good reasons for choosing not to share.

Imaging, or visualisation? Make it clear: 'This will be *imaging*.'[213] Some people will be much quicker in their response than others. Will images come in terms of feelings, body reactions, words, the sound of a voice, smells? Or in pictures?

---

213 Imaging and visualisation, See p. 18.

Starting. Invite them to relax and ease out tensions in their own way; don't offer any particular relaxation procedure. Speak aloud but not loudly, voice firm and resonant, keeping a slow pace, with a mythological, fairy-story ring to it if you can. This is about evocation and magic: 'Once upon a time....' However, it's easy to raise material. Anyone can do that: lying people out, lights dim, magic in the voice – powerful stuff. The danger of too much concentration should be known, both within the workshop and before the next: there should be at least a month between, probably more.

Allow time. This is absolutely crucial.[214] If time is short, save it elsewhere, not in the explorations. Give five, seven, even ten minutes after each suggestion you make – slightly more than you feel is needed. Images come up in the last minute and all need processing. Give at least half to three-quarters of an hour for an exploration. More time, and people go deeper; less, and they surface. During the imaging, try saying, 'I'm going to give the next instruction twice', and repeating it pithily. If more than five minutes have passed, warn, 'You have another minute – ' and then, 'Now, move on when you're ready.' Allow yourself to vary the speed if need be, sensing the atmosphere, any movements of body or eye, even the colour of people's skin. In timing the conclusion, say, 'In your own time – ' and guide people out as well as in. They may wish to adopt the foetal position. Don't be too quick with the light.

Sharing. For short imaging sessions, share in pairs immediately. For longer journeys, it is fine to have a first general, large-group discussion afterwards, giving people more chance to digest. Then, small groups of three, four or five are most suitable for the later main sharing; three is ideal, but may not be practicable. You might suggest they avoid being with people they already know well.[215]

DESIGNING IMAGING EXPLORATIONS

Structure. If you are creating your own imaging journeys or explorations (terms preferable to 'exercises'), keep them simple and brief. Not all explorations are equally useful. Aim to illumine theory, accelerate development and lead to self-discovery. The structure contains the journey, and its containment confers freedom. Unless you can write down your

---
214 IGB really did do this, fully allowing the times indicated for the explorations in these workshops. If necessary he cut back on time for the talks – but not for the imaging. Ed.
215 More on the imaging explorations given for the first four workshops, Appendices 1 and 2.

exercises, you shouldn't give them. You have to handle the results.

Spirit and ethos. You are the magician and imagination is the key to creating the energy field for magic. A good journey evokes a wide *range of images*. Suggest them from the Bible (the Garden of Eden, for instance) or from fairy stories (helpful animals). Look to dreams, myths, legends, parables, which have a long archetypal race memory attached. Some real-life situations also have great potential for evoking magic. The simpler, shorter and older the words you use, the better. For example, 'Find yourself in a meadow.'

The talisman. It may be appropriate with a group, as well as with individuals, before the start of a journey to evoke this wise, compassionate observer and companion.

Places. What does a house, wood, shrine, island or garden symbolise? For one person, home, sanctuary, the goal, the origin, the Self; for someone else, a place of confrontation. Avoid suggesting they go under the earth, or into a cave – not at least until you know them well. Only when you're working one-to-one with experienced people do you go deliberately to the domain of the lower personal unconscious. (We fear the dark, believing it's the way to the devil, not realising that the devil has things for our salvation. We're afraid we'll see what we are really like.)

Unresolved conflicts. People can be asked to find the major crises or polarities of their lives and characterise them, discovering images and names. 'What crisis most affected your *body*? Return and re-experience that time, noting its physical effect.' Someone may, for example, recall their wedding, or the birth of their first child, or the death of parents or others. Do the same for their emotional and for their mental nature, inviting the Self to show which crises were most important for their development. We are controlled by things with which we identify; but dis-identify, disengage, and *they* are controlled by *us*. Then, energy transforms till inside and outside are one.

Travelling. Explorations often involve journeys by vehicle, ship, aeroplane, on foot, being transported, changing from one mode to another. Ask: 'What are for you the qualities of land, sea, air, space? Is it hard or easy to be there?'

Tasks and tests. They confront participants with themselves – or with others, which is the same thing. The tests may find *them*. Or you can build tasks in, inviting people to meet inner figures representing say the shadow, the light side, the instinctual part of themselves. They can experience the elements, journeying into Earth, Water, Air and Fire to meet the body, emotional life, the mind and the spiritual part. At a later stage they might, like Alice, go through the looking glass to find unknown parts of themselves; however, make sure they can get back.

End on a positive note. It is usually possible, without manipulating, to help people to transform negative energy. Catharsis is ideally followed by a peak which can be helped towards but not induced.

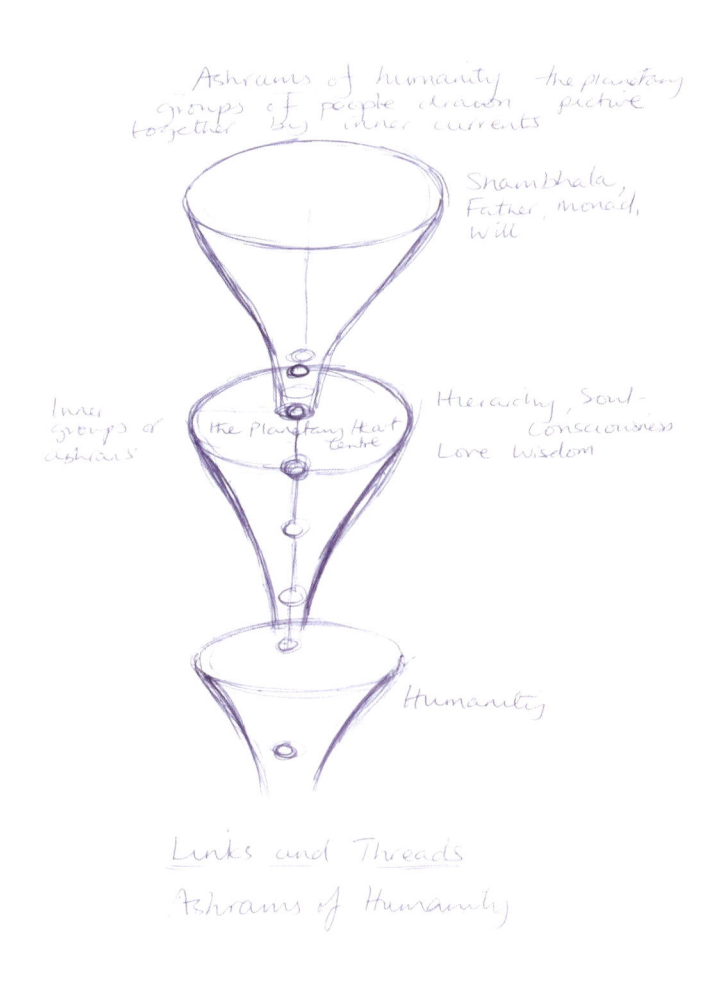

Hand-rendered drawings: Alison Gaffney

PART III

Advanced Workshops

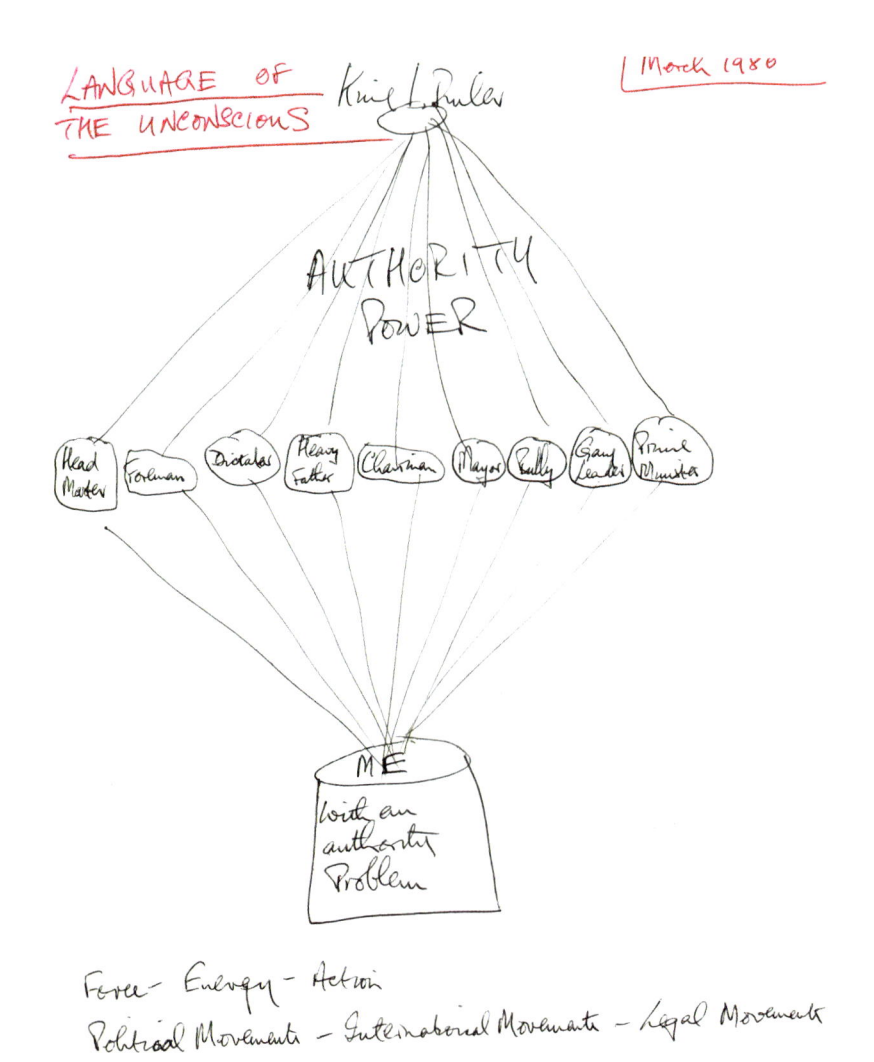

Facsimile of notes: Ian Gordon-Brown

CHAPTER SEVEN

Archetypes

Ian Gordon-Brown

*There was a young man who said, 'Though
I seems that I know that I know,
What I* would *like to see
Is the 'I' that knows 'Me'
When I* know *that I know that I know.*[216A]

INTRODUCTION

Of what stuff am I made?

Human needs, inborn impulses, fundamental drives motivate us all: the will to meaning, the thrust to wholeness, the will to be, to live. Yet we are not all made of the same stuff. An archetype is a model, a fundamental imprint, a prototype, a shape, a container. Neither good nor bad, it is an energy-form, a design-plan of the Architect of the Universe. The Platonic notion is that it is stored as an eternal, transcendent *form*, an *idea* that pre-shapes and continually influences our thoughts, feelings and actions. Jung comments that such archetypal patterns are inherited, historically predating all personal experience. Themselves unconscious, they constitute a mould, as it were, for the expressions of consciousness; they possess a natural numinosity, an emotional value, a degree of autonomy. He points to Plato's Cave parable to illustrate this.[216B]

For Jung, Mother Earth, Father Wind and the Sun god are not mere delusions: they are expressions of the underlying structure of conscious experience. From the sun and moon, the stars and planets, the springs and rivers, come messages from time immemorial. There is a pre-formed *tendency to create images* – the highest mountains, the deepest valleys, the vast oceans, the endless sky, the healing spirit of numinous moments and transcendent experiences. These *are* the archetypes. Any specific image is just one of many possible *contents* of an archetype. Jung

---

216A Alan Watts, 1969, p. 54
216B Plato's Myth of the Cave, Appendix 11. See Jung's letter to Lang, 1957, 'Letters', Vol. 2, pp. 372 n. 2 and 371.

compared the archetype to a dry river bed.[217] The rain gives the flow and direction. We name the river, but it is never clearly located; it is a form, always changing, never the same. Yet it *is* a river, and we know that rivers ultimately flow into oceans, which are symbolic of the unconscious. It can also be compared to a super-saturated solution which forms specific crystals around a *nidus*, the symbolic breeding point of formations characteristic of that kind of liquid and no other.[218]

The great sagas and myths, the divine symbols, the creativity of geniuses and of great men and women – all point to the archetype of the Self, reminding us of the godhead within each of us. It appears in images and numinous visions: as a divine child, as a mandala representing wholeness and totality, as Christ. We see it in the uniting quaternary symbol of four, in the cross, circle or sphere, epitomising the total union of opposites.[219] Religious symbols from time before history are treasures of mythology, archetypal images among the highest values of the human soul. Once, seeing the heavens – eclipses, storms and lightning – or hearing thunder, we knew magic and divine power. They are now lost in the delusion that we have mastered space, conquered mountains, and are hot on the trail of knowledge of life itself. But we have not even begun to conquer ourselves.

The inner world has two realms: the personal, subjective unconscious, which Freud pointed up; and the collective, objective unconscious, discovered by Jung. These contain the whole range of our experience, noblest to darkest. The *personal* unconscious is inhabited by images, memories, feelings and ideas once conscious but now repressed and so not directly accessible to consciousness. The *collective* unconscious takes us into the invisible, archetypal world of humanity that we have never seen, yet know. This deepest archetypal realm has power to evoke images of a more or less predictable nature. We find ourselves in a living myth. The underlying archetypes appear in infinitely variable symbolic expression and make their collective presence known by powerful personal feeling.[220]

Images and events antithetical to science are at home in the soul. We

---

217 Jung 1922, 'On the Relation of Analytical Psychology to Poetry', *CW 15*, para 127; and Jung 1936, 'Wotan', *CW 10*, para 395.
218 For example, a super-saturated solution of ordinary salt will precipitate out only the square-faced crystals characteristic of salt. The cubes come in different sizes and are sometimes graphed on to other cubes in odd building-block shapes, but they are only cubes – you might imagine that sodium chloride is the archetype of a reactionary, super-conservative psyche…
    Wilmer 1987, *Practical Jung*, p. 57. See also Jung 1929, *CW 8*, para 221.
219 Some masculine and feminine elements in the archetypal context, Appendix 17.
220 In the so-called 'Akashic Records', where the divine and the human are said to meet, such archetypes are real: whether by subtle ether or by evolution via DNA, the 'many things' of creation – including us – are brought into being by breath and by radiance; and our souls are seeking to return to the One Self, the Creator – playing, creating for the joy of creating.

know them through these myths and fairy tales, sagas, legends and stories told the world over: the quest for the treasure in a place hard to find, guarded by powerful, mysterious forces; superhuman, supernatural beings casting spells; heroes and prophets – these have from time immemorial recurred worldwide in the psyche of all peoples.

The great Danish physicist Niels Bohr said that the clarity of a statement is in inverse ratio to its rightness: too clear and it contains something false. And Jung, that only immanent objects can be described unequivocally; transcendental ones require paradox.[221] Again, that an unknown or unconscious content can only be apprehended by discriminating its opposite. Once an archetypal symbol is made conscious, the paradox in it falls apart and its latent opposites become manifest. Since our language needs to be ambiguous and have two meanings to be fair to the dual aspect of the psyche, he strove deliberately for that superior ambiguity which reflects the nature of life.[222]

Since archetypes are not equally present at all times, we come under the spell of one of them and for a time resonate together with it. There are many archetypal energies: the *dramatis personae* and their supporting cast present themselves in thousands. There may be a wise old man among them, an earth mother, a father figure, *animus* or *anima, bête noir*, trickster, guide or sceptic, a divine child or an eternal boy or girl. Perhaps a grand-vizier, a courtesan, a warrior, high priest, hero or witch. There are kings and queens and paupers, demons, daimons, monsters, the shadow, the serpent, the Antichrist, Satan. More, there are gods and goddesses and images of God: redeemer, saviour, *imago Dei*. We find the tree of knowledge and the tree of life, the fish, the tornado, earthquake, flood and storm. Or the muse, the maiden, *senex*, hermit, psyche, fool, rebirth. The list is endless. Here is a-causal ordered-ness; here are the sacred mountain and the night sea journey, the mandala, the Trinity, the quaternary, *hieros gamos*, soul, persona, rebirth, spirit... *ad infinitum*.

EXPLORATION
ARCHETYPAL IMAGES
(25 minutes)

So, with notebook by you, relax down, close your eyes. The aim is to begin to approach the archetype of the Self. Sense into what archetypal

---

[221] See Jung 1955, 'Mysterium Coniunctionis', *CW 14*, para 715.
[222] See letter to Werblowsky, 1952. Jung Letters, Vol. 2, p. 70.

images may be around for you. What is your own god; your own energy or will; your method of work; your esoteric group; your mode of organisation? What makes them resonate? Ask the images questions like:

>Who are you?
>Did you always look like this?
>Are you a mental or an intuitive type?
>How old are you?
>How long have you been around?
>Are you connected with my feeling nature?

And so on. You can even ask the images to form threes and have a discussion. Someone may have a dragon; talk to the image. Ask, 'What are dragons?' Don't try to kill it.[223]

MAPPING THE ARCHETYPES

Though as we have seen, maps are not the country, yet here is an ancient map:

>*Shiva* is about the fiery will to power and the truth of power. Here we find boss-figures, military men who become generals, statesmen, political figures, those with authority, mediating purpose and direction. Even in a small way they are law-makers, law-enforcers, law-destroyers. Shiva is to do with *justice*.
>
>*Vishnu* involves the will to love and the truth of love. Here, where the values of the heart are honoured, is the teacher who nurtures and cultivates consciousness, recognised by deep study and efforts to raise consciousness. Here too the priest, the healer, the counsellor, doctor, ambassador, the one who says, 'he didn't really mean it' – the Buddha, Christ, full of compassion, wisdom and understanding. Vishnu carries *mercy*.
>
>*Brahma*. The will to knowledge and the truth of knowledge are here, where the mind is valued. People under Brahma's influence are head-oriented, characterised by deep thought – and rarely found in the transpersonal field. A pity, since the mind badly needs revaluing. Here are philosopher and metaphysician, informed by

---

[223] See Somers & Gordon-Brown 2002, *Journey in Depth*, pp. 215-216 and 223.

the will to know; people in business, making money, in the universities, in the civil service; theoreticians, those who love systems.

The will to perfection and the will to wholeness

The Archetypes are about our fundamental will to Live and to Be. As the more recently-known physical elements derive from four fundamental elements, so the Will derives from four main aspects: the will to Power, the will to Love, the will to Knowledge and the will to Truth. Together these four lead to *the will to Wholeness* and to the seven main archetypal energies which have been known as the Seven Paths of Unfolding, or the Seven Spirits before the Throne of God. We can see the urge that motivates a person under its influence; the techniques they employ; what such a person may need for integration; and the image of the archetype in the world. For each, we can map the highest value – the god that is worshipped by those under this archetype: power, love, knowledge, harmony and beauty, truth, manifestation.

However, in the last two thousand years another, the *will to Perfection*, has been elevated above the will to Wholeness. And the god of the Devotee is perfection. 'Be ye therefore perfect....' Enormous damage has been done by this Biblical translation.[224] We feel consumed with guilt when we are not the ideal, 'perfect' – in other words, when we are in our inferior function. So we deny half of our nature. The Transpersonal, however, is for wholeness.

Seven Core Archetypes [225]

Ruler: power, human rights, authority
Priest-healer: consciousness, love, relationship
Thinker: ideas, mind, intelligence
Mediator: harmony, peace, beauty, art
Scientist: truth, objective knowledge, alchemy
Devotee: perfection, the ideal, following
Magician: manifestation, efficiency, organisation

King, ruler – power and will

The will to power is about direction and purpose, force, energy and action. The will to rule motivates the king, the empress, the great queen,

---

224 Be ye therefore perfect, even as your Father which is in heaven is perfect. Matthew 5:48.
225 These seven archetypes were introduced in Workshop 3, pp.155-158. And see the Seven Rays of Alice Bailey, Appendix 18.

the emperor, the conquering hero and heroine. Also the general, statesman, politician – many in government and law have the electrically-charged auras of monarchs. Under the influence of Shiva or Kali, their *God is power* and their will is to overcome and conquer. Large-minded, one-pointed, they wait for no detail, no analysis but hit the spot directly, in a line as with a sword, with lightning. Concerned with fundamental principles and values, they are oriented towards the goal, not the journey. The *symbols* are masculine: strength, rock, diamond, fire, violence. For the Ruler, grasping situations, assertively enunciating with undeviating will, the wind of God is rushing up the cliff.

As forces for justice, they are bent upon human rights and freedoms, valuing the power to accomplish – and using it well, as did, for example, William Wilberforce, Elizabeth Fry, President Gorbachev. For Roosevelt, power was 'to set the people free'. They have included Moses, Caesar, Joan of Arc, Napoleon, Churchill, Kennedy, Thatcher.

The *drawbacks* of natural rulers include isolation – up on their own in pursuit of a task, ceasing to notice individuals at all. Authoritarian, impersonal, detached, they can be ruthless, even cruel – Hitler, Stalin, Mao, Saddam – destroyed in turn by a life-force which breaks up forms. They may be short-winded: 'He shouted his ideas in the market place. No one responded. So he knew they must be true.' Blustering, or quiet and cold, their method is still violent and separatist and it isolates them. Boxed in, they can't let their energy out. They are not liked; no one cheers as they pass by, unless police see they do.

Is power 'bad'? Certainly, it is often used badly; attempts have been made throughout history to curb it (the Magna Carta, the 1789 Bill of Human Rights, the American Declaration of Independence, the Universal Declaration of Human Rights after the Second World War.) In its *shadow* are violence, destructiveness and brute force. Having to achieve their goals, rulers do it by imposition, manipulation, clean sweeps, no compromise – till something tempers it. They go for hierarchies rather than networks. They start their own large enterprises, having begun in small ones, and run them – as prime minister, director, chairman, foreman, mayor, headmaster, yes; but also as godfather, controller, dictator, gang boss, bully. Occultists may be found among them; and heavy father, cowardly, weak at a certain level, letting others make decisions while he keeps control.

Rulers *need* love but don't get it. They have to learn that it's not people who must be changed, but limitation. They need to link with other people – become inclusive, heart-based, de-centralised, asking, 'Is it *right*?' What of ourselves? Someone with a rational mind may yet be Ruler at the feeling level. When we begin to come on to our centre, our being resonates.

Priest-healer, teacher of consciousness – love and wisdom

The will to love fills with its more feminine energy doctors, healers, nurses, ambassadors, listeners, those bent upon health and wholeness. Motivated by the need for expansion, initiation and fulfilment, longing for awareness and wisdom, they pursue the truth of the heart. They communicate by empathy, attracting and radiating, inspiring others with their compassion. Almost in spite of themselves they let others be drawn to their healing power. For them, *God is love* – Christ, Buddha, Krishna, Vishnu. They follow St. Francis of Assisi, Mother Teresa, Pope John XXIII. They teach, not facts but relationship, mysticism, consciousness of the inner life.[226] Voluntary workers, members of goodwill groups, they do counselling and therapy. Positively, they are calm, open, sensitive, responsive to real need in the other. Universal, not personal, patient and open, their *symbols* include the heart, the circle, the Caduceus, the rose, lotus, pen, book.

Their *drawbacks* cluster mainly round invasion. Too wide open to 'helping' everyone, too inclusive (unlike the rulers), what matters to them is relationship; so they can become fearful and oversensitive with all the wrong attachments. They love to be loved. Easily drawn off-centre, too open, too loving, their floppy boundaries are invaded by everyone. Loving persons, not causes, they can be sentimental.

Inflation is in the *shadow* of their longing for inner, subjective truth. Group leaders, therapists, teachers of consciousness, mistaking themselves for the wisdom they mediate, can be full of self-satisfaction, which is pleasurable – or self-pity, which isn't. Vishnu is about caring, yes and those moved by the Priest-healer energy work out of love, both for the subject and for humanity. However, a certain ruthlessness underlies the archetype. They are tuned to *eros* rather than *logos*, so the relationships must be right. They love everyone with bright energy – but it can be a jealous, intense, interfering love that says, 'I want to love them more than you do!' They need not to be shining *too* brightly.

---

226 They include people such as Alice Bailey and the Theosophists.

They *need* protection, to be pulled back from people with tremendous neurotic or psychotic needs. And it doesn't take a King or Ruler to do it; some sub-personality will do fine, helping them develop and remember their *own* space and boundaries. To be contained, less invaded and invading, less sapped and sapping, is to move towards true initiation.

Thinker, philosopher – intelligence (higher mind)

The will to knowledge characterises a different kind of teacher, one who values consciousness, the light of the mind and pure understanding. To know and to impart knowledge is all-important; the thrust is towards ideas and intelligence. Thinkers are influenced by Brahma. *God is thought* and God is all-knowing. Though related to the Scientists, whose God is truth (see below), for Thinkers truth changes as you look at it. They are the pattern-makers, weavers, archivists, keepers of the records. Here are the entrepreneur, the communicator, educator, skilled in planning and effective communication. Valuing the intelligent use of mind rather than heart, they understand beauty and the elegance of the good theory. They are concerned with adaptation, development and evolution.

They are moved by words, loving the subject, generating ideas and concepts, longing for knowledge. Less open than the Priest-healer, their love is also of the heart. Here are Aristotle, Wittgenstein, Russell, Chomsky, Rodin, the Rothschilds. Philosophers, theoreticians, model-builders, planners, they *select*. They include tradesmen and bankers affected by money and gold; writers, metaphysicians and systems-builders (cybernetics, think-tanks); those teaching anthroposophy and the Kabbala, lovers of mathematics. They like to see where everything fits in. Astrologers are on this archetype, with their need to understand, define and be clear, exploring balance. However, absorbed in the beauty and elegance of the chart, they tend to forget the person – unlike counsellors, who may lose proportion and judgment by being lost in the client.

The *drawbacks* for people under this archetype lie in the very activity of their thought processes, the constant mental manipulation of what they are doing. This is *citta*, mind-stuff. When things change, truth changes with it. Some work slowly and are extremely cautious; great philosophers or metaphysicians they may be, yet the accounts don't add up and the papers are in a mess. Others think quickly, adapting flexibly enough to meet demands, processing schemes for getting out of holes. Never still, always busy, they hurry, weave, scheme, reaching solutions through mixes of ideas. Their minds keep them running. They become careless, over-active, taking on too much and scattering their forces. 'What's going on?' Go-go!

In the *shadow* of the Thinker lies a dogmatic manipulator who may try to brainwash other people; the mind, the stuff of thought, has taken over. 'These are *my* ideas, not yours!'

They *need* to select and discriminate, to be still. Profundity develops them; not meditation but thinking it through, reflecting on the problem or issue or need. The true intellectual is lost in deep thought, *pondering*. The aim is the stillness of the lake when wind is absent – a flat calm; then they reflect perfectly whatever may be of light and shadow.

Mediator, conciliator – harmony through conflict

'Is it *acceptable*?' ask those affected by this archetype. 'Does everyone agree? How do you feel?' They are mixers; they understand by tuning in. Instinctual as well as intuitive, they jump to the point and land on the truth. Moved by the *will to harmony*, they seek peace *through* conflict and its resolution. They long for things to flow, for relationship between others. They negotiate the resolution of dissonance, seeking at-one-ment, atunement, 'both this and that'. Their *God is harmony*. At best, the Scriptures are full of it: Christ, Buddha, Krishna. So are the social sciences, town planning, architecture, ecology.

Here are peace workers, ecologists, solvers of problems. Diplomatic, prepared to take risks and move around, they negotiate using game theory to see that everyone benefits.[227] They stand firm. Between management and labour they often work in pairs to bridge the unbridgeable, reconcile the irreconcilable. Though not out to con anyone by this, they still avoid being seen too close together.... All cultural movements and peace movements, all declarations of the Rights of Man, need this harmonising energy. The United Nations has its share of such mediating, reconciling visionaries. So do voluntary organisations, religious orders, most adult education and consciousness-raising movements in psychology. Whereas those working for human rights have Ruler energy, people exploring human relationships have the energy of Conciliators.

Here too are *explorers*, whose *God is adventure* and whose motive is to dare; and *artists*, seeking to capture vision harmoniously through music, acting, painting. Their *God is beauty*, the elegance of expression in

---

[227] In game theory, people on Ray Four go for the 'positive-sum' situation (where the whole somehow becomes greater than the sum of the parts), not the 'zero-sum' or 'negative-sum' game where one side is bound to lose). See John Nash, b. 1928, the game theorist who in 1994 won a Nobel Prize in Economics. (He is the subject of the 2001 film *A Beautiful Mind*, about his mathematical genius and his struggles with schizophrenia. Ed.)

form. Their motive is to make visible the invisible. Moved and motivated by the will to create, artists, craftspeople and explorers seek expression for their ideas. Subjective, keenly aware of the vibrations of things, they are in touch with what seems beyond the individual – with the collective unconscious, the well-springs of creation. Here are Arjuna – Orpheus – Mozart who *is* the harmoniser – Leonardo da Vinci, the archetypal expression of this energy.

The *drawback* for those moved by this archetype, whether harmoniser, explorer or artist, involves a falling into chaos and despair. Full of vision, they may lack application, with too low a ratio of perspiration to inspiration. Dealing with opposites, split to one end or other of the pole, they gamble with life. Subject to bi-polar swings, they lurch from over-enthusiasm and recklessness into a *shadow* of depression and self-flagellation. It's both yes-and-no; going for peace at any price, they get stuck on fences, seeing both sides till decisions become impossible: '*You* decide!' Their *need* is to make decisions and to act, to develop steadfastness. The keynote is 'stand steady'.

Scientist, alchemist – knowledge through research

The will to truth is behind this, the objective practical fact, the nature of a thing. Those under this archetypal energy discriminate and differentiate, searching, analysing, experimenting, measuring, seeking to find out, discover, prove, and only so to know. For them, 'E = MC squared' is as important as 'God is love'. Their *God is truth*.

Here are engineers, chemists, electricians and surgeons, scientists in pursuit of truth – Newton, Darwin, Edison. Manipulators not of ideas but of things, infinitely patient, loving precision, they ask, 'Will it *work*?' Not sloppy but careful like the Curies, they experiment and test, though not knowing the consequences of their research. Their value is practical: 'suck it and see'. Fact-oriented, they run trials, wanting evidence, enjoying technicality and analysis. They are cautious, not jumping to conclusions but differentiating, discriminating, spotting inconsistencies, choosing either this or that. Categorising, sorting and pigeonholing, they have a passion for measurable and repeatable outcomes.

Through facts, engineering and the production of *things*, these immensely keen, hard-working lovers of truth have brought about vast changes: anaesthetics, electricity, astronomical knowledge. They have created modern industry. Ironmongers all, neat and exact with their microscopes, telescopes and flasks, they are practical men and women, accurate, intelligent, full of craft. Physical, 'body' knowledge is what's sought. Psychology was taken into the laboratory by behavioural scientists and made academic; Jung, to have it accepted, made it look more scientific than it was. The meaning lay both within and behind the form. Our education system would like to be seen to be based here – showing which archetype may move the nation. Perhaps the alchemist is the feminine counterpart of the scientist. Many an esoteric group – Rosicrucians, astrologers, metaphysicians, psychical researchers – seek factual truth in their healing methods and approaches to the psyche.

The *drawbacks* include a possible lack of ethics to match their skill; witness the creation of the atom bomb. Head types, out of touch with their feelings, they may forget the microcosm in the interest of a wider search for facts for facts' sake. Critical and arrogant about the virtues of their path, they may concentrate overmuch on form, irritable with those not quite like themselves. The *shadow* of science is that there *is* no shadow. Wedded to their research, some seekers after truth may be less detached than they believe: the unconscious investment is in science itself. Dismissing a topic for study before looking at it makes it hard for these narrow researchers to see that their method is not very scientific. And they can be pedantic, long-winded, full of wearisome detail.

Detachment is needed. Science is changing. There are new paradigms. Scientists themselves, taking a new position, have begun to speak the language of consciousness. While the early image was of someone concerned with outer form, it is now accepted that the fact of the observer changes what is seen. The bias of the experimenter has to be taken into account. The physicist Stephen Hawking said, 'For me, physics is about seeing better, further and deeper.' Where scientists used to be at variance with religious thinkers, they may now be at the very forefront of knowledge, at a place where physics meets mysticism.

Devotee, idealist – perfection and adoration

The energy of *the will to perfection* has given rise to the idealists and adorers of the Christian era. The last two thousand warlike years have elevated this ideal above the archetype of wholeness (which would have led us to integrate, not fight). When a minor archetype is lifted over a major, problems ensue.

Those influenced by this archetype are about salvation and self-sacrifice. They include saint and missionary, martyr and preacher, for whom *God is perfection*, God is the ideal. Sympathy and tolerance are valued, but the real motivation is to perfect devotion and abstraction. Here are the divine warriors, crusaders with their targeted love, robbers and sword-bearers for the *logos*, Knights Templar all. The very religious are here, church workers, volunteers – reverent, serving others, full of faith and prayer – and followers, responding with persistence and purity: disciples, students, apprentices, devoted servants of a person, a cause, a family, perfect backroom girls and boys – like, perhaps, those found at Bletchley Park during the Second World War.[228]

Seeking perfection as their god, those of this era have tended to cluster around a central favourite teacher: Buddha; Jesus (rather than Christ); Milarepa, St. Paul, St. Francis; or, more recently, various holy men and extreme cults. Here are the churches with their monasteries and nunneries, and many esoteric and psychic movements. The Devotee can be devoted to anything – to gurus and ashrams, to Sufis, yoga, Christianity – to baked beans. Hospitals are filled with Devotees – along with Ruler-Kings. The Salvation Army offers an example of this archetype at its best: it's the work that counts; devoted without pushing their devotion (which is rare), they really are motivated by their will to idealise and perfect.

But the *drawbacks* are many. Devotees love those they love. They love particularly and selectively, deeply loyal to the chosen cause, teacher, ideal – the rest can go hang.... In the language of astrology, for the last two thousand years Pisces and Virgo have been the dominant archetypes, causing much psychological damage. Devotees both positive and negative have flourished in the Christian world, as well as in Judaism and Islam. Some men still publicly thank God daily that they were not born women. Christ's ideas have been twisted. 'Be ye therefore perfect' came to mean, 'Be ye therefore masculine, as woman is imperfect'.

Their *shadow* includes bigotry and exclusivity; their supreme god must be the supreme god for everybody. 'My god's better than yours.' Devotees can readily become fundamentalists, even fanatics. The Cross has the longest arm; at its worst, the Inquisition follows. 'God is on my side!' Perfectionists are not tolerant; one-pointed and narrow, sentimental, often emotionally tense – and intense – they are jealous and hurt when rejected or feeling themselves not accepted. Full of religious instincts and

---

[228] Cryptographers, decoding war-time secrets. See Harris 1995, *Enigma*.

impulses – 'Christian enthusiasm' – their extremes of view can be intolerable: 'I want to love them more than you do – don't get in my way!' Loyal workers, yes – and organisations depend on them – but they *need* tolerance and sympathy for other people's views. The task: to stop following and become leaders themselves.

Saints are after pain. Their eagerness to respond, their devotion to causes and ideals, their fanatical energy, are both splendid and terrifying. People on this archetype may be the most difficult of all. But the impulse to perfection is secondary to the will to *wholeness*; though some archetypes dominate for a long time, it is on the wane now, at the turn of the millennium. The energy of the Magician is coming in.

Magician – making manifest

So this seventh main archetype is constellating and coming into consciousness – into manifestation – now, in this era. Whenever a new archetype constellates, it appears to be divine. Those under this archetype can anchor and earth, bringing components together coherently, understanding people. The Magician's wand is the wand of touch. Certain individuals never seem to do much or work hard, yet things happen all around them; for their *God makes manifest*, deftly. By subtle moves and unerring touch they unlock trouble. The *will to wholeness* shapes and organises matter systematically, efficiently, economically. They love the economical deployment of force. If a thing has to happen, let it be with the least possible expenditure of energy: no waste, no sledgehammers cracking nuts.

British state occasions demonstrate a modern magic; unlike their Russian or German counterparts (one sided, goose-stepping their rigid organisation), these are flowing, artistic, dancing. People with this energy include theatrical producers, choreographers, business entrepreneurs – and, again, some teachers. Tennyson, that poet of emotions, was here; Lord Beaverbrook, an organising individual; Sheikh Yamani, a skilled diplomat;[229] Lyndon Johnson. Masonry and magic, ritual and courtesy, care over detail – all appear when Magicians wave their wands. Here are effortless efficiency, economy of movement, systematic organisation, co-ordination, bringing together.

A Magician is different from those under the archetypes of either power or love. The king needs a Magician around: a court chamberlain, a

---

[229] Yamani, Saudi Arabian Oil Minister (1962-1986), close adviser to the Saudi government and with a colourful international reputation for diplomatic skills. He was taken hostage in 1975 by notorious terrorist Carlos the Jackal. Carlos was ordered by his superiors to execute Yamani, but after two days in an aeroplane with him, he released him.

grand vizier. Arthur had Merlin, the Czar had Rasputin. And a Priest-healer combined with a Magician makes the best healer of all. What's happened to the Magician's energy? To manifestation and the proper ordering of things? Merlin went to sleep; where's he been during the Christian era? Now he is returning, attempting to bring order to the world through *networks*. However, since the idealists of the departing era are so much caught up with their forms, Magicians can't readily get in. Is the Magician, then, the fool? Some practise white magic – spiritualism, the Western mystical tradition – and some practise dark. Their fundamental aims are different. The fool loves the *thing*; and manifesting for your own purposes – if you're any good at it – will cause trouble.

Their *drawbacks* include inflexibility. They know about incubation, manifesting with such skill and ease that they may forget why they are doing it, so that the manifesting itself becomes central. A ritualistic dimension can creep in – 'I'm absolutely sure you mustn't alter the ceremony!' – and rituals that run out of energy become dry form. Though precise, appearances must be right. People under this archetype can be slow to change, iconoclastic, secretive and rigid, putting control, form and organisation first. They hold superstitiously to the rules, valuing the manner before the matter. The *shadow* of the Magician includes inflation, manipulation and deception. Here is the inhuman technocrat. This is a major, collective impulse, wider than just a few people. It affects everyone according to their consciousness. Magicians can misuse power to bring about dark ends and render other people, including their family members, mad.

This incoming archetype has (stupidly!) sent apprentice sorcerers ahead. They come in like children and go out like old men. These would-be magicians don't know their stuff; they wave wands and cause havoc. Still at the apprentice stage, they respond by producing a mass of stuff and not knowing what to do with it. Take some important movement led by a small number of pioneers. The second generation is almost bound to foul it up. The problems become bigger than the people and most of what goes on is apprentice sorcery. The hope is that the third generation will redress the balance. Do we need smaller organisations – or bigger people? It's insoluble. These apprentice sorcerers need not dignifying but, rather, calling for what they are. And the *zeitgeist* pays them for the work they do....

The Magician is subtly different from the *manager*, who structures and organises energy systematically. With a Magician behind to inspire him, he'll be excellent at his job – as financier, economist, middleman or dealer. Management lacks good white magicians with orderly, rhythmic energy, sensitive to pattern, doing things punctually, carefully, in the right order. One such organisation man, a quiet and gentle chairman, who chose his subordinates well and worked always through the team, was both a Conciliator and a Magician in his own right. The manager-Magician understands that people are more important than systems and computers. And all Magicians *need* humane purpose – to develop true magic, true ritual.

ARCHETYPES OF THE SELF

I laugh when I hear that the fish in the water is thirsty.
You don't grasp the fact that what is most alive of all
is inside your own house.
And so you walk from one holy city to the next with a confused look!
Kabir will tell you the truth: go wherever you like, to Calcutta or Tibet.
If you can't find where your soul is hidden
For you, the world will never be real.
Kabir[230]

To reiterate: we *are not* the archetypal energy – that is the potential within us. Our images bring us archetypal *figures*, not the archetypes themselves – consciousness teachers, priest-healers, scientists, magicians or mediators rarely appear as such in our dreams. Jung talked about the god-*image*, not about the god. So we get the hero, the muse, the guide; a wise person appears, or a trickster, rather than God or the devil.

These seven archetypal energies constitute one system among many. Esoteric groups love to put things into systems. There are other systems (transcenders and actualisers,[231] for instance, or to do with the chakras[232]) but they don't work for everyone.[233]

---

230 Kabir, 15th Century Hindu/Sufi mystic.
231 More types of people, see transcenders and actualisers, Appendix 8.
232 See Chapter 8 below.
233 For addicts of the 'Star Trek' films, here is an observation from a colleague of the authors. The first 'Star Trek' series, from the days of Humanistic Psychology, involved three main characters: the Captain (perhaps symbolic of Body), Mr Spock (Mind), and Dr McCoy (Emotions). At about the time when Transpersonal Psychology was taking hold, this was followed by a series called 'Star Trek, the Next Generation'. The new characters seem to represent archetypes: Captain Picard (King), Commander Riker (Hero), Worff (Warrior, Devotee), the engineer (Magician), Data (Scientist, Truth), Guinan (Wisdom), the doctor (Healer), Counsellor Troi (Priestess, or perhaps Love/Compassion). (With grateful acknowledgement to Hazel Guest. Ed.)

Vocation

Once more, 'Who am I?' No chart can answer that question. The task of finding the archetype of the Self is equal to that of finding our vocation. Our archetypal energy sends us each to our own trade. It may be easier to discover who you're *not*. Not a scientist – then are you a mediator or a thinker? If you can't get love, is it that you want power? Does one of your ego's sub-personalities (some Happy Bastard, perhaps?) like to rule, but your true Self does not? Are you a devotee at the personal level, but a healer or teacher of consciousness at the level of the Self? Are you in the wrong stream of life altogether?

In the first half of life we're moved by the personal centre, in the second, by the transpersonal Self, speaking in dreams, in things we enjoy, in consciousness. Early on, though we heard it only indirectly, its voice may have been peremptory and punishing, giving us pain. Then, a midlife crisis and a new factor comes into consciousness, a touch of the soul, telling you perhaps to change your career – or change the way you are in your existing career? Someone in medicine, for instance – is their energy that of a surgeon, a scientist? Or are they at heart a physician, a priest-healer? We differ in our healing methods, as much as in our approaches to the psyche.

Archetypes come in and out. We may well be under the spell of more than one, resonating then moving on. Which?[234] Are ego and Self on different lines – magical, scholarly, scientific or whatever. The ego may be under several archetypes; the Self, just one. Do you respond more to the priest-healer, or to the ruler? Good partners when brought together. How about perfection, the devotee? Maybe it's the artist, in touch with harmony, exploration, with what seems beyond the individual, with the collective unconscious, the well-springs of creation – the subjective. Do you then lack application, the perspiration to match the inspiration?

We tend, mistakenly perhaps, to live amongst people of our own kind; if we're always with, say, a set of priest-healers and consciousness teachers, never meeting a ruler or a thinker, where is the sceptic in us nourished?

---

[234] See Jung, *CW 9* Part I, 'Archetypes of the Collective Unconscious'. 'I recommend that you skip the first twenty pages, then start!' (IGB).

EXPLORATION
ARCHETYPES OF THE SELF
(35 minutes)

This aims to get in touch at a deeper level with two or three of the archetypes which have a particular meaning for you: first, some energies of the *personality*, then perhaps the core archetype of the *Self*. Looking in turn at Mind, Emotions and Body (maybe Intuition too), ask yourself: 'To which archetypal energies do I particularly resonate?' Let *them* come to *you*.[235]

Minutes

3 Begin by closing your eyes and finding yourself in a safe place. Let go of the thinking function, which has had a good go at doing what it enjoys, and enter instead the imaging mode. Take some time to enter your inner world. *Be* there. Feel the atmosphere, scents, sounds, season. When you are ready, choose your Talisman.[236]

7 Let your Talisman take you where you can meet the parts of yourself that resonate to archetypal energies. Here, expect to meet with that part of your nature which resonates to your first archetype. Is it an impression, or a person – is it an inner space, a dwelling, a garden, part of nature? Tune in to the quality, energy and character of this aspect of yourself. Invite a sense of what archetype may be around – allow it to present itself, let it come to you. It may be the one you expect – or not. Allow an image, symbol or picture to form to represent it. Note the setting, the atmosphere, your physical feelings, your emotions, as you come into the presence of this energy. At what level does it work?

4 Where, in your life in the world, does this archetype have influence? What would happen if you let it be more prominent in your life? Prepare to let it move on, and rest in your safe place.

7 When you are ready, and if it's appropriate, invite another archetypal energy that is close to you. Once again, get an image,

---

[235] IGB writes: 'As an example, when I did this exercise I found at the level of personality the extravert, the man of action, the attention-seeker, doer and achiever with the power and authority of the first archetype. The body felt neglected, uncared for, the Ruler taking it for granted as a workhorse. The emotions were relaxed, tranquil, lazy, clear and light, suggesting the second archetype, but occasionally disturbed by tension and by the eruptions of the attention-seeker, indicating that both Ruler and Perfectionist were sometimes present at this level too. The mental level of logic and reason – the front of my mind – resonated to the analytical energy of the scientist. At the top of my mind, on the other hand, I sensed a receptive, reflective energy bent towards synthesis, the discovery of the total pattern. This tended more towards the Thinker archetype. Looking more deeply, towards the level of the Self, I found that for me, the archetype is love and human consciousness.'

[236] The talisman, see Chapter 6, p. 270.

symbol, picture, note the atmosphere, your feelings, the level of being of this archetype. Observe any changes in energy.

4 Where does this archetype have influence in your life? What would happen if you let it be more prominent?
Let this second archetype move on, and rest once again in your safe place.

7 Again if it's appropriate, invite a third archetype to come in. Once more, see an image, symbol, picture. Note the atmosphere, your feelings, the level of being of this archetype.

3 Note the area of your life where it has influence. Are there any changes in energy?

Eventually, note, draw and, if it's appropriate, do some body work. Though there's nothing orderly about the way this presents itself, once you are aware of the collective streams and dance the dance of the psyche, you can see a marvellous order emerging.

ARCHETYPES AND PSYCHOTHERAPY

Try to explain what an archetype is; it's like trying to tell someone what a ghost is; a ghost in Plato's cave.[237] Coleridge, when asked if he believed in ghosts, said no, he'd known too many of them. An archetype is known to us by the company it keeps, projected onto outer objects, persons, or events. Jung wrote that those who speak archetypal language stir us because their voices are stronger than ours, overpowering and enthralling us with a thousand primordial images, raising the transitory and the occasional into the everlasting. They evoke beneficent forces that offer refuge from all perils, enabling us to outlive the longest nights; they transmute our personal destiny into that of all mankind.[238]

Particularly in the great, inescapable, archetypal moments – birth, adolescence, love, hate, danger, opportunity, death, rebirth – we emerge from our context. Our Selves and our clients respond both personally and by resonating in a collective, human way. Each single human individual knows all this; it is lying behind them, though they may never touch on it. At such times our experience is the same as our roots and the roots of all humanity.

---
237 Plato's Myth of the Cave, Appendix 11.
238 See Jung 1922, *CW 15*, para 129.

Those on a particularly deep journey will be tapping archetypal energies (different from the archetype itself). A lot of counsellors back off at this point, preferring not to work with such energies, calling the whole thing a nonsense. Given insight into their shadow and personal complexes, they may recover without ever having heard of an archetype. Jung never looked for archetypes when working with his patients – enough when they came all by themselves.[239] And they sometimes do, and most vehemently, especially if therapy has gone on too long, or the client has a vivacious mind, when things archetypal will sooner or later appear. Can the person be helped to hold the energy?

Archetypal energy and psychosis

In ancient times people spoke of being possessed by demons. To the patient, psychosis or severe neurosis still seems like being possessed by a mysterious, invading power (though psychiatric diagnoses can now be made according to numbers![240]) A *complex*, according to Jung, is the sum of all the associated ideas and feelings that are attracted to an archetype. The complex gives the archetype a form of expression; and the complex is powered by affect. Feeling this affect, we believe we are experiencing the archetype itself. Trumpets! Enter the King! Thunder and lightning! As we've seen, for someone to become *identified* with the archetype, to feel they *are* the archetype, is dangerous. To say, 'I think I know what was the nature and quality of Mary Magdalene', is very different from saying, 'I *am* Mary Magdalene'. Perhaps clients for whom this happens a lot may indeed have broken through some barrier and be contacting archetypal energies – or not. They may have no barrier at all and be on the edge of psychosis. Which?

Perhaps, as the consciousness of the race changes, those suffering from psychosis – those with no boundaries, no containers – hold something for the rest of us. They need certainly to be treated with respect and helped to relate to the positive energies of the archetype. The person helping needs to ground them, strongly relating the inner with the outer, encouraging the client to anchor it by keeping a workbook, a dream book – painting, sculpting, doing psychodrama. It needs long, gentle, slow, common-sense handling.

---

239 See letter to Dr. D. Cappon, 1954. Jung, Letters, Vol.2, pp. 160-161.
240 See the *Diagnostic and Statistical Manual of Mental Disorders* or DSM-III (now IV), published by the American Psychiatric Association.

SPIRIT OF PLACE – COMMUNITIES AND LOCATIONS

People who are ill may simply be living in the wrong place

Are sick or unhappy people in a geographically alien energy-field – the wrong district, even the wrong country?[241] Are they on the wrong kind of rock – or is a granite person living on clay, a sand person on limestone? Sea people may be stuck inland, plains people in the mountains and mountain people in the Fens. Is this a city person forcibly isolated in the country, a village person confined to the town? One person from the North of England, forced to live in the South, was always unwell till she went to Manchester, where she was fine (despite the fact that her troublesome family lived there). She needed look no further for the root of her malaise.

Explorers of earth-energy, aiming to relate to the planet as a whole, are on the edge of something important. In China, the houses have to suit the Dragon Spirit, being built so that no evil spirits can enter – indeed, mirrors are put up to scare them off....

Spirit of Cities

Places like Glastonbury are no longer the powerful energy centres of Great Britain. The truly major magnetic and spiritual centres for the collective are the big cities. They are like chakras in the country's total energy system, while the ley-lines, crossing at power-points across the land, are its acupuncture meridians. Each town and city is a sacred site with its different geology and topography, like a lotus with an initiating triangle at its centre, the 'jewel in the lotus'. Each petal has a different energy, its own cellular structure.

Cities have regions which correspond to different areas of consciousness. London, for instance, consists of villages that have grown together, each with its own spirit: Westminster for Government, the City for money and banking, Bloomsbury for education and medicine, Lincoln's Inn for justice. (And south of the river lies the shadow, where the Redeemer lives....[242]) All are different; we sense it as we cross streets that represent boundaries. The *local* spirits are very important both for the people and for the organisations there. Until quite recently, the postman was a walking, Tolkien-style *ent*, like a tree;[243] there were corner-shop

---

241 IGB's sources for Spirit of Place, see n. 86, p. 152.
242 As the least differentiated function, p. 234.
243 'Ents' or tree-people, Tolkien 1954, *The Two Towers*, pp. 484 ff..

people, porters, caretakers, dustmen, milkmen, street-cleaners. Love them, support them, become one of them – they are being crowded out. Little room is left for them when the cellular structure of a city is destroyed. The centre fades as huge motorways and car parks appear on the edges, breaking up the archetypal shapes, cutting into the squares and circles and crescents, shattering its structure.

Spirit of nations

They, too, have different collective national energies. For the United Kingdom, Alice Bailey suggested *love* and *wisdom* were the soul energies while *power* was that of the ego-personality which had been dominant in the age of Empire. Recently, Great Britain had been shifting towards the energy of the soul or Self of the country. In the United States, love and wisdom were again the soul's energies, but the personality was that of the *devotee*. In Russia, the *magician* was the soul's energy and, again, devotion the ego's; both Russia and America were shifting towards their soul energies. China had power for the soul and *ideas* for the ego; India, again, power for the soul but *mediation* for the ego.[244]

As nations, towns and cities differ, and the areas within cities – and individual people – so too do organisations.

LIFE-CYCLES OF GROUPS AND ORGANISATIONS

There is genuine good will in industry,
but in esoteric groups they cut each other's throats....

Important movements tend to be led by a small number of pioneers. The second generation are almost bound to foul it up; then the third generation redresses the balance.

There are parallels between the behaviour of the individual and behaviour in the collective. In the individual, the borderline between conscious and unconscious is varied and fluid, where in the collective it is more distinctly marked. Groups, like individuals, have their journeys and their cycles: the goal, the energy used and the style of management depend on the archetype, and the group must meet the test of the market place, each activity serving a real need. When we consider an organisation,

---

244   See Alice Bailey on the Nations and the Rays, Appendix 19.

we need to remember not only its conscious side, but its unconscious purpose, its structure, leadership, size, way of communication, relations and life-cycle.[245]

Purpose. What is the keynote of the group? Is it a voluntary organisation, or an industry? Organisations designed for love – those which, on the surface, care for spirituality – tend to have the knives out underneath in the unconscious. And in esoteric groups, people cut each other's throats. On the contrary, in those organisations designed for *profit* the battles are less destructive. People who have worked in both the industrial and the therapy worlds have tended to find more genuine love and good will in industry, where power-trippers get their legs pulled, than in 'helping' groups where they are stabbed in the back. What's in the unconscious of a competitive, cut-throat organisation? The answer is, *love*.

Structure. In our society, well-functioning groups are usually hierarchical: democracy still turns out that way. Balancing a strong central energy with group involvement is difficult, and few are yet ready for it; organising and tightening up the structure brings up quarrels. Although the interplay of power and money is crucial in all organisations, one is normally set against the other. And in voluntary and 'New Age' groups, they are both in the shadow: 'If we make appeals, we should send out accounts'. Or should we?

Leadership. Are the leaders charismatic? Charisma is what we beam out – it makes it possible for others to project on to us. Charismatic leaders set up groups which become extensions of themselves; they can touch and feel what's going on. This is an instinctual phase in the life of the group: the leader carries not only the life force but the masculine and feminine principles too. Are they tight, disciplined and hierarchical; or, as in certain types of network, do they keep a looser hold? Both are useful and necessary – but which is appropriate? It depends on the archetype under which the group functions.[246]

Charismatic leaders, whether men or women, tend to be entrepreneurs, not managers. But a charismatic man needs a colleague, often a woman, who *can* manage; and the charismatic woman will remain just a wise woman of the *village* unless she has a manager, usually a man. If each has the other, a *sect* grows.

Size. With fewer than about twenty-five, everyone knows everyone. When the number grows above that, the group becomes an organisation

---

245 Again, for IGB's sources, see n. 86, p. 152.
246 See Handy 1985, *Gods of Management*. Each god – Zeus, Apollo, Athena, Dionysus – rules a different kind of organisation.

and charismatic leaders often can't cope. Earlier than one might think, starting in the second seven-year cycle, the work increases, numbers rise and problems multiply. As soon as the archetypal structure gets spoilt, relationships are ruined. The secret is, make haste *slowly*. On a bigger scale, two to five hundred is a critical size. An organisation is 'small' if it's under five hundred; over that, and it's inhuman, non-organic, and doesn't work. Other ways – the way of the network, the way of the matrix – must be found.

Communication. Within organisations there are process people and there are project people. Lines of communication between them need to be kept open. Process people mind the shop and get pleasure thereby; project people undertake a task, and when that is accomplished they want another, different task. There are project and process *organisations*, too. Their breakdowns can be compared with those of individuals: at odds with their purpose, everything gets too much, too big for them. Communication fails. The organisation needs the small things again, till it can begin to extend lines of communication within itself, and finally with others.

Relations. Within the archetypal field of the organisation, people mix in inner groups. Each archetype needs to be present at some level, a balance giving effective action. The masculine and feminine principles are both crucial for success. Hospitals, schools, industry and so on traditionally allowed women only menial tasks: the feminine was carried by the secretaries and the tea ladies and canteen staff and porters. But organisations which have ignored, suppressed or barred the feminine principle in this way are organisations in trouble.

Life-cycles of groups and organisations

There are cycles in the lives of groups as well as of people. The first six nursery years ground the vision. Expansion takes place from seven to thirteen. In the next seven years – the adolescent, apprentice stage – the children rebel and leave home. From twenty-one to twenty-seven is the first stage of the hero's journey, when group generation takes place. Groups and organisations multiply because the founder doesn't prepare adequately for the succession – he can't let go. People come and go; very few stay for more than one seven-year cycle. However, to be prepared for the central energy of leadership a person needs to be there for *two* seven-year cycles. Most candidates for the succession won't hang around that long. They break away.

What happens? Many organisations – the Club, the Mafia – simply bring in like-minded people, family, friends; the Old Boy network makes history, through trust based on personal contact. This spider's web of nepotism enables speedy decisions and is cheap and effective. How do industrial and financial, head-type organisations multiply? The love is in the unconscious and groups spin off from each other quite amicably as individuals feel a need to be left to themselves. For example, a bank has money in the coffers and uses it to fund bright enterprises. Networking is the way; people are left free, and if one of them gets successful, that endeavour grows and the bank *wants* to float it off – rather like a spider-plant. It's seen as good that individuals go off and do their own thing. Of course, splits do also take place in industry; there are takeovers, as well as deliberate divisions by the originator. But in these 'for-profit' organisations, a genuine group sexual process, a mating, is sometimes possible.

They certainly have something to teach many 'love' organisations, which, not yet at this evolutionary mating stage, tend to be more like amoeba: they multiply by *splitting*. Within five years of the retirement or death of the founder, trouble arises. As new groups evolve out of the old, feelings of betrayal arise. It's painful. Many knives go in backs. The second generation, as we saw, has good intentions but is without charisma. Group-think and planning are substituted for inspiration. People divide into two ideological factions, one saying: 'Our Leader taught thus, and we must remain true to that!' The other, 'If he were here, he wouldn't *want* us to stick to the old ways. It's stupid!'

And so they split and start new organisations. This way seems to be natural for our age. How are we to use and respond to such unavoidable splits? The subsequent decline of the organisation is not necessarily a disaster. It can lead to a scattering of the seed. It might even be quite nice to look back at twenty-five years on when the protagonists are dead and the creative energy has been released. For the split may yet prove good for the future – and it does stop the leader from becoming a poor old *senex*.

Secondary Archetypes

The splitting of groups is not difficult at the level of the Self, the *primary* archetype of a group's personality. For example, in Psychosynthesis, Assagioli was first and foremost a priest-healer.[247] But ask, which *subsidiary* archetypes lend energy to organisations? This is very

---

[247] See Assagioli 1987, *Transpersonal Development*, on Psychosynthesis and the esoteric roots of Transpersonal Psychology.

difficult. Where some groups have 'power' or 'thinker' second, others have 'magician' or 'conciliator'. It makes a difference. In some kinds of group everyone falls over themselves to be helpful, while in others no one at all will volunteer to help new and ignorant members. Again, Humanistic psychology is under a different secondary archetype, more social and political, from Transpersonal psychology which leans more towards relationship and the spiritual. Humanistic people advertise more than transpersonal people, who believe that advertising even gets in the way. Could it be that 'psychology people' have more heart and less head, while 'astrology people' are the other way round? The god of the Scientist is truth, but what about the god of the transport organisations? Of engineering, sculpting, philosophy groups, poets' societies? They all differ in archetypal energy.

Leadership. Some leaders are better than others over questions of networks *versus* hierarchies. Political groups such as most governments, running on power and tight organisation, need Harmonisers among the Idealists. Yes, Rulers are required for focus and purpose, but also the heart of the Priest-healer, the clear analysis of the Scientist, the Magician to organise, and the Devotee to keep the show on the road. Educational groups need Conciliators to blend the harsh outlines of schools, universities, colleges; they need Science for clarity and they need Love to relate people with each other. Scientific groups need Thinkers for clarity, and Harmonisers too. Who is in charge of the health service? Take hospitals. The consultants are usually Ruler types, often trying to be Magicians too. But where are the Healers?

It needs a mix. In successful organisations, the leaders often succeed in blending the archetypes *within themselves*. If they don't, they will need the combined energies of two or three other people; otherwise, a lopsided organisation and a lot of trouble follow. The right archetype must be in charge, within the individuals and thus in the group. Its outer form must be compatible with its spirit. In applying for an apparently ideal job, ask: does the resonance of this group really match this individual? We recall Jung's concept of the accidental and the chosen family.[248] We are not all of the same stuff, but have our spiritual families. At a certain stage we find our own people – and come home.

Again, it may be appropriate to end this workshop with the Universal Blessing of Buddhism.[249]

---

248 See Somers & Gordon-Brown 2002, p. 136
249 The Universal Blessing of Buddhism, see Chapter 10, p. 365.

Facsimile of notes: Ian Gordon-Brown

CHAPTER EIGHT

The Chakra System

Ian Gordon-Brown

Door to experience and gateway to the mysteries

INTRODUCTION

…ephemeral and intuitive consciousness has an energy – tangible, like a feather or a breath of wind…

Energy in the human body

Just as the map is not the country, so not everyone fits every map. However, the basic chakra system, though still primitive and certainly not rigid, may despite its variability be considered among the most sophisticated of approaches to the psyche. It embraces all human energies, charting not only our development but the apparently inexplicable movements of energy within us.[250] What can the ancient science of the chakras tell us about our evolution and our next spiritual steps? That man is an energy system, and each person a unit of energy within the universal field of the cosmos, is now widely accepted. Esoteric schools and Eastern teachers have always known it, expressing it in terms of these chakras.

Exploring the nature, quality and function of these major concentrations of energy in the human being, we begin to learn their language. Registering and tuning in to energy in certain parts of the body, we become conscious of the effects of these centres in daily living. What of their relationships to each other; to the spiritual paths of individuals, groups, communities, cities, nations and races; to the planet and the cosmos? Be encouraged to undertake some safe and gentle experiential work to discover more about your own energies and their creative development. Discover how each centre speaks within you; listen to what it says; involve the soul.

What are chakras?

The chakras are energy centres in the human body. Energy and

---

[250] It is a Tantric Buddhist map, but even older than the roots of Tantric Buddhism.

consciousness are two sides of the same coin, as we saw above: consciousness has energy; energy is a form of consciousness. This is paralleled in modern physics; we may not understand waves and particles, time and space, yet we trust the paradox. We're surrounded by energy, receiving and communicating it at all levels. The planet's field (the ionosphere, the etheric, the field of *prana* [251]– energies of place, magnetic spots) is much wider than the individual's. Recent science suggests substance itself is conscious. A stone, a grain of sand – each has its potential for consciousness, as Leibniz suggested.[252] And even the most ephemeral and intuitive consciousness has an energy. It can be almost touched – it's tangible, like a feather or a breath of wind. With heavier energies like rage you can feel 'stuff' coming off a person as if they were throwing it at you. One day, sensitive instruments will be able to measure this.

The energy field of the human being is known as the aura. We have access to a wide range of sources of energy, including all kinds of enjoyment, among which is the sexual, and much of our thinking. Intuition carries energy, and so do emotions such as anger and fear. Time as it passes is the measure of intensity of interest. Negative energy is carried particularly, perhaps, by boredom: yet more washing up, cleaning, furniture-shifting.... As the positive arises and radiates out to the edge of our own aura, our interest is awakened, no longer triggering boredom but clear, strong purpose, drive and endurance. The atmosphere around us is charged.

Storehouses of energy and consciousness, chakras express and represent a particular dimension of awareness. They can be seen as whirling discs of colour – saucers, flowers, gateways through which we receive communication. They have been described as vehicles or focal points for the soul. Ernest Wood sees them as cohering wheels threaded upon a very thin channel in the spine and spinning in a horizontal plane.[253] A pre-scientific Eastern image likens a chakra to a lotus or rose gradually opening; a jewel lies within the lotus, the jewel of the spirit, the keynote of the chakra. The 'I' can centre around this 'jewel in the lotus', as around a circular magnetic field. The petals are the substance or matter of the system, each symbolising a particular quality, and the number of petals in each centre differs. A chakra may still be unopened, like a lotus bud; as each petal unfurls, excessive energy comes into play.

Cosmology provides images for the chakra system: a spiral nebula, a galaxy, a solar system, concentric ellipses expanding and rotating.

---

251 Prana is etheric energy in a bioplasmic energy field.
252 Leibniz, the 'Monad', Appendix 13.
253 Ernest Wood gives a lot of very good information about the chakras. See Wood 1959, *Yoga*, pp. 143 ff.

Technology too: a radio is receiving and transmitting from a full range of wavebands, tuning in to and regulating both individual and collective energies. Whether a sophisticated, multi-wavelength gadget with a wide range of vibrations, tuned to many stations, or a simple, undeveloped cat's whisker wireless getting a single station, as receiver it is reactive, as broadcaster pro-active. In one person, a particular centre, say the Solar Plexus, may experience just one weak emotion. Maybe nervous anxiety passed the time when waiting for the breast or the bottle, and that became a pattern. Another has energy only in the Sexual centre. Someone who has not yet developed, or has closed down some too-painful area, may lack much energy at all.

What happens to consciousness when energy is fed into a chakra? That *something* happens there's no doubt. The experience may be light or heavy, warm or cool; we may have learnt to associate warm energy with

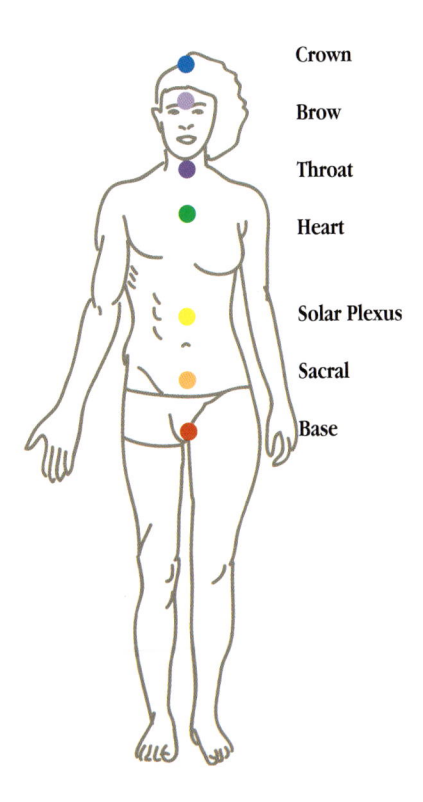

Chart 8:01 – Seven Chakras

love, cool with seeing things as they are. There are no rules. The chakras may be associated with colours, with planets, with musical resonances or notes. There are many variations depending on the individual's stage of development and inner archetypal orientation (Priest-healer, Magician, Scientist and so on).

Chakras are centred *behind the spine*. People often mistakenly picture them towards the front of the body, enabling the emotional openness and responsiveness of the Solar Plexus, say, to blow a person in all directions, including the negative. It is safer to sense them about an inch behind the physical, centred on the etheric spine where the jewel is located. By practising the qualities of a particular chakra, each may be gradually opened. Our state of consciousness is crucial. Let the rose come to flower; to engineer its opening by pulling at the petals kills it. *Wait* for it, mulch it, water it, sun it. The path is through balance and harmony.

The traditional chakra systems offer different numbers of these energy-centres in different bodily locations. Some follow the endocrine system.[254] Seven is a special number in Hinduism, Buddhism and Sufism. The Bible is full of references to *seven* as sacred, indicating perfection or

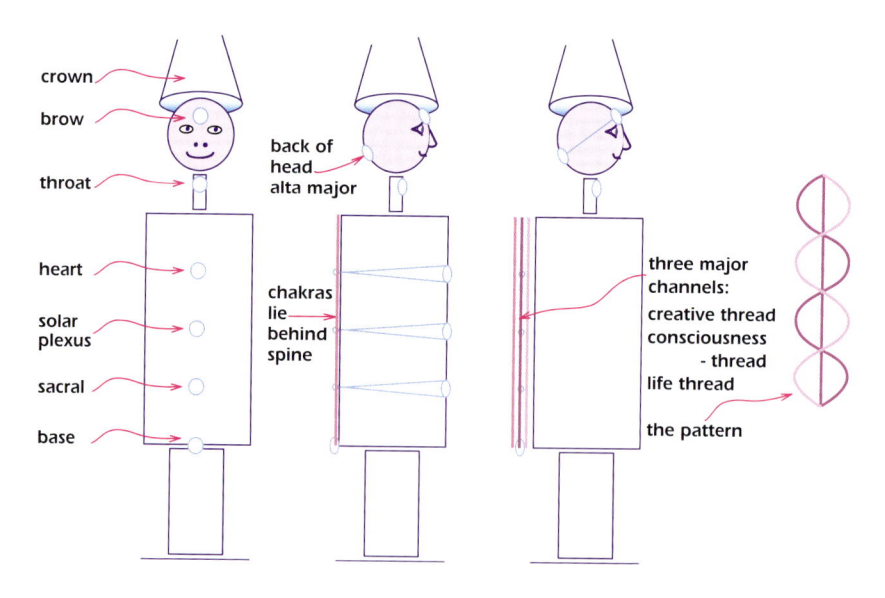

Chart 8:02 – Eight Chakras

---

254 Links between chakras and glands, Appendix 20.

completion, symbolising the *whole* of a thing – altars, trumpets, Sabbaths, years, tribes, cities. In the dream interpreted by Joseph there were seven of each sort of kine and seven ears of corn. The New Testament has seven baskets of bits left over, seven angels, seven golden candlesticks.

However, our preferred model includes an *eighth* centre, for which there is considerable evidence: the Alta Major. This, in descending order, is still only a map, but one of the most sophisticated and traditional:

> *The Crown or Highest Head Centre*
> *The Alta Major or Back of Head Centre*
> *The Brow Centre*
> *The Throat Centre*
> *The Heart Centre*
> *The Solar Plexus Centre*
> *The Sexual or Sacral Centre*
> *The Base of the Spine or Root Centre*

From the transpersonal perspective the Self is not on the chart. Yet every chakra has its counterpart in the highest Head centre, known as the thousand-petalled lotus, so the map may be seen as reflecting our own 'solar system'. For convenience we deal with them 'from bottom up', though that is not the order in which they generally awaken (see below).

Base

Presented first, the Base or Root chakra is usually almost the last to open. Linked with the Adrenals, it is to do with survival. Enormous spiritual and physical energy is stored here at the lowest point of the spine, between sacrum and perineum. While life is in the Heart and consciousness in the Head, the Base anchors us in the will to live and to be, until we become conscious. The immense strength physiologically generated here may lift a car to rescue a child, for example, or leap the fence out of the bull's field. Extraordinary extra energy can be pulled out after a shock, a 'white rage'. It operates all through our lives, pumping in the adrenalin, active when we get up and dance. It is the male servant within us, guarding the treasure, rescuing the princess. And it does so for our sakes, since it cannot itself access either treasure or princess.

When the time comes for its awakening, we'll know it. If we don't know, the time hasn't come. The awakening of the Head centre may show that it will come soonish.

Warning. This Root chakra is the seat of *kundalini*, the powerhouse of the dense, physical system. *Kundalini* holds our spiritual energies entrapped, so that they are not generally usable; and it's a very good thing that they do. We could not handle it at full power. The word *kundalini* means 'coiled'. It involves Shakti, a force, a 'goddess', a most powerful feminine energy within this masculine centre – and it is like an atom bomb. *Kundalini* is awakened by the Self when the time is ready. It comes from the Base, not from the Sex centre, and the energy spirals up to the head and down again. Given an imbalance, a person may be hostage to an accidental awakening of *kundalini*, whether by chance, or by overestimating where they are, or through stress. The thrust of the psyche is towards wholeness but some people are like lightning conductors for the collective; those who get caught unawares are weak on grounding in some part of their nature. The rousing of *kundalini* may well indicate that the system is not yet integrated, since the higher centres in the head are not yet linked to those in the spine.

Gopi Krishna describes first-hand and in great detail, in his book '*Kundalini*'[255] the dangerous and devastating experiences and the years of near-madness which followed when he accidentally, almost innocently, aroused it. He did this by a faithful and rigorous practice of meditation over many years. His book contains a most fascinating warning: artificial stimulation of this chakra is dangerous. We may raise more energy than we need to use; its raising must be linked with life – as must meditation.

Be careful of exercises. Playing about with the system, hurrying, leads to trouble. Being ruled by the Base centre leads to an adrenaline-fuelled overdrive, putting us under pressure to achieve and accomplish, pushing us beyond our capacity. Burnout may well follow.[256] The Base needs to be a steady glow, clear and open, requiring no special focus. (One dowser's intuitive image for this chakra was a monkey's tail, whose roots grew into the earth and helped them at work.) The final integration takes place when all the chakras are very much activated and, starting at the Crown, energy spirals down and *back up again*.

Sacral

The Sacral or Sexual centre often awakens after the Solar Plexus and the Throat. Again behind the spine, this chakra is to do with the Gonads, and is of the body. Exchange of generative energy at the reproductive area is about enjoyment on the physical plane of creativity, pleasure and

---

255 Krishna 1971, *Kundalini*. The author's account of his awakening, with commentary by James Hillman.
256 See Peter Nixon, Chart 4:09, The Human Function Curve, above.

procreation and the survival of the species. It carries much physical energy; the range of sensitivity is relatively limited. For most people the Sacral centre operates happily and well, is relatively simple to deal with and rarely needs deliberate stimulation. Usually all too easy to awaken, it flows naturally and looks after itself. However, the physical act of sex is but a symbol for something deeper and wider. The opening of this chakra involves the relationship between sexual and etheric energy.

Problems mostly originate in some other chakra, though individual sexual difficulties may perhaps reflect some difficulty in the Sacral centre. The Magician archetype has to do with the magic of sex, yet the mind may inhibit it; or it can become over-active. Modern industry and commerce are constantly *creating*: reproduction through the assembly line is a kind of sexual activity. Is it repetitive and dull, or creative and joyful? How, collectively and physically, do we relate to possessions and to sexuality, to which society gives so much attention? Sex is often connected with money and aggression, goods and exchange, transactions on the physical plane. Does the way people handle finance reflect their sexuality? What about joint bank accounts? Since money is energy manifest on the physical plane, a block on money can lead to a block on sexuality, and *vice versa*. The need is for common sense, earthing and practical activity.

Solar Plexus

This is the very first chakra of which many of us become aware.[257] We mostly experience it above the navel, in front of the body rather than behind. A clearing house between lower and higher centres, our relations to the world are felt here at a fairly physical level. Transition to the higher chakras starts here. And it *protects* us.

The Solar Plexus involves the Pancreas, and is capable of a wide range of feelings, often with truth in them. Ordinary emotions flow here, painful or pleasant – not only pain and anxiety, fear and anger but happiness, nervous excitement, anticipation. We feel a lift towards the Heart, towards joy and laughter. Although the energies of most of the chakras are difficult to reach (and this one too, for some people), yet personal feelings are usually readily accessible. We need only to hear, control and direct them. They don't have to be acted on, they just want to be listened to and so, released. Take grief; crying can provide a transpersonal energy which is not inflation but enlargement.

---

257 Neither it nor the Sacral chakra is to be confused with the 'hara', which is halfway between the belly button and the pubis. Appendix 20.

Problems. The Solar Plexus is our psychic dustbin. Too much use leads to over-sensitivity, emotional hysteria, dreams, visions and fears. It can cause splits involving hallucination and nervous disorder. Projection comes in here, devotion and fanaticism and issues around boundaries and invasion; reality, versus unrealistic hopes and expectations. Repressed Heart energy goes into the Solar Plexus, turning from purity to grubbiness and a feeling of being battered. By deliberately dwelling on emotions, our minds can inflate and nourish them and set up actual physical states – as energy follows thought, so the body follows energy. This is certainly true for destructive thoughts. Rather, go thoroughly into them, watch them arise, sense and own them, before letting them go.

Solar Plexus activity is often from an outside source. Some mediums use this level of energy – it involves power of a certain kind, a low-level clairvoyance adept at feeding back the wish life (and many contents of the emotional body do manifest anyway).

Like the radio receiving on several wavebands, individuals particularly receptive to a wide range of emotions may also be *broadcasting* those energies. The original child lives in the Heart but is vulnerable; so the hurt child in the adult moves down for cover. The Solar Plexus thus carries a large lump of shadow which, when broadcast, hooks other people in. When we are with such people, our Solar Plexus picks up their states – anxiety, for example, is infectious. Or we may be hit by headache or stomach-ache; our insides are the buffers and the other person is the train, coming to get us in the Solar Plexus. Healing for both of us may require psychotherapy.

As therapists, where do *we* project, what is our shadow side? Sensitive to the state of our own Solar Plexus, we seek the positive counterpart to its troubles. Colours can help: to move from irritation to serenity, visualise red changing to pale green; to clear the chattering mind, image a calm lake. Do this in small doses, regularly, lightly.

Heart

The Heart is also home to feelings, but more collective and transpersonal ones: the spiritual virtues, compassion, joy, empathic understanding. Etheric and associated with peak experiences, its energy line is of the feminine principle. It goes with the Thymus gland which, once thought to be vestigial, is now seen as importantly connected with the immune system. It usually opens after the Solar Plexus, Sacral and

Throat centres.

The Heart is the safest of the centres. In cultivating its qualities, we attend to the business of being understanding and compassionate, aware of our neighbours' consciousness. We need to develop objective love, helping transform the pain of another because, though sensitive, we are not identified with it. (Consider also that it may be better to let them stew in it – the Heart can differentiate. The Zen master Kennett Roshi was detached, described as being informed by *ruthless compassion*.)

The Heart centre lies again *behind* the spine. We feel our function as heart-based people in our *backs*, anchored in the etheric spine one or two inches behind the physical backbone, generating energy around our shoulder blades. In the old days it too was imaged in the front of the body, so that a person didn't have to go in towards the deep centre and was in danger of developing too much psychic sensitivity. But truly to experience is to go in towards the heart of the thing.

Visualise the lotus of the Heart, perhaps as a pool of electric-blue light, or as the blossoming of a rose. It is closed – see it opening under the light of the sun. Visualise there your image of perfection, or your wise teacher, or an impersonal symbol for the Self – a vase, chalice or jewel.

The opening lotus, twelve-petalled, first faces forward to the world; but as we reach a deeper level, closer to its heart and roots, it begins to look upwards towards the highest Head centre.[258] It leads to awareness of higher values; its qualities – spontaneity, altruism, service, good will, love of peace, tenderness, purity, humility, sympathy, tolerance – are of the soul, relating us to the higher Self, binding and linking us to the collective to work on behalf of other people. And there's a lot of emotion in it as well, moving us to relate and to function in groups. Priest-healers and teachers of consciousness are open to the feminine Heart centre; they know we learn to love by loving.

Problems. Emotional instability results when life is not carrying the whole energy of the heart; and so follows the mid-life crisis. In the Body, Emotion, Mind, Observer quartet, the *Mind* tends to take over the Observer's higher role. And the Heart reacts in the Solar Plexus. If we learn consciously to differentiate, to co-operate with moments of contact with energy, then we can hold situations, carry through change and make the breakthrough. Releasing our feelings through the *Heart* centre, open to the energy of love, is what matters.

---

[258] And see Wood 1959, ibid, p. 165.

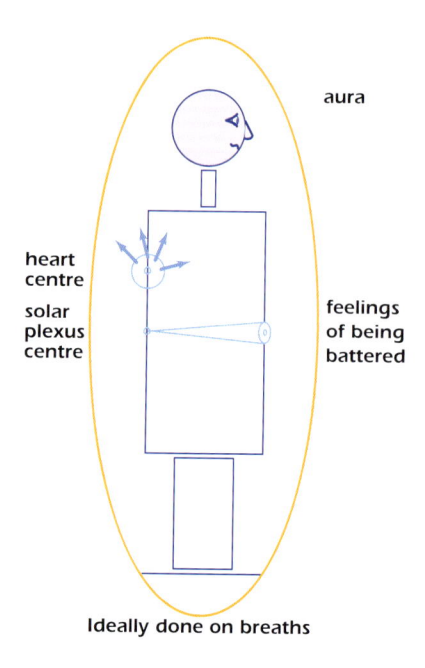

[Diagram with labels: aura, heart centre, solar plexus centre, feelings of being battered; caption "Ideally done on breaths"]

Chart 8:03 – Solar Plexus and Heart

One business man, pretty ruthless, had handpicked his team for their toughness. He ran a successful firm. However, when crisis struck, he came as a client for counselling and began to open to transpersonal energies. Though he was a 'mind' man, these energies chose the Heart centre. He became uncomfortable in his own firm. He could no longer be ruthless to his ruthless subordinates nor harsh to his workforce – he had started to relate to people through the Heart centre. His subordinates thought him nuts. He had either to abandon the business, or change it. So he sacked them all, started again and moved on.

Like the other chakras, it can be over-used. Learning to love by loving, yet we may throw ourselves too much into group responsibility, compensating for over-sensitivity with defensive coldness. People carrying responsibility for healing and therapy in groups, for example – heart-based rather than head-based, radiating concern for others – are often unconscious of the weight they carry. They are the centre, the life-blood, of the group. Their physical hearts, their blood-pressure, will feel the stress on the system. Pain in the heart can indicate that it feels too far forward, too open and vulnerable. Take it back to behind the spine and turn it *up*, not forward.

Throat

The higher in the body, the more complex the energies flowing through the system. The Throat, an integrating centre, often opens second, soon after the Solar Plexus. Western man usually has both of these complex chakras opened. The Throat is the bridge between head and body, thinking and feeling. At the back of the neck is a connection to the sacred.

The Throat chakra, linked with the Thyroid gland, is associated with both intellect and higher creativity. Here we learn to think things through. In this prime centre for the logical and analytical, for objectivity and detached thought, the mind works out its plans. Though speaking often with a legal or academic voice, it is also a centre for art, for the receptivity of telepathy and clairaudience, and for intuitive listening.

Problems. Inspiration is anchored in the Throat centre where energy flows in. But Throat energy can spill over into the Sacral, so sexual drive may be increased if there isn't enough creative outlet. This can lead to the charged-up sexuality of some artists. Too much sexual energy? Then emphasise creative art, creative living and thinking, drawing the energy up into the throat. Conversely, too little, and too *much* energy may be going on creativity.

Blocked creativity may be sexual, involving the axis from Throat to Sacral; difficulties with swallowing and breathing may show that the Throat chakra is becoming activated, energy flowing up as far as the throat then being suppressed and retreating, blocking creativity. The voices of academics are rarely full and rounded; they're thin and reedy, representing the narrow band of the intellectual. Thinking has taught them discipline and control of emotion which, rising up into the throat, has been choked back again and again. Since they learned so well to control excessive feelings – and never to cry – they limit themselves to the thinking function and the lump in the throat. Thus the thyroid may be affected.

If thinking is hard, it may be our 'inferior' function. No philosophical base for our attitudes or assumptions, and we fall into a logic-chopping confusion. We need quiet, to be in a receptive state, take it slowly. Similarly with feeling: those who have an inferior Feeling function may learn by doing. Energy grows with use.

It may be that the *transpersonal* component that works through the

Throat centre is weak. The resulting imbalance can lead to an over-dominant personality.

Do you experience your creativity as a bore – or a joy? Take an analytic look at your thought processes. Here is the energy of your creative mind, the willingness to carry on trying. Ask, 'But how much feeling, how much subjectivity, is in this?' You may need to take up some artistic expression, some creative activity however small, to contrast with your usual habits of thinking and feeling. Otherwise, splits may follow; one singer dreamed that his mother was coming up behind him to cut his head off. What's going on in the chakras when you have that kind of split? We become creative by creating something. To learn how to do it – do it.

Brow

This is the 'third eye' within. Seen in consciousness, intuitive and mystical, it is the Self looking at us. It is linked with the Pituitary gland, said to be very active in deep meditation. Like the Heart centre, it usually opens after the Solar Plexus, Sacral and Throat centres. The Brow chakra is said to be to the front of the forehead, marked by the triangle of Intuition, Thinking and Feeling. An eternity symbol characterises its central energy, two wing-like petals reminding us of an aeroplane propeller – also of the caste mark of the Brahmins and of the cobra on the Pharaonic headdress of the Egyptians.[259]

The Brow is the seat of the Observer, co-ordinating all the chakras. Leaning to the future, it focuses and integrates, sending a searchlight forward like a laser, restoring the clear sight of reality. When Tiresias saw two snakes coupling in a wood, Zeus and Hera asked him who had most sexual enjoyment, the male or the female. Turned first into a woman for seven years, then back to a man for seven more, he finally announced: 'Woman has the most enjoyment.' Hera was predictably angry and struck him blind for his impiety – but Zeus gave him second sight.[260]

To awaken this chakra we need to be persistent, carrying on but then laying our studies aside, allowing the flow of intuition with its quicksilver quality, catching it out of the air. As the Heart and Brow develop, we begin to tune in to the Other. The Brow can be associated with mystical

---

[259] A relationship is sometimes perceived between these petals and the eyes, right and left being seen to cross over at the cranial base so that the left eye goes with the left brain and vice versa. The left eye, Manas, then is mental and masculine, about intellect and thinking; the right eye, Buddhi, is feeling and feminine, about emotion and intuition. The Brow chakra works best out of the feminine, being receptive rather than active; so, checking the balance, we must set aside the analytical mind and find time, leisure and space for the incubation of intuitive sensitivity, which is related to the higher mind.

[260] The study of myths and symbols awakens the 'third eye'. I believe that in future both psychology and human development will increasingly carry mythological material.

experiences of the void type: at the centre of a brilliant light is darkness and within the dark is more light, from which the original light is dark.

Problems. The Brow chakra is manic, a polar opposite to the Alta Major. Medical difficulties are of ear, nose and eye; sinus troubles arise here. Counsellors, for instance, may well find themselves drained of energy through the eyes.

Alta Major

This is not written about much. Hardly surprisingly: we have lost touch with it. The Alta Major[261] joins us to the earth, to the race, perhaps to the collective unconscious. Here we experience the flow of an ancient intuition – heavy, slow, dense – through the mind and through feeling. It goes back into the distant past of the tribe: 'I have heard of that before....' It is about clairvoyance. And, equally, depression. We can note people's body language when they are in touch with this centre. They rock back, putting a hand behind the head, almost listening for something in the back of their minds; whereas conversely, when searching for the unknown in the future, they lean forward, hand to forehead.

The Alta Major involves an area of the reptilian 'old brain', the 'hindbrain' of anatomy, to do with evolution, self-preservation, assertiveness. It is less about 'gut feelings' than about the intuition of our instinct, spontaneous and off the cuff. Related to the pre-intellectual faculties of the *deva* kingdom, it is where we get in touch with the natural world and the instinctual nature of humanity. The key function of the Alta Major is control of the spine, linking and integrating the centres. Bailey suggested it acts like a sparking plug in a car's engine: when it's functioning well and healthily, it 'sparks' well, connecting the lower chakras (Root to Throat) with the higher (Brow to Crown); if it doesn't spark well – then you're in trouble![262]

Together with the Solar Plexus it is a warning centre, receiving messages of danger, 'something in the wind'. We listen to land, trees, water, we walk consciously with the animals, we pick up intimations. When this chakra opens in people close to nature, a different line of intuition awakens, the ruling energies of the etheric run in prickles up and down the spine and the hair stands up on the back of the head.

Problems. Habitually using the intellect instead of the intuition can cause tension in the Alta Major chakra and headaches in the backs of our

---

261 Note the spelling: following Alice Bailey, IGB employed 'Alta Major', high; it is also written 'Alter Major', other. See Bailey 1962, 'A Treatise on Cosmic Fire', pp. 960-966. Ed.

262 IGB was pioneering here: since then, this chakra has been increasingly seen as very important. This sentence is from a private conversation between Anthony Thorley and IGB.

heads – our instincts are blocked, our activity draining their energies. However, feelings of headache can follow *increase* of energy – it's often instinctual people who get such headaches.

Crown

This highest Head centre faces downwards, a cone of light like a magician's hat. A tuft on top of the head is all that represents it, and the saints' haloes, and dunces' caps, monks' shaven and tonsured heads, cardinals' caps, bishops' mitres, the fontanelles of babies. Here is the cap of the Buddha, representing not the intellect but the core essence of the being. Liverpool's Roman Catholic Cathedral is built in the shape of the Crown chakra. While some yoga systems have sixteen petals for the Solar Plexus and twelve for the Heart, the Crown chakra is known as the thousand-petalled lotus. The energy of both Priest-healer and Magician flows through it.

The transpersonal Self cannot be charted, but if it could it would be here at the top. The Crown is the ruler of the other chakras, central controller of all the radio stations, containing within itself a counterpart or original pattern for even the minor ones and the acupuncture meridians. As one centre begins to open, so does its counterpart in the thousand-petalled lotus; though experienced most strongly in the head, it is not itself necessarily one of the Head chakras.

The Crown, associated with the Pineal gland, is of the spirit, love and the archetypal will. It is experienced as the flow of a powerful, sun-like energy, stimulating growth from without till the archetype of the Self takes a hand – the *centre* of the soul, not just the stream of the soul – and a door is opened to a vertical passage to the *inner* world. Working from the Crown through all the chakras, the Self charges its energy into one of them in particular. Then that centre begins to unfold from within, as if the elemental fire goes to the jewel in the middle, and it resonates, bringing spiritual enlightenment and awareness.

The Crown opens late on the path of individuation; not till we begin to discover our own approach and the teaching which speaks to us inwardly. We are seeking our own fundamental archetype, our God, our destiny and purpose, the nature of ourselves. Then the will of the transpersonal Self can start to course through Heart and Throat[263] and at last through the highest head centre. Its movement is experienced through

---

263 Not perhaps the Brow centre so much.

the imagination, perhaps in esoteric groups, and in the contemplation which enlarges the container and heals the Crown centre itself. We may visualise a connection between the head and 'something up there' – perhaps a cone with a stream of energy coming in and, beyond it, a link with a wider collective consciousness.

If you lack energy, or love, then visualise according to the reality and it will come back. Say, 'Let love come in' and it will, through the Crown to the Heart. Make the connection, act *as if* energy were being projected imaginatively through the Crown chakra, and its descending light may stimulate the Heart centre with odd, unaccountable flows. Sometimes it is like an electric drill, with pressure and lights flashing; or it runs up and down the spine, or goes so far and stops at a block. The Self is saying, 'Clear the channels, balance your development, get the flow going'. Many people for whom the Heart chakra is opening may have a sense of lightness, as if something were trying to get in; or it may be something from inside trying to get out. They may experience pressure in the head – heat, tightness, an iron or steel band around it, perhaps as a result of resistance. In either case, the door is opened to a powerful energy.

Physical exercise is useful, or a colour that calms, or cooling water, letting it flow into all parts of our nature. As energy follows thought, so we may switch the thought process, asking the energy to let up, or show us why it should continue and what it is trying to do, so that we can co-operate. Let it happen. Experiment cautiously with facilitating it. Eventually the Self will activate each centre from the Crown, reaching the Base, setting in motion the energy there and returning up. The Base is the Great Mother, the Crown the Father in Heaven. Their union leads to tremendous energy, as described by Jung and by Alice Bailey, among many others. This is the Transfiguration. The important thing is to remain centred and allow it to happen.

The chakras and the Self

Invocation means drawing energy down, evocation means drawing it up till it is flowing both ways, by both invocation and evocation, a state even beyond prayer. Just as in Assagioli's Egg-map the transpersonal Self pours energy down into the personal centre, so now the highest Head centre, the primary anchoring-point for the Self or Soul, pours down its energy. As consciousness expands, the centres open.

Energy or *prana* circles around the Crown, moving from the side or centrally, travelling along the etheric spine through three subtle channels, *ida, pingala* and *sushumna*.[264] Not everyone can experience energy in this sense. The thread of *ida* carries *intuition*, aspiration and insight. It is of the soul, of perception, of understanding, of relationship. The thread of *pingala* is about *inspiration*, about substance, matter, form-building, manifestation in the body, the linking of inner and outer. Here are the petals of the lotus. The central thread of *sushumna* is to do with the *will* in daily life, with psychological energies, spiritual libido, the central energy of a being in incarnation or man in a system. This is the jewel in the lotus.

So we become aware of these transforming, vitalising, effective energies pouring in from the Self, finding creative outlets, expanding the world of our inner and outer relationships. The process of *kundalini* is a long one, involving much clearing and opening up. And we have seen how it can burn – an electric, or atomic, or solar fire, a fire of friction. It may involve only one chakra at first, or perhaps two. The centres do not always open sequentially; blockages and channels need to be cleared by the natural process of growth – by our becoming creative. However, when they are cleared out, it will flow without burning. It takes a long time, but at the end of the process lie the descent and ascent of life.

EXPLORATION
EXPLORING THE CHAKRAS
(20 minutes)

This simple exercise aims to raise energy to the Heart.

Adopting a comfortable posture, be in touch with the Heart centre. Visualise an opening rose, with energy at its centre. What symbol represents the energy? Join with the symbol. Find out:

Which chakras are the most visited?
Which chakras are alien to you?
If you have had a health trauma, where was it located – in which chakras?
In which chakras do *you* feel most at home?
Where is *your Self* most at home? Are these two the same?

Now, take the energy to the Brow; there, reflect on the qualities of the Heart. Recall people who attract you and affect others in a loving way.

---

264 These subtle channels are the nadis; threads respectively of Consciousness, Creativity and Life. Chapter 9, p. 338.

THE OPENING OF THE CHAKRAS

The whole spiritual journey is a continual falling on our face

Order of awakening

For each of us it's different. The archetype of the Self – ruler, scientist, entrepreneur, mediator, artist, organiser – takes precedence, modifying the chakras. Though we are on many archetypes and need to become multi-functional, we clearly have a dominant mode. The complications cannot be mapped. All simple rules and systems (such as allocating a particular colour or astrological sign or planet to a particular chakra) are wrong.

We have taken the chakras in rising order. However, we know that in our primitive ancestors the energy operated first on the Sexual centre, then the Solar Plexus. We know for instance that Priest-healers will tend to have Heart, Alta Major and Solar Plexus awakened; the King will have Crown, Base, Alta Major and Throat; and Thinkers (philosophers, metaphysicians) will probably use Alta Major and Throat, as well as the Sacral chakra. Racially and individually, a relatively normal order of opening for Westerners may now be this:

The Solar Plexus	Power, dominance: 'We all'.
The Sacral or Sexual Centre	Personal desires: 'You and me'.
The Throat	Creativity.
The Heart	Love and spiritual values; putting others' welfare above one's own.
The Brow	Spiritual vision.
The Crown, Highest Head Centre	Individual consciousness merging with spirit, leading to universal consciousness.
The Alta Major, Back of Head Centre	Intuition and Instinct.
The Base of the Spine, or Root	Basic survival: 'Me consciousness'.

In adolescence, an *emotional* awakening of the Solar Plexus is usually followed by a *sexual* awakening of the Sacral, and a *mystical* awakening when our Throat and Heart centres are at least somewhat involved. So most of us are happily aware of our sexual consciousness in the Sacral centre and can express it. We are generally open to our emotions in the Solar Plexus and Heart centres, even if they are repressed somewhat. Most of us can reach our thinking, even our mystical, consciousness in the Throat.

At around twenty-eight an *intuitive* crisis may follow, a critical point of awakening to the Self after the emotional clearing of the Baptism.[265] Difficulties come at us, leading either to growth or to regression – the whole spiritual journey is a continual falling on our face. But as the energy of the Self starts its transforming work, there is a thrust towards the godhead: *I must be about my Father's business.* A reconstitution and transmutation of the chakra system itself begins to take place and peak experiences may follow. Now, the intuitional awareness associated with the Brow chakra awakens as the head is roused to balance the system. The Brow becomes a reality, a 'backbone', an experiential energy to be tuned into. Notice where something is trying to break out; a ripple or flow, a fizzing round the heart, bubbles of light – the Self determines how we experience it. Heavier energies are lost, more subtle ones awakened in preparation for the final synthesis. It's now that the Self may say, 'Aha, I have here an instrument that is usable!' So Christ started his ministry; only then could he move towards the ultimate stage of his life, not now searching for the godhead but letting the godhead work through him.

We probably know less about the final three chakras: Crown, Alta Major and Base. The Self through the highest Head centre raises the Base at last and awakens the 'serpent fire', clearing away the dross so that the higher marriage can take place between matter and spirit, the Mother and the Father, soul and personality. Now the Alta Major can fully open us to our ancient and intuitive instincts.

Kundalini may come in when the Crown as King and the Base as Queen relate to each other.[266] Usually, the petals of the various centres open, in whatever order, without touching *kundalini*. However, after the Crown centre is opened, its jewel is activated. Then, we need to work down again, activating all the other jewels. It is the Base jewel that releases the snake, which rushes up and down, fusing all the chakras. From then on, an adept will work from the Crown, which is the receiver of all chakras.

Always close down these centres of energy: imagine the petals of the open lotus gradually closing till the light is held safely within.

---

265 Chapter 4, pp. 179-181.
266 Again, beware. As already stated, there are warnings to do with the awakening of kundalini by artificial means, indulging in exercises which do not have any outlet in life. When, all unprepared, energy rises from Base to Heart to Crown, very real burnout can follow. It is quite possible to become psychotic, opening to it before we are ready. It truly is an electrical fire with thousands of volts pouring through. And it is irreversible – we can't be rewired. See again Krishna 1971, *Kundalini*.

WORKING WITH THE CHAKRAS

Is each of them getting its oats?

Again, no one who had learned the lesson would be having to attend the class. However, it's a rare person who lives every centre. Balancing first comes as an unbalancing. Keep going back to base, as if re-tuning a guitar from the bottom up. Indeed, as mentioned above, the chakras are sometimes said to go with musical notes or resonances.[267] Start by working with your *consciousness* – it's safe. Which chakra dominates? At different stages of life, different centres act as co-ordinators; for instance, a child sub-personality may be found in Solar Plexus or Heart and an authoritarian parent and controller in the Throat. Or there may be an adolescent in the Solar Plexus or Sexual centre and a crisis-stricken adult in the Heart.

Learn to distinguish the energies and their physical location. For instance, energy rising from Sacral to Throat leads to creativity; from Solar Plexus to Heart, to group service. The Solar Plexus may[268] go with the sexual organs of the Sacral centre, as well as with the higher senses of the Heart. Self-identity goes with Heart and Brow. Rarer is that pressure in the head that runs up and down the spine. Those on a spiritual path will become aware of energy being transferred through Heart and Alta Major, from personal will at the Base to the Crown chakra.

Each level of consciousness has a paranormal function for which it needs space and leisure.[269] For direct perception and clairvoyance, *intuition* uses Crown and Brow, activating the Throat, Heart and Alta Major. The *mind's* telepathy needs the Throat centre. The *emotions* use the Solar Plexus for mediumistic psychism; the *body*, healing through the Heart, uses touch; and the psychometry and dowsing of *instinct* needs the Alta Major and finally the Base. Crossing these levels, the chakra system maps many different qualities: sexual drive, heart values, creativity.

Some people try, and results come; for others, to think is to prevent results. In either case, work till it becomes automatic, like swimming or cycling, typing or driving. Using the *animus* is not usually very satisfactory; the will is a useful tool, but we fear its failure. If necessary, it

---

267 Musically, it is interesting to conceive a major triad rising from Base to Sacral to Solar Plexus, with the top octave at the Heart; another major triad rising from Heart to Throat to Brow, with the top octave at the Crown and the seventh at the Alta Major; and a major triad rising from the Crown and going on up, with a Healing chakra next above at the third. The Sacral, the Throat, and the Healing chakra are horizontal centres (leading outwards), while Base and Crown are vertical ones. The Heart can be seen as more omni-directional, rather like the queen in chess, but with a strong vertical function in relationship to Base and Crown. (With grateful acknowledgement to Monica Anthony for these insights into music and the chakras. Ed.)

268 See Bailey 1953, 'Esoteric Healing', pp. 138 and 171.

269 See Chart 4:01, Levels of Consciousness 4, p. 169.

can go into action, but *gently*. Better if the masculine principle remain within as support – an iron hand, but in a velvet glove. The *feminine* principle rather – instinct, feelings, intuition – is the most sensitive guide. Learn to recognise Ariadne's thread and trace it back. Incubation is fundamental; relax and let go – sleep on it. Love is the carrier.

To develop, balance and manage the qualities of some of the higher chakras ask, 'Is each of them getting its oats?' To nourish the *Heart*, encourage love, compassion and sensitivity but without repression of other energies such as anger. For the *Throat*, develop artistic expression, in life as well as art – for example, in cooking. Follow your intellectual aspirations with sustained, clear, logical thought, without intrusion from the emotions, slowly and carefully thinking things through. For the *Brow*, listen, be receptive, study symbols and myths, seek for what lies behind the forms. Is the Brow's energy cool and light – or the razor-sharp energy of the will – or is it touched by the heart's warmth? Later it becomes Observer, controlling, leading, integrating, carrying the energies of the other chakras, agent of the Self. Nourish the instinctual roots of the *Alta Major* in earth – water, nature, the land. Start being creative in a small way: make a room, make a garden, pursue music or painting. Develop your relationships; with a certain degree of openness, energy begins to flow into them and can be consciously used.

Between them, psychologists have been concerned with raising the level of psychological thinking and so activating all the chakras. It has been said that while Behavioural psychology was about the Base, Freud raised energy to the level of the Sacral chakra, Adler to the Solar Plexus, and Jung to the Heart. Yogic, transpersonal and esoteric schools may be concerned with raising it to the Crown chakra.

EXPLORATION
THE CHAKRAS AND THEIR SYMBOLS
(30 minutes)

Take some time to be in touch with your own being. Be in a meditative state, and get in touch with the chakras:
    What symbol do you associate with each chakra in an ideal state?
    What jewel symbolises the energy at the centre of it?
    With which of the five senses is it associated?
Draw what came up for you in the exercise, and if possible spend some time discussing it.

CHAKRAS AND HEALTH – SYMPTOM AS SYMBOL

*Know that love protects you:
if you love your Self, illness has nothing in you to look after it.*

Health is of course an individual matter, depending on more than this system. Illness may have many origins. But the chakras can be both diagnostic and therapeutic, viewing and reflecting the soul's relation to the body. When a centre needs development or is newly opening up in the unconscious, the transpersonal energies may affect that area of the body, choosing that particular centre for any symptoms. So the parallel psycho-somatic processes can be mapped at the bottom of the Egg. For instance, eye trouble might accompany awakening of the Brow. This is often unexpected and uncomfortable. Although psychological wounds and major changes often inhibit us and damp us down, yet lethargy or restlessness, tiredness, muscular locks, aches and pains and general malaise may rather be the key to approaching *health*. A physical illness or accident may finally release and shift our energy, heralding that the battle is now over.

Over-activity of the chakras

Introverted, intuitive people are prone to stress. Shock or excessive stimulation can make extra adrenaline rush through the body, perhaps uncontrollably, whipping up energy and leading to over-activity where late nights destroy sleep patterns. This artificial and emotional situation can lead to trouble. Indeed, *back problems* almost always involve stress. At what level does the spine go out? The lower back is related to the Solar Plexus, the hips to the Sacral centre. It helps to become aware of the feet and the need for earthing. Explore at the level of the chakras for a clue to the symptom's cause.

Over-activity in the *Crown* centre can lead to pain in the head, too much energy surging through too small a channel. May this go with the First Ray?[270] Premature awakening and inflammation of the brain can follow.

Eye and ear trouble may follow over-stimulation of the *Brow*, perhaps associated with the Fourth Ray of art and harmony, or the Third Ray of the thinker; headache, migraine, forms of neuritis, nervous trouble and pituitary problems may follow if mysticism gets mixed with selfishness and dogmatism.

---

270 The Seven Rays of Alice Bailey, Appendix 18.

Whereas falling in love develops the *Heart* centre and true loving certainly releases Heart energy, yet its over-emphasis may lead to exaggeration of the higher values so that we find ourselves playing God, full of compassion and caring but heading for self-destruction. In over-responsible leaders of a group, for example – loved, hated, swamped, invaded, smothered – trouble with stomach, heart and blood pressure can result from a Second Ray type of over-activity in this chakra.

Over-activity of the *Throat* can lead to difficulty in swallowing, possibly linked with the Fifth Ray of Knowledge. The wrong metabolism can follow a lower kind of psychism, potentially leading to hyperthyroidism, goitre, respiratory tract congestion and laryngitis.

The damaged child within, over-active in the *Solar Plexus*, can cause an over-emotional response, so that we become weepy or excitable or angry. Some people keep and operate their symptoms at this level. Ulcers, adult diabetes, stomach, liver and intestinal difficulties and troubles with the bloodstream may follow. The Sixth Ray of Devotion is possibly linked. If the ego is prone to drama, sacrifice and self-pity, its emotionalism can lead to nervous diseases.

Too much instinctual energy in the *Sacral* centre can, obviously, cause sexual diseases. These last two chakras are really quite 'young'.

In the *Base* of the spine, energy is associated not with stress exactly but with struggle. If the Root centre opens too rapidly, nervous disorders, spinal disease, brain trouble and inflammation of the tissues may follow. Pure selfishness, self-interest and black magic linked with the Seventh Ray can cause heart and other disease, glamour and illusion working through to the physical level.

Imbalance in the chakras. The higher Self may send an inflow of energy into a particular centre. If more flows in than out, the balance is disrupted. A constipated, over-sensitive chakra results and these exercises are not enough – more strength is required. By becoming conscious we begin to change the energy paths. Where is the imbalance or one-sidedness? Practitioners of Hatha and Tantric Yoga hold that it is *thinking* upon or within the chakras that can either quieten or stimulate them.[271] Work on your emotional nature, learn to use say anger impersonally and without harm, and the imbalance will go. Certain chakras may need to hibernate while it is corrected. Have humility about your limits. Time and space, solitude and awareness are needed, so that creativity, conscious-

---

271 Wood 1959, *Yoga*, p. 150.

ness and life can come together.

Transference of energy within the system. Should you feel tension, or referred pain, then relax. Where is the pain? Is it perhaps energy in the wrong place? A sudden inexplicable cough, say, may be Heart energy stuck in the Throat – you are coping in one chakra with the misplaced energy of another. The same may be true for migraine, sickness, tension in the muscles and so on. Where does it want to go – out – or in? Ask perhaps by visualising a lotus in a closed bud on the head and the petals opening to form a chalice. And let it go.

Emotional energy gets misplaced from stomach to head. One client came in with a migraine. 'Get in touch with it, ask it where it would like to go.' 'To my stomach!' 'Let it, then.' She burst into tears and immediately the headache went away. However, alas, as soon as she stopped crying back came the headache.... *Healing* in certain forms may merely shift the symptom around the body, as indeed may hypnotism. Another migraine sufferer went for healing and found it 'explosively effective'. However, her blood pressure immediately rose instead. She had been putting the lid on her energy, driving it into her head. Now, the healing was putting the lid on the energy in her head *as well* – and it had to go somewhere.

A young man asked his state of confusion, 'Where do you want to go?' 'To your stomach,' it replied. This time it did go, and for good. Returning the energy to its proper place where it could be worked on consciously, he discovered what the pain was trying to say. Would he accept it, would he overcome it? Offered a choice, he elected to be left with a pain in the stomach, for sure, but a clear head; and his life did change.

Under-activity of the chakras

Lack of life in a particular area of consciousness is generally due to under-activity of the chakras rather than any constitutional or hereditary weakness:

The bypassing of centres. Sometimes a certain area (emotion, say, or sexuality) is almost inactive, even vestigial. It is completely disallowed and missed out. Energy cannot flow there. Feelings, when listened to, don't play games, but usually we aren't listening to them – or rather, consciousness hears, where our heads just think about our feelings and churn them over. By getting Heart and Head confused, so all confusion arises. Knowing *about* our feelings is not the same as hearing them and then owning them.

Repression of centres. A congested chakra, on the other hand, is 'allowed' but cannot open because of suppression, inhibition or fear. It is under-active and one-sided, especially in relation to emotional, etheric or physical balance. We need to discover the positive side of blocked or malfunctioning chakras and practise with them. Is the block on the right side or the left, is it upper or lower, front or back? The aberrant cell growth that is *cancer* – what may cause it? Could it be that some channel is being blocked and the energy building up? Could emotional inhibition – suppression, dammed energy – lead to it, perhaps? With stomach cancer there is very often a damaged child involved, representing the person's heart-nature. As noted above, this child runs for cover into the Solar Plexus and hides there as in a cave, locked in by control mechanisms. It wants to come into the Heart, if only it were allowed to. Could throat cancer be the opposite, maybe, and too much energy going that way that should be going elsewhere? In either case, try to shift the energy.

Leaking of energy. Lack of co-ordination and integration may indicate a loose etheric connection with the physical vehicle, so that energy is being drained. At what level is the loss of energy? Could this be linked with kidney trouble?

Chakras and the Collective

The chakras are related to the dream or etheric body which, though protective, can be rent and allow harmful effects. Some people lack intelligence here. Playing manipulative games, making predictions, employing exercises, drugs and hallucinogens, they invoke and evoke energies they do not understand. Being unconscious, they live only a portion of the chart.

Neglect the unconscious and our resonance links up with synchronistic events, making it hard to differentiate our own problems from those of the collective, which seems to act like outside fate. Many are swamped by it. Our energy bodies differ in weakness and vitality. Perhaps we just have very finely tuned apparatus; but we differ in degrees and areas of sensitivity [272] and in the ability to defend ourselves.

Dangle out hooks, and people will hang their coats. Sometimes, hit through the Solar Plexus with signals from troublesome people, we seem to *grapple* any negativity coming in. As a short-term correction for oversensitivity to the vibrations of others, imagine bands, boxes, shields

---

272 For example, to noise, particularly sub-sonic noise.

around you. But better, learn to let the energy go to the right place, closing down a chakra by seeing an open lotus with the petals gradually folding down and enclosing the light within. Thus, practise stillness, observe the need for privacy, and get in touch with the energy, visualising it going back behind the spine to the Heart and *changing when it gets there*. See the positive energy going out from the Heart, clarifying the aura; then feed the positive energy back into the Solar Plexus. If arrows are coming at you from other people, this next practice can help you deflect them down into the ground.

A FIRST AID EXPLORATION
FOR PANIC, FEAR AND ANXIETY
(25 minutes)

The aim is to close down the Solar Plexus and deal with negative energies. Remembering your breathing, adopt a meditative posture. Again, the intention is to raise energy to the Heart.

Minutes

5   Tune in to the Solar Plexus and Heart centres. How would you name the troubling energy? What is the feeling? Identify and reflect on it.

10   When it's identified, consider what would be the opposite side of that energy. Begin to reflect on the *other* face of it – be with the positive counterpart of that energy.

Now, on the inward breath, imagine any powerful stuff being taken back just behind the spine. As you deliberately take it back to the core, feel it flowing up – just behind your back – up the etheric spine towards the Heart, which becomes a positive pole and balances the Solar Plexus. If your attempts to take it up the *back* don't work, try taking it up the centre. Stay in touch with that positive counterpart of the energy.

Raise the energy up into the very centre of the Heart chakra. As it flows up, see the energy changing into its opposite quality, losing the rubbish on the way.

Next, imagine this positive energy radiating out, to clear the aura. Send it out on the out-going breath.

Work out a feedback loop, seeing the energy flowing again from the Heart centre to the Solar Plexus.

10 When you are ready, repeat the whole process, doing it together with the breathing.

Attack

If you're still feeling attacked, ask, is it really the person, or simply that your energy-field and theirs don't work together. Connect with other souls in your own group, becoming closer to them. Note that in groups the energy-field may be reversed. If this is the case, don't be open; simply preoccupy yourself with the inner business and so be unavailable to potentially draining people. Create a protective field around yourself, and so avoid invasion and claustrophobia.

Beware of those psychotic individuals who have an uncanny knack of hitting you on your weak spot. Don't try to work with them unless you have a special gift, because this is 'people-poisoning' and they will get you. You have to be specially trained to cope with such sappers, such intensely needy people. You can't beat them; the problem won't be solved until they are forced to go inside themselves.

Is the attacker yourself – from within, to do with your own shadow? If so, and you don't know it, it'll get to you in time. Protection and 'blocking off' techniques may make matters worse, since yet another encasing layer is added. Meditation can help, but meditation is not usually the way to deal with projections; it simply strengthens the barrier against them. So, recognise the shadow – peak experiences are more likely to shake it. Acknowledge synchronicity; withdraw projections, helpful messages as they are and not to be blocked off altogether. Protect your space and boundaries. Every mature person using themselves for others needs physical space in order to survive, be creative, connected with their own centre. Make private space and private time. Do you feel attacked? You probably haven't enough of either.

Though rather rare, there are *collective* forces of attack which are nothing to do with the personal unconscious. Again, imagine the quality of attack, and then its opposite. See and feel the attacking quality travelling back on the inward breath and up the spine, and there transforming into its opposite. It may change colour. Feed positive energy back to its negative source, and the attack has been a helpful message. Other people can help here; powerfully creative people whose tasks are to do with energy and force and use of the will can often afford protection to those on the priest-healer line, who are very sensitive and open to attack.

Change the substance

There's something in us that attracts repeating patterns. People who are frequently burgled, for instance, may well have a difficult attitude to possessions. The Self is beaming out the message: 'I have a lesson to learn, please take my stuff!' *Karma* is substance but, more, it is transfiguration; it transmutes, and we are no longer on the wheel of repeating experience. Change the language, become aware, and it won't happen again. There are techniques for balancing the chakra system and the magnetic polarity of your own energy fields and so gaining a degree of control of your aura, your sensitivity and your need for self-protection. Is the balance right between introversion and extraversion? How is your capacity to be centred, clarity of vision, confidence, wholeness, singleness of mind? Visualisation is a real energy. Given proper centring and confidence in what you are doing, an imaged shield can actually shield you.... See your aura and its boundaries; see yourself being filled with light, or love.

People have different perceptions of *colour*. Generally, however, *violet* is experienced as toning up the etheric body; *blue* is calming and good for lower back pain. Applied to the brow, *green* soothes headaches; it calms the nervous system, while *yellow* stimulates it. *Red* and *orange* give energy to the circulatory system via the Heart chakra.

Sound is very closely related to spirit. Tell your truth, sound out your inner note as vibration, spoken invocation or prayer. The creative power of music and of the word evokes a positive energy-field, tuning you in to the collective resonance. Listen; note the energies as you become aware of them. While the petals are related to light, the essence, the jewel in the lotus, is *sound*, the note of the soul; and the sound is at the centre.[273]

CHAKRAS, PLACES AND ORGANISATIONS

The spirit of places

Remember the psychic cleanliness of your place of work: look after the atmosphere, make sure the energy field is suitable. Avoid places where groups have quickly spilt out pent-up emotions; the opposite might be a church, where the atmosphere is helpful. Lighting, music, plants, animals

---
[273] Almost as if sound were to attach to the nucleus of the atom rather than to the electrons?

can all cleanse the area, as can fragrances. You may find you drink a lot of water in a 'heavy' group. Water has to do with the exchange of ions; positive ionisation of the atmosphere is depressing, while negative ionisation is elating. Sappers take energy from you – Christ knew when virtue had gone out of him.[274] Since running water has a negative charge, splash your face in it.

Remember that the atmosphere of certain geographical regions and areas may not suit you – indeed, can be inimical to you. The energy field is planetary, even solar. Both individual and collective, it embraces people and groups, communities and nations with its power and influence. Its quality and chemistry have a trigger effect, anchoring, channelling and manifesting threads of energy. It is as if Gaia had a central impulse or will, a quality of consciousness, seeming material substance, specialised focal points of force. As we saw, the cities are the truly major magnetic spots, the chakras if you like, in this total energy system.

In Britain, for instance, Liverpool and Glasgow can be seen as linked to the Solar Plexus; Leeds, and Glasgow again, to the Heart. Manchester, always one step ahead of everywhere, is the Brow centre, together with Oxford and Cambridge; while Newcastle and Edinburgh are at Throat and Head respectively. And what about old Birmingham, sunk below the Bull Ring? London is at both the Head and Heart of the country: the Queen and the Commonwealth. May there not be more spiritual work in London now than anywhere else in the world?

Other cities linked with the Heart may include Genoa, Madras and Los Angeles, while Nuremberg, Darjeeling and Washington DC are for the Head. So are Geneva, New York, Ottawa, Toronto, Johannesburg, Calcutta, Delhi, Madras, Jamaica. Like London, Rome and Moscow are each both Heart and Head; New York and Berlin are Throat and Head. Paris too has a strong Throat connection. Addis Ababa is for the Brow centre and Chicago and Sydney may be linked with the Solar Plexus.

Organisations

The Head is for consciousness, the Heart for life, and the Throat and Brow for creativity. So in public life, within governments and firms, the cabinet or the board of directors are ruled by the Head, while the Brow is the thinktank of researchers and developers. The Throat, linked with education and social science, is represented by the planners, the office

---

274 Luke 8:45-6; Mark 5:30.

managers and their staff. The Alta Major is in the environment department and round the back with the tea ladies, porters and caretakers. At the Heart are personnel and welfare workers, and also the Foreign Office and the diplomatic service. Solar Plexus energy is carried by supervisors and shop-stewards; and the Sacral is where the workforce of industry has its energy. The Base has been linked with both the Home Office and the Trades Unions, as well as with capitalists and high finance.

It could be said that in Parliament the Head rules; also in the United Nations and the Commonwealth. In education the intelligentsia, the professional people, are usually linked with the Throat centre. The healing professions and the social services need the link with the Heart. However, none of these may any longer fit – considering the state of some of our public services, people just laugh.

Explore the raising of consciousness – see what it does

The chakras are a self-regulating system moved by the Self. When the Self, which is interested in consciousness, begins to take note of the instruments and processes of transformation, things change. Start by working with the energy offered. There are receptive ways of consciousness, and there are active. Visualise the Heart chakra, at the same time invoking energy through the Head. Like the sun, it causes the petals to open and emphasises your *aura*.[275] Use imagination, use words to make a connection. Invoke love by both verbalisation and imagination. To draw in light, let visualisation together with a mantric phrase invoke it, illuminating more. When the channels are sufficiently purified, the *kundalini* energies begin to flow – not from outside, but from your own soul.

How do we get there? 'Going up', we get to know who we are. 'Coming back' – work, let go. Ask, *are you having fun*? Energy can get diverted; blocked; come too powerfully; be congested; change. It may be transmuted, or transposed from one chakra to another. Remember the danger – warning: *Here is no ordinary conflagration; it is electrical, even atomic fire*. People have always courted it, perhaps by playing with Eastern practices. It's never awakened totally accidentally.

Once more it may be appropriate to end this workshop with the Universal Blessing of Buddhism.[276]

---

[275] The aura is a name given by researchers to the electromagnetic field that is present as long as we are alive.
[276] The Universal Blessing of Buddhism, see Chapter 10, p. 365.

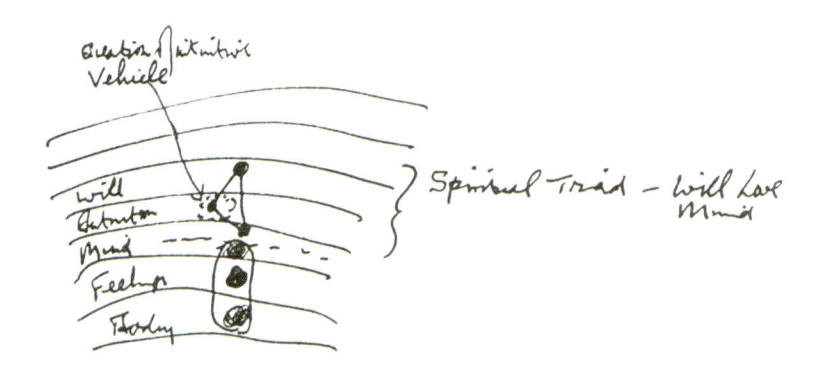

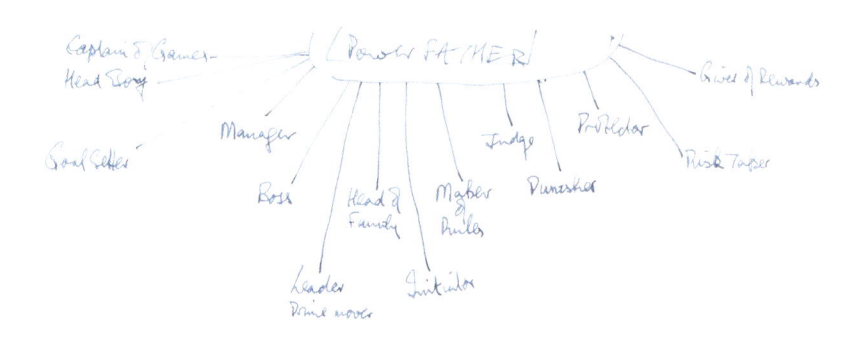

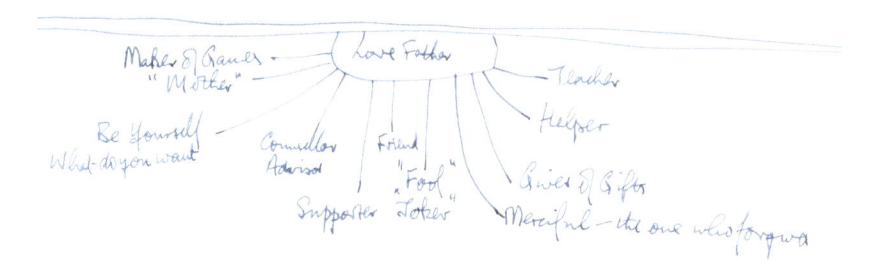

Facsimilies of notes: Ian Gordon-Brown

CHAPTER NINE

Intuition, Inspiration and the Will

Ian Gordon-Brown [277]

We grow from the personal to the Transpersonal
by the integration of the different aspects of the personality,
until the personal centre becomes the Transpersonal centre.
Then we may be in a fit state to be used by the Self

INTRODUCTION

Energy-threads

In the Eastern tradition, three fundamental lines or threads of energy link the Crown chakra with the Self. They are the Consciousness thread of *Intuition*, the Creative thread of *Inspiration* and the Life thread of *Will*.

Intuition	Inspiration	Will
Consciousness	Creation, Form	Life
Soul	Body, Mind	Spirit
Love	Intelligence	Will
Light	Number	Sound
Compassion	Creativity	Divine Purpose
Vishnu	*Brahma*	*Shiva*
Buddhi	*Manas*	*Atma*
High Priest	King or Queen	Grand Vizier
Heart	Throat	Crown
Pingala	*Ida*	*Shushumna*

Chart 9:01 – Three Threads of Energy

---

[277] This chapter consists of a digest of the talks IGB gave at a workshop of this title which he ran several times, and summaries of the explorations he offered.

The three threads have their origin in the Self, but find outer expression in and through the personality. They function on their own plane; they are aspects or emanations of Spirit – the One, the Three in One. How to understand these threads?

Intuition, Inspiration and the *Will* form a spiritual triad. They are aspects of the Holy Trinity, emanations of Spirit, the Monad, the One,[278] energies that function on their own plane but find outer expression in and through the personality. Intuition, on the Soul thread of consciousness, goes with feminine energy and with the Heart centre; it also has to do with the Brow chakra, and particularly with the right eye. Inspiration, the Creative thread, goes with masculine energy, with the Throat and Brow chakras, and particularly with the left eye. And Will, the Life thread, goes with Spirit and with the Crown and Base chakras.

In Eastern maps, the trinity is various. In one of them, it consists of the Soul, the Body or Mind, and the Spirit. What is Spirit? What is the real me? If the transpersonal Self is spirit, *where's the soul*? Another offers the trinity of Love, Intelligence and Will: Intuition goes with Love, Inspiration with Intelligence, and Will with Spirit. The Kabbala suggests Light, Number and Sound, or Soul, Form and Spirit.

The Hindus have Vishnu, Brahma and Shiva, whose archetypal representatives are High Priestess or Priest, King or Queen, and Grand Vizier. Vishnu is about Intuition, soul and consciousness; he is the Preserver, the sleeping figure awakening in response to need. Brahma the Creator goes with Inspiration, form, the new vision. Shiva, who is Destroyer, is of Will, life and the body. Again, they have *Buddhi*, the will to compassion, to love; *Manas*, the will to create, inspire and make manifest; and *Atma*, spirit, divine purpose, destiny. Or consider the chakras, Heart, Throat and Crown. And the *nadis* go with the three threads of the Soul: *pingala*, for consciousness and Intuition; *Ida*, for creative Inspiration; *sushumna*, for life and Will. And so on.[279]

EXPLORATION
INTUITION, INSPIRATION AND WILL
(25 minutes)

Minutes

6   Go inwardly to a quiet place and there, by spot imaging, be in touch

---

278   Leibniz, the 'Monad', Appendix 13.
279   For example, the collective energies of Hierarchy, Humanity and Shambhala, connecting respectively with Intuition, Inspiration and the Will.

with Intuition, Inspiration and Will in turn. For each, seek to get a symbol or image, a word or phrase, a colour, a sound, and a representative of:
>   the animal kingdom,
>   the vegetable kingdom,
>   the mineral kingdom,
>   the human kingdom,
>   the kingdom of souls.

6   Now, find your Talisman: one who knows your Will, your inspiration and your Intuition. Centre yourself with the Talisman, and there be in touch with your own *Intuition*.
>   Go within, into your body. Seek for your Intuition there.
>   Go out, to the world outside.
>   Go up, to the realm above.
>   Go down, into the earth beneath.

6   Once again, centre yourself. Now seek to be in touch with what *Inspiration* is for you.
>   Again, explore within, in your own body.
>   Seek for your Inspiration outside, in the world beyond.
>   Go up, to the realm above.
>   And down, into the earth beneath.

7   Return to your own Centre and the Talisman. Contact the *Will*.
>   Explore within, your body.
>   Outside, in the world.
>   Above, in the higher realm.
>   Seek for your Will below, in the earth beneath.

INTUITION – THE CONSCIOUSNESS THREAD

Weaving in the Light
Alice Bailey

In the areas of intuition [280] and inspiration, we are not alone. Things strongly felt around the Heart centre can sometimes break through as if shattering concrete. However, in Eastern thought *intuition* is elusive,

---

280   The subject of Intuition was originally addressed as part of Workshop 2, pp. 104 et seq.

coming and going in response to need. We struggle for our soul's contact with this thread, needing the light of consciousness to unite life and substance; for Vishnu, the Preserver, is a sleeping figure.

The rainbow bridge of light

Alice Bailey writes of how we have to build this *antahkarana* to make access more possible.[281] Pontifex is the Bridge-maker. We picture the smoke of incense – of sacrifice, intercession, prayer, the axis of aspiration – forming a spiral staircase, a ladder of ascension. This 'weaving in the light' builds at the intuitive level, filling gaps from earlier stages and involving continuity. An atmosphere of *love* has to be present as we reach for the reality to be contacted and our consciousness responds to what it meets; scepticism's static interference gets in the way. So suspend judgment, set the analytic mind to one side and become *receptive*. Let consciousness be as a container; feel for signals, make connections. The Brow chakra and the right eye play a part here, and the Solar Plexus is good at picking up atmospheres.

Images of intuition touch you so gently – a butterfly, a feather – you almost don't know they are there, like the images of dreams. *Expect* something to come; wait with anticipation for this strong but subtle energy. Anxiety will act as a powerful and subtle barrier. Expectancy and striving are mutually exclusive: don't strive for intuitive insight, or grab it. Just gently await it. Set your work to your own daily rhythms. When are you at your best – early morning – evening? If it's important to you, put it first and do other things later. Act on the message or hunch or flash, or it will come only sporadically. This helps the faculty to develop and grow.

How can I tell when my intuitive instrument is on pitch? What is its energy? What's my measure, in which of the chakras is my gut level? It's quite difficult, but important, to know other peoples' unconscious processes and *their* signals as well as our own. It requires an impersonality on our part.

The practice of awareness enables us to connect with, plug into, the energy of the Collective. The Alta Major guides us, warning of danger and offering its protection. Note the protective power of the will when it is connected to spiritual work: it makes an invisible shield around us, a diamond, a magnetic field which keeps things afloat, keeps the wolf from the door, lets us hold the centre as… what? A fist; a fire; the Rock of St. Peter.

---

281 The antahkarana is to do with the thread of consciousness and involves continuity, the response of our consciousness to what it meets, the union of life and substance. By endeavouring to visualise the entire process, we may set up a definite rapport (if successful) between the Buddhic intuition and the creative imagination of the astral body.

Different types of intuition

There is a hierarchy, requiring different sensitivity. At what level of consciousness do we experience extrasensory impressions?[282] In considering true impulses of the soul, we need to distinguish instinct from intuition, lower mind from higher, desire from spiritual impulse, selfish aspiration from divine incentive and (in Alice Bailey's terms) urges by the Lunar Lords from the unfolding by the Solar Lord. Is our hunch a direct knowing, a *spiritual* impulse at the level of the Heart? Is it a knowing by telepathy at the Throat, the *mental* level? Is it at a *feeling* level, the astral with its psychism centred in the Solar Plexus? Psychometry operating at the *physical* or *instinctual* level may be moved by self-aspiration rather than any divine incentive – it may even employ force.[283]

The boundaries of mind and emotions, body and instinct, are hazy; but, while other types of consciousness are easily confused with intuition, each of the levels on the map does have its intuitive counterpart.

> *The Intuition of the Instinct.* Given intuition, instinct can become our very conscience – our wise instinct. 'Animal instincts', appreciably determined by heredity, concern drive-motivated behaviour and its goals. In the West they are thought to need sublimation since they are 'bad', and to be replaced by the cognitive as we go up the evolutionary scale. But we have many strong and active instincts which may well be endowed with intuition. Maslow suggests that they are socially beneficial, *not* anti-society. Healthy instincts and healthy reason go together. The urge to understand is as instinctual as the drives involving hunger and sex and our need to love and be loved, whereas the urge to choose subject or behaviour can be acquired or learned.

> *The Intuition of the Body.* While an ability to dowse, use the pendulum or practise psychometry can come from an intuitive wisdom in the body, yet its energy may just be of the sensation function. A quarter of the population can do these things.

> *The Intuition of the Emotions* is the psychic hunch, our feeling nature's own intuitive leap. Our feelings already convey our psychic sensitivity; but again, we may simply be picking up energy from the atmosphere, mere emotional stuff. Those 'psychics' who usually work through the solar plexus at this emotional level are tuning into

---

283 However, our hands can become transmitters of spiritual energy in healing, in the stimulation of a specific Centre, in the work of linking a person with their soul, and in group work, where energy may come from the soul via Crown, Throat and Base of Spine.

the wish-life of the person. This is not good for the future.

The Intuition of the Mind reveals and illumines what is there in shadow form. It involves interest, thinking, premonition – the flash. Like the feelings, our minds already function as vehicles for the intuition. What brings the mind alive? It may be telepathic, a lively interplay between people at the mental level, communication expressed through the mind.

The Intuition of the Intuition itself. Depending on neither mind nor feelings, it is direct knowing, pre-cognition, a perceiving from the inside, a down-pouring of inspiration. 'Primitive' people went straight from instinct to intuition, by-passing other levels of consciousness, tuning in to the natural world with a pure perception. For Jung, it was direct perception via the *un*conscious. People are now making intuition *conscious* and so going beyond Jung. This is an important step in human development.

EXPLORATION
IN SEARCH OF YOUR INTUITION
(25 minutes)

2 Go inwardly to a quiet place where, by imaging, you may be in touch with your Intuition.

15 Review any *intuitive moments* or flashes or periods in your life.
Take five minutes to check what was happening in your life at the time of each event:
Where did you register the flash: where did it land?
How did you register it: voice – image or symbol – energy impulse?
At what *level*: mind – feeling – body?
Was the intuition *helpful*: did it work out?
What was the *time factor*: near future – distant future?

8 Return to your inner space. Invite an image or figure that personifies your intuition. Dialogue with this figure:
What does it *need*, to develop its nature more fully?
What in your life *blocks* its functioning?
How can you *nurture* it?

INSPIRATION – THE CREATIVE THREAD

Inspiration means bringing the future in over the hill

To inspire means to breathe in; to be inspired is to be awake to supernatural prompting and divine influence. Creation is to make manifest. Brahma the Creator links spirit and matter, heaven and earth, bringing in the new vision. To act on *inspiration* is to use our creative imagination, make something new, work from above downwards to come to another mode of consciousness. Inspiration comes in on the vertical plane but it flows out horizontally. Like intuition, it needs listening to, anchoring and grounding; but perhaps it is more masculine than the elusive intuition, which comes in a flash of consciousness, a touch. And intuition *needs* it – needs not only space and the feminine but inspiration, the generating of creative energy, to bring it to life and make it flow.

If what we are doing is worthy, both intuition and inspiration can come through. Creative inspiration needs:

> *Preparation*: finding the facts, asking the right questions, exploring the topic.
> *Incubation*: catching the inspiration and letting it alone.
> *Relaxation*: setting the mind to one side, following our curiosity.
> *Elaboration*: developing it for use.
> *Verification*: testing it out – does it work?

Where does our inspiration come from?

Remember the occult law, *energy follows thought*. Ask yourself, through which channel does the creative thread run? Is it in contrast to the wants of the small self and in tune with the psyche? Is there a horizontal, telepathic connection with someone else? Which chakras are involved (remembering that all of them have their counterpart in the Crown)? It may involve the Throat and the mental level, also the Brow chakra; and this time the left eye.

Is it a rusty faculty in you? Inspiration is often unconscious – the full tank is upstairs, but clogged with neglect so the taps won't work.[284] Work breeds inspiration, not *vice versa*. Use it, exercise it on a daily basis, ground and anchor it – there is a time-limit beyond which it withdraws. Some authors write every day, regularly *employing* their mode of work, keeping

---

284 As we saw in Workshop I, p. 63.

the doors open. It takes endurance. When writing, say, we may ask: 'But *who* is writing all this?' It seems *it* is writing – *it* knows best. Inspiration, the in-breathing spirit, Crown chakra energy flows down and in. Sentences form themselves, words scarcely need changing. Again, why? Who am I writing *for*? Where is it going? Creativity makes manifest. Is it serving the ego-personality, or a wider purpose? There is a population out there. Inspiration means bringing the future in over the hill – to *people*.

A *ritual* without inspiration makes no sense; if significant, it starts from within. Be aligned, tune in to the energy seeking expression. Then the energy and the ritual function as a unity, the ritual both serving the energy and providing an appropriate form for manifestation on its chosen plane.

Changing images in the different art forms – or *life* forms – pose difficulties for any artist; and a confusion of archetypes is hitting us at the dawning of the current age. In the '50's, the composer Sir Michael Tippett said that the archetypes seeking to be anchored were not clear: some had been withdrawn, while others hadn't yet found their way through. Therefore he didn't know what kind of music to write. Old images were dying, new ones yet unformed, and artists struggling to convey what was happening.[285] How do new patterns come into the old-patterned substance? Inspiration is not just art, but *the art of life*, creative, purposeful and conscious. There *are* people of vision; but it has been harder to be sure than it perhaps was in the earlier part of the twentieth century.

It takes the *magician* to make inspiration manifest. It needs exercise, practice and skill to manifest the energy of the idea, the archetype, the time cycle, linking spirit and matter. The stages of creation follow when a subjective thought-form becomes clothed with a sheath of desire and seeks an objective existence. This vibrant, subjective form attracts material to give it organisation on the physical plane, becoming an etheric vehicle with its dense gaseous envelope. Creation from the down-flowing spirit brings together a group, or society, or money, or an idea. Manifestation requires power, detachment, non-criticism and above all, precipitation. *Potencies produce precipitation*. Then, self-expression becomes expression of the Self. Do not be concerned about results; though your project may not succeed, it is still a contribution to the bridge that is being built.

The tension of inspiration often borders on pain, *the pain of the creative process*. Perhaps the pain of a thin skin is the inspiration – *is* the

---

[285] Tippett 1959, broadcast: 'Moving into Aquarius'.

inner impulse in all its uncertainty? How to reach the place where we can say, 'I *know* this thing is right – at least, as good as it can get'?

Anger is said to be locked-up creativity, or blocked inspiration. Our whole being holds the tension, the 'reaction of substance to descending impressions'. If inspiration then appears, it may resolve the conflict, solve the problem.

After conception, time in the womb, inspiration requires *incubation*. Working on a theme, building the form, at some point set the task aside and allow the unconscious space to come up with the answer. Cultivate the attitude of the onlooker, the silent watcher.

In starting a project or organisation, *timing* is vital. Many inspired ventures never get off the ground because they are left too late or pushed too hard too early. Do we pull on it, or open to it – push it, or allow it?

Who is to be *midwife*? Mind and feeling may go along with a project, but appropriate energy is needed to give it birth. One danger is to ignore the etheric level of energy. Too violent, too purposive, and birth is premature; forced growth leads to destruction by fire. Too little, and there are too few roots; without enough directed attention to bring the form into being, it may be stillborn.

On which plane is this project, this point of risk? Is it a physical creation, or the emotional creativity of a relationship, or the mental activity of an idea, a paradigm, a brain-child? Is the source the Self, or the ego? We hear ourselves saying things we didn't know we knew; they are all there in our consciousness. Don't kill the sound. *By premature speech and too much talk he slays what he has attempted to create.*[286] Don't let it be too perfect – leave in a flaw....

Did we get it right? Is it good? Does it feel fair? We know the answer. Having let the work take over, inspiration has flowed with intuition, emotion and sensation and given the project its form. Only now may we stand back and *evaluate* with mind and feelings, judging our creation. When the four functions are operating in the right way, we tune into many different levels of reality.

So the boat is released to run down the slipway. Attached we may be, but we need not identify with what we have created. Detachment is required; our attempts will sail in their own way. In the end we let them go.

---

286 See Bailey 1955, *Discipleship in the New Age*, Vol.II, p. 552 (2 & 3).

EXPLORATION
IN SEARCH OF YOUR INSPIRATION
(25 minutes)

2 Again, go inwardly to the quiet place. Prepare to be, through imagination, in touch with your Inspira

15 Review your times of *inspiration and creative flow*. Again, take five minutes each for several of the most important events, noting and recording:
>What was going on in your life?
>What was your role?
>How did it start?
>How did you register it?
>What was the result?
>What or who was being served?
>Is your inspiration random, or can it be turned on? If so how?
>Does work for you breed inspiration?

8 Return to your inner space. Seek for an image, figure, representative or personification of your inspiration. Dialogue with it:
>What does it *need*?
>What *blocks* it?
>How can you *nurture* it so that it can become more effective and useful?

WILL – THE LIFE THREAD

If thine eye be single, thy whole body shall be full of light[287]

The will is always mysterious. In the West it often implies self-will, having our own way. In the Indian tradition the will that unites and synthesises is the very thread of life, always available and present, keeping us going. The spirit of our nature, it holds the meaning of our life and makes us whole. *I assert the fact, I enunciate a collective purpose*, are its esoteric intentions. Such singleness of purpose maintains the inner link: *as above so below*.

Shiva is here, the Destroyer, banishing compromise, allowing no

---

[287] Matt 6:22; Luke 11:34.

'halfwayness'. Yet the will is also about protection: it prevents invasion, clears away all impediments and sets people free. Patiently it preserves values, holds steady, stands firm.

Will; spirit; life force – they're all the same thing. Located in the Crown with its connection with the Base, the will requires a channel, so it works through the spine. By continued visualisation a transpersonal link is made; we become *conscious of consciousness itself*, and the different levels of consciousness. When the life force is there, energy charges the moment and creates a sense of authority. The will both invokes, focussing upwards upon the down-pouring will; and evokes, drawing out from within. Indeed, invocation leads directly to evocation, mobilising the collective will of the people. If the vision can be stabilised, resurrection may follow.

Projection constitutes a primary block, rendering us quite unable to use the will. And, though it has authority, guard against associating the strong will with *power*. The conductor of the orchestra is simply a conductor. Instead, be in touch with the words of power associated with your own Ray.[288] Esoteric schools develop the will aspect of the spirit, giving it shape and direction; it is made meaningful when attached to something:

The will to be – to be the Self.
The will to wholeness.
The will to meaning.
The will to live.
The strong, powerful will.
The focussed, concentrated will: outward, inward, upward.
The will that *asserts the fact*; the reality principle.
The will that is the channel for a higher will.
The will that initiates.
The will that protects and prevents invasion.
The will that patiently persists, endures and holds steady.
The will that preserves values.
The will that unites and synthesises.
The will that chooses and evaluates.
The disciplined will, its expression regulated.
The peaceful, silent will.

---

288 Alice Bailey's 'Words of Power':
    I   'I assert the fact' – the line of will and power
    II   'I see the greatest Light' – the line of love and compassion
    III   'Purpose itself am I' – the line of thought
    IV   'Two merge with One' – the energy of harmony through conflict
    V   'Three Minds Unite' – the line of the scientist
    VI   'The Highest Light controls' – the line of devotion
    VII 'The Highest and the Lowest meet' – the ray of the magician.
Bailey 1960, 'Rays V', pp. 515-518. And see Appendix 18.

Who am I?

What is the purpose of my life? At Transpersonal workshops we consider the will to *wholeness*, to 'become what thou art' – become the Self. We also look at the will to *meaning*, remembering Jung: *loss of meaning is the neurosis of our age*. The will to wholeness and meaning constitute Assagioli's Egg, with the will to be above and the will to live underlying it all. As Assagioli said, unless they develop their inner powers, humans may become victim of their own achievements, losing control of the tremendous natural forces at their disposal.[289] The will of the ego-personality may contradict and counteract the will of the Self. To follow the inner daemon we need to be persistent and relatively free of self-interest. *Thy will be done*. The will to the highest good is to our own inner god, pulling us to be open to meaning – to make manifest, make music, paint, write – to be a still centre in the eye of the storm. The peaceful, silent will creates a centre where energy is available. *There can be no integration without a centre*.

The will is both personal and collective; it plugs us in to our *planetary* destiny, putting us in touch with the life of the world and the spirit of our time, making us accessible to other forms of will. There are *pressures* that go with the collective.

Pause again and ask yourself:
> which *archetype* are you under?
> What is your *personal* will to create?
> Your *collective* will to meaning?

EXPLORATION
IN SEARCH OF YOUR WILL
(35 minutes)

This highly individual journey involves your will, no one else's. It takes you close to the essence of your being.

---

[289] See Ferrucci 1982, 'What We May Be', p. 71.

Minutes
- 2 Know that you have helpers:
  The *Talisman*.
  Your *intuition*, perhaps represented by the symbol which you found for it.
  Your *inspiration*, perhaps also represented by a symbol.
- 7 *Exploring the past*. The will may have travelled with you for a long time and been present at many decisive moments, yet not have been recognised for who or what it is. Take some time now to review other journeys you have made, paths you have followed; and any past Talismans, perhaps involving family stuff and old feelings. Go within to a quiet place where, inwardly, you may be in touch with your Will.
- 7 *Where is your will today?* Explore its present state and its more recent influences. Find an image for its feelings and its current state.
- 7 *Exploring the future*. Invite an image for the future state of your will.
  Where is your will taking you – or driving you?
  What is your life's journey and tendency?
  What is your own spiritual path?
- 7 Note the difference between symbolic material from imaging, and real life. Seek to discover some of these things:
  What sort of will is it – what is the feel of it?
  What is the direction of your will?
  Where within you does the will live?
  What causes arousal of the will?
  At what level of consciousness is the will?
  What is its creative energy at each level: artistic?
                                                  relational?
                                         mental or ideational?
  What does the will give you?
  What does your will want?
  Is it the same at different times, at turning points, decisive moments?
  Are there different wills? Can you personify more than one?
  Does the will wish not to be found?
- 5 Seeking to know the will better, move towards finding a final personification or symbol for it.

The Raincloud of Knowable Things

[Facsimile of handwritten notes]

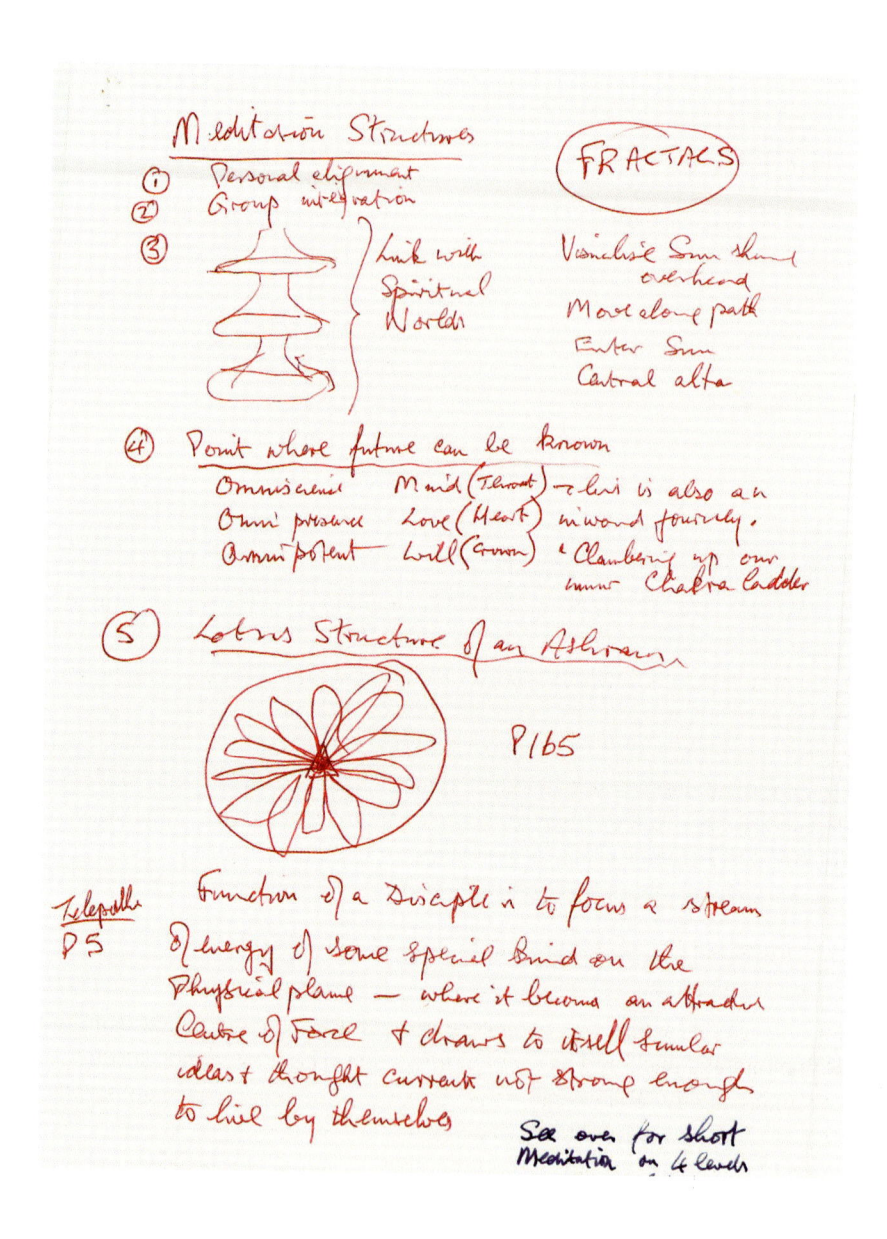

Meditation Structures

1. Personal alignment
2. Group integration
3. [diagram of tiered structure] Link with Spiritual Worlds

FRACTALS

Visualise Sun shape overhead
Move along path
Enter Sun
Central altar

4. Point where future can be known

   Omniscience — Mind (Throat)
   Omnipresence — Love (Heart)
   Omnipotent — Will (Crown)

   — this is also an inward journey.
   "Clambering up our inner Chakra ladder"

5. Lotus Structure of an Ashram

   [lotus diagram]   P165

Telepathy P 5 — Function of a Disciple is to focus a stream of energy of some special kind on the Physical plane — where it becomes an attractive Cause of Force & draws to itself similar ideas & thought currents not strong enough to live by themselves.

See over for short Meditation on 4 levels

Facsimile of notes: Ian Gordon-Brown

CHAPTER TEN

The Raincloud of Knowable Things
A Workshop on the Expanding of Consciousness

Ian Gordon-Brown [290]

Then to the inner ear will speak the voice of silence
Patanjali

INTRODUCTION

The personal and the planetary

We see, not so much ourselves as moving into the future, but the relatively immediate future approaching *us*, bringing not only a raincloud, but a raincloud of knowable things.[291] The immediate future is coming into the present. How can we tune in, how help it to descend? And is it descending – or is it in fact *surfacing*? A familiar image is of going up the mountain and there reaching out. We need the Other, 'the other half', our consciousness. Rather than our moving towards it, consciousness is moving to meet us. *It* is coming towards us. The building is done both from inside outwards and from outside inwards – perhaps at the same time?[292]

All substance is living substance

When the stage of the 'raincloud of knowable things' is reached, hindrances and *karma* are overcome. Something new is brought from the Raincloud and anchored as usable knowledge. The very *plan* is substance, dynamic energy. Recipients must become sensitive to this substantial energy and repudiate what is not right for the current time-cycle. The divine plan may lead to something that won't be recognised for five hundred years, something that cannot be grounded because its time has not

---

290 IGB gave this workshop once only, on 20-21 November 1995. Unlike most of the workshops, it was held over just one and a half days. Afterwards, someone remarked that several people had found it 'different'. Ian, hearing this as implying 'hard to understand', immediately responded: 'Ah, then they were not ready for it.'
291 A phrase from Bailey 1927, 'The Light of the Soul: The Yoga Sutras of Patanjali'. When a man can detach his eyes from all that concerns the physical, emotional and mental, and will raise his eyes and direct them away from himself, he will become aware of 'the overshadowing cloud of spiritual knowledge,'... the 'raincloud of knowable things'. Bailey 1927, *The Light of the Soul*, Book IV, Sutra 29, p. 425.
292 IGB acknowledged that this workshop draws heavily on Alice Bailey, 'Rays V'. See also Bailey 1934, *A Treatise on White Magic*.

yet come.[293] Personal centring and contact with the Self through practices for raising awareness (the use of *mantras*, words of power, visualisation) are only the beginning of our inner work. They are preludes to participation in the creative world process of contemplation. Patanjali's famous saying (above) expresses the need for the individual to move beyond personal transformation to become part of this great world movement, bringing the patterns, archetypes and symbols of the future into present manifestation. Then the science of invocation and evocation can be used to go beyond our *personal* contract with the soul, which is just the beginning. Thus we may help build the *planetary*, the rainbow bridge between heaven and earth, the *antahkarana* linking the worlds of the gods and of humanity.

The magnetic field

By 'tuning' our being and becoming more alive, we become magnetic, beginning to create a magnetic field that starts to sing – to zing. It's an aura on which energy can play and link to the wider magnetic field. This aura tries to form as we each find contact with our soul and become more sensitive to impressions. We attract thoughts and images into a field of consciousness; they drop into that field because of the aura we have developed – things pop in at the needed moment. Assagioli said of meditation that it's not usually recognised that it is *inner action* – the exploration of inner worlds. The West has defined *nirvana* as 'nothing'. Certainly Nirvana is 'no thing'; yet it is full of energies and qualities, of cause and meaning more real than that to be found in the visible world.

The avatars of history

Who are they, the great avatars, those who embody principles – Alpha to Omega, Omega to Alpha, invoking and evoking? Krishna, Lao Tzu, the Buddha, Confucius, Christ, Muhammad Akbar.[294] From 1400 onwards in the West there was a whole series of revolutions: the Renaissance, the Reformation, the rise of printing, the spread of the English language, each brought about by a group of great figures of the time. Such avatars brought a big theme into the consciousness of the planet and embodied profound principles. Groups were involved in the development of science, in the Industrial Revolution, in the American and French Revolutions, the wakening of democracy, the Russian Revolution in 1919 and the mixing

---

293 This workshop has already, in the light of changing world consciousness since 1995, been seen as a prescient primer in Transpersonal manifestation. Now is the time for the Raincloud. Ed.
294 Akbar the Great, 1542-1605, ruled from 1556 until 1605; considered the greatest of the Mughal emperors.

up of East and West. There have been cultural revolutions such as that informed by the Impressionists or, more recently, by those adopting alternative lifestyles

Individual movements form different streams of the one river. Their avatars are manifest in such great pioneers as Abraham Lincoln, who embody a necessary principle or energy. Groups emerge, followed by a phase of integration. The present era can trace itself back to the founding of the Royal Society in 1660, and of the Masons soon after.[295] Links go back to Benjamin Franklin, leading printer, scientist, inventor, civic activist, diplomat and candlemaker who, more than anyone, invented the idea of an American nation.[296] Also to Tom Paine and his pamphlet, where common sense set the bush-fires alight in America;[297] and the Marquis de Lafayette in France, hero of two revolutions.[298]

Between 1789 and 1989, dominoes toppled in Europe. The river flowed via mechanical geniuses, via poets, musicians and painters of the eighteenth and nineteenth centuries, to the beginning of the Labour movement, the Luddites, and the rise of modern physics. It is arguable that physicists have done more to transform the consciousness of nations than any other group. World Communism followed and, in 1948, the Declaration of Human Rights. Consider Blavatsky and the Theosophical Society, Dag Hammarskjold and the United Nations.[299] Then the psychological field was activated (though with relatively few names – psychology has had good aspects and bad); and the women's movements, the feminine principle, Gaia and ecology, the awareness of tides and cycles. In 1981, Marilyn Ferguson introduced her Aquarian Conspiracy[300] – *con spiro*, breathing together, creating a network – and Alison Barnard inspired the Scientific and Medical Network. There has been a process enabling it to happen, and it has happened in good humour.

Death and rebirth

There are times and seasons for all things. All substance is living, as we have seen; the Raincloud involves life in *form*, and all forms die as part of

---

295 The formation of the Grand Lodge of Freemasonry in 1717 was followed by the creation of hundreds of Grand Lodges that spread rapidly worldwide.
296 Benjamin Franklin, 1706-1790, one of the best-known Founding Fathers of the United States.
297 Thomas Paine (1737-1809), English intellectual, scholar, revolutionary, deist and radical, often in America and France. Paine anticipated and helped foment the American Revolution through his powerful writings, most notably 'Common Sense', an incendiary pamphlet advocating independence from Great Britain.
298 The Marquis de La Fayette, 1757-1834, a French aristocrat considered a national hero in both France and the United States for his participation in the American and French revolutions.
299 Dag Hammarskjold, 1905-1961, 2nd Secretary-General of the United Nations from 1953-1961.
300 Ferguson 1981, *The Aquarian Conspiracy*.

creation. Destruction prepares the way for the infusion of new life; hence the important and necessary cycles of Brahma the Creator, Vishnu the Preserver, and Shiva the destroyer. When the life-force is stimulated and energised, it can be released from form. Shiva and Kali destroy, and thus stimulate energy within. We certainly need them, for Vishnu is lying asleep; without Shiva we would be shocked, for the Self would have to do the destroying.

The last taboo was sex; now it is death. Death and longevity are major themes reflected in the Tibetan science of dying, as in the rise of the hospices. The Raincloud may be about *help* in the destruction and releasing of life, the death of the form. No crop is successful without ploughing and manuring at the right time of the year, suitable soil and weather, good quality seed – and people to do the job, usually too few in number, who just get on with it, unbothered. Not only are individuals, families and small groups subject to birth, death and rebirth, but organisations and communities, movements, churches, races, nations, religions. We are born, grow, reach maturity and usefulness, live our cycle, our age, our wisdom, decline and die.

Transformational groups

There will be manifestations of any avatar whose principle is about to come into being. It is as if the spiritual guides of the race were beyond the Raincloud but had their agents in the Raincloud; as if they had regular meetings. It is as if individuals come into incarnation, learn lessons and go back. Groups incarnate to accomplish transformational ends – a warming notion. Such groups include not only those who brought about the great revolutions, but clusters of musicians, writers, poets and painters. The overall plan of the avatars is to bring in four freedoms: the transformation of human consciousness; the education of the mind of man; world peace and brotherhood (no more war); and beauty.

Schools of initiation

So our work for the Raincloud is in preparation for the mystery schools of the twenty-first century. This is my personal goal, working in the area of heart-consciousness. Much work has to be done before we can plant seeds and get a suitable crop. The early stages of ploughing and seeding have to be repeated many times. Not all clouds are rainclouds; some yield only droplets rather than a decent shower. There will be many groups aiming for initiation; timing is important. Some things can go forward, others are held back. We may have to step *down* the rates of vibration. Being sensitive to the Raincloud means being sensitive to an ocean of energies. What's moving, what's not moving? Do we need to change what we are doing a little bit? We put ourselves in the position of world leaders: 'What would *I* do if faced with this situation?'

Shambala, Father, Monad, Will

Hierarchy, Soul-consciousness, Love, Wisdom

Humanity

Chart 9:02 – Links and Threads

Networks of people serving the world

Such a network is organised not outwardly but inwardly, by an inner structure of thought, a telepathic medium of inter-relation. Where, inwardly, is this structure coming from? What's really going on behind the scenes? Is it more organised than we realise; are possibilities being allowed to grow? The timing often seems uncanny: time, tide, destiny and their cycles – millennial cycles, hundred-year cycles, seven-year cycles. Members of the human family make links and threads at the personal level, at the level of soul and the hierarchy, up to the highest levels of all. We remember that the chakras are involved. And life *makes* us make changes. As someone remarked: 'It's as if there's a Personnel Department on the "other side".'

Ashrams of humanity [301]

The planetary picture involves three downward-radiating levels: the Crown chakra (Shambhala, the centre of the world); the planetary Heart centre (the Buddha, Christ, consciousness and initiation) which, in Alice Bailey's terms, forms the hierarchy or the group integration process; and the Throat centre of humanity and the collective (inner groups or ashrams). Each ashram with its lotus structure receives a different type of message from the hierarchy and each movement towards the centre is paralleled by a movement out into the world. Where are we drawn? We tend to be attracted by the energy field of a group that does a particular sort of work; we can distinguish impulses that come from our own inner tribe and teacher. What is our field or style – our archetype or Ray? Are we aware of our role, our part, task, Dharma? On which side of the bridge are we most comfortable, the orthodox or the unorthodox? Which drums do we hear? Are we with those taking orthodoxy into the future, or with those on the other side of the bridge, bringing the future to the present – working within the cracks in the system? *Many are called, but few are chosen.* [302]

Disciples

There are the *great avatars*, then *avatars, lesser avatars* and *disciples* or helpers.[303] The function of a disciple is to focus a stream of special energy on the physical plane where it becomes an attractive centre of force and draws to itself similar ideas and thought currents not strong enough to live by themselves. But watch for inflation and the over-stimulation that leads to it.

The Antahkarana

So we build the Rainbow Bridge of light and substance, of some subtle matter that is within it.[304] We build it from the ego to the Self, channelling

---

301 I use the term 'ashram' not in a narrowly religious way, but to signify any group of people drawn together by inner currents.
302 St. Matthew, 22:14 (and 20:16).
303 See the Chela, Appendix 10.
304 Antahkarana, see n. 51 and n. 281.

energy, constructing a reliable channel of conscious communication from the heart to the soul. We prepare our consciousness by looking to our personal alignment and having our own individual picture of the Raincloud; by connecting with the energy of the group and its integration; and by aiming towards a link with the spiritual worlds. We focus on tension and attention. We clamber up our inner chakra ladder, becoming aware of omniscience (mind and Throat); omnipresence (love and the Heart); and omnipotence (will and the Crown). We call in the will; building the bridge involves a mental focus, holding the energy substance at the point of projection. We put our thread up from the Crown chakra to our friends on the 'other side', stabilising it and holding the tension. And traffic crosses the bridge in each direction, a Jacob's Ladder on which angels both ascend and descend.

Seed thoughts

They come to us. As we focus our energy on the mental plane, what is our intention, our orientation, our mental understanding? Meditating on *the seed*, we aim to think clearly; we gather energy, holding the greatest tension without any pressure on the cells of the brain, enlarging and solidifying our consciousness, creating a kind of ring-pass-not. Take each seed; it will render its meaning in time. We identify our own thoughts with the fundamental thoughts going on around the planet – perhaps those concerning, for example, the world's armed conflicts. We may pick an idea or a theme (sound, light, number); a quality of aliveness; a feeling; an element; colour, beauty, meaning. It may have mental appeal, teaching value, soul purpose, human rights and freedoms, astrology, telepathy, a chakra. It may be an outer place – a city, a sacred spot. Or the petal of a lotus, a plane of consciousness, an inner sanctum. So there is brought into being a magnetic aura on which higher impressions can play.

However, *meditating without seed* (not putting a seed thought in the middle) is also an important way of holding in the light.

Sound

Sound is spirit; it has power and it can be used. Sound your note. Sound your name. Sound the mantra of light, love and will – of consciousness, form, and image. Some forms of prayer have mantric power. In Mantra Yoga the sound goes out and comes back, creating a sculpture of vibrations. Sound the Om; doing it silently is just as powerful as doing it externally.

Power-words

We need to organise the powerful energy of words. In Alice Bailey's teaching, certain words of power correspond with the seven main archetypes.[305] Which for you represents the essence?

How to generate the magnetic field?

Energy follows thought: thinking in a certain way will bring in light, love and the will. To energise the heart centre, for instance, *think* love. Love the Alta Major and it will start to flower. Simplistic? Simplistic processes have a reality.

Visualisation

The imagination, an aspect of intuition, pictures the focussed energies. As we have seen, visualisation is different from imaging, where we relax, let go and let what's waiting there come to the surface. In visualisation, on the other hand, we *construct* a form to represent a spiritual symbol, drawing on the imaginative processes of the emotional vehicle. For example, we might deliberately visualise a rapport between Buddhic intuition and creative imagination.[306] This ability to use mental energy together with the creative powers of imagination is an important starting point. Penetration leads to visualisation, from which comes the seed on which we reflect. It holds consciousness at the Crown chakra. Allow it; allow energy to flow down more and more. *Upon a beam of light can the energy of mind materialise.* If we are receptive, precipitation follows, for the thinker has potency and the quality of that potency brings about the precipitation. The gathering of energy is followed by the attaining and maintaining of focus as we picture a *form*. Our minds give life and direction to the form, and the form embodies purpose. When the soul is creative in this planned and constructive way, a rapport is set up between the mind and the inner world. What sounds, what words of power may be projected from our hearts with the energy of love and wisdom, or from the Crown as energy of the will?

The thousand-petalled lotus

What form do we visualise and how do we place it? Perhaps the blossoming of a rose; or a golden lotus, closed, resting in the heart centre.[307] See it, closed. See the light of the soul shining on it; watch it open petal by

---

305 Alice Bailey's Words of Power, see n. 288, and The Seven Rays, Appendix 18.
306 Intuition operates on the plane of Buddhi.
307 An antidote for headaches, this, where there is a feeling of a tight band, or of being out of control and frightened, or of being attacked from behind with an electric drill by something desperate to be released.

petal, a kingfisher-blue light in the middle. See the opening of the thousand-petalled lotus above the head, the petals rising to let the energy *out*; and then imagine a reversed lotus letting it flow down and *in*. Build an image of light in the lotus, a figure of light, of the master of the heart, full of the qualities and attributes of the Heart chakra, an image or symbol of what is for you the perfection of the heart. Become one with the figure of light. Visualise a bridge – from body to soul, ego to soul. Do not bother about the form the answer comes in; remain detached from any results.[308]

Organisations

Any *outer organisation* of co-workers need not exist. The work is held together by telepathy and inner magnetism, by breathing together. Take an energy appropriate to any particular chakra and see what it does to the energy fields. The power to communicate is to be found in the very substance of stuff itself; and substance is omnipresent, omnipotent, omniscient. *Only what we know and consciously experience for ourselves constitutes our truth.* Personal 'stuff', as opposed to what we do for the Collective, may come into our consciousness, and not in quite the way we expect. How do we hold our consciousness and build the bigger picture? If we look outside ourselves, thinking: 'Someone else can do one bit while I do another?' then what happens when our spiritual colleagues are no longer here? Other people can at best enhance or corroborate it; they may rather create illusion. The answers are always inside us; we can find out what the energy wants to do by an *inner* dialogue. When the disciple has reached a certain stage, he or she doesn't need to refer to the teacher very often, being too busy getting on with the work.

Moon rhythms

The cycles of New and Full Moon offer helpful rhythms for sowing and reaping. At the New Moon, we concentrate on activities of good will. Words flow more easily now than at other times in the month, and understanding, receptivity and the power to visualise. At Full Moon, meditation may involve adequate preparation, then elevation to the mountain – the inner mountain – which leads to the sun and out into world. The symbol of the mountain also involves spiritual renewal, from above downwards.

---

308 See Bailey, *A Treatise on White Magic*', and also *Discipleship in the New Age I*, pp. 89-91.

Danger

Remember – *energy is substance*. There is, as we know, a point of danger in all creative work where the vibrant, subjective thought-form has to attract to itself the form it needs for an outlet in the world. This must happen with neither too much energy, nor too little. Too much, and the infant burns in a death by fire; too little and it is stillborn. Often both the *anchoring* and the *timing* are difficult. Don't push too fast – yet if you leave it too long, you've got words, not life. None of us is good enough; none of us has our head above the water; and there is a protective function in standing firm. So – *stand firm*. Keep the channel open; remain aware of the Rainbow Bridge and the traffic on it to and fro.

The Plan

As the disciple develops soul quality, she or he attracts into consciousness from the Raincloud an outline of 'the plan', and, thence, of the purpose. This plan is a reservoir on which we can draw. When we make contact with our souls, we become more sensitive to impressions, developing a magnetic relationship with it, invoking both plan and purpose. So, without effort, we create on the physical plane a magnetic aura that draws to itself thoughts not strong enough to live by themselves.[309]

> *Here we have, esoterically and symbolically given, the indication that there lies before the initiate (advanced as he is) a still further progress, another veil to be penetrated. He has made a great at-one-ment and has unified soul and body. He stands (as regards the three worlds) at the stage called that of isolated unity. But another union becomes possible, that of the soul with the spirit. The Master must become the Christ and to do this the raincloud of spiritual knowledge must be reached, used and penetrated. What lies on the other side of that veil which hides the Father it is needless for us to consider. In our New Testament, when the Father communicated with the Christ, the voice issued out of a cloud.*
>
> (St. Matthew 17:5) [310]

---

309 Bailey 1950, *Telepathy*, pp. 95-96. ,
310 Bailey 1927, *The Light of the Soul: The Yoga Sutras of Patanjali*, pp. 425-426.

FOUR EXPLORATIONS FOR GROUPS

Creation – Manifestation – Generation

These four journeys for the Raincloud of Knowable Things (which may be used in any order as required, together or separately) are aimed at *alignment*, going straight into and through the Raincloud and into the Temple in the Sun, linking with Ashrams and the Hierarchy. The first is *personal*, the second for the *group*, and the third acknowledges the *spiritual path*. In each, be in touch with the process of creative imagination – contemplative, anchoring, catching – creating. Seek to make your energy field magnetic, involving both invocation and evocation, preserving the state accomplished. Let it open up all areas – body, mind and feelings – so that the future can make an impression on you. Use soul energy and words of power to project across the gap.

Prayer and invocation are important in setting up these journeys, individually or for the group. So, first a period of reflection, followed by reception of the blessings which follow.

EXPLORATION
MY PERSONAL PLACE OF CREATION
(25 minutes)

Begin by making a journey to the Self, to the world where *creation* is happening. Move into the future to explore the Raincloud of Knowable Things. You can take with you a guide and a Talisman.

> Go inward, look around, scan the horizon about you. Look and see. Seek an image for the Raincloud, and for the Knowable things.
>
> Now take the path that attracts your soul, following it to the place to which you are drawn, where your friends are. Discover where it is: an inner place, such as a chakra, the petal of a lotus, an inner sanctum; or an outer place – a city, a sacred spot.
>
> Visit each part of it separately. Which resonates? Recognise that both the place and its function may change.
>
> Invite a general picture, or images, in response to this question: 'What am I supposed to be doing?' Your Talisman or wise person is there to help.

EXPLORATION
THE GROUP AND THE ASHRAM
(25 minutes)

What part of the Raincloud are you drawn to?

Be in touch with the process of creative *manifestation* as you know it. Invite a picture of the world. Take an overview; see images of its government, religion, culture, science, economy.

Connect with what is for you the Ashram. This is where you will be led to discover your vocation and learn your trade. Sense your place and function – it may change. Are you shaping, designing, creating an atmosphere for it to be present, leading towards reality? Are you group worker, teacher, apprentice, journeyman, master craftsman? Connect also with the hierarchy; be in touch with your tutor or teacher, fellow pilgrim in the process of becoming a wise being. Find an image or visualisation that is helpful as you ask yourself:

What is my Ashram, my Group?
How do I make this manifest, shape and anchor it in the world?
What are my problems in doing this?
What do I need to develop to do this?
Is the time right?
As I look ahead, will my task or function change?

EXPLORATION
THE TEMPLE IN THE SUN
(25 minutes)

Go behind the manifestation to the place of *generation*. What happens if you put it into practice – will it change? Don't push it too fast or it won't happen – it's a delicate process. As we know, there is a point of danger in all creative work. 'Not too little, not too much' – beware the destruction of energy by fire. Begin to recognise a stage that lies *beyond* the hierarchy.[311]

Again, invite images or pictures as you go. Know that this is an *inward* journey and remember that it involves the chakras:

Visualise the Sun shining overhead.

---

311 Described by Alice Bailey as Shambhala.

> See yourself moving along a path towards it.
> Enter the Sun.
> There, you find yourself in an inner Temple, at a central altar; this is a point where the future can be known.

We recall Patanjali: *Then to the inner ear will speak the voice of silence.*

EXPLORATION
ORIENTING THE SELF
(25 minutes)

You may wish to make a map for the orientation of the Self. So choose an image or picture, a word or phrase, and become deeply aware of it:
> Study its form, symbolically, as a word-picture or image.
> Study it from the angle of quality – beauty, clarity, colour, desire.
> Study its teaching value and mental appeal, its more fundamental meaning.
> Study its very being, its soul-element or sound. Identify yourself with its divine underlying purpose.

Contemplate while you draw.

SOME WAYS TO THE CENTRE OF LIFE

Love is a process of self-enlargement. It may include the disciplines of meditation and the inner way – of service and of study. 'Who am I? Who am I not?' When meditation becomes part of life, then you become your own guide – you wait for the Self to speak. Reviewing daily, monthly or annually shows how time may stretch, crises cease to repeat, opportunities not be lost. A journal or workbook can record desired qualities, evocative words, dialogues with sub-personalities; help to nourish body, feelings, mind and instincts; encourage us to enjoy our leisure and have fun.

On the journey, the Way, the Tao, we follow a 'path with heart', meet masculine and feminine symbols, adopt different modes of travel, see our goal afar. We encounter inner figures for good or ill – including heroes, the true intermediaries. Images certainly help; but don't become hooked on them – it's their energy that's important. They point up polarities: dismemberment, scattering, dissolving, loss; and taking up, incorporation, gathering.

Don't help the flowers to grow by pulling them upwards. Forgetting and remembering, we move towards integration. Personal qualities are replaced by transpersonal qualities – inclusion, centralisation, stillness. As one participant commented, 'My whole life has been informed, knowingly or unknowingly, by my commitment to the journey of self-discovery – and it's been hard work too!'

Transpersonal workshops

They are not for everyone. They are about non-expectation, living with no reward except that of the journey. The impact of the Transpersonal is that we come to know our task. If positive, energy, health, calm and radiance follow and our capacity as catalyst is enhanced. If negative, a fuse blows; defective events occur, and flights of ideas, hyper-activity, depression, *idées fixes*, excessive sensitivity – even a messiah complex. However, our hope is to become more loving and creative, our full lives marked by a spontaneous outflow of joy, simplicity, energy, participation and service to humanity.

The Workshops offer us the chance to sit with our fellows, but at the end we all go our different ways. Confucius said: 'When will you realise that the way out is through the door?' The following came from participants:

'As ye reap, so shall ye sow.'
'Many are called, but few choose.'
'When the dragon is slain, let the sword rest.'
'Don't push the river.'
'Stand back; the door opens towards you!'
'Am I part of the problem, or part of the solution?'
'Listen, don't whimper.'
'I need to care for my own internal child, not seek for adoption.'
'The lazy are the best on earth – they do the least damage.'
'Go with the mystery of life.'
'I intend to go on dreaming; it's not the same as taking action.'
'Trust, attention and silence....'

'The greatest gift from life is your Self.'

You may wish to end with this transformative magical action.

EXPLORATION
THE UNIVERSAL BLESSING OF BUDDHISM

Peace to all beings, North – South – East – West, above – below
    Peace to all beings.
Love to all beings, North – South – East – West, above – below
    Love to all beings.
Compassion to all beings, North – South – East – West, above – below
    Compassion to all beings.
Joy to all beings, North – South – East – West, above – below
    Joy to all beings.
Serenity to all beings, North – South – East – West, above – below
    Serenity to all beings.

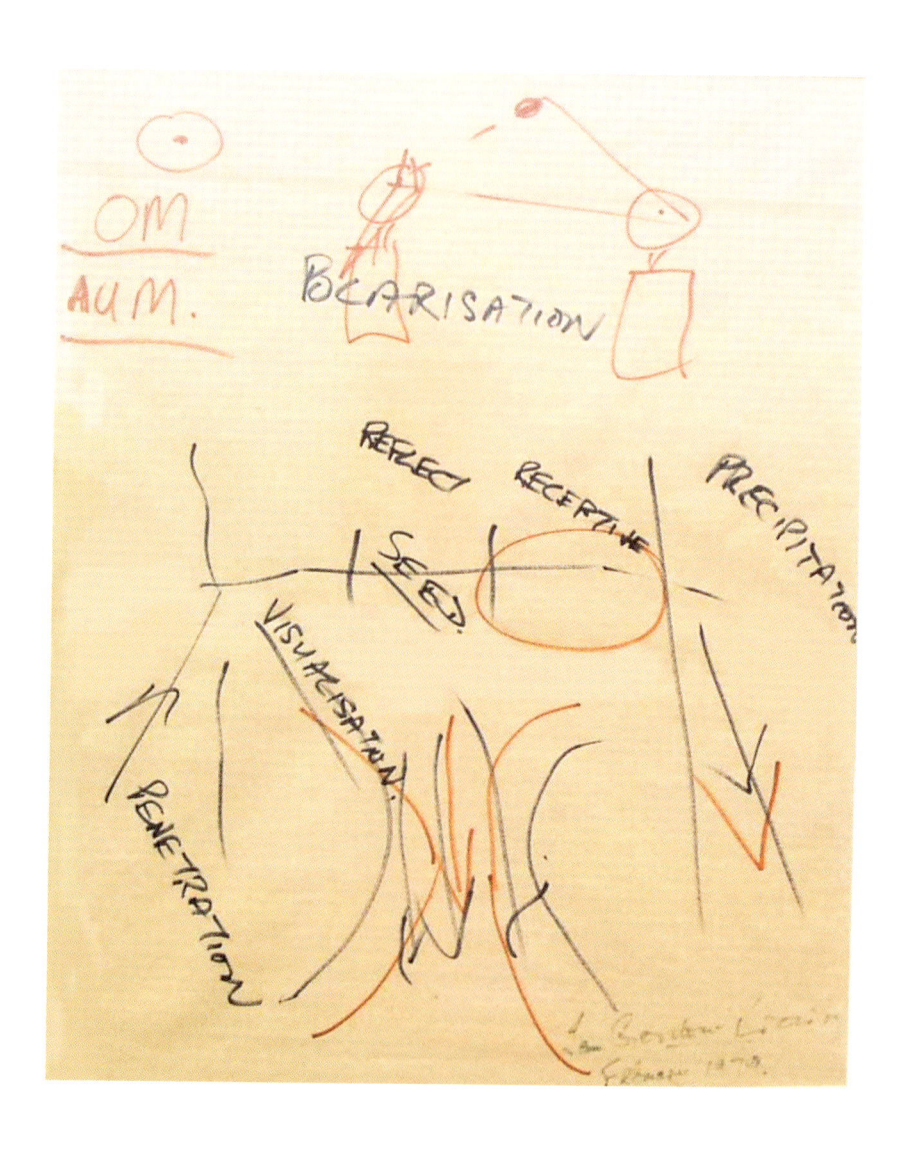

Facsimile of flipchart: Ian Gordon-Brown

PART IV
Appendices

Facsimile of chart: Ian Gordon-Brown

APPENDIX 1

CHECKLIST FOR RUNNING TRANSPERSONAL WORKSHOPS

Ian Gordon-Brown

It is very important that, before running transpersonal workshops, the reader is aware of some essentials. They are summarised here for convenience:

Contra-indication. Active imagination is a very powerful tool for exploring the depths of the unconscious. Do not use it on anyone with a serious mental disorder.

Provision of therapy. Unconscious material that is stimulated can take several days or weeks to emerge. Ideally there should be some one-to-one therapy available for dealing with this if needed.

Leaders. It is preferable, if possible, that at least the first three workshops be run by two people, a man and a woman. Those at the beginning of their journey of self-discovery may well have unresolved issues about gender.

Group discussion and sharing. It is held in some quarters that the leader's job is to interpret clients' material for them; also, that the significance is probably sexual. In transpersonal workshops neither of these is the case. It is important to ensure that participants understand that they should not attempt to interpret for somebody else, nor ask leading questions. Again, interpretations must come only from the person.

For the explorations:

Provide a pleasant and welcoming room, preferably with flowers – a room free as far as possible from traffic and neighbour noise.

A floor comfortable for lying down, with enough space so participants are not crowded.

Tissues available.

Participants might need extra clothing or a blanket during long guided journeys; lying down and relaxing deeply will make them cooler.

Dim lights and curtains drawn.

For the earliest explorations in each workshop, give plenty of time for people to relax down. This can be speeded up in later journeys when they have become accustomed to the procedure.

Speak calmly in a clear voice. Make sure everyone can hear.

Do give all the time suggested – which can seem long. Insights often emerge during the final minutes.

So that people don't get left behind during long periods of silence say quietly, 'Another minute before we move on.'

At the end of an imagery session, give participants time to come out of it calmly and quietly without being rushed, maybe inviting them to adopt the foetal position.

Provide plenty of coloured crayons (wax pastels are suitable), boards if possible and large drawing paper.

Recording. Encourage people to record in pictures as well as words. Avoid having a break between an imagery session and its recording, lest the material become contaminated by discussion with others. Where the exploration (like the Sub-personality exploration in Workshop I) is in two parts, invite them not to discuss the material itself during the break, but save it for later.

APPENDIX 2
COMMENTARY ON SOME OF THE WORKSHOP EXPLORATIONS
Ian Gordon-Brown

EXPLORATIONS FOR WORKSHOP I, APPROACHING THE SELF

It's well to start this workshop with at least twenty minutes' discussion on the conscious and the unconscious. Then say, 'You can map this', and lead into:

The Traveller on Life's Journey

Several of our original exercises came out of Psychosynthesis as evolved in California. The first six of these simple questions came that way; we added 'Who am I?' as well as the theme of the *journey* and the *traveller*. It's our own journey – our goal, our blocks, our assets, our weaknesses. And it's also the hero's journey: 'Where am I going? Which way?' It's important to know each person's *direction*. Are they moving up – or perhaps down? Is the movement inwards, or outwards?

If people lie down, the level is more likely to deepen. However, this first exploration gives a chance not only to explain about imaging, but to offer a *way* of imaging. It's a teach-in. So, for this one, invite them alternately to lie down and sit up, recording as they go. This keeps them aware and awake, secure because up into their heads, not lying down for long with strangers. People are usually scared at the beginning, and need to be told things several times. Always repeat the questions, and even have them up on a board.

And, right from the beginning, establish *drawing* as a method of recording what comes up. It sets the pattern for all the workshops. Artistic talent is not the point. Say: 'You may wish to do just a diagram, to remind you.'

The Sub-personality exploration

The primary can-opener for all the workshops, this. To be all goodness – to admit nothing negative – leaves space for seven devils to occupy the room when the one is driven out. Conversely, to express and let out a great deal of negative energy (dark material, rubbish, *stuff*) without allowing its positive face to reveal itself, equally leaves a hole in the unconscious for the devils to get in.

Going *into* the house of the sub-personalities often changes the depth of the imaging; staying outside, people go less deep.

Going up the column of light, there to find a wise person or presence, requires a good six or seven minutes. Say: 'If no wise person comes, then experience this as a place where wisdom is possible; and there consider the sub-personalities and your relation with them'.

It's too simplistic to ask people to befriend and love all their sub-personalities. In the end, maybe – but first, there may be too much real pain.

At the end, say (not too emphatically): 'See your sub-personalities go back into the house and the door close behind them'. If they won't (and they sometimes refuse to, preferring to run around outside) people may worry. So, explore the meaning of their not going back in; it's often that they have been locked away far too long. Let them loose.... The person usually then feels good, with more energy than usual. So, while keeping the instruction, be open to alternatives. It's inappropriate – too heavy – to say, 'Make sure the door closes firmly behind them all!' [312]

The Gestalt exploration

Towards the end of each of the first two workshops (also in the 'Archetypes' workshop of Chapter 7) we added a Gestalt exploration into Body, Emotions and Mind.[313] Explain beforehand what happens, demon-

---

312 Guidelines for writing up sub-personalities, Appendix 1.
313 I used to invite people to get an image for Body, Emotions and Mind, but changed to a Gestalt framework to prevent too much imaging. However, images do work very well for them too: for instance, someone had a tree for the emotions, a saw for the mind and a clam for the body!

strating the whole layout in advance and saying: 'This is about your present life-style.' Set cushions or chairs for Body, Emotions and Mind, and place a fourth for the wise, intuitive Observer, inwardly putting it in a column of light if desired. Be alert to medical problems, offering people a choice of positions: will they sit, lie or stand?

This exploration benefits thinking-oriented people who have problems with imaging, encouraging as it does differentiation and interaction between the different aspects in the presence of the Observer.

The Inner Sanctuary

This is important in *each* workshop. Ask people to find somewhere such as a temple, a grotto, a grove, an island. You might say: 'Find yourself in a place you'd like to go to for quiet and intimate conversation.'

EXPLORATIONS FOR WORKSHOP II, THE MASCULINE AND FEMININE WITHIN

Do you begin a workshop by talking about the map of the psyche – or with the imaging, the journey itself? Different maps explain different things. Do people have the wrong map in mind? They may need the chance to think about the content beforehand. *Or not....*

The Cup and Sword

Whereas in Workshop I the Sub-personality Exploration certainly needs the talk first, here the Cup and Sword needs to come *before* the talks. Explain merely that this will be a journey of exploration, looking for these things. To say more leads people to visualise it all at once, then and there.

Afterwards. The more archetypal the journey, the longer the period of life to which it relates. The Chalice, the Sword and the Mountain may symbolise the crisis which follows when, out from the unconscious, comes what has been disregarded and suppressed – when we realise that, as Joseph Campbell commented, we're not only up the wrong ladder, but it's leaning on the wrong wall. This crisis often seems to have a positive intention, inviting us to bring together what was separated, becoming more whole and in the round. Ask:

Which of the objects was found first? There may be a paradox here.

Was it the one with which you are most familiar, or the one for

which you have the greatest need?
Water wasn't mentioned at all – did it appear? Or wine, or blood, which may represent energy or life force?
Did the two symbols come together in some way? For example, was the sword put into the cup? Was it curved or moon-shaped? Were either embellished?
What about the wise person?
Was going up the mountain about moving out of daily living?
Is it time to change or update your earlier scripting?

The Gestalt exploration

This one is similar to that in Workshop I, but looks at the *nourishment and development needs* of each aspect, thus helping to offset psychosomatic symptoms.

The Grounding exercise

This sensitivity exercise can be given especially to intuitive, feeling people for their own use. It aims towards the balance (indicated by the *yin-yang* symbol) of feminine with masculine, being with doing. It aims to cleanse us, restore our relationship to others and to life, link our heads to our hearts and establish our feet on the ground. And, finally, to end in a good place.

EXPLORATIONS FOR WORKSHOP III, CYCLES AND STAGES

The Self-image exploration

Though it is preferable to talk about the principle of projection *before* the exploration, this can be impracticable because of the timing.

The Road of your Life

This can be a good exercise to use diagnostically, since it suggests more than one alternative.

Beforehand, it is well to mention the present road, the intersection and the roads into the future, explaining the outline of the journey. I finish with: 'Now, I will say all that again in slow stages, giving time for the imaging of it.' This exercise aims at the future. It lets someone unable to change their geographical location build a compensatory inner landscape.

Afterwards, consider the road, the vehicle and the journey. What was the nature of the countryside? What did you see, hear, sense? How did you *feel* at each stage? Invite further insights into:

> The *road* – bumpy, hilly, misty, straight? Were you surprised by it? Were you driving on the left or the right of it – to another continent's set of rules? Was it an actual road you know? If so, what is the symbolism, the cluster of feelings around that particular road?
>
> The *countryside*. What was the view? Could you see where you were going? Was there a changing element – swimming through water, flying through air – which might indicate feeling, the unconscious?
>
> The *intersection*? Was it a crossroads, a fork, another road as well? How many possibilities were there? Did you go from a major to a minor route, or *vice versa*? Moving to the right may indicate a leading towards the conscious, the masculine; and to the left, towards the unconscious, the feminine. Check it out.
>
> The *crossroads* can have a deeper, collective meaning. Crucial meetings occur where the inner interacts in one reality with the outer and time coincides with eternity. As we saw, criminals were buried here, the limbo between two worlds; crossed sticks were placed by the Aborigines, signalling: 'Be alert – the gods are nearby'.
>
> Going on past the junction *into the future* for the second journey, what were your feelings – disappointment, relief? And what about the alternative road of the final journey? Was there a view far ahead, could you see where you were going? Was it blocked? Our image of the future is not necessarily about what *will* happen, but rather what we would like to happen – or possibly what we fear may happen.
>
> Then, the *vehicle*, your portable psychic space. What was the power under the engine, its energy? Was it designed to take you a long way – or a short? Were you on foot, on a horse, a pedal cycle, a motorbike? Were you in an a boat, ship or aeroplane? The vehicle might indicate something about the physical vehicle, the body itself, saying something about your vital energy, your pace, lifestyle, space, the way you present yourself.
>
> And what was your *feeling* about the vehicle? Was it pleasing? Or was your response, 'Typical!' or ' Oh, rubbish!' Were you carrying passengers – was it a bus or train? If so, who is being carried? You pay your way on the bus, but you don't do the driving. However, a collective means of transport may be good, not bad: for instance, leaving a sports car for a bus could mean leaving hurry for responsibility. Did you change vehicle, or set off on foot and later get into something? What does it signify? For instance, a cycle and a helicopter offer different perspectives. How close to the ground were you? The change-over point may be worth considering, and the ground you would be able to cover.

EXPLORATIONS FOR WORKSHOP IV, INITIATION

Places feature largely in these journeys – cave and plain, water, desert and mountain top. The cave is the place both of birth in the stable and resurrection from the tomb, as early Christian writers, particularly Origen, pointed out. The plain of the Baptism and the River Jordan and its water symbolise the everyday world. Masons to this day meet on the level. The hill and the mountain top are places of both transfiguration and crucifixion.

The Door of Second Birth and Initiation in the Cave

The *door* is a portal into a different energy field, a gateway through which the hero passes, searching for his vocation. It is to do with expansion of consciousness, the ability to hold a steady state through attraction and repulsion. Basic requirements include aspiration, morality, intellectual development, personality integration.

Who is the *initiator*? Who presents the candidate; what helper, guide, spiritual teacher? There may be more than one, the first to do with recognition, with the soul, the Self, and the second being a world teacher. The third initiator is lord of the world. The *rod of initiation* concerns the will. It is a conducting rod, carrying energy, electricity; a magician's wand, precious as diamond.

Trials and conflicts inevitably follow initiation, a testing after the event, reinforcing our dependability, 'livingness' and vitality. Perhaps unexpectedly, we experience both death and rebirth, light and deep shadow, even pitch darkness as our roots winter in the earth. As St. Paul's vision was blinded, so the blindfold candidate has to sense and to feel. Consciousness is the goal; that which has never been raised to the light seeks recognition, and so we project onto the outer world and other people. We are on the thread.

The Water of our Emotional Life

For this second journey, say nothing more than: 'Find yourself by water. You are looking at an image of your emotional life'.

The Desert and the Journey to the Mountain

On the other hand, it's well to talk in advance about the meaning of the third journey, and thus help prevent people falling asleep. Talk about the desert, the shadow, the companions on the path – about affinity, about the Father's business, and how the person and the Work have chosen each other. The journey is not all even but, like the curate's egg, bad in bits. Humanity is travelling a path of transition with steps ahead, a goal, a direction. As disciples, we face its challenges and problems. And we have to do it on our own – become our own guides, teachers, initiators. Later on, we may meet with our own special tribe; after that, again there may be no group. Real learning on a planetary scale only *gradually* enters our bones, our structure, our substance. Development, that necessary feature of life and learning, is not sudden; we should expect the offering of a launching pad for the new to take time, and a lot of recapitulation.

AN EXPLORATION FOR WORKSHOP V, THE OTHER SELF

The Door and the Mirror

Afterwards, you may note that the *door* is one of hope and opportunity. It is feminine, a birthing, a gateway, a passage from one state to another. Directional, it leads to somewhere. There is a two-way entrance and exit, affording communication between two worlds. The *mirror* is magical; indeed, it may offer illusion. It too is feminine, but represents a gateway to 'otherness'. It is lunar, about Self-reflection, a watery wisdom. We may not be able to get back – it's risky. As Jean Cocteau remarked: 'A mirror should think before it reflects'.

APPENDIX 3
WRITING UP SUB-PERSONALITIES
Ian Gordon-Brown

It is probably as well not to repeat the Sub-personality exploration in full at home, though people may be warmly encouraged to follow up their individual sub-personalities.[314]

How to become aware of your sub-personalities [315]

What different 'faces' do you present to the world under different circumstances? What different roles do you play with authority figures, younger people, your peers, a companion of the opposite sex, your subordinates, someone you admire; and under different conditions – at

---

314 Commentary on the Sub-personality exploration, Appendix 2.
315 This section is from a letter from IGB November 1985, 7 Pembridge Place, London W2 4XB, to the Canadian Institute of Psychosynthesis Inc, 3496 Avenue Marlowe, Montréal 260, Québec.

home, at work, on vacation, at church? Write them down, and the sub-personalities generally start to become clear. Some may be difficult to contact from a conscious level. Ask, 'What important sub-personalities have I missed?' and review the recent ones using mental imagery, which may be:

- visual, (pictures or words written on a screen);
- auditory, (words spoken or heard);
- a combination, addressing your question to a symbol of inner wisdom;
- or by spontaneous movement, drawing, writing, or sounding.

List as many sub-personalities as you can, and focus on a selection for detailed analysis. Which seem to play the most important roles? Which cause the greatest conflict? Several may be considered together as different versions of the same thing.

Questions to answer about your sub-personalities

Consider the following for each, adding any other relevant questions or techniques:

Naming. For example, 'The Guru', 'Clinging Vine', 'Bitchy Bertha', 'Doormat', 'Harry the Haggler'. Humour can facilitate detachment and dis-identification from the sub-personality, making it less overwhelming and more subject to conscious direction.

General character sketch. What does it look like, how behave? What feelings does it have and thoughts does it think? What does it tell you, or others? What image does it try to project? What physical posture does it assume? How does it dress? What expression does it wear on its face? How does it feel inside its body? Where does it experience tension? What does it like to do? What would your life be like if this sub-personality had its way all the time? Ideally, how would it like to live?

Needs and desires. What are they for this sub-personality? How does it seek to fulfil them? Does it use direct or devious, effective or ineffective, even destructive methods? Are there more constructive ways?

Drawing. Express graphically its essential qualities.

Circumstances that evoke the sub-personality. When does it emerge? In what social roles does it express itself? With which specific people does it interact? What is it about these people that evokes the sub-personality? Does the 'demand' to behave in this way come from them or from within yourself?

Strengths and weaknesses. Every sub-personality has both valuable and limiting or negative aspects. What are the strengths of this sub-personality and what are its weaknesses and limitations? How could it develop and use its strong points more effectively? How overcome its weaknesses?

Centrality and prominence. How important is its role in your life? What proportion of the time is it on stage? Has it been part of you for many years or is it fairly recent? When and under what circumstances did it begin to manifest itself? Is it fairly deep in your personality structure, or more superficial and transient? How much are you identified with this sub-personality; do you think of it as really 'you', or can you stand back from it and see it as a pattern over which you have control, which you can choose or refuse to act out?

Interaction with other sub-personalities. Which of them reinforce this one? With which does it conflict? How are these conflicts resolved? How do the sub-personalities in conflict with it help to sustain it – are they two sides of a coin?

Integration. Do you, as the Self, actively mediate the conflicts of this sub-personality? Does this go with how far you feel identified with or dis-identified from it? As an objective yet compassionate observer, what suggestions would you give it? What could it learn from other sub-personalities? How could it interact with them more harmoniously? How express more fully the will of the Self?

Dialogue. The sub-personalities and the Self may communicate by:
> written correspondence in both directions;
> spoken dialogue, whether aloud or silently;
> acting out the two parts, switching between seats as you alternately play the two roles, assuming the physical posture, tone of voice and expression of the sub-personality and attempting to become centred and aligned in playing the role of the Self.

APPENDIX 4
SOME ROOTS OF TRANSPERSONAL PSYCHOLOGY
Ian Gordon-Brown

Where did Transpersonal psychology come from?

Transpersonal psychology came out of Humanistic psychology, which developed in turn from Freudian and Behavioural psychologies. This development could be mapped onto IGB's egg diagram.

Behavioural psychology is positivistic, mechanistic and often very effective. Man is a product of his conditioning, and therefore available for de-conditioning. Concerned with the interaction between the organism and the environment, it could be mapped across the middle unconscious.

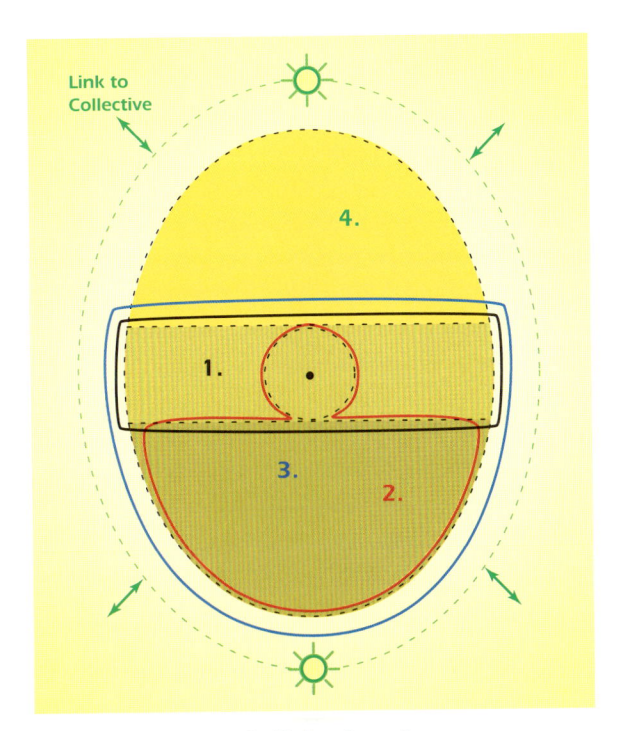

1. Behavioural
2. Freudian
3. Humanistic
4. Transpersonal

Chart 11:01 – Assagioli's Egg 3

Modern attempts at mapping the *personality* began with the great work of Sigmund Freud. *Psychoanalytic psychology*, his classical approach, followed by Adler and Klein, holds that at the source lie our inherited characteristics and instincts, the *id*. The personality or *ego* has to balance the force of the irrational id, which comes first, with other pulls such as those from the *super-ego*. Indeed, the ego is merely a middle-man; the driving force is the energy, the *libido*. So first comes the id, followed by the super-ego, energetically countering the id; then the suffering ego, the 'I', has to come in to sort it all out.[316] Freud's followers often explained things in terms of infancy, tending to reduce experience to 'nothing but'. This could be mapped in the lower and everyday unconscious only.

Carl Jung, asking, 'How do I see my self?', threw out the super-ego and, drawing closer to the inner world, added the *collective unconscious* and the *higher self*. He held that it was lack of *meaning* that is the soul-sickness of our times. *Viktor Frankl*, survivor of the death camps of the 1940's, wrote of the will to meaning.[317]

Humanistic psychology, which is about the here and now and is very much to do with feelings, would have its place in the lower unconscious and the whole of the middle unconscious. Dating from the 1960's, it brought the person back to the centre, looking at the interpersonal – at relationship, needs, creativity. *Carl Rogers* said the person himself is the best expert on himself. *George Kelley* talked about the self concept or self-picture: maybe it is this self-image which in fact controls us?

By 1962, *Abraham Maslow* and *Anthony Sutich* were reaching out from the Humanistic movement towards what they first called 'Transhumanistic' and soon changed to 'Transpersonal'. Maslow postulated a higher unconscious as well as a lower. Well known for his 'hierarchy of needs', he was deeply interested in the farther reaches of human nature and in peak experiences.[318] Writing of the possibility for transformation in a person, he wondered how the individual fitted into the universe. We need a relationship to a wider context. Asking not only 'Who am I?', but 'Who may I become?' he pointed to the possibility for self-transcendence and to the values of the spirit, of awe and wonder. He was also concerned to study not only pathology but mentally healthy and well-functioning people.[319] So he came out of and went beyond what was then the field of Humanistic psychology, to found *Transpersonal*

---

316 For an analogy, see n. 73, p. 134.
317 Frankl 1946, *Man's Search for Meaning*.
318 Maslow 1971, *The Further Reaches of Human Nature*.
319 Maslow 1954, *Motivation and Personality*.

psychology. With Sutich, he began in 1960-61 by drawing up a mailing list; and that led to the setting up of a Transpersonal journal in 1969, then to the Transpersonal Association.

Mapping the personality

People have long tried to do this. Some early attempts included the typing of everyone according to the four elements – earthy, fiery, airy and watery people. Then there were the 'humours': people might be choleric, melancholic, phlegmatic, sanguine. Much later, ectomorphic, mesomorphic and endomorphic types could be discerned; people's body structure was said to define them.[320] These all described the outside of the person, how they appeared. More recently, modern astrology, for example, maps the personality.

APPENDIX 5
SUGGESTED PROGRAMMES FOR
THE FIRST FOUR WORKSHOPS
(laid out overleaf as a workshop per page)

---

320 Endomorphs are the little, fat dumpy ones with small hands and feet who get depression and tend to smooth things over. Ectomorphs are the thin ones, and Mesomorphs the athletic ones.

WORKSHOP I – APPROACHING THE SELF

Friday evening

6.30	Welcome	short meditation
	Introductions	individual, and introducing the workshop
7.10	Talk	MAPS OF THE PSYCHE:
7.50	Short exploration	two questions about myself
8.15	BREAK	- and sharing in pairs
8.45	Exploration	THE TRAVELLER ON LIFE'S JOURNEY
		drawing as you go, sharing tomorrow
9.40	Discussion and	
	Talk	SUB-PERSONALITIES 1 (feminine)
10.00	CLOSE	

Saturday morning

10.00	Meditation	re-gather, dreams
10.20	Talk	SUB-PERSONALITIES 2 (masculine)
10.30	Exploration	SUB-PERSONALITIES 1
11.15	BREAK	- including bodywork and drawing
11.45	Exploration	SUB-PERSONALITIES 2 - inc. drawing
12.30	Discussion	whole group
12.40	Talk	SYMBOLS AND IMAGES
1.15	LUNCH	

Saturday afternoon

2.30	Discussion	and sharing in small groups of the 'Traveller'
		and 'Sub-personality' explorations, including:
	TEA BREAK	
5.15	Discussion	whole group
5.25	Talk	THE FOUR-BALL MAP
5.50		and prepare for Gestalt exploration tomorrow
6.00	CLOSE	

Sunday morning

10.00	Meditation	re-gather, dreams
10.30	Exploration	THE FOUR POSITIONS (GESTALT)
		and sharing in pairs
11.30	BREAK	including suggested books
12.00	Discussion	whole group
12.20	Talk	THE FOUR FUNCTIONS
1.00	SHORT BREAK	
1.20	Final talk	EXPERIENCING THE TRANSPERSONAL
1.50	Meditation	THE INNER SANCTUARY
2.00	END	

WORKSHOP II – THE MASCULINE AND FEMININE WITHIN

Friday evening
6.30	Welcome	short meditation
	Introductions	individual, and introducing the workshop
7.15	Talk	MASCULINE AND FEMININE
7.30	Exploration	THE CUP AND SWORD
8.15	BREAK	including bodywork, drawing and sharing in 2's
8.45	Discussion	whole group
9.00	Talk	THE FEMININE PRINCIPLE
10.00	CLOSE	

Saturday morning
10.00	Meditation	re-gather, dreams
10.20	Talk	THE MASCULINE PRINCIPLE
10.35	Exploration	THE MASCULINE & FEMININE JOURNEY ('Met on the Road')
11.30	BREAK	including drawing
12.00	Discussion	whole group
12.10	Talks	CONTAINER AND CONTAINED, and THE FOUR PEOPLE AT THE WEDDING
1.15	LUNCH	

Saturday afternoon
2.30	Discussion	and sharing in small groups of the 'Cup & Sword' and 'Met on the Road' explorations. Including:
	TEA BREAK	
5.15	Discussion	whole group
5.25	Talk	INTUITION
5.50		and prepare for Gestalt exploration tomorrow
6.00	CLOSE.	

Sunday morning
10.00	Meditation	re-gather, dreams
10.30	Exploration	THE FOUR POSITIONS (GESTALT) and sharing in pairs
11.30	BREAK	including suggested books
12.00	Discussion	whole group
12.20	Talk	SYMPTOM AS SYMBOL
1.00	SHORT BREAK	including future programme of workshops
1.20	Final talk	IDENTITY – 'WHO AM I?'
1.40	Meditation	THE GROUNDING EXERCISE
2.00	END	

WORKSHOP III – CYCLES AND STAGES

Friday evening
6.30	Welcome	short meditation
	Introductions	individual, & introducing the workshop
7.10	Talk	PATTERNS AND CYCLES OF GROWTH
7.50	Short exploration	the pattern of your life
8.00	BREAK	and sharing in pairs
8.30	Exploration	SELF-IMAGE
		drawing as you go, including bodywork; sharing tomorrow.
9.20	Discussion	whole group
9.30	Talk	PROJECTION and introduction to 'The Shape of your Life'
10.00	CLOSE	

Saturday morning
10.00	Meditation	re-gather, dreams
10.30	Exploration	THE SHAPE OF YOUR LIFE 1
11.20	BREAK	including bodywork, and drawing
11.50	Exploration	THE SHAPE OF YOUR LIFE 2 inc. drawing
12.30	Discussion	the symbolism of 'The Shape of your Life'
12.45	Talk	CONTROL PATTERNS
1.15	LUNCH	

Saturday afternoon
2.30	Discussion	and sharing in small groups of the 'Self-Image' and 'Shape of your Life' explorations, including:
	TEA BREAK	
5.15	Discussion	whole group
5.25	Talk	CHANGE
6.00	CLOSE	

Sunday morning
10.00	Meditation	re-gather, dreams
10.30	Exploration	THE ROAD OF YOUR LIFE
		and sharing in pairs
11.30	BREAK	including suggested books
12.00	Discussion	whole group
12.20	Talk	ARCHETYPAL ENERGIES
12.50	Exploration	CORE ENERGY, and sharing in pairs
1.00	SHORT BREAK	including future programme of workshops
1.20	Final Talk	WORKSHOP REVIEW
1.50	Meditation	THE SANCTUARY
2.00	END	

WORKSHOP IV – INITIATION

Friday evening
6.30	Welcome	short meditation
	Introductions	individual, and introducing the workshop
7.10	Talks	THE STORY OF BUDDHA
		STAGES IN THE LIFE OF CHRIST
7.50	Short activity	stages in your life
8.00	BREAK	and sharing in pairs
8.30	Exploration	THE DOOR AND THE CAVE
		and recording; sharing tomorrow
9.20	Discussion	whole group
9.30	Talk	RITES OF PASSAGE 1
10.00	CLOSE	

Saturday morning
10.00	Meditation	re-gather, dreams
10.35	Talk	RITES OF PASSAGE 2
11.25	BREAK	
11.55	Exploration	THE WATER OF EMOTIONS
		and recording; sharing this afternoon
12.45	Discussion	whole group
1.15	LUNCH	

Saturday afternoon
2.30	Discussion	and sharing in small groups of 'The Door and the Cave' and 'The Water of Emotions' explorations, including:
	TEA BREAK	
5.15	Discussion	Whole group
5.25	Talk	INITIATION AND THERAPY
6.00	CLOSE	

Sunday morning
10.00	Meditation	re-gather, dreams
10.30	Talk	INITIATION IN MYTH AND LEGEND: THE HERO'S JOURNEY
11.10	Discussion	whole group
11.30	BREAK	including suggested books
12.00	Exploration	THE DESERT AND THE MOUNTAIN
		record as we go, longer sharing in threes
1.00	SHORT BREAK	
1.20	Closing Talk	THE INITIATES
1.50	Meditation	CONTEMPLATION
2.00	END	

APPENDIX 6
ORIGINAL READING LISTS
FOR THE FIRST FIVE WORKSHOPS

WORKSHOP I – APPROACHING THE SELF

Roberto I 1965, *Psychosynthesis: A Manual of Principles and Techniques*,
London: Turnstone Books, 1965
Bly, Robert 1988, *A Little Book on the Human Shadow*,
first published USA: Harper & Row. Dorset: Element Books, 1992
Campbell, Joseph 1949, *The Hero with a Thousand Faces*,
NY: Bollingen Foundation, 1949. USA: Princeton University Press, 1972
Cooper, J. C. 1978, *An Illustrated Encyclopaedia of Traditional Symbols*,
London: Thames & Hudson.
Faraday, Ann 1974, *The Dream Game*, (also *Dream Power*),
UK: Maurice Temple Smith. Harmondsworth: Penguin Books, 1976
Ferrucci, P. 1982, *What We May Be: the Vision & Techniques of Psychosynthesis*,
London: Mandala, 1990
Frankl, Viktor 1946, *Man's Search for Meaning*, NewYork: Insight Books, 1959
Johnson, Robert A. 1991, *Owning Your Own Shadow: Understanding the Dark Side of the Psyche*, San Francisco: Harper Collins
Jung, Carl. G. 1963, *Memories, Dreams, Reflections*,
London: Collins and Routledge & Kegan Paul, 1963
Martin, P. W. 1955, *Experiment in Depth*, Boston: Routledge & Kegan Paul, 1976
Maslow, Abraham 1954, *Motivation and Personality*, New York: Harper & Row
Miller, Alice 1979, *The Drama of Being a Child*, London: Virago Press, 1987
Mindell, Arnold 1987, *The Dreambody in Relationships*,
London: Routledge & Kegan Paul
Progoff, Ira 1963, *The Symbolic & The Real*, New York: McGraw Hill
Sandford, John A. 1968, *Dreams: God's Forgotten Language*, NY: Crossroad, 1982
Singer, June 1973, *Boundaries of the Soul: The Practice of Jung's Psychology*,
London: Victor Golancz
Von Franz, Marie Louise & James Hillman 1971, *Lectures on Jung's Typology*,
Zürich & NY: Spring Publications, 1975
Wickes, Frances G. 1927, *The Inner World of Childhood*, London: Coventure 1977
Wickes, Frances G. 1963, *The Inner World of Choice*, London: Coventure 1977

WORKSHOP II – THE MASCULINE AND FEMININE WITHIN

Bly, Robert & Keith Thompson, 'What Men Really Want', a chapter about Iron John, in John Welwood 1985, *Challenge of the Heart: Love, Sex and Intimacy in Changing Times*, Boston: Shambhala, p. 100.

Bolen, Jean Shinoda 1984, *Goddesses in Everywoman*, NY: Harper Colophon, 1985
Bolen, Jean Shinoda 1989, *Gods in Everyman*, NY: Harper Perennial
Claremont de Castillejo, Irene 1973, *Knowing Woman*,
London: Hodder & Stoughton Ltd
Estes, Clarissa Pinkola 1992, *Women Who Run with the Wolves*, London: Rider
Greene, Liz 1977, *Relating: An Astrological Guide to Living with Others on a Small Planet*, London: Coventure
Hall, Nor 1980, *The Moon and the Virgin*, NY: The Women's Press
Harding, Esther 1933, *The Way of All Women: A Psychological Interpretation*,
New York: Rider & Co, 1971
Johnson, Robert A. 1974, *He: Understanding Masculine Psychology*
(on Parsifal and the Grail), USA: Harper & Row, 1977
Johnson, Robert A. 1976, *She: Understanding Feminine Psychology*
(on Amor and Psyche), USA: Harper & Row, 1977
Johnson, Robert A. 1983, *We: Understanding the Psychology of Romantic Love*
(on Tristan and Isolde), USA: Harper & Row, 1977
Johnson, Robert A. 1993, *The Fisher King and the Handless Maiden: Understanding the Wounded Feeling Function in Masculine and FemininePsychology*,
San Francisco: Harper,
Jung, Carl. G. 1982, *Aspects of the Feminine*. (this book is extracted from CW 6, 7, 9i, 9ii, 10, 17) London: Routledge & Kegan Paul
McCormick, Elizabeth Wilde 1988, *Breakdown: Coping, Healing and Rebuilding after Nervous Breakdown*, England: Unwin Hyman 1988, Optima 1993
Moore, Robert L. & Douglas Gillette 1990, *King, Warrior, Magician, Lover*,
New York: Harper Collins
Neumann, Erich 1956, *Amor and Psyche: The Psychic Development of the Feminine*,
New York: Bollingen Foundation
Norwood, Robin 1985, *Women Who Love Too Much*, London: Arrow Books
Pelletier, Kenneth R. 1977, *Mind as Healer, Mind as Slayer: A Holistic Approach to Preventing Stress Disorders*, NY: Delacorte and Delta, revised 1992
Perera, Sylvia Brinton 1981, *Descent to the Goddess: A Way of Initiation for Women*,
Toronto: Inner City Books
Pintar, Judith 1992, *The Halved Soul: Retelling the Myths of Romantic Love*,
London: Pandora
Rowe, Dorothy 1983, *Depression: The Way out of Your Prison*,
London: Routledge & Kegan Paul
Singer, June 1977, *Androgyny: Towards a New Theory of Sexuality*,
London: Routledge & Kegan Paul
Von Franz, Marie-Louise 1970, *Puer Aeternus: A Psychological Study of the Adult Struggle with the Paradise of Childhood*, Santa Monica CA: Sigo Press, 1970, 1981
Woodman, Marion 1982, *Addiction to Perfection: the Still Unravished Bride*,
Canada: Inner City Books

WORKSHOP III – CYCLES AND STAGES

Bettelheim, Bruno 1976, *The Uses of Enchantment*, London: Penguin, 1991
Edinger, Edward 1972, *Ego and Archetype: Individuation and the Religious Function of the Psyche*, London: Random Century Group, 1972. Boston: Shambhala Publications Inc, 1992
Frankl, Viktor 1955, *The Doctor and the Soul*, USA: Random House, 1955. NY: Vintage Books, 1973
Hannah, Barbara 1974, *Jung: His Life and Work*, USA: Chiron, 1997
Johnson, Robert A. 1986, *Inner Work: Using Dreams & Active Imagination for Personal Growth*, San Francisco: Harper
Jung, C. G. 1954, 'The Psychology of the Transference', in *CW 16 The Practice of Psychotherapy*. NY: Bollingen Foundation Inc.
Jung, C. G. 1954, 'Answer to Job', in *CW 11*. London: Routledge & Kegan Paul
Jung, C. G. 1972, 'Four Archetypes: Mother, Rebirth, Spirit, Trickster'. This book is extracted from *Archetypes of the Collective Unconscious, CW Vol. 9 Part 1* London: Routledge & Kegan Paul
Keen, Sam 1983, *The Passionate Life: Stages of Loving*, London: Gateway Books
Kopp, Sheldon 1974, *If You Meet the Buddha on the Road, Kill Him*, London: Sheldon Press
Moore, Thomas 1982, *The Planets Within: the Astrological Psychology of Marsilio Ficino'*, USA: Bucknell University Press, 1982. England: Lindisfarne Press, 1990
Moore, Thomas 1992, *The Care of the Soul*, London: Piatkus
Pearson, Carol S. 1986, *The Hero Within: Six Archetypes we Live By*, San Francisco: Harper
Perera, Sylvia Brinton 1986, *The Scapegoat Complex: Toward a Mythology of Shadow and Guilt*, Canada: Inner City Books
Peck, M. Scott 1978, *The Road Less Travelled: A New Psychology of Love, Traditional Values and Spiritual Growth'*, USA: Simon & Schuster, 1978. London: Rider, Century Hutchinson, 1985
Storr, Anthony 1988, *Solitude*, London: Harper Collins, 1997.
Vaughan, Frances 1985, *The Inward Arc*, USA: New Science Library
Von Franz, Marie-Louise 1970, *Apuleius and the Golden Ass*, Dallas: Spring Publications 1980
Von Franz, Marie-Louise & James Hillman 1971, *Lectures on Jung's Typology*, Zürich & NY: Spring Publications, 1975
Von Franz, Marie-Louise 1977, *Individuation in Fairy Tales*, New York: Spring Publications (and all her books on the interpretation of fairy tales).
Von Franz, Marie-Louise 1984, *On Dreams and Death'*, Boston: Shambhala
Welwood, John 1983, Ed., *Awakening the Heart: Approaches to Psychotherapy and the Healing Relationship East/West*, Boston: Shambhala

WORKSHOP IV – INITIATION

Bailey, Alice 1960, 'The Rays and The Initiations', Vol. V,
        A Treatise on the Seven Rays. London: Lucis Trust
Campbell, Joseph 1972, *Myths to Live By*,
        Harmondsworth: Penguin Books, 1993. London: Souvenir Books 1995.
Campbell, Joseph with Bill Moyers 1988, *The Power of Myth*,
        ed. Betty Sue Flowers, New York: Doubleday
Eliade, Mircea 1954, *Cosmos and History: The Myth of the Eternal Return*,
tr. Willard Trask. NJ: Princeton University Press (on rites and symbols of initiation)
Eliade, Mircea 1959, *The Sacred and the Profane: The Nature of Religion*,
        tr. Willard Trask. London: Harcourt Brace Jovanovich
Eliade, Mircea 1963, *Myth and Reality*,
        tr. Willard Trask, New York: Harper and Row
Eliot, T. S. 1943, *Four Quartets*. London: Faber & Faber, 1959.
Fenwick, Peter and Elizabeth 1995, *The Truth in the Light: An Investigation of over 300 Near-Death Experiences*, London: Headline Book Publishing
Grof, Stanislav 1977, (with Joan Halifax), *The Human Encounter with Death*.
        New York: E. P. Dutton
Grof, Stanislav 1988, *The Adventure of Self-Discovery: Dimensions of Consciousness and New Perspectives in Psychotherapy*,
        SUNY series in Transpersonal and Humanistic Psychology.
Leboyer, Frederick 1974, *Birth without Violence*, Wildwood House, 1975.
Moody, Raymond Jr. 1975, *Life after Life*, New York: Bantam
Rinpoche, Sogyal 1992, *Tibetan Book of Living and Dying*,
        San Franscisco: Rigpa Fellowship 1992
Somers, Barbara 2004, *The Fires of Alchemy*, England: Archive Publishing, 2002
Von Franz, Marie-Louise 1977, *Individuation in Fairy Tales*,
        New York: Spring Publications,

WORKSHOP V – THE OTHER SELF

Argüelles, José & Miriam 1972, *Mandala*, Berkeley & London: Shambhala
Campbell, Joseph 1959-1968, *The Masks of God*, Vol. 4, Creative Mythology, 1968.
　　　New York: Viking Press, 1968. London, Harmondsworth: Penguin Books, 1982
Campbell, Joseph with Bill Moyers 1988, *The Power of Myth*,
　　　　　　　　　　　　　　　　　ed. Betty Sue Flowers. New York: Doubleday
Clarke, Lindsay 1989, *The Chymical Wedding*,
　　　　　　　　　　　　　　　　　London: Jonathan Cape, Picador, 1990.
Edinger, Edward 1985, *Anatomy of the Psyche: Alchemical Symbolism in
　　　　　　　　　　Psychotherapy*, Chicago: Open Court
Jung, C. G. 1931, 'Commentary on "The Secret of the Golden Flower"',
　　　tr. Richard Wilhelm, Routledge & Kegan Paul, London 1962 & 1975;
　　　　　　　　　　　　　　　in *CW 13, 'Alchemical Studies'*.
Jung, C. G. 1944, 'Psychology & Alchemy'; in *CW 12*.
Jung, C. G. 1963, *Memories, Dreams, Reflections*,
　　　　　　　　　　　　London: Collins and Routledge & Kegan Paul
Keirsey, David & Marilyn Bates 1984, *Please Understand Me: Character &
　　　　　Temperament Types'*, Del Mar, CA: Gnosology Books Ltd
Klossowski de Rola, Stanislas 1991, *Alchemy: The Secret Art*,
　　　　　　　　　　　　　　　　　　London: Thames & Hudson
Maslow, Abraham 1968, *Towards a Psychology of Being*,
　　　　　　　　　　　　　　　　New York: D. Van Nostrand Co
Storm, Hyemeyohsts 1972, *Seven Arrows*, New York: Harper & Row
Von Franz, Marie Louise 1979, *Alchemical Active Imagination*,
　　　　　　　　　　　　　　　　Dallas: Spring Publications
Von Franz, Marie Louise 1980, *Alchemy: An Introduction to the Symbolism and the
　　　　　　　　　　　　Psychology'*, Toronto: Inner City Books

APPENDIX 7
PROJECTION EXPLORATION (11:1)
ALTERNATIVE SELF-IMAGE EXPLORATION
Ian Gordon-Brown
(35 minutes)

Get an image, picture, a name and a sensing for:

The kind of people who most *repel* me are like this....
And when you have your answer, draw and write the name.
The kind of people who most *attract* me....
Again, draw and write.
Who or what, out there or in me, most *motivates* my life?
Draw and write.
Who or what, out there or in me, most *undermines* my life?
Again, record.
Who or what, out there or in me, most *enriches and enhances* my life?
Record.

Look back over the names given, the sensing, the images that arose. Be in touch with each and with the whole.
Now, stand. Rattle the images, give them a good shake and a brush; clear anything you want to get rid of. Then, lie down once again.
Who or what is *really, truly* you, your *true* Self. That's not a 'for ever' question, but a *now* question. Rest with the real, true you.

APPENDIX 8
TRANSCENDERS AND ACTUALISERS
Ian Gordon-Brown [321]

Another way of understanding people is to note how they react to crisis. This is when the Transpersonal may be activated. Do they respond as 'actualisers' or as 'transcenders'?

Actualisers. Those who express their capacities externally and make things happen, are, so to speak, executors in the outside world. Maslow, in his study of healthy and well-functioning people, found that such 'actualisers' are both independent and good at relationships. Solitude is

---

[321] IGB originally introduced this theme in Workshop 1, but discontinued it.

for them no mere indulgence – it is necessary. Realistic in their judgments, not sentimental, able to take tough action towards people and circumstances, they are achievers, though personal ambition is not particularly important to them. And they are likely to have had at least one peak experience which has transformed their view of the world. They function mainly through mind and will. For them, time leads to success, which leads to success which leads to success – which leads to crisis, which will take an existential form. Life becomes meaningless.

Finding that the only way out is up, they will *rise*; and what they ascend towards is self-crystallisation. The impact on the personality from such a crisis may well be positive, manifesting in renewed energy and health; now they may become yet more effective catalysts, radiating a loving calm. If on the other hand there is a negative outcome, it is as if a fuse blows, or the current becomes defective. This may show as a flight of ideas, *idées fixes*. They may develop a messianic complex, or an excessive sensitivity manifesting as either hyperactivity or depression. The hope is that, having sought power for themselves, they are led to use it benevolently.

Transcenders, on the other hand, have the ability to enter *inner* space. Moving naturally towards the Transpersonal, they tend to live more in the higher, supra-conscious part of IGB's map. They may have had several peak experiences, even peak after peak, marked less by mind and will than by devotion and love. For them, the crisis when it comes will be about the immense difficulty of being grounded and earthed. Their recovery will be marked by a necessary descent to mundane actuality. The hope is that the initial love that soared up so blindly will eventually lead to an intelligent love.

These are extremes. The aim for both is to build a bridge towards the centre. 'As above so below.' Inclusiveness, centralisation, stillness are necessary. The instrument needs organising. Methods of integrating body, mind and feelings will need to be adopted, symbols noted, inner dialogue listened to. For some, a meditative way of exploring how they actualise, how they transcend, may be an effective therapy. 'Is the map the same for the first and second half of my life? What is the pattern for the whole of my life?'

APPENDIX 9
SOME BUDDHIST TEACHINGS

The Noble Eightfold Path (The Way to the End of Suffering)
>Right Understanding
>Right Thought
>Right Speech
>Right Action
>Right Livelihood
>Right Effort
>Right Mindfulness
>Right Meditation

The Four Great Vows of a Bodhisattva

However innumerable beings are,
>I vow to save them.
However inexhaustible the passions,
>I vow to extinguish them.
However immeasurable the Dharmas are,
>I vow to master them.
However incomparable the Buddha-truth is,
>I vow to attain it.

APPENDIX 10
SIX STAGES OF DISCIPLESHIP
Based on the work of Alice Bailey

The stages in membership of spiritual groups are said to parallel the six stages of discipleship for the *chela* or disciple:[322]

>Firstly, the *little chela*, the aspirant or Probationary *chela*, makes contact with the group on the physical plane. His task is to accept the teaching and the group and, as an apprentice, learn the tools of the trade. *The chela in the light*. The light flashes – and it is the light of glamour. Full of aspiration and karmic agitation, his soul intensifies his interest in the personality. This is equivalent to the first initiation. Under the supervision of a more senior disciple who has accepted the teaching, the

---

[322] The Six Stages of Discipleship: see Bailey 1944, *Discipleship in the New Age*, pp. 713-773.

task of the novice is to dissipate the glamour, sustain the pairs of opposites and find his work in the world. The bridge of light, the *antahkarana* or rainbow bridge of consciousness, now appears.

At the third stage the *chela's discipleship is accepted*. He moves towards becoming a master. This may be either before or after the Baptism. Dreams and images may follow, direct contact in meditation with the inner world. This is the symbolic leading by the thought form or image of the inner teacher, the inner interview with the Master.

Fourthly, the *chela* is *on the thread*. Soon after the Baptism and well before the Transfiguration, being 'on the thread' he can in emergencies attract the attention or help of the inner teacher. Interest in his own development is now transcended. His inner life takes outer form and he is fully occupied in the work of the world.

The *chela* is said to be *within the aura* of the ashram as he approaches the Transfiguration. By now he can readily arrange an interview with the master. He is full of serenity and a new radiating of the soul.

At last, the *chela* is *within the master's heart*. This is a later initiation and a specialised work. Christ's ministry began here, in the spirit of this place. The *chela* within the heart can give dependable service. Spiritual maturity is achieved. Now the dove of God descends.

APPENDIX 11
PLATO'S MYTH OF THE CAVE [323]

Man is compared to an underground creature, bound immovably hand and foot, chained in dim fire-light in the cave where he was born. At his back is the cave's entrance; he can see nothing but the shadows of forms passing outside, thrown on the wall in front of him. Mistakenly, he and his fellows believe the shadows to be the real things.

At last one of these prisoners frees himself, escapes from the cave and begins to look around. At first he can see only shadows; then he manages reflections in water, and finally the things themselves. At first it is easier for him to look upon the stars by night than upon the sun by day. But eventually he can see the sun, not merely its reflection in the water.

He starts by thinking that it must be the sun which causes the seasons and the years, and is the guardian of everything he and his fellows have formerly seen. Remembering the cave and his fellow-prisoners, he pities

---

323 Plato, *The Republic*, Book VII.

them and is happy about his change. He would rather suffer anything than accept their false notions and live in that miserable manner.

And if he had to return to his old place in the cave, his eyes would be full of darkness, his sight still weak and he would seem ridiculous. They would say his adventure had destroyed his eyesight. Best not leave the cave.... And if they caught anyone trying to free another and lead him up to the light, they would put the offender to death.

The prison-house or cave is the world of sight; the light of the fire within the cave is the sun. The journey upwards is the ascent of the soul into the intelligible world. Only God knows whether or not my description is accurate; but whether true or false, my opinion is that in the world of knowledge the Form of the Good appears last of all, and is seen only with an effort. When seen, however, it can only lead us to the conclusion that it is the universal author of all things beautiful and right, that it is the origin of the source of light in the visible world, and the immediate source of reason and truth in the intelligible world. Without having seen the Form of the Good and having fixed his eye upon it, one will not be able to act wisely either in public affairs or in private life.

APPENDIX 12
FAITHS OF THE CHEYENNE PEOPLE
Based on the work of Hyemeyohsts Storm [324]

The Cheyenne people have this scheme: at birth, each has a beginning place on the Great Medicine Wheel at one of the Four Great Directions. This gives our first way of perceiving:

North, buffalo, white. Place of head. Wise, cold, without feeling. Power and wisdom.

West, bear, black. Place of hooks within. Introspection, going over the same thing again and again without decision or action. Introverted, unanchored.

East, eagle, yellow. Place of illumination. Clear, far-sighted vision, aloof, never close to things. Separative, not touched or touching.

South, mouse, green. Place of heart. Growing. Innocence, too close to ground. Near-sighted, personal, seeing only what is whisker-touch.

---

[324] See Hyemeyohsts Storm 1972, *Seven Arrows*.

None can be all four at once, but only two or three. For example, one could be a Golden Bear of the North but lacking the personal touch, earthing. Or a Black Eagle of the South, but without wisdom, or a Bear-person from the East, or a Mouse from the North and so on. None is whole. Each of us is a Living Medicine Wheel, powerful, but limited and placed on earth to touch, experience and learn. We were placed on earth to learn things of the heart, by touching.

Stories are magical teachers on the Way, flowers of truth to be unfolded by the Seeker without end. When you question, the Medicine Wheel is turned for you. Because there was no written language, allegorical, symbolic stories were remembered and told, through countless generations. The understanding of the Way is not from memorising the stories or symbols. It is a living, growing thing that comes from touching and experiencing the Four Great Directions within. They are learned not by studying archaic tradition, but by seeking understanding and then allowing it to grow within your heart and mind.

For instance, Coyote is the Gentle Trickster, who tricks us all into learning. Mouse sees close up but not the distance, with limited vision. He gathers things, facts, information, ideas, but misses their connection with the Great Prairie. If Mouse is born in the North, he will have the gift of mind. To become whole, he must go South, to the place of the Heart, to unite this Gift with his Beginning Gift. Going towards the East brings illumination, and to the West, to the place of hooks within.

One can live one's entire life without finding more within than the Beginning Gift: to grow, one seeks the other ways and the different medicines. All uniquely different, we possess only one thing equally – loneliness, our desire to be needed and loved. We can only overcome our loneliness through touching. Only then can we be total beings.

APPENDIX 13 [325]
SOME PIONEERS

Alfred Adler (1870 – 1937), Austrian medical doctor and psychologist, founded the School of Individual Psychology in 1912. With Freud

---

[325] This Appendix is not the authors'. It was put together in 2007 by the editor, in order to offer the reader a note on some of those mentioned in the text.

and other colleagues, he was in at the beginnings of the psychoanalytic movement, but disengaged from it in 1911. He admired Freud's thinking on dreams, but on power and inferiority he stood closer to Nietzsche than did Freud. The concept of the inferiority complex was his. A social idealist, he abandoned the analytic couch for two equal chairs. He helped bring psychology to the lay person; an early supporter of feminism, he worked to prevent psychological difficulties in children by allowing them to exercise power through reasoned decision and co-operation.

Roberto Assagioli (1888 – 1974) was an influential Italian psychiatrist and the founder of the transpersonal psychology movement known as Psychosynthesis. A student of Sigmund Freud, he introduced Freud's teachings to the medical fraternity in Venice in 1910. He is one of three Italians credited with being pioneers of the psychoanalytic movement. At the same time, around 1910, he laid the groundwork for Psychosynthesis. He saw that there was a need for something beyond analysis: it was the need for a person to become whole – to be united in synthesis. Just as there was a lower unconscious, there was also a superconscious, a realm of the psyche which contains our deepest potential, the source of the unfolding pattern of our unique human path of development. The term psychosynthesis of course distinguishes it from psychoanalysis; but Assagioli did not mean thereby to replace psychoanalysis – rather to complement and include it. Assagioli was also involved in the Theosophical Society.

Josef Breuer (1842 – 1925) was an Austrian physician whose works laid the foundation of psychoanalysis. A close friend and collaborator with Sigmund Freud, Breuer is perhaps best known for his work with 'Anna O.', a woman suffering with symptoms of paralysis, anaesthesia and disturbances of vision and speech. Breuer noted that her symptoms disappeared or were reduced after she had described them, and it was this 'chimney-sweeping' which led him to explore hypnosis as a method of enhancing the process. The discussions of Anna O. between Freud and Breuer were documented in their 1895 work, Studies in Hysteria, and became a formative basis of Freudian theory and psychoanalytic practice especially with regard to fantasy, hysteria and catharsis, where Breuer's major contributions lay.

William C. Dement (born 1928), is a pioneering sleep researcher and founder of the world's first sleep laboratory at Stanford University. He is a leading authority on sleep, sleep deprivation, and the diagnosis and treatment of sleep disorders. As a medical student, together with Nathaniel Kleitman and others, he studied intensively the connection between rapid eye movement (REM) and dreaming and in 1950 discovered and described REM sleep. Having an interest in psychiatry, which in those days considered dreams to be important, he was excited by the discovery and was eager to pursue it. He began his work in sleep deprivation at Mount Sinai Hospital in the late 1950's and early 1960's: 'I believe that the study of sleep became a true scientific field in 1953, when I was finally able to make all-night, continuous recordings of brain and eye activity during sleep'. From them he discovered and named the five stages of sleep. Dement is the author of numerous books, including *The Promise of Sleep*. He commented: 'Dreaming permits each and every one of us to be quietly and safely insane every night of our lives' (*Newsweek* 30 Nov '59).

Robert Desoille (1890 – 1966) developed a method known as the Guided Waking Dream. The subject would be put into a state of relaxation, lying down with eyes closed, in order to create an imaginary scene in which he himself is the principal or only hero. Desoille believed that healing and transforming ecstatic states could only be obtained by symbolic *ascent*. The therapist, sitting behind the client, would intervene from time to time, to clarify the inner scene or suggest a possible change of direction. He, or the client, would write down what had happened in order to make the session clearer and explore the significance of the imaging face to face. On the theoretical level, Desoille was influenced first by Sigmund Freud, then Jung; however, later on, his adherence to the French Communist Party meant that he had to confine himself to more Pavlovian theories. His students defined themselves as analysts, understanding their practice as having a Freudian, Freudian/Lacanian or Jungian orientation. His works include 1961, *Theorie Et Pratique Du Rêve Eveillé Dirigé*, Geneva; and 1966, *The Directed Daydream*, Psychosynthesis Research Foundation, New York.

James Fadiman (b. 1939) is, with Abraham Maslow and Michael Murphy, one of the founding Professors of the Institute of Transpersonal Psychology and a pioneering teacher in the Sufi tradition. He has authored numerous books and articles including: *Personality and Personal Growth* (with Bob Frager), *Health for the Whole Person*, and *Unlimit Your Life*. He was involved with the International Foundation for Advanced Study in the late 1960's and later served as president of the Institute of Noetic Sciences.

Piero Ferrucci (b. 1946) is a psychologist who lives with his wife and two children in the country near Florence. His book *What We May Be*, makes the work of Assagioli more accessible.

Théodore Flournoy (1854 – 1920) was a Professor of Psychology at the University of Geneva and author of books on spiritism and psychic phenomena. He is most known for his study of the medium Helen Smith, who relayed information about past lives through a trance state. He presented this information as being 'romances of the subliminal imagination', and a product of the unconscious mind. Flournoy was a contemporary of Freud, and his work influenced C. G. Jung's study of another medium – Jung's own cousin Hélène Preiswerk – which was turned into Jung's doctoral dissertation in 1902.

Michael Fordham (1905 – 1995) edited the Journal of Analytical Psychology and co-edited the Collected Works of Jung. In 1980 he published *Analytical Psychology: A Modern Science*. For his work and ideas, especially in linking the work of Jung with that of the Kleinians, see James Astor 1995, *Michael Fordham*.

Viktor Emil Frankl M.D., Ph.D., (1905 – 1997) was an Austrian neurologist and psychiatrist as well as a Holocaust survivor. Frankl was the founder of Logotherapy and Existential Analysis, the Third Viennese School of Psychotherapy. His book *Man's Search for Meaning* (first published in 1946) chronicles his experiences as a concentration camp inmate and describes his psychotherapeutic method of finding meaning in all forms of existence, even the most sordid ones, and thus a reason to continue living. He was one of the key figures in existential therapy.

Sigmund Freud (1856 – 1939), Austrian neurologist and co-founder of the psychoanalytic school of psychology, is best known for his theories of the unconscious mind, especially involving the mechanism of repression, his redefinition of sexual desire as mobile and directed towards a wide variety of objects; and his therapeutic technique, especially his understanding of transference in the therapeutic relationship and the presumed value of dreams as sources of insight into unconscious desires.

Stanislav Grof (born 1931) is one of the founders of the field of Transpersonal psychology and a pioneering researcher into the use of altered states of consciousness for purposes of healing, growth, and insight. Grof constructed a theoretical framework for pre- and perinatal psychology and transpersonal psychology, in which powerful emotional experiences were mapped onto a person's early foetal and neonatal experiences. Over time, this theory developed into an in-depth cartography of the deep human psyche. Many states of mind can be explored by using certain breathing techniques in a supportive environment. He continues this work today under the title 'Holotropic Breathwork'. Being the founding president of the International Transpersonal Association (founded in 1977), he went on to become distinguished adjunct faculty member of the Department of Philosophy, Cosmology and Consciousness at the California Institute of Integral Studies, a position he remains in today. His books include *Beyond the Brain, The Adventure of Self-Discovery* and, more recently, *The Transpersonal Vision*.

Marc Guillery,[326] a doctor, led the way in Switzerland in the therapeutic use of guided mental imagery techniques. By 1925 he was employing what he called *guided reverie*; though, feeling Desoille's method was too directive, he later dropped the 'guided' and allowed people to develop their own images with little intervention from him.

Carl Happich's technique is meditation of a most systematic kind, yet also of the widest human scope. It begins with physiology and ends in religion. Happich developed it out of his literary and practical knowledge of Oriental techniques, combining their wisdom with the experience of modern depth psychology. That his system of meditation is based on sound psychological principles is confirmed by the work of the Jungian school. He evoked particularly images of meadow, mountain, and chapel: dreams have been recorded where a mountain is seen in a landscape of meadows, and on the mountain stands a church. Such symbolic pictures have been valued psychically as an indication of the end of the process of

---

326 For mention of Guillery, see Crampton 1974, Quebec Center for Psychosynthesis.

individuation, the attainment of spirituality. But in meditation Happich did not wait until the needed symbols were produced spontaneously, as during dream analysis. Rather, the meditator was *made* to occupy himself with certain symbols selected by the therapist until he had explored the fullness of their meaning. The goal of Happich's *mandala meditation* was not the production of extensive fantasy, but rather a lively contemplation of the central meaning of the design. Eventually, the meditator was directed to identify himself psychically with the symbol and to integrate the meaning of the symbol with his psychic life. Properly speaking, these designs are used less as a technique of therapy than in furthering the highest development of personality. Happich set forth his fundamental principles in two small works (Happich, 1932, 1939), and beyond these left only a short *Introduction to Meditation* - (Happich, 1948), which is concerned with religious symbolism.

James Hillman (born 1926) is considered to be one of the most original psychologists of the twentieth century. Trained at the C. G. Jung Institute in Zürich, where he later became Director of Studies until 1969, he developed archetypal psychology, looking at polytheistic myth as psychology. In 1970 Hillman became editor of Spring Publications, a publishing company devoted to advancing Archetypal Psychology as well as publishing books on mythology, philosophy and art. His magnum opus, *Re-visioning Psychology*, 1975, was nominated for the Pulitzer Prize. *The Soul's Code* came later, in 1997.

William James (1842 – 1910) was a pioneering American psychologist and philosopher who claimed that religious *experience* should be the primary topic in the study of religion, rather than religious institutions, since institutions are merely the social descendant of genius. He wrote that the intense, even pathological varieties of experience (religious or otherwise) should be sought by psychologists, because they represent the closest thing to a microscope of the mind—that is, they show us in drastically enlarged form the normal processes of things; and that, in order to interpret usefully the realm of common, shared experience and history, we must each make certain 'over-beliefs' in things which, while they cannot be proven on the basis of experience, help us to live fuller and better lives. James concluded that while the revelations of the mystic hold true, they hold true only for the mystic; for others, they are certainly ideas to be considered, but have no claim to truth without personal experience of such. James has been a significant influence for the New Age and Human Potential movements of the 1960's and 1970's.

Pierre Marie Félix Janet (1859 – 1947), a French psychologist in the field of dissociation and traumatic memory, was one of the first persons to draw a connection between events in the subject's past life and their present day trauma. He coined the words 'dissociation' and 'subconscious'. In several ways, he preceded Sigmund Freud: many consider Janet, rather than Freud, the true 'founder' of psychoanalysis and psychotherapy. In 1919 he published a definitive text on suggestion, *Les Médications Psychologiques*.

Carl Jung (1875 – 1961). The overarching goal of Jungian psychology is the reconciliation of the life of the individual with the world of the supra-personal archetypes. Central to this process is the individual's encounter with the unconscious. The human experiences the unconscious through symbols encountered in all aspects of life: in dreams, art, religion, and the symbolic dramas we enact in our relationships and life pursuits. Essential to the encounter with the unconscious, and the reconciliation of the individual's consciousness with this broader world, is learning the language of symbols. Only through attention and openness to their world can the individual's life be harmonised with these suprapersonal archetypal forces.

George Kelley (1905 – 1967) conceived Personal Construct Theory, believing that ultimately a person measures his own freedom and bondage by the level at which he chooses to establish his convictions. The world is perceived in terms of whatever meaning that person applies to it. We have the *freedom to choose* a different meaning, as we want. Therefore, we are not prisoners of our past, and can liberate ourselves from the misery of miserable events, if we desire, by re-construing, reinterpreting and redefining them. He published *The Psychology of Personal Constructs* in 1955.

Melanie Klein (1882 – 1960), Austrian-born British psychoanalyst, had great impact on contemporary methods of child care and rearing. Considered one of the co-founders of object relations theory, Klein and her followers have had a lasting influence upon child psychology and psychoanalysis. Her theoretical work gradually centered on a highly speculative hypothesis propounded by Freud, which stated that life may be an anomaly – that it is drawn toward an inorganic state, and therefore, in an unspecified sense, contains an instinct to die. In psychological terms Eros, the sustaining and uniting principle of life, is thereby postulated to have a companion force, Thanatos, which seeks to terminate and disintegrate life. Melanie Klein put forth the interpretation that the human psyche is in a constant oscillation depending on whether Eros or Thanatos is in the fore. She calls the state of the psyche when the sustaining principle of life is in domination, the depressive position. To the psychological state corresponding to the disintegrating tendency of life she gives the name the paranoid-schizoid position. Melanie Klein's works are collected in four volumes.

Wolfgang Kretschmer held that the psychotherapist who wants to employ techniques of meditation must first be able to meditate himself. Kretschmer published *Meditative Techniques in Psychotherapy*.

Gottfried Leibniz (1646 – 1716), great German philosopher and mathematician, proposed his philosophy of 'monads' which has similarities with the philosophies of the Orient. He held that physical matter is illusory; also, that every particle of which the universe is composed is a living, growing entity or being. He was a true evolutionist: 'matter' is not dead, but is the semblance or outward and visible appearance of an invisible (to us) superphysical reality composed of metaphysical or 'spiritual' points which he called monads. Each monad is a distinct individual possessing its own kind or degree of consciousness and existence. Life is everywhere, rising in grades of intelligence from the most primitive monad to the ineffable glory of the 'monad of monads', the incomprehensible Divine Unity or One – the word *monad* being derived from the Greek *monas*, or one.

Hanscarl Leuner (1918 – 1996), developed a special interest in guided mental imagery, in the interaction of mental contents and emotional processes, and in dreams and daydreams. He developed a standardized treatment technique based on this research called *Guided Affective Imagery*. In 1985, together with other important researchers in the field, Leuner founded the European College for the Study of Consciousness (ECSC) and acted as its president. He was an important pioneer of the medicinal use of psychedelics. In 1984 he published *Guided Affective Imagery: Mental Imagery in Short-Term Psychotherapy*.

Abraham Maslow (1908 – 1970) taught at Brooklyn College where he came into contact with the many European intellectuals who were immigrating to America at that time: Adler, Fromm and Horney, as well as several Gestalt and Freudian psychologists. Serving as chair of the psychology department at Brandeis from 1951 to 1969, he met Kurt Goldstein, who had originated the idea of self-actualization in his famous book, *The Organism* (1934). So he began his crusade for a humanistic psychology, later developing self-actualization into an area for research and application. Maslow dedicated 'Toward a Psychology of Being' (1968) to Kurt Goldstein.

Franz Anton Mesmer (1734 – 1815) discovered what he called *animal magnetism*. Others often called it *mesmerism*. In 1774, Mesmer felt that he had contributed the animal magnetism which had accumulated in his own body to one of his patients. He wrote an 88-page book, *Mémoire sur la découverte du magnétisme animal*, outlining his theory at that time. He understood health as the free flow of the process of life through thousands of channels in our bodies; illness was caused by obstacles to this flow. Overcoming these obstacles and restoring flow produced crises, which restored health. When nature failed to do this spontaneously, contact with a conductor of animal magnetism was a necessary and sufficient remedy. Mesmer aimed to aid or provoke the efforts of nature. In 1784, King Louis XVI appointed commissioners to investigate animal magnetism. They conducted a series of experiments aimed not at determining whether Mesmer's treatment worked, but whether he had discovered a new physical fluid. The commission concluded that there was no evidence for such a fluid. Whatever benefit the treatment produced was attributed to 'imagination'. The evolution of Mesmer's ideas and practices led James Braid (physician, 1795-1860) in 1842 to develop hypnosis.

Arnold Mindell (born 1940) is an American psychotherapist, writer and the founder of Process Oriented Psychology. While in Zurich, he shifted his emphasis to study analytical psychology at the C. G. Jung Institute, where he graduated as a Jungian analyst. He became fascinated with body experiences, particularly physical symptoms, and how they are mirrored in dreams. In 1982, Mindell published his first book, *Dreambody: The*

Body's Role in Revealing the Self, looking at how the dreaming mind produces unconscious or 'double signals' in us while we are in relationship to others. He found that bringing those signals from the background to the foreground made interpersonal communication easier. His interest in relationships evolved into the study of conflict in large groups. After writing a series of books on his discoveries, including *The Dreambody in Relationships*, he explored again the interconnections of psychology with theoretical physics, seeking to find new ways of working with subtle states of consciousness. Mindell said of his own motivation, 'I am still in love with the idea of nature, and following the Tao seems to remain the haunting and romantic background to all I do.'

Jacob Levy Moreno (1892 – 1974), the originator of *Psychodrama*, was born in Romania, grew up in Vienna and in 1925 settled in New York. He had had experience with storytelling in children's groups, with the children acting out the stories. He later used this method with adults, founding in 1921 a theatre in which actors and audiences played out real and imagined stories. In the 1920's, charting how people interact in groups, Moreno introduced psychodrama, an original form of psychotherapy. In the process of acting out conflicts and problems in interpersonal relations, the actors gained insight and were helped by the group process to remedy problem behaviour patterns and improve coping skills. In 1953 he published *Who Shall Survive?* elaborating his psychodrama approach. Moreno was critical of psychoanalysis as a therapeutic technique, though he related free association to spontaneous acting out. To this day, group therapy flourishes in many forms.

Michael Murphy (b. 1930) at Stanford University had mistakenly wandered into a lecture on comparative religions, which so fanned the flame of his interest in the integration of Eastern and Western thought that he enrolled in the class and subsequently began meditation. In 1951 he experienced 'a hinge moment' which gave him a new vision for the purpose of his life. In 1962, together with Dick Price, he was the driving force behind the founding of the Esalen Institute. In 1969 he was on the Editorial Staff of the first issue of the Journal of Transpersonal Psychology, along with Anthony Sutich (editor) and Miles Vich. Chairman of the board at the institute, he continued to be a key contributor to research projects at the Esalen Center for Theory and Research.

Frederick William Henry Myers (1843 – 1901), English poet and essayist, in 1882 together with others founded the Society for Psychical Research. He continued for many years to be an admired, fervid, fluent and alert mouthpiece of the society, steering a mid-course between extreme sceptics on the one hand, and enthusiastic spiritualists on the other. He was also an early member of the Theosophical Society, possibly leaving about 1886. He left a posthumous and provisional work, *Human Personality and its Survival of Bodily Death*, and a small collection of essays, *Science and a Future Life* (1893).

Wilder Graves Penfield (1891 – 1976) was an American-born Canadian neurosurgeon, and a groundbreaking researcher who in 1951 published the landmark Epilepsy and the Functional Anatomy of the Human Brain. During his life he was called 'the greatest living Canadian'. He devoted much thinking to the functioning of the mind, and continued until his death to contemplate whether there was any scientific basis for the existence of the human soul. He retired in 1960 and turned his attention to writing, producing a novel as well as his autobiography, *No Man Alone*.

Fritz Perls (1893 – 1970) was a German-born psychiatrist and psychotherapist. He coined the term Gestalt Therapy for the approach he developed with his wife Laura Perls from the 1940's, and in 1964 became associated with the Esalen Institute in California. At the core of Gestalt Therapy is the promotion of the awareness of the unity of all present feelings and behaviours, and the contact between the self and its environment. Among other books he wrote *Gestalt Therapy Verbatim*.

Dick Price (1930 – 1985). With Michael Murphy, Price co-founded the Esalen Institute, to which he invited course leaders such as Alan Watts. He had himself undergone an episode of psychosis and been in a mental hospital for eighteen months until 1957. He saw in Esalen an alternative to current mental health practice, especially the practices of mental hospitals, a place where inner process could move forward safely and without interruption.

Ira Progoff (1921 – 1988) was an American psychotherapist best known for his development of the Intensive Journal Method. His main interest was in depth psychology, particularly the humanistic adaptation of Jungian ideas to the lives of ordinary people. He founded Dialogue House in New York City to help promote this method, and wrote and published many books, among them *The Symbolic and the Real* and *Jung, Synchronicity and Human Destiny*.

Hermann Rorschach (1884 – 1922) developed the Rorschach Inkblot projective test. Like many young people in his native Switzerland, he enjoyed Klecksography, the making of fanciful inkblot 'pictures'; in high school, he had even been called Klecks, or 'inkblot', by his friends. However, unlike other young people, he was to make inkblots his life's work. He showed great talent at painting and drawing conventional pictures, but he enrolled in medical school at the University of Zurich and studied under eminent psychiatrist Eugen Bleuler, who had taught Carl Jung. The excitement in intellectual circles over psychoanalysis constantly reminded Rorschach of his childhood inkblots. He wondered why different people often see entirely different things in the same inkblots. While still a medical student, he began showing inkblots to schoolchildren and analyzing their results.

J. H. Schultz (1884 – 1970) was a German psychiatrist offering a step-by-step introduction to his Autogenic Training, one technique of meditation. However, with meditation, as with psychotherapy, a study of the literature is seldom enough; a personal dedication is necessary, or there are dangers. In the advanced stages of Schultz's meditation, after a general bodily relaxation had been achieved, symbolic fantasies were skillfully induced, colours and objects visualised and a symbolic representation of ideas sought. Meditation is quicker than dreams in gaining the reaction of the unconscious. What is the goal of meditation? Schultz sees this question clearly, but does not conclude that it is connected with religion. He limits himself, rather, to the formulation of *basic existential values*, aiming towards a reasonable view of life, self-realization, psychic freedom and harmony, as well as a lively creativity. At best, the meditator may achieve Nirvana-like joy and release.

Anthony Sutich (1907 – 1976) was a pioneer in Transpersonal psychology because he had the intelligence, vision, interpersonal skills, and the persistence to create the infrastructure for both the humanistic and the transpersonal. Together with Abraham Maslow, Stanislav Grof and others, Anthony Sutich in 1969 founded the *Journal of Transpersonal Psychology*; also the Transpersonal Institute, which in 1972 became the

Association for Transpersonal Psychology.

Miles Vich was editor with Sage Publications, serving as consulting and technical editor during the initial preparation of the manuscript of Abraham Maslow's book 'The Farther Reaches of Human Nature'. This was during the early months of 1970. After Maslow's death in June of that year, Vich continued to provide general editorial assistance. With Anthony Sutich, he in 1969 edited 'Readings in Humanistic Psychology'.

APPENDIX 14
GUIDED IMAGING AND FANTASY TECHNIQUES
Desoille, Leuner and Assagioli

A   DESOILLE'S DIRECTED DAYDREAM

Robert Desoille adopted a series of standard themes to evoke symbolic situations:

a) *Confronting one's more obvious characteristics*: for a man, a sword; for a woman, a vessel or container, such as a cup.

b) *Confronting one's more suppressed characteristics*: for both sexes, a descent into the depths of the ocean.

c) *Coming to terms with the parent of the opposite sex*: for a man, a descent into a cave to find a witch or sorceress; for a woman, a descent into a cave to find a wizard or magician.

d) *Coming to terms with the parent of one's own sex*: for a man, a descent into a cave to find a wizard or magician; for a woman, a descent into a cave to find a witch or sorceress.

e) *Coming to terms with societal constraints*: for both sexes, a descent into a cave to find the fabled dragon.

f) *Coming to terms with the Oedipal situation*: for both sexes, the castle of the Sleeping Beauty, in a forest.

He pointed out that while clients can describe their imagery, they will often not be aware of its meaning. This allows material to emerge that would otherwise be censored. He asked them therefore to write a full account of each directed daydream.

B LEUNER'S STANDARD SITUATIONS

Hans-Carl Leuner used these situations for *training*; for *diagnostic purposes*, where all relevant standard situations are explored one after the other, the imagery that emerges being noted for later exploration; and, by *associated imagery*, for encouraging clients to let images develop in a free and spontaneous way, linking them with past events as well as the here and now, noting feelings that arise, and understanding the messages which the fantasy situations and associations suggest. Then negative energies locked up in the symbols can be released and transformed.

1) A meadow.
2) Climbing a mountain.
3) Following the course of a stream.
4) Visiting a house.
5) The ideal personality – hearing in imagination the first name of a person of the same sex.
6) Unconscious affective relationships symbolised by animals.
7) Unconscious attitudes to sexuality: for men a rosebush, for women being offered a lift on a country road at dusk.
8) A pool of water in a swamp.
9) Waiting for a figure to emerge from a cave.
10) Eruption of a volcano.
11) Confronting the lion – people who oppose the client in outer life.
12) An old picture book in a cellar.

Leuner observed and sought to evoke an *inner psychic pacemaker*, an aspect of consciousness which knows the real nature of the client's problem and what to do about it. For dealing with initially threatening figures he suggested *confrontation*, *feeding*, the use of *magic fluids* applied both to the images and to the patient himself, and *reconciliation*, making friends with hostile figures.

C ASSAGIOLI'S SYMBOLS OF TRANSPERSONAL EXPERIENCE

Roberto Assagioli originally suggested fourteen types of transpersonal symbol:

a) Symbols of introversion, or *inner orientation*. Introversion is an urgent need for modern and extraverted western man, and is recognised by the growing use of such terms as 'inner life', 'inner quality', 'inner space' and 'subtle energies'. The inner room, hidden sanctuary, meditation hall, private chapel or shrine, forest glade, can all be used as aids to inward focusing.

b) Deepening or descent. Related mostly to the lower unconscious and to be used with care. For example the cave, tunnel, passage to the underworld or centre of the earth. Such symbolic places may evoke the shadow, which can be difficult to manage. Symbols of descent are important because of the client's need to integrate all aspects of their nature on the path to individuation.

c) Elevation or ascent. Classic and universal symbols of the spiritual life include climbing the mountain, the castle at the summit, tall spires on churches or cathedrals, being lifted into the air, the flight to the sun.

d) Expansion. Broadening the consciousness to embrace ever-larger wholes, from our immediate group of friends and colleagues to include humanity, the planet and beyond: the drop of water absorbed into the ocean; the spark merging with the flame; the present embracing past and future.

e) Awakening. The image of the person asleep, gradually awakening, becoming aware of body and feelings; then their immediate environment; next their thought processes; then the life of the wider community; and gradually becoming alive to deeper and higher states of consciousness.

f) Light or illumination. More than by any other form of symbolism, the evolution of consciousness can be defined in terms of expansion of vision, of light, illumination and insight. Symbols of light sources (the moon, the sun, a candle, a light shining in darkness), light networks and bodies of light are universal. Blinding precedes the gift of illumination in many initiation rituals. This is paralleled in life where periods of pain, darkness and testing often precede a breakthrough of enlightenment.

g) Fire. A universal symbol of the spirit, of God as consuming Fire, and of purification. Here are the furnace, the phoenix, the sun, the atom, lightning, a supernova explosion. Agni Yoga, the Yoga of Fire, is said to be the highest of all the yogas.[327]

h) Evolutionary development. The unfolding lotus or rose is a universal symbol for development from child to adult, seed to flower, design to finished construction, acorn to oak.

i) Strengthening, intensification. Charging with a new or higher energy; plugging into a more powerful electric circuit. Access of energy, power, radiance.

---

[327] Some Yogas: Jnana (awareness); Mantra (sound); Bhakti (prayer); Karma (action); Raja (mind); Prana (breath); Hatha (body); Tantra (vital sexual); Kundalini (energy); Agni (fire).

j) Love. The identification of 'I' and 'thou'. The loss of self, or transcendence. The part becoming the whole. The circulation of the blood, bringing life to all bodily organs; the cup or grail; the heart; and the twelve-petalled lotus of the heart.

k) The way, or path. Especially any path or road going straight, or upwards, over mountain passes and towards mountain peaks. Symbolic journeys, such as the Pilgrim's Progress. Also such inner pathways as the rainbow bridge over which the gods passed; and the *antahkarana*, the bridge of inner consciousness woven at a certain stage along the spiritual path between the egoic lotus (the body of the soul) and the spiritual triad.

l) Transmutation. Symbolism of alchemy; changes in the quality and nature of the substance of the mental, emotional and bodily vehicles of the psyche. Transmutation is for the most part brought about by the 'lifting up' or sublimation of energies on the one hand, and the 'descent' or down-flow of energies from the supra-conscious on the other. Our form-nature is the crucible within which, by a mix of inner energies, the transformation of consciousness is brought about.

m) Regeneration or rebirth. The 'new man', or 'second birth', as it is called in the East. Shedding old skins, taking on a new name; from chrysalis to butterfly; the revelation of the self at the centre.

n) Liberation. Discarding masks, images, idols; throwing off hindrances; breaking out of imprisoning bonds – from being tied by ropes, or from a prison or confining space, out of a tomb, coffin, box, cave, locked room or house; release into the open and from dark places into the light.

APPENDIX 15
SOME SYMBOLIC SITUATIONS FOR GUIDED IMAGING
Ian Gordon-Brown

The Meadow.[328] The meadow is often used as a point of departure for the inner traveller. It initiates visualisation, standing as a psychological Garden of Eden, a place of early beginnings. It usually offers a positive, happy, or at least neutral centre to start from and return to. Its nature, the length and greenness of grass and flowers, or their lack, are indicative of the client's present psychological state. Short, closely-clipped grass, for example, can indicate unhealthy psychological mechanisms. Those whose

---
328 Also Leuner's Standard Situations, Appendix 9.

inner life is barren may find a desert, or stony ground with very little vegetation at all. A meadow over-lush or swampy may symbolise an over-emotional nature, with insufficient opportunities for release. Always relate any interpretation to the client.

The House may represent the ego or personal self, or their self-image or life style. The number and size of rooms, the furnishings, the number of floors, whether there is a basement or attic, the feeling tone of the different rooms, and whether the inside and the outside match or are incongruous, all have meaning. Again, avoid standard or stereotyped interpretations. Note the feeling tone: yes, a large house may indicate an enlarged consciousness, or capacity for enlargement – or it could mean inflation. A small house *may* mean limited capacity – but not necessarily; it could signify modest demands or expectations of life; or the person's undervaluing of their own nature; or even, should the house differ substantially from those they have lived in, fears for the future. Similarly, do empty rooms symbolise a barren state of mind or feeling? Or have they been emptied in readiness for something new or different? Many rooms apparently without specific function could indicate resources untapped by consciousness – or an undisciplined and uncoordinated nature. The state of certain key rooms such as the kitchen, for example, where raw materials are prepared and transformed for assimilation, may signify transformation processes occurring within the psyche.

The Cave and the Tunnel. To go into or under the ground usually symbolises the exploration of the middle, lower or even the collective unconscious. Generally, the deeper into the cave, or further into a cave system, the deeper into the lower unconscious. Images evoked by such an inward and downward journey will penetrate successive layers, eventually reaching archetypal and primordial depths. Tunnels may differ, being places of transit, passages through some level of the lower unconscious.

The Mountain has traditionally symbolised a place apart from the everyday world where only the brave and the strong can go. Does it indicate peaks or heights of experience – or of aspiration and ambition? The ease or difficulty of the climb, the obstacles to be confronted and surmounted, may speak of challenges faced by the individual. A small hill can indicate poor levels of aspiration; encourage them to climb to the top and look around. Is any higher peak now visible? Ascent of the mountain generally symbolises the passage into supra-conscious and transcendent levels of awareness.

The River. Whether small streams or wide and flowing rivers, these normally signify the subtle psychic energy available to the individual. Obstacles upstream may speak of blocks in the flow of energy from the higher consciousness to the personal; obstacles downstream, of blocks in its flow into the lower unconscious. Note its depth or shallowness, clarity or muddiness, turbulence and so on.

The Lake, landlocked and fed from streams that spring in the surrounding country, has a different connotation from the river. Again, take note of its size, shape, its temperature, feeling, colour and so forth. Water often relates to the feminine and the feeling aspects of the psyche.[329]

The Marsh or Swamp. How beautiful and dramatic are the statements made by symbols once we get the hang of them.... Earth and water are here combined; the water is trapped. Is there too much water in relation to the earth? Is the earth so heavy that it cannot drain away? Does some feature of the surrounding land contain and hold the water? Water that stands becomes dank and foetid. Sticking to clothes and body, mud is difficult to wash off. A marsh sucks a person in and down; the more they struggle the harder it is to escape; and it's deceptive, covered with vegetation. Even close up it looks no different from many an ordinary field, trapping unwary travellers. If for water we read 'emotions and feelings', and remember that marshes and swamps have been there for a longish time, we have some of the keys to their meaning in someone's imagery.

The Volcano usually refers to 'affective tension'. The ease with which the client visualises an eruption, and its power and duration, indicate how much energy is locked up and the degree of repression or inhibition. A skilled therapist can accompany someone on a journey into the volcano, entering not necessarily from the mouth (which may be blocked), but from some cave or tunnel at the side or base. Such an exploration can reveal the original source of the energy and how it may be permanently harnessed, released or redirected. An extinct volcano may indicate a revisiting of old and worked-out emotions, no longer dominant and without power.

Mandalas evoke material relating to the future – to becoming whole. Symmetrical in shape, bearing from periphery to centre, they are commonly four-sided, or circular, or a combination of both, with some key symbol at the centre – a circular clearing, a pool, altar, statue or stone. A guided daydream can be structured so that towards its conclusion the client

---

[329] See Alice Bailey's meditation on the lake, Bailey 1944, *Discipleship in the New Age* Vol. 1. p. 535.

comes towards something like a mandala. Symbols of integration and individuation both East and West, mandalas are very specially important to all who are responding to the transpersonal Self. Note their presence with special care and interest, using them to invoke and evoke the Centre.

The Centre. As the centre of a mandala can symbolise the spirit of wholeness in a person, representing the highest, the deepest, the core essence in man, so the centre of the earth, the middle of the meadow, the tops of mountains, the sources of rivers – all may be such symbolic locations. So may valleys surrounded by high mountains, islands particularly if they have a central peak, springs or fountains, oases in deserts, clearings in forests, groves of trees; and the centres of towns or villages, market squares, often with fountains in the middle, central courtyards of castles or large houses. And of course monasteries, cathedrals, temples, mosques with their archetypal shapes and structures; and chapels, meditation halls, altars, shrines – all can stand in for and represent wholeness. As they emerge in guided fantasy, approach them with special reverence, recognising that you and the client are in the presence of the life source; and consciously tune to and co-operate with whatever that life source chooses to say.

However, as testified in myth and legend, that which appears at first to be the Centre is frequently only the *outer* court. The true Centre, the Holy of Holies, can be entered only through another, sometimes secret door. The client, or the talisman, may know the procedure to follow to enter the inner chamber; if not, the guide may suggest some invocation or simple ritual to allow the possibility of entry to the innermost centre.

Experience at the Centre. Something of a profoundly transpersonal or spiritual nature may happen quite spontaneously – the guide doesn't need to suggest it, and must be especially careful not to interfere and spoil it. They may find themselves before an altar, performing some ritual. A wise teacher may appear, a being of light, an angel, the archetypal Christ or Buddha. It may take non-human form – a Grail cup or chalice from which they drink. Some jewel may appear, a diamond, a pearl or a white stone which may be recognised as the *lapis*. The equal-armed cross in its various forms frequently recurs at the centre. Some negative feature or image met on the way may be turned into its positive counterpart; or the talisman which has accompanied them on the journey may itself be transformed. If no symbol or ritual occurs spontaneously, the counsellor can suggest one: 'Stand at the centre; visualise the light of the spiritual sun pouring down and filling the centre, and you, with its energy and radiance.'

APPENDIX 16

WORKING WITH INDIVIDUALS
THE STRUCTURE OF THE JOURNEY
Ian Gordon-Brown

Some guided daydreams need very little structure; counsellor and client together know which area or areas they wish to explore. They may be encouraged to move from neutral ground, perhaps the meadow, towards some place from which they can move on. Or there may be slightly more structure, an encounter being suggested, for instance, with two or three people who will tell them about any *tests and trials* they are to undergo; this allows their unconscious to do the choosing. There is much to commend this. Still more structure may involve challenges and a *goal* to be sought, a treasure at the end of a symbolic journey that takes them to *the Centre* where they find the gift of the heart's desire. The *country* through which they travel can be structured beforehand to throw light on any core problems. For difficulties in the lower unconscious, the journey may go partly 'under the earth'. Perhaps it requires them to cross water, so looking at emotional problems. It may take them into the world of meaning; for this, a convenient starting point is to ask them to go through a mirror to the 'inner side of life', whether to explore the meaning their life has, or to search for some particular meaning. Facing the mirror at the start is an interesting and sometimes fruitful way for them to confront themselves, or at least one of their self-images. Again, an *exploration into the body* can be particularly helpful, visiting sites of tension, or health difficulties suspected to be of psychosomatic origin.

Both in the full guided daydream and in shorter periods of spot imaging during didactic work, the counsellor's task includes helping the client to *stay with the image*. Exploring the borderland of conscious and unconscious requires an attitude of reverence. It is this that evokes the unconscious, both lower and higher, and enables it to speak to us. Prior to deep exploration, use such phrases as:

'Could you hold the image of ... before you.'
'Describe ... to me. What colour is it – what size – shape?'
'What is the feeling ... gives you?'
'See if you can stay with that feeling.'

Talking with the image. A wealth of material may be offered. Watch for significant *symbols and images* representing some important aspect and

encourage the person to enter into a dialogue with them:
- 'Ask the ... why it is here.'
- 'Ask it what it represents in your life.'
- 'Does it have any message to give you?'
- 'Can it give you another image or a symbol that will tell you about its meaning for you?'
- 'Can the Talisman get it to reveal who or what it is?'

If it does not speak, it can be asked to give its message or meaning in the form of another image, or by changing its shape or colour. Ask them to get closer to the image, to bring it into better focus, perhaps to look into its eyes and see what is there. A more detailed inspection may reveal important features that were not at first noticed, leading towards its meaning.

Confronting it. The image will sometimes be so frightening or disturbing that there is great difficulty in staying with it, and certainly no hope of establishing a dialogue. *Leuner* quotes the example of a large snake coming out of a swamp to attack his client. Reminding him that the talisman was available as a help of last resort, he encouraged him to suppress his anxiety, stand his ground and employ the ancient and magical practice of neutralising it by staring into its eyes, rather than running away or attempting to overcome it . Firstly, prevent attack; secondly, discover its message or meaning. Some quite remarkable transformations can occur, the image becoming less hostile, perhaps changing into a new animal, usually one higher up the scale of development. Any successful fantasy confrontation will strengthen the individual's ability to stand on his own feet and work from his own centre.

Feeding it. Another way of dealing with an angry or disturbing image is to provide it with as much food as it wants – indeed, overfeed an aggressive creature till it becomes incapable of aggression. Feeding implies symbolic acceptance of the negative element in the psyche represented by the creature, and a willingness to search together for a way forward. At a deeper level, feeding means loving; to give love to a rejected or partially split-off component of the psyche is an important stage in the process of assimilation and integration. It also leads to the discovery of a more benign symbol and energy underlying the negative.

Becoming it. We have seen how consciousness and energy are two aspects of a single reality: consciousness has energy, and energy is consciousness. The image is embodying our energy, and we need it to grow towards individuation. *Become* it, and its energy is ours again.

Reconciliation. This consists in showing tenderness and understanding to hostile figures, talking to them, asking what they want, in imagination even touching and stroking them. This can also be done with our images of real people. The negative idea of others that we carry around with us form a major part of our troubles. There may indeed be a sound basis in reality for these images; but, when we meet such people it's the images we react to, rather than the person. To ease such troubles we have to reverse this, responding to the person rather than the image. Making friends with, and understanding, our image of the other is an important and helpful aid to this.

Enlarging or miniaturising. Enlarging an image to permit closer and more detailed inspection, or making it smaller and therefore more manageable, and if necessary portable, may be useful.

Ascent and descent. Much movement is in the vertical dimension. Although ascending can be difficult at first, later it may invoke luminous images expressing open and generous feelings and a sense of calm, serenity and joy. On the other hand, to imagine a *descent* evokes increasingly sombre images, sometimes unpleasant, even quite distressing. By ascending, the client discovers ways of sublimating or transforming his problems; by descending he is helped to face up to the reality of things as they are in everyday life, and to uncover and deal with the actual roots of his conflicts.

Attacking, exhausting and killing. To damage or kill people or creatures who appear during the journey is generally to be avoided. It is one of the most difficult and potentially dangerous tools in guided fantasy. There is a risk that the negative figure may represent an important but not-yet-integrated component of the psyche, so that the client will experience the attempt to kill or exhaust it as an attack against himself. Such figures usually want, rather, to be transformed. However, should it be simply a peripheral negative energy, a 'hanger-on', it may be dealt with successfully in this way. Leuner reports the case of an image representing death that was kept on the run until it fell exhausted into a stream and there dissolved, with immediately beneficial effects. However, only experienced therapists should ever encourage this.

Use of (imaginary) magic fluids. These may be applied, for example, to relieve bodily aches and pains; or the patient can be asked to imagine they are bathing in healing or health-giving water.

The cutting of the umbilicus. This makes it easier to sever the links, both positive and negative, with parent figures. First, visualise the parent. See a golden cord, and pour affirmation through it. Though *positive*, like every umbilicus this old link still needs to be cut. Sever it. Experience being separate. Then set up a *negative* umbilicus and cut that. Send it up, with fire. The aim is that energy begin to flow freely between child and parent *from heart to heart* instead of via the outmoded channel.

Fear. It is normal to edge away from painful or threatening images and energies. If, instead, we face or approach that which we dread, it often proves to be benign and instructive. It is our own fear and the *fear of fear* itself which invest it with energy.

Resistance. While some clients move rapidly into painful areas, there are others who hold back. This is not always obvious to the guide; it may be spotted by feeling or intuition, though unrecognised by the intellect. Forcing the issue, pressing too hard at the blocked area, may simply increase the resistance. The talisman can be invoked, but this may not help either. A shift of approach from imaging to awareness of the body, or the feeling-tone of the situation, may sometimes do the trick. But not always. Try asking them to rest, to relax, go deep into their inner space, and simply to report whatever image or feeling comes to the top of their mind. This may be related to the area of resistance and provide a way into it. Or not. Its origin may emerge at the end of the daydream, from the perspective of the Centre or Self. Or it may have to wait until later.

Blocking. Distortion and the generation of negative forces are part and parcel of growing. The strongest and most rooted growth generally occurs when there is a degree of opposition to 'grow against'; few can generate their own motivation without any outside pressure. Thus the psyche finds circumstances and people against which it can test its strength. This may be useful; but it can also lead to the least helpful kind of sensitivity, and to the blocking, suppression and repression of the individual's psychic forces.

Genuine *transformations* in consciousness are of supreme importance – even the possibility augurs well for the future. What is transformed will be *negative energy*. Nearly all negative energies began by having positive value, but were blocked, sidetracked or twisted by circumstances, parental pressures or limitations within the individual. Now they take this troublesome form. When understood for what they are, they can be released and re-directed. *Desoille's* technique of ascent[330] will frequently initiate a transformation, showing the higher, positive counterpart of a negative energy. The client can be asked to imagine a light shining on dark or regressive objects, when they may be shown to be beautiful and valuable. If sordid or sticky, they may be washed or scraped clean to reveal value hitherto unrecognised through lack of use.

Ending on a 'high'. A long guided daydream should, ideally, end on a positive note. You might build in a ritual, inviting them to go up a mountain to meet a wise person; or to find themselves at a Centre of peace, joy and serenity where they may undergo some integrative experience; or to be bathed in a healing light which enters all the dark places of the inner world, dispelling gloom. Remember the healing power of transpersonal symbols of synthesis and integration – mandala forms, the quaternary, the lotus or the rose, the sanctuary, the sun – and employ them. Move back or forward to rescuing symbols such as the healing fountain, chapel, star, gold or jewel.

'We are now drawing to the end of the journey. Find yourself again
    with your rose, daffodil, daisy –
    in a sunny clearing in the heart of this dark forest –
    back by the fountain in the square –
    on your way back to the meadow.'

'We are going to call upon the energy of the Talisman to give meaning
    to the experience you have just had.... Thank your Talisman.'

Or:

'You have had a deep experience with much pain. Your Talisman will
    help you to understand its meaning.'

'We can return to this later ... now you should rest ... feel the warmth
    of the sun ... experience it....'

Completion. Taking up the *foetal position* at the end, particularly after regressive work, helps the post-dream earthing process. Ground them if necessary, saying, 'Touch the couch, feel your fingers, say your name....' A short break allows them a few minutes alone to come out of the daydream and return to everyday reality – and a cup of tea, if that fits your style. Go through the notes just enough to ensure that all the important features can be remembered and built on. What comes up can fade like a dream and significant features be forgotten. A minority of people go so

---

330 Desoille, see Chapter 6, p. 255, and Appendix 9.

deep into parts of the daydream that they have real difficulty in recall. Do not interpret nor, usually, discuss it now. Offer the client your notes, affirm them and send them safely home.

Aftermath. Try to organise a follow-up session reasonably soon, when you may discuss the meaning of the dream (some clients can do this immediately after it is finished). Encourage them to write up, or make a tape-recording about, the experience and do related drawings; remind them to call on the talisman if subsequent difficulty arises.

APPENDIX 17
MASCULINE AND FEMININE ASPECTS IN THE ARCHETYPAL CONTEXT

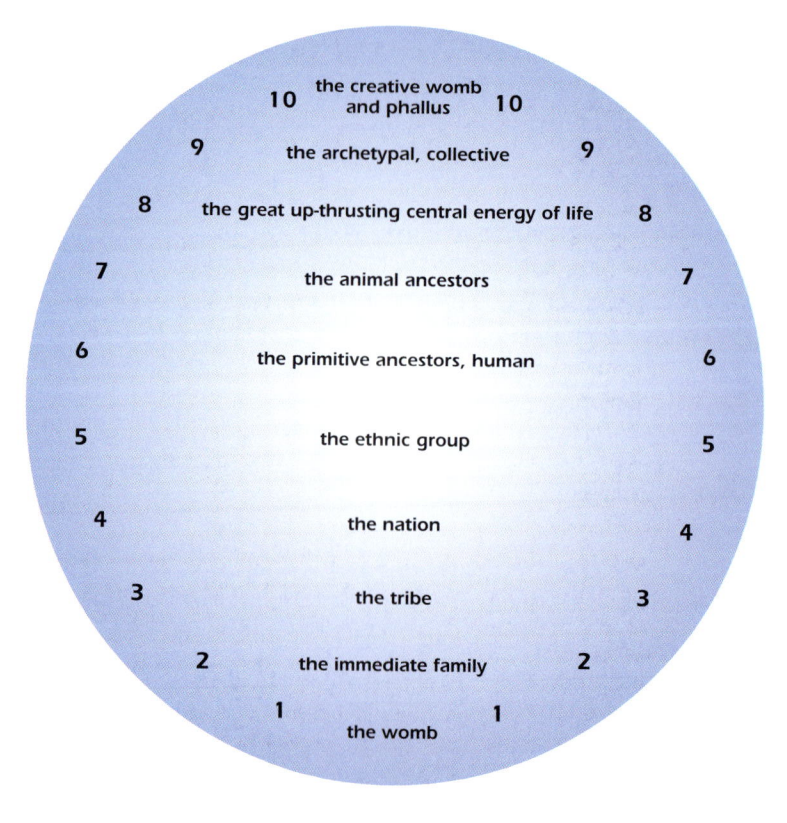

```
              10   the creative womb    10
                     and phallus
           9        the archetypal, collective       9
        8     the great up-thrusting central energy of life    8
     7              the animal ancestors                  7
    6             the primitive ancestors, human           6
    5                 the ethnic group                    5
    4                    the nation                       4
     3                   the tribe                       3
        2          the immediate family          2
              1                          1
                       the womb
```

Chart 11:02 – The One

The hero who goes on the journey of life is the masculine principle; the journey itself is the feminine. Reading upwards, we see that the individual welled or emerged from the layer below.[331] In more detail, starting with:

1. The personal masculine and the personal feminine. The mother from whom we are born.
2. The personal father and the personal mother and the close family.
3. The widening family; widening the feminine to the tribe; grandmothers and aunts, sisters, teachers; and widening the masculine to grandfathers, to brothers, teachers, uncles.
4. The ancestral father and the ancestral mother. On the one hand, law and order, society's *mores*, judges, the police; on the other, our national and cultural roots. The idea of the soil, of plants and their rooting, often comes up for people.
5. Beyond that lie the cultural father and the cultural mother. Feminine images at this ethnic level include the Madonna, Kali, the Earth Mother; and the masculine, the images of our tribe: Jehovah, Christ, Shri Krishna, Shiva, God.
6. Then, at the phallic level, the mythical masculine with its pointed, directional objects and its bulls, stags and stallions. And the mythical feminine, going deeper into the container, the cup, the shell, the basket, the Grail. Here are helpful plants, animals and people, as well as negative symbols from folk lore, legend and myth.
7. At the religious or spiritual level, we find the priest, the shaman, the guru. Here are the tempter, the trickster, the witch doctor with his *tremendum* of demonic power. But also, lying behind the whale, the cave, the mine and the labyrinth is the matrix out of which rise initiators and rituals of initiation. It is the *chthonic* level from which the ore is drawn. Here, in the place of initiation, are found feminine religious figures.
8. The eighth level is about the *quest*, thrusting itself up like mountains, soaring into air and fire. It is also about the journey down into earth and water. Motifs of the journey often include witches, fairies, divine maidens, naiads and fish that swallow you up.
9. The collective ninth level is itself archetypal. It is about light, day, the sun, and consciousness. It is active and of the right hand. But on the left hand, it is also feminine at a deeper, archetypal, collective level; it embraces the dark, the night, the moon and all that is unconscious. Passive, it is about the return to the masculine at a deeper level.
10. Here we come to the creative womb of life itself, source of humanity's creation myths. And at the top is the One, which links them. And so at the climax Sol and Luna meet once more and disport themselves in the heavens, then fall out of bed the other side in their ecstasy.

---

331 And see Jacobi 1942, *The Psychology of C. G. Jung*, p. 44

APPENDIX 18
SEVEN ARCHETYPES, SEVEN RAYS
Based on the work of Alice Bailey

Ray I
Name. Ruler, gardener, destroyer, Wind of God.
Words of Power. 'I assert the fact.'
Energy and purpose. Will to power, will to rule, will to initiate. Will-power. Tendency to synthesis.
Path to the centre. Fire, energy, head centre, authority.
Archetypal task. Statesman, general, director, boss, human rights, general chairman, politician.
'God' or highest value. Power, human rights and freedoms. Zeus, Jahweh, Shiva.
Highest realisation. Initiation, freedom.
Function. Assertion, purpose, direction and control, law. Destroying and releasing.
Method. Force, violence, imposition. Grasping, taking hold.
Starting a work. Force, energy, action, (occultist). Grasping.
Key problems, shadow. Pride, ambition, willfulness, hardness, arrogance, desire to control others, obstinacy, anger.
Technique of integration. Inclusion, discipline, inclusiveness, tenderness, humility, sympathy, tolerance, patience. Develop the *gardener*.
Movements. Agni yoga.

Ray II
Name. Priest-healer, consciousness teacher, scholar.
Words of Power. 'I see the greatest light.'
Energy and purpose. Love and wisdom, will to love, will to understand, will to unification.
Path to the centre. Heart, deep study, consciousness, vision, expansion. Compassion, unselfishness, energy.
Archetypal task. Priest, healer, teacher, ambassador, scholar.
'God' or highest value. Relationship, love, consciousness, wisdom. Christ, Buddha, Vishnu.
Highest realisation. Mystical vision.
Function. Build, nurture, cultivate, preserve.
Method. Radiation, absorption. Scholar, knows the truth, surrounded by books.
Starting a work. True psychic initiation. Attracting, centralising.
Key problems, shadow. Over-absorption in study, coldness, indifference to others, contempt of mental limitations in others.
Technique of integration. Opening up to love, centralising, relating. Develop the *quality of the hidden vision*.
Movements. World religions.

Ray III

Name. Thinker, weaver.

Words of Power. 'Purpose itself am I.'

Energy and purpose. Higher mind, active intelligence, will to know, will to understand, will to evolution. Adaptation, development. Instinct to formulate a plan.

Path to the centre. Mind, deep thought, philosophising.

Archetypal task. Philosopher, metaphysician, thinker, entrepreneur, academic, intellectual.

'God' or highest value. Knowledge, ideas, mind, intelligence. Brahma.

Highest realisation. Education.

Function. Planning and design, theory-building, model-building, communicator, manipulator, educator.

Method. Deep thought, planning, communication, pattern.

Starting a work. Evolution, (magician). Selecting. 'This *not* that'.

Key problems, shadow. Schemer. Intellectual pride, coldness, isolation, inaccuracy in details, absent-mindedness, obstinacy, selfishness, overmuch criticism of others.

Technique of integration. Stillness, sympathy, tolerance, devotion, accuracy, energy and common-sense. Develop the *weaver*.

Movements. Systems of thought, systems of administration.

Ray IV

Name. Conciliator, mediator, mixer, artist, explorer.

Words of Power. 'Two merge with one.'

Energy and purpose. Harmony through conflict. Will to harmonise, relate, co-operate. Vibration and response.

Path to the centre. Steadfastness, serenity, confidence, self-control, purity, unselfishness, accuracy, mental and moral balance.

Archetypal task. Negotiator, harmoniser. Messenger and intermediary, counsellor and consultant.

'God' or highest value. Peace, beauty, harmony. Leonardo.

Highest realisation. Harmonisation and creativity.

Function. Peace, conflict-resolution, at-oneing, imagining, attuning, blending.

Method. Creative: 'This *and* that'.

Starting a work. Expression (artist).

Key problems, shadow. Self-centredness, worrying, inaccuracy, lack of moral courage, strong passions, indolence, extravagance.

Technique of integration. Steadfastness, exploration, bridging, relating, creating. Develop the urge to creative life through divine faculty of imagination. Unseen beauty.

Movements. Gurdjieff.

Ray V
Name. Scientist, alchemist, worker.
Words of Power. 'Three Minds Unite.'
Energy and purpose. Will to truth, will to know. Mentation, science, concrete knowledge.
Path to the centre. Research, analysis, experiment.
Archetypal task. Scientist, alchemist, analyst, academic, engineer.
'God' or highest value. Truth, science, concrete knowledge, objective knowledge.
Highest realisation. Liberation.
Function. Knowledge, educational processes, technology.
Method. Researching, analysing, differentiating, pigeon-holing. Worker (toiling deep in a Pyramid); practical, detached.
Starting a work. Differentiating.
Key problems, shadow. Harsh criticism, narrowness, arrogance, unforgiving temper, lack of sympathy and reverence, prejudice.
Technique of integration. Develop detachment. Reverence, devotion, sympathy, love, wide-mindedness.
Movements. Rosicrucian, alchemy.

Ray VI
Name. Idealist, devotee, follower.
Words of Power. 'The highest light controls.'
Energy and purpose. Idealism, will to perfect, will to persist, will to causation, devotion, abstraction.
Path to the centre. Faith and prayer, devotion to a cause, self-sacrifice. Strength, purity, truth, serenity,
Archetypal task. Devotion; saint, sinner, missionary, priest, preacher, monk, nun, guru.
'God' or highest value. Perfection, the abstract ideal.
Highest realisation. Idealism.
Function. Religious systems, ideologies.
Method. Following, faith and prayer.
Starting a work. Devotion, responding.
Key problems, shadow. Selfish and jealous love, over-leaning on others, partiality, self-deception, sectarianism. Frenzied follower, superstition, prejudice, over-rapid conclusions, fiery anger.
Technique of integration. Sympathy, tolerance, imaging, becoming leader yourself. Develop balance and common sense.
Movements. Esoteric Christianity.

Ray VII
Name. Magician.
Words of Power. 'The highest and the lowest meet.'
Energy and purpose. Will to manifest, will to organise, will to express. Music, ceremonial order.
Path to the centre. Wide-mindedness, tolerance, humility, gentleness and love.
Archetypal task. Magician, manager, ritualist, arranger.
'God' or highest value. Efficiency, economy, perfect form, order.
Highest realisation. Manifestation.
Function. Relating, coordinating polarities. Linking spirit and matter.
Method. Systematic organisation (bringing together). Ritual.
Starting a work. Incantation, ritual.
Key problems, shadow. Formalism, bigotry, pride, narrowness, superficial judgments, self-opinion over-indulged.
Technique of integration. Humane purpose, realisation of unity. Develop awareness of interplay of the great dualities.
Movements. Magic.

Relationships between the Rays

The only ray which stands alone and has no close relationship with any of the others is the fourth. Between the third and fifth rays there is a close relationship. In the search after knowledge, for example, the most laborious and minute study of detail is the path that will be followed, whether in philosophy, the higher mathematics or in the pursuit of practical science. The correspondence between the second and the sixth rays shows itself in the intuitive grasp of synthesised knowledge and in the common bond of faithfulness and loyalty. Masterfulness, steadfastness, and perseverance are the corresponding characteristics of the first and seventh rays.

APPENDIX 19
THE NATIONS AND THE RAYS
Based on the work of Alice Bailey [332]

Nation	Personality Ray	Soul Ray National	Motto
India	4th Ray of Harmony	1st Ray of Power	I hide the Light through Conflict
China	3rd Ray of Intelligence	1st Ray of Power	I indicate the Way
Germany	1st Ray of Power	4th Ray of Harmony	I preserve through Conflict
France	3rd Ray of Intelligence	5th Ray of Knowledge	I release the Light
Great Britain	1st Ray of Power	2nd Ray of Love	I serve
Italy	4th Ray of Harmony	6th Ray of Idealism	I carve the Paths through Conflict
U.S.A	6th Ray of Idealism	2nd Ray of Love	I light the Way
Russia	6th Ray of Idealism	7th Ray of Order	I link two Ways
Austria	5th Ray of Knowledge	4th Ray of Harmony	I serve the lighted Way through Conflict
Spain	7th Ray of Order	6th Ray of Idealism	I disperse the Clouds
Brazil	2nd Ray of Love	4th Ray of Harmony	I hide the Seed through Conflict

---

332 See Bailey 1949, *The Destiny of Nations*, p. 50.

APPENDIX 20
THE CHAKRAS AND THE GLANDS
Ian Gordon-Brown

Order of Opening	Centre	Gland	Traditional Name	Spirit or Core Essence
6	Crown	Pineal	Brahmaranda	-
5	Brow	Pituitary	Ajna	Intuition
2	Throat	Thyroid	(Vishuddha)	Mind and Sex
4	Heart	Thymus	Anahata	Love
1	Solar Plexus	Pancreas	(Manipura)	Emotions
3	Sacral or Sex	Gonads	(Swadhisthanna)	Body, Creativity
7	Base of Spine	Adrenals	Muladhara	Survival

Chart 11:03 – Major Endocrine Glands

Each of the seven main chakras lying along the line of the spine chakra can be taken to have its connection with the endocrine system.[333]

The numbers refer to a possibly typical order in which the centres open. It is interesting to consider: Why that order? What may be the stages of unfolding?

The Pineal Gland has been linked with the Crown. From the esoteric perspective, this Highest Head centre is to do with latent functions of the will and becomes dominant after the Third Initiation.[334] Its opening, which is very rare, goes with a state of perfect balance, perfect health: when in it, disease can't get at a person. In mere occultists, it is not yet active. Becoming conscious of 'something else', of archetypal worlds and patterns, is the key to its awakening; then the *disciple* can go on into

---
333 See Bailey 1953, *Esoteric Healing*, p. 45.
334 The Five Initiations. Out of the mass of undeveloped humanity, with only Base and Sacral chakras open, comes the First Initiation for the average person, when energy awakens mainly in the Solar Plexus. The Second Initiation is for Aspirants, with the soul's energy running from the Solar Plexus below the diaphragm to the Throat. The Third is for Disciples, involving Throat and Heart till the energy of the soul is transferred to the Ajna centre. The Fourth is for Advanced Disciples: it runs from all the centres into the Head, and then from the soul via the Head into the human frame. The Fifth is for initiated Masters. See Bailey 1953, 'Esoteric Healing', pp.144-145 and 152.

initiation, and at last move towards becoming a *master*. The pineal gland is also to do with our concept of time. If the balance between the Brow and the head is upset, it can make people manic; while depressed people over estimate the passage of time, those in a manic state underestimate it. This chakra is often seen as purple or violet in colour.

The Pituitary Gland. The Pituitary can be linked with the *Ajna* or Brow centre.[335] It is to do with soul force. It carries a magnetic quality of love, light and intuition. It opens in the *aspirant*, who is on his or her way to becoming a *disciple*, and becomes dominant after the Second Initiation. Most people are limited and function only partially; indeed, many of us are psychologically dormant or even unconscious, so that only our physical functions are active. The problem with this chakra is that it can also be about mastery and control. It is linked with the colour indigo.

The Thyroid Gland is to do with the Throat centre (sometimes known as *Vishuddha*). It carries creative energy, maturation and consciousness of the Self. It resonates to sound. It opens in creative artists and all 'advanced' human beings, those we might call the *intelligentsia*. It goes with the colour blue.

The Thymus Gland. The Heart chakra, *Anahata*, is related to love, balance and good health. Only recently have *heart-centred* people been numerous enough to make its discovery.[336] The Thymus is to do with the life force and with group consciousness. Green in colour, this chakra is awakened among all 'spiritual' people, and becomes dominant after the First Initiation.

The Pancreas is linked with the Solar Plexus chakra (*Manipura* as it's sometimes known), and mediates astral force, emotion and desire. Yellow in colour and linked, obviously, with digestion, it is open in most 'ordinary' people – in *average humanity*.

The Gonads are to do with the Sacral or Sex centre (which some call *Swadhisthanna*), bearing life-force and vital energy. They affect moods, and are awake in relatively undeveloped men and women and in all *animal* life. It goes with the colour orange.

The Adrenals are situated at the Base of the Spine in the *Muludhara* chakra, and are to do with the will to survival and with *universal* life. They are near the seat of *kundalini*, Mother of the World and can be associated with the colour red.

The Spleen is to do with the *hara*, which I do not include among the

---

335 Some of the many different chakra systems have the first two reversed, suggesting that the pineal goes with the Brow, and the pituitary with the Crown.
336 In the same way, when the consciousness of the race is aware of the energy of an unknown planet, only then is that planet discovered.

chakras. Traditionally linked with perception of the *paranormal*, the hara is said to lie below the navel, half-way between belly-button and pubis, between the second and third lumbar vertebrae where the spine bends in below the Solar Plexus. The hara is where you experience it: some regard it as the centre for physical balance and action, and experience it as moving towards the front of the body – the Root, Sex and Solar Plexus centres are all further back; others hold that it is the field-centre or hub of the body, the life-force of the physical, to do with the spacious aspect of physical being, a combination of Base and Sacral centres. Sensing that it is not a chakra, we suggest that the hara derives from a combination of systems, fitting the masculine psyche and the aggression of the male sex-centre and the Solar Plexus.

ORIGINAL BIBLIOGRAPHY

Argüelles, José & Miriam., *Mandala*, Berkeley & London: Shambhala, 1972.

Assagioli, Roberto., *Psychosynthesis: A Manual of Principles andTechniques*, London: Turnstone Books, 1965

Assagioli, Roberto., *The Act of Will: A Guide to Self-Actualisation and Self-Realisation*, Psychosynthesis Books, 1973

Assagioli, Roberto., *Transpersonal Development: The Dimension Beyond Psychosynthesis*, Harper Collins, Crucible, 1987

Bailey, Alice., *A Treatise on Cosmic Fire*, 1925

Bailey, Alice., *The Light of the Soul: A Paraphrase of the Yoga Sutras of Patanjali*, with a commentary by Alice Bailey. London: Lucis Press, 1927

Bailey, Alice., *A Treatise on White Magic: or the Way of the Disciple*. London: Lucis Press, 1934

Bailey, Alice., *Discipleship in the New Age*, Vol. 1. London: Lucis Press, 1944

Bailey, Alice., *The Destiny of Nations*. London: Lucis Press, 1949

Bailey, Alice., *Telepathy and the Etheric Vehicle*. London: Lucis Press, 1950

Bailey, Alice., *Esoteric Healing*. London: Lucis Press, 1953

Bailey, Alice., *The Rays and The Initiations,* Vol. V, *A Treatise on the Seven Rays*. London: Lucis Press, 1960,

Bettelheim, Bruno., *The Uses of Enchantment*, London: Penguin Psychology, 1991.

Bly, Robert & Keith Thompson., 'What Men Really Want', a chapter about Iron John, in John Welwood, *Challenge of the Heart: Love, Sex and Intimacy in Changing Times*, Boston: Shambhala, 1985. p. 100.

Bly, Robert., *A Little Book on the Human Shadow*, Dorset: Element Books, 1992.

Bly, Robert., *Iron John: A Book about Men*, (The Wild Man), Reading, Ma: Addison-Wesley,1990

Bolen, Jean Shinoda., *Goddesses in Everywoman*, NY: Harper Colophon,1985

Bolen, Jean Shinoda., *Gods in Everyman*, NY: Harper Perennial, 1989

Breuer & Freud., *Studies in Hysteria*, ed. James Strachey, trans. Nicola Luckhurst, London: Penguin Classics, 2004.

Campbell, Joseph., *The Masks of God*, (4 Vols: *Primitive Mythology* 1959, *Oriental Mythology* 1962, *Occidental Mythology* 1964, *Creative Mythology* 1968), London: Penguin Books, 1982.

Campbell, Joseph., *The Hero with a Thousand Faces*, USA: Princeton University Press, 1972

Campbell, Joseph., *Myths to Live By*, Harmondsworth: Penguin Books, 1993

Campbell, Joseph., & Bill Moyers *The Power of Myth*, ed. Betty Sue Flowers, New York: Doubleday, 1988,

Claremont de Castillejo, Irene., *Knowing Woman*, London: Hodder & Stoughton, 1973

Clarke, Lindsay., *The Chymical Wedding*, London: Jonathan Cape, 1990.

Cooper, J. C., *An Illustrated Encyclopaedia of Traditional Symbols*, London: Thames & Hudson, 1978

Crampton, Martha., *History and Manual for Practitioners*, Montreal: Quebec Center for Psychosynthesis Inc, Canadian Institute of Psychosynthesis Inc., 2005

Alighieri, Dante (1300-1320)., *The Divine Comedy*, trans. John Sinclair, London: OUP, 1961.

Desoille, Robert., *Theorie Et Pratique Du Rêve Eveillé Dirige*, Geneva:1961

Desoille, Robert., *The Directed Daydream*, New York: Psychosynthesis Research Foundation, 1966

Dolf & Kieser., *Art and Science: Modes of Thinking: Visual Perception and Art: Vision: Art Forms in Nature: Art and the Unconscious Mind*, London: Studio Vista, 1972

Edinger, Edward., *Ego and Archetype: Individuation and the Religious Function of the Psyche*, London: Random Century Group, 1972

Edinger, Edward., *Anatomy of the Psyche: Alchemical Symbolism in Psychotherapy*, Chicago: Open Court, 1985

Eliade, Mircea., *Cosmos and History: The Myth of the Eternal Return*, trans. Willard Trask, New Jersey: Princeton University Press, 1954

Eliade, Mircea., *The Sacred and the Profane: The Nature of Religion*, trans. Willard Trask, London: Harcourt Brace Jovanovich, 1959,

Eliade, Mircea., *Myth and Reality*, trans. Willard Trask, New York: Harper and Row, 1963

Eliot, T. S., *Four Quartets*. London: Faber & Faber, 1959

Epstein, Gerald., *Waking Dream Therapy*, New York: ACMI Press, 1992

Estes, Clarissa Pinkola., *Women Who Run with the Wolves*, London: Rider, 1992

Faraday, Ann., *The Dream Game*, Harmondsworth: Penguin Books, 1976.

Fenwick, Peter and Elizabeth., *The Truth in the Light: An Investigation of Over 300 Near-Death Experiences'*, London: Headline Book Publishing, 1995

Ferguson, Marilyn., *The Aquarian Conspiracy: Personal and Social Transformation in the 1980's*, London: Routledge, 1982

Ferrucci, Pierro., *What We May Be: the Vision & Techniques of Psychosynthesis*, London: Mandala, 1990

Fordham, Michael., *Analytical Psychology: A Modern Science*, London: Library of Analytical Psychology, 1980

Frankl, Viktor., *Man's Search for Meaning* New York: Insight Books, 1959

Frankl, Viktor., *The Doctor and the Soul*, New York: Vintage Books, 1973

Gordon-Brown, Ian & Barbara Somers., 'Transpersonal Psychotherapy', in Rowan & Dryden, eds., *Innovative Therapy in Britain*, Milton Keynes: Open University Press, 1988

Graves, Robert., *The Greek Myths*, 2 Vols., Harmondsworth: Penguin Books, 1955

Greene, Liz., *Relating: An Astrological Guide to Living with Others on a Small Planet*, London: Coventure, 1977

Grof, Stanislav., *Realms of the Human Unconscious: Observations from LSD Research'*, New York: E. P. Dutton, 1976

Grof, Stanislav and Joan Halifax., *The Human Encounter with Death'*, New York: E. P. Dutton, 1977

Grof, Stanislav & Christina Grof., *Beyond Death: Gates of Consciousness.* London: Thames & Hudson, 1980

Grof, Stanislav., *The Adventure of Self-Discovery: Dimensions of Consciousness and New Perspectives in Psychotherapy'*, SUNY series in Transpersonal and Humanistic Psychology, 1988,

Hall, Nor., *The Moon and the Virgin*, New York: The Women's Press, 1980

Handy, Charles., *Gods of Management*, London: Souvenir Press 1978

Hannah, Barbara., *Jung: His Life and Work'*, USA: Chiron, 1997

Hannah, Barbara., *Encounters with the Soul: Active Imagination as developed by C. G. Jung*, USA: Sigo Press, 1981

Harding, Esther., *The Way of All Women: A Psychological Interpretation*, New York: Rider & Co, 1971

Harris, Robert., *Enigma*, London: Arrow Books, 2001

Jacobi, David., *The Psychology of C. G. Jung*, London: Routledge & Kegan Paul, 1968

James, William., *The Varieties of Religious Experience: a Study in Human Nature'* (The Gifford Lectures 1901-2). London: Fontana, 1960

Janov, Arthur., *Primal Scream: Primal Therapy, The Cure for Neurosis*, Abacus Books, 1991

Johnson, Robert A., *He: Understanding Masculine Psychology*, (on Parsifal and the Grail), USA: Harper & Row, 1977

Johnson, Robert A., *She: Understanding Feminine Psychology*, (on Amor and Psyche), USA: Harper & Row, 1977

Johnson, Robert A., *We: Understanding the Psychology of Romantic Love*, (on Tristan and Isolde), USA: Harper & Row, 1983

Johnson, Robert A., *Inner Work: Using Dreams & Active Imagination for Personal Growth*, San Francisco: Harper, 1986

Johnson, Robert A., *Owning Your Own Shadow: Understanding the Dark Side of the Psyche*, San Francisco: Harper, 1991

Johnson, Robert A., *The Fisher King and the Handless Maiden: Understanding the Wounded Feeling Function in Masculine and Feminine Psychology'*, San Francisco: Harper, 1993

Jung, C. G., *Collected Works* (CW) in 20 volumes, trans. R. F. C. Hull, London: Routledge & Kegan Paul 1953, revised 1968

Jung, C. G., 'Marriage as a Psychological Relationship'; in *CW 17, The Development of Personality*. London: Routledge & Kegan Paul, 1909-10

Jung, C. G., 'The Role of the Unconscious'; in *CW 10, Civilisation in Transition*. London: Routledge & Kegan Paul, 1918

Jung, C. G., 'Psychological Types'; *CW 6*. London: Routledge & Kegan Paul, 1921

Jung, C. G., 'On the Relation of Analytical Psychology to Poetry'; in *CW 15, The Spirit in Man, Art, and Literature*. London: Routledge & Kegan Paul, 1922

Jung, C. G., 'The Significance of Constitution and Heredity in Psychology'; in *CW 8, The Structure and Dynamics of the Psyche*. London: Routledge & Kegan Paul, 1929

Jung, C. G., *Commentary on 'The Secret of the Golden Flower'*, trans. Richard Wilhelm, London: Routledge & Kegan Paul, 1962 & 1975; in *CW 13, Alchemical Studies*. 1931

Jung, C. G., 'The Meaning of Psychology for Modern Man'; in *CW 10, Civilisation in Transition*. London: Routledge & Kegan Paul, 1933-1934

Jung, C. G., 'Archetypes of the Collective Unconscious'; in *CW 9i, The Archetypes and the Collective Unconscious*. London: Routledge & Kegan Paul, 1934 and 1954

Jung, C. G., 'The Tavistock Lectures'; in *CW 18, The Symbolic Life: Miscellaneous Writings*. London: Routledge & Kegan Paul, 1935

Jung, C. G., 'Wotan'; in *CW 10, Civilisation in Transition*. London: Routledge & Kegan Paul, 1936

Jung, C. G., 'Psychology & Alchemy'; in *CW 12*. London: Routledge & Kegan Paul, 1944

Jung, C. G., 'The Shadow'; in *CW 9ii, Aion: Researches into the Phenomenology of the Self*. London: Routledge & Kegan Paul, 1951

Jung, C. G., *Letters* Vol. 2, London: Routledge & Kegan Paul, 1951-1961,

Jung, C. G., 'The Psychology of the Transference', in *CW 16, The Practice of Psychotherapy*. London: Routledge & Kegan Paul, 1954

Jung, C. G., 'Answer to Job', in *CW 11*. London: Routledge & Kegan Paul, 1954

Jung, C. G., *Mysterium Coniunctionis*, in *CW 14*, London: Routledge & Kegan Paul, 1955, (1963)

Jung, C. G., *Man and His Symbols*, London: Aldus Books, 1964. As 'Symbols and the Interpretation of Dreams' in *CW 18, The Symbolic Life: Miscellaneous Writings*. London: Routledge & Kegan Paul, 1961,

Jung, C. G.,,, *Memories, Dreams, Reflections*, London: Collins and Routledge & Kegan Paul, 1963

Jung, C. G., 'Four Archetypes: Mother, Rebirth, Spirit, Trickster'. This book is extracted from *Archetypes of the Collective Unconscious, CW Vol. 9i*, London: Routledge & Kegan Paul, 1972

Jung, C. G., 'Aspects of the Feminine'. This book is extracted from *CW 6, 7, 9i, 9ii, 10, 17*, London: Routledge & Kegan Paul, 1982

Kabîr. *Songs of Kabîr*, trans. Rabindranath Tagore, Intro. Evelyn Underhill, New York: The Macmillan Company, 1915.

Keen, Sam, *The Passionate Life: Stages of Loving*, London: Gateway Books, 1983

Keirsey, David & Marilyn Bates, *Please Understand Me: Character & Temperament Types*, Del Mar, Canada: Gnosology Books Ltd, 1984

Klossowski de Rola, Stanislas, *Alchemy: The Secret Art*, London: Thames & Hudson, 1991

Kopp, Sheldon , *If you meet the Buddha on the Road, Kill Him*, London: Sheldon Press, 1974

Krishna, Gopi, *Kundalini, the Evolutionary Energy in Man*, Boulder and London: Shambhala, 1971

The Divided Self: An Existential Study in Sanity and Madness, Harmondsworth: Penguin, 1960

Laing, R. D., *The Politics of Experience and the Bird of Paradise*, Harmondsworth: Penguin, 1967,

Leboyer, Frederick, *Birth without Violence*, Wildwood House, 1975

Leuner, Hanscarl, *Guided Affective Imagery: Mental Imagery in Short-Term Psychotherapy*.1984

Martin, P. W., *Experiment in Depth*, Boston: Routledge & Kegan Paul, 1976

Maslow, Abraham, *Motivation and Personality*, New York: Harper & Row, 1954

Maslow, Abraham., *Towards a Psychology of Being*, New York: D. Van Nostrand Co., 1968

Maslow, Abraham., *The Farther Reaches of Human Nature*, Harmondsworth: Penguin Books, 1973

McCann, Abbott Justin (ed)., *Cloud of Unknowing*, by an English Mystic of the 14th Century. London: Burns & Oates, 1924 & 1952.

McCormick, Elizabeth Wilde., *Breakdown: Coping, Healing and Rebuilding after Nervous Breakdown*, Unwin Hyman 1988, Optima 1993.

McCormick, Elizabeth Wilde., *Change for the Better: Self-Help through Practical Psychotherapy*, London: Cassell, 1990.

Miller, Alice., *The Drama of Being a Child*, London: Virago Press, 1987

Mindell, Arnold., *The Dreambody in Relationships*, London: Routledge & Kegan Paul, 1987

Moody, Raymond Jr., *Life after Life*, New York: Bantam, 1975

Moore, Robert L. & Douglas Gillette, *King, Warrior, Magician, Lover*, New York: Harper Collins, 1990

Moore, Thomas, *The Planets Within: the Astrological Psychology of Marsilio Ficino*, USA: Bucknell University Press. Lindisfarne Press, 1990

Moore, Thomas, 'The Care of the Soul', London: Piatkus, 1992

Myers, Isabel Briggs, *Manual: The Myers-Briggs Type Indicator*, Consulting Psychologists Press, Palo Alto, Ca. 1962

Neumann, Erich, *Amor and Psyche: The Psychic Development of the Feminine*, New York: Bollingen Foundation, 1956.

Norwood, Robin, *Women Who Love Too Much'*, London: Arrow Books, 1985

Patanjali, Yoga Sutras, in Alice Bailey 1927, *The Light of the Soul: Paraphrase of the Yoga Sutras of Patanjali*, London: Lucis Press,1927

Pearson, Carol S., *The Hero Within: Six Archetypes we Live By*, San Francisco: Harper, 1986

Pelletier, Kenneth R., *Mind as Healer, Mind as Slayer: A Holistic Approach to Preventing Stress Disorders*, New York: Delacorte and Delta, 1992

Perera, Sylvia Brinton, *Descent to the Goddess: A Way of Initiation for Women*, Toronto: Inner City Books, 1991

Perera, Sylvia Brinton, *The Scapegoat Complex: Toward a Mythology of Shadow and Guilt*, Canada: Inner City Books, 1986

Pintar, Judith, *The Halved Soul: Retelling the Myths of Romantic Love*, London: Pandora, 1992

Plato, 360 BCE, *The Republic*, Book 7, trans. Benjamin Jowett 1871, eBooks@Adelaide, 2004

Progoff, Ira, *The Symbolic & The Real*, New York: McGraw Hill, 1963,
Progoff, Ira, *Jung, Synchronicity, and Human Destiny: C. G. Jung's Theory of Meaningful Coincidence*, New York: Dell, 1973
Rilke, Rainer Maria, *Letters to a Young Poet*, trans. Stephen Mitchell 1984, London: Random House, 1913.
Rosarium philosophorum, 16th St. Gallen: C. Stadt-bibliothek Vadiana,
Rowan & Dryden (eds.), *Innovative Therapy in Britain*, Milton Keynes: OUP, 1988
Dorothy Rowe, *Depression: The Way out of Your Prison*, London: Routledge & Kegan Paul, 1983
Sandford, John A., *Dreams: God's Forgotten Language*, New York: Crossroad, 1982
Schultz, J. H., *Das Autogene Training*, Stuttgart: Georg Thieme, 1950.
Schultz, J. H. and Luthe, *Autogenic Training*, New York: Grune & Stratton, 1959
Scott Peck, M., *The Road Less Travelled: A New Psychology of Love, Traditional Values and Spiritual Growth*, USA: Simon & Schuster, 1978
Sheehy, *Passages: Predictable Crises of Adult Life*, New York: Bantam/ E.P. Dutton & Co. Inc. 1976
Singer, June, *Boundaries of the Soul: The Practice of Jung's Psychology*, London: Golancz, 1973
Singer, June, *Androgyny: Towards a New Theory of Sexuality*, London: Routledge & Kegan Paul, 1977,
Rinpoche, Sogyal, *Tibetan Book of Living and Dying*, Rigpa Fellowship 1992, San Francisco: Harper, 1992
Somers, Barbara, 'Dreaming in Depth', chapter in Nigel Wellings & Elizabeth Wilde McCormick (eds.), *Transpersonal Psychotherapy: Theory and Practice*, London: Continuum,2000
Somers, Barbara, & Ian Gordon-Brown, *Journey in Depth: A Transpersonal Perspective*, UK: Archive Publishing, 2002
Somers, Barbara, *The Fires of Alchemy*, UK: Archive Publishing, 2002
Stevens, Anthony, *Jung, a Very Short Introduction*, Oxford & New York: Oxford University Press, 1994
Storm, Hyemeyohsts, *Seven Arrows*, New York: Harper & Row, 1972
Storr, Anthony, *Solitude*, London: Harper Collins, 1997
Sutich, Anthony, 'Some considerations regarding Transpersonal Psychology', *Journal of Transpersonal Psychology No.1*, Spring 1969. Pp.11-20.
Thompson, Francis 'In No Strange Land', *Oxford Book of English Verse 1250-1918*, (ed. Arthur Quiller-Couch 1900), London: OUP, 1939

Tippett, Sir Michael, *Moving into Aquarius*, London: Routledge & Kegan Paul. Expanded edition. England: St. Albans, Paladin, 1974

Tolkien, J. R. R., 'The Two Towers', *The Lord of the Rings* Part 2, London: Allen & Unwin, 1969

Vaughan, Frances, *The Inward Arc*, USA: New Science Library, 1985

Vich, Miles & Anthony Sutich, eds. *Readings in Humanistic Psychology*, Free Press, June 1969

von Franz, Marie-Louise, *Puer Aeternus: A Psychological Study of the Adult Struggle with the Paradise of Childhood*, Santa Monica CA: Sigo Press, 1970, 1981

von Franz, Marie-Louise, *Apuleius and the Golden Ass*, Dallas: Spring Publications, 1970, 1980

von Franz, Marie-Louise, & James Hillman, *Lectures on Jung's Typology*, Zürich & New York: Spring Publications, 1975.

von Franz, Marie-Louise, *The Feminine in Fairy Tales*, Zürich: Foundation for Jungian Psychology, 1972

von Franz, Marie-Louise, *Shadow and Evil in Fairy Tales*, Zürich: Foundation for Jungian Psychology, 1974

von Franz, Marie-Louise, *Individuation in Fairy Tales*, New York: Spring Publications, 1977

von Franz, Marie-Louise, *Alchemical Active Imagination*, Dallas: Spring Publications, 1979

von Franz, Marie-Louise, *Alchemy: An Introduction to the Symbolism and the Psychology*, Toronto: Inner City Books, 1980

von Franz, Marie-Louise, lectures pre 1980, *Archetypal Patterns in Fairy Tales*', republished Zürich: Foundation for Jungian Psychology, 1997

von Franz, Marie-Louise, *On Dreams and Death*, Boston: Shambhala, 1984

Watts, Alan, *The Book on the Taboo Against Knowing Who You Are*, London: Abacus, 1969. p. 54.

Welwood, John ed., *Awakening the Heart: Approaches to Psychotherapy and the Healing Relationship East\West*, Boston: Shambhala, 1983

Welwood, John, *Challenge of the Heart: Love, Sex and Intimacy in Changing Times*, Boston: Shambhala, 1985

Wickes, Frances G., *The Inner World of Childhood*, London: Coventure, 1977.

Wickes, Frances G., *The Inner World of Choice*, London: Coventure, 1977 trans. of 'The Secret of the Golden Flower', (1931), rendered into English by Cary Baynes, London: Routledge & Kegan Paul Ltd., 1962. C. G. Jung's commentary included; see also CW 13.

Wilhelm, Richard, trans. *The I Ching or Book of Changes*, (1923), rendered into English by Cary Baynes, London: Routledge & Kegan Paul Ltd., 1951

Wilmer, Harry A., *Practical Jung: Nuts and Bolts of Jungian Psychotherapy*, New York: Chiron Publications, 1987

Wood, Ernest, *Yoga*, Harmondsworth: Penguin Books, 1973

Woodman, Marion, *Addiction to Perfection: the Still Unravished Bride*, Canada: Inner City Books, 1982

Wordsworth, William, 'Ode: Intimations of Immortality, from Recollections of Early Childhood', *Oxford Book of English Verse 1250-1918*, (ed. Arthur Quiller-Couch 1900), London: OUP, 1939

Apocryphal 'Gospel of Eve', possibly the Gospel of Perfection, an almost completely lost Gnostic and pantheistic text.

INDEX

'Assagioli's Egg', 379
active imagination, 8, 18, 263, 253–66
Adler, Alfred, 326, 380, 396
advertising, 274, 305
Aesculapius, 96
'Akashic Records', *n*, 282
Akbar the Great, 352
alchemy, 73, 237–43, 411
    stages of, 239
antahkarana, Rainbow Bridge, 218, 340, 352, 356, 394, 411
Anthony, Monica, *n*, 325
anxiety, 4, 37, 44, 105, 255, 340
Apollo, 201
Aquarian Conspiracy, 353
archetypal energies, 152–61, 165
archetypal levels, 17, 75, 87, 93, 94, 121
archetype of the Self, 84, 154, 295, 297, 320, 323
archetypes, 281–305
    Amazon, 80, 160
    Apprentice, 88
    Boy child, 87
    Devotee, 157, 180, 291, 424
    Divine Child, 283
    Earth Mother, 21, 283
    Girl child, 77
    Hetaira or courtesan, 160
    Journeyman, 88
    Magician, 158, 293, 425
    Maiden, 78
    Master craftsman, 89
    Maternal, 79, 159
    Mediator, 156, 289, 423
    Medium, 160
    Muse, 21
    Old father, 89
    Priest-healer, 155, 422
    Psyche, 21, 81
    Ruler, King, 155, 285, 422
    Scientist, Alchemist, 157, 290, 424
    Senex, Poor old man, 89, 128, 135, 304
    Serpent, 21
    Thinker, 156, 288, 423
    Trickster, 65, 283, 295
    Wise old man, 90, 283
    Wise woman, 24, 83
    Young father, 89
Archimedes, 62, 105
Ariadne and Theseus, 24, 82, 171, 214
Arjuna, 16
art materials, 274
ashram, 177, 356, 362, 394
    n, 356
Assagioli, Roberto, 3, 12, 13, 104, 253, 258, 259, 304, 352, 397, 399, 409, *n*, 272
'Assagioli's Egg', 13, 14, 36, 321, 327, 348
attack, 332, 333
aura, 308, *n*, 335

Bailey, Alice, 273, 301, 321, 340, 356, 393, 422, 426, *n*, 152, 287, 347, 351
Bates, Thelma, *n*, 206
Beaverbrook, Lord, 293
Blavatsky, Helena, 353
Bohr, Neils, 283
boy child, 24, 78, 193, 194
Brahma, 156, 172, 284, 288, 338, 343, 354
Breuer, Josef, 397
Buddha, 15, 62, 170–72, 187, 209, 218, 246, 249
Buddhism, 310
    of Tibet, 224, 273
        Universal Blessing, 249, 305, 335
    Zen, 90, 273, 315

Campbell, Joseph, 155, 227, 372
cancer, 330
career woman, 23, 81, 160
cave, 37, 173, 175, 187, 188, 194, 205, 255, 277, 394, 410, 412
celibacy, 101, 198
chakra
    Alta Major, 311, 319, 324, 326, 335, 340
    Base or Root, 185, 311, 324, 328, 335, 428
    Brow, 318, 324, 327, 334, 338, 343, 428
    Crown, 185, 320, 324, 326, 327, 337, 343, 356, 427
    Heart, 62, 314, 321, 322, 323, 328, 331, 335, 428
    Sacral, 312, 317, 323, 328, 335, 428
    Solar Plexus, 313, 323, 328, 331, 335, 428
    Throat, 317, 323, 328, 343, 428
chakras, 106, 307–35, 338, 362
    and endocrine system, 427 *n*, 310
    and music, 310, *n*, 325
change, 39, 122, 145–51, 177, 201, 223, 248, 315, 333
Chartres, 216, 247
chela, 393, See disciple
Cheyenne people, 395, *n*, 227
chosen family, 148, 177, 184, 305
Christ, 15, 62, 172–88, 220, 243, 282, 324, 334, 360, 394
Christianity, 158, 204, 292
cities, 300
Cocteau, Jean, 376
confrontation, 258, 271, 416
Confucius, 249, 364
consciousness, 3
Copernicus, 244
creativity, 27, 63, 82, 282, 290, 317, 325, 344
crystal, 12, 40, 282
Curie, Marie, 290

Dalai Lama, *n*, 206
danger, 299, 312, 319, 335, 340, 345, 360, 417
    and opportunity, 126, 145, 165, 192, 241
Dante, 204
    and Beatrice, 24, 82

Darwin, Charles, 290
de Castillejo, Irene Claremont, 138
de Chardin, Theilard, 14, 187
Dement, William C., 259, 398
Desoille, Robert, 255, 258, 398, 408, 419, *n*, 270
Diagnostic and Statistical Manual *n*, 299
disciple, 158, 161, 356, 359, 376, 393, 427
divine child, 7, 40, 242, 282
dreams, 7, 35–40, 92–96, 130, 162, 186, 202, 253–60, 340, 394, 397–404
   amplification, 36
   association, 258
Dummling, 212

Earth Mother, 118, 192, 205
Edison, Thomas, 290
ego, 16
Einstein, Albert, 62, 105
Eliot, T.S., 217, 221, 225, 246
endocrine system, 310
energy, 4
ents, Tolkien's tree people, *n*, 300
Epidaurus, 96
Erikson, Milton, 127
explorations, xiv
   Archetypal Images, 283
   Archetypes of the Self, 297
   Chakras, 322, 326
   Contemplation, 225
   Core Energy, 161
   Cup and Sword, 71, 372
   Desert and Mountain, 221
   Door and Cave, 188
   Door and Mirror, 236, 376
   Drawing, 363
   First Aid for Panic, 331
   Gestalt, 46, 107, 371, 373
   Grounding Exercise, 118
   Inner Sanctuary, 372
   Intuition, Inspiration and Will, 338, 342, 346, 348
   Journey through Elements, 229
   Journey to the Other Self, 243
   Met on the Road, 94
   Place of Creation, 361
   Road of your Life, 151
   Sanctuary, 66, 166
   Self-Image, 131, 373, 391
   Shape of your Life, 138, 141
   Sub-personalities, 28, 30, 371
   Temple in the Sun, 362
   Traveller on Life's Journey, 18, 370
   Two Questions, 18
   Universal Blessing, 365
   Water of Emotions, 207

Fadiman, James, 398
Fenwick, Peter and Elizabeth *n*, 206
Ferrucci, Piero, 259, 399
Fordham, Michael, 262, 399
Four Functions, 48–59, 105, 231–34, 239, 245, 345
Frankl, Viktor, 253, 380, 399
Franklin, Benjamin, 353
Frederic Myers, 254, 406
Freemasonry, *n*, 353

Freud, Sigmund, 3, 12, 48, 254, 256, 282, 326, 396, 399, 402
Frost, Robert, 76

Galileo, 244
game theory, 289
Garden of Eden, 219, 277, 411
Gestalt, 164, 259, 270, 406
girl child, 23, 43, 78, 193, 195
glands
    adrenals, 311, 428
    gonads, 312, 428
    pancreas, 313, 428
    pineal, 320, 427, *n*, 428
    pituitary, 318, 327, 428, *n*, 428
    spleen, 428
    thymus, 314, 428
    thyroid, 317, 328, 428
gold and silver, *n*, 199
Golden Age, *n*, 196
Greenfield, Susan, 111
Grof, Stanislav, 253, 259, 400, 407, *n*, 193, 206
groups, 301–5, 315, 332, 354, 361, 393
Guest, Hazel, *n*, 295
guided daydream, 8, 18, 254, 255, 258, 259, 398
    full, 263–72, 415–20
Guillery, Marc, 255, 400

Hammarskjold, Dag, 353
Hannah, Barbara, 260
Happich, Carl, 255, 400
hara, 428
harlequin, 25
hero and heroine, 18, 196, 211, 219, 286, *n*, 212

hero's journey, 56, 87, 212–15, 267, 303, 370
Hillman, James, 137, 259, 401
Hinduism, 224, 310, 338
hospice movement, 206
house, 30, 33, 38, 300, 371, 409, 412

I Ching, *n*, 84
identity, 4, 62, 85, 117, 124, 325
Ignatius Loyola, 123
imaging, 263–70
    and visualisation, 18, 86, 259, 263, 275, 358
    guided, 254, 256, 260, 262, 261–63, 266, 400, 403, 408, 411
Inanna and Ereshkigal, 219
'inferior function', 52, 55, 58, 233, 234, 236, 245, 256, 285
inspiration, 63, 157, 322, 337, 342–46
intuition, 8, 34, 42, 43, 46, 54, 74, 82, 104–6, 110, 125, 179, 185, 215, 221, 318–22, 337–43, 428
Islam, 135, 292
island, 3, 11, 269, 414

James, William, 254, 401
Janet, Pierre, 254, 402
jewel in the lotus, 246, 300, 308, 322, 333
Johnson, Lyndon, 293
Judaism, 135, 154, 292
Jung, Carl, 3, 10–13, 48–53, 96–100, 181, 231–33, 249, 253, 254–61, 273,

291, 321, 399–406
alchemy, 238
anima and animus, 73
archetypes, 281, 299
depression, 149
dream of lopsided people
   n, 70
dream of underground
   chamber, 37
ego and Self, 245
Heart chakra, 326
image of God, 295
individual and collective, 191
intuition, 104, 342
meaning, 208, 348, 380
nekyia, 204
paradox, 283
projection, 136
second half of life, 200
shadow, 164
symbols, 32
'Jung's map', 9–12, 13, 52, 122,
   129, 192, 232

Kabbala, 288, 338
Kabir, *n*, 227, 295
karma, 223, 333, 351
Kekulé, August, 62, 105
Kelley, George, 380, 402, *n*, 20
Klein, Melanie, 255, 380, 399, 402
Kleitman, Nathaniel, 259, 398
Koestler, Arthur, 253
Kretschmer, Wolfgang, 255, 403
Kübler-Ross, Dr. Elisabeth., 206
Kuhn, Maggie, 130
kundalini, 180, 185, 322, 335, 428
   warning, 311, 312, *n*, 324
Kwan Yin, 79

labyrinth, 82, 214, 216, 223, 231, 246
lake, 269, 289, 314, 413
Lao-tzu, 249
Leibniz, Gottfried, 308, 403
Leonardo da Vinci, 14
Leuner, Hans Carl, 256, 270, 403, 409, 416, 417, *n*, 411
levels of consciousness, 85, 116, 169, 342, 347
Leviathan, 21
London, 334
lopsidedness, 11, 33, 41, 43, 145, 150

maiden, 23
mandala, 40, 231, 239, 244, 246, 282, 401, 413, 419
Marquis de Lafayette, 353
marsh, 413
Maslow, Abraham, 208, 253, 341, 380, 391, 404, 407
McGee, Brian, 111
meadow, 33, 255, 269, 400, 409, 411, 415
Medusa, 21
Mesmer, Anton, 254, 404
midwife of the spirit, 45, 83, 196, 209, 210
Mindell, Arnold, 259, 267, 404
Minotaur, 214, 215
mirror, 236, 269, 376, 415
mirrors
   hall of, 134

Monad, the, 338, 403, *n*, 308
Moore, Henry, 63, 224
Moreno, Jacob Levy, 259, 405
mountain, 92, 93, 183, 212, 223, 255, 269, 283, 300, 351, 400, 409, 412, 419
Murphy, Michael, 253, 398, 405, 406
music, 34, 147, 247, 333, 344
and the chakras, *n*, 325
Myers-Briggs typology, *n*, 51
mystery, 3
mystery schools, 168, 176, 307, 326, 347, 354

nadis, 338, *n*, 322
Nash, John *n*, 289
Newton, Isaac, 290
Night Sea Journey, nekyia, 204, 206, 283
Nirvana, 13, 60, 204, 352, 407
n, 172

observer, 20, 46–48, 107, 106–12, 266, 270, 277, 291, 315, 326, 372
Ocean of Dark Things, 122, 127, 130, 200
Odysseus, 79, 214, 215
Oedipus, 214, 219, 255
'Onion map', 15, 163
opportunity, 126, 129, 140, 146, 165, 192, 241
organisations, 87, 206, 301–5, 334
Osiris, 204, 218
oxherd, the, 210

Paine, Thomas, 353
panic attacks, 115, 149, 331
Paracelsus, *n*, 199
parental images, 17
Patanjali, 13, 352, 363, *n*, 351
Pegasus, 21, 93
Penfield, Wilder Graves, 259, 406
Perls, Fritz, 259, 406
Persephone, 140, 219
persona, 15
philosopher's stone, 242, 247
n, 247
Plato, 198
myth of the cave, 209, 210, 281, 298, 394
Plotinus, 249
Pluto, 201
Pontifex, 172, 212, 340
prana, 308, 321
Price, Dick, 405, 406
Procrustes, 201
Prodigal Son, 219, 246
Progoff, Ira, 253, 259, 406
Prometheus, 214, 219
protection, 288, 332, 340, 347
Psyche, 24, 75, 82
psyche and soma, 110, 113
psychosis, 134, 183, 273, 299
puer aeternus, eternal boy, 88

'raincloud of knowable things', 13
reconciliation, 258, 409, 417
resistance, 247, 321, 418
responsible breadwinner, 25
river, 39, 171, 178, 205, 413
Jordan, 179, 375
Rogers, Carl, 380

Rorschach, 255, 406
Rudolf Steiner, 123

salt crystals, *n*, 282
samadhi, 13, 61
Saunders, Dame Cicely, 206
Schopenhauer, Arthur, 245
Schultz, J. H., 255, 406
Seven Rays, *n*, 285, 327, 358
shadow, 16, 37, 137, 138, 164, 169, 183, 247, 299, 314, 332
Shaman, 190, 196, 254, *n*, 190
Shambhala, 204, 356, *n*, 362
sharing, 8, 19, 275, 276
Sheikh Yamani, 293
Shiva, 155, 224, 284, 286, 338, 346, 354
Singing Stone, 227, 228, 231, 243, 246
Sioux, 194, 227
Sogyal Rinpoche, *n*, 206
soul, 24, 82, 137, 209, 262, 282, 301, 322, 333, 395
    dark night of, 204
spirit, 61, 347
    and matter, 32, 73, 84, 198, 209, 324, 344
    and soul, 185, 338, 360
    in drink, 245
    of cities, 300, 334
    of nations, 191, 301, 334, 426
    of place, 300, 333
spot imaging, 265, 267, 338, 415
Sri Krishna, 15, 187
St. Paul, 53, 62
St. Teresa of Avila, 210
Star Trek, *n*, 295

sub-personalities, 20–34, 85, 155, 164, 288, 296, 325, 376–78
Sufism, 310
Sutich, Anthony, 253, 380, 405, 407, 408
Swallow, Joan, *n*, 41, 42, 152, 211
swamp, 409, 413
symbols, 7, 31–40
symptom as symbol, 109–15

Tai Chi, 202
talisman, 188, 207, 236, 243, 259, 261, 270–72, 277, 297, 339, 361, 413–20
Tantra, 328, *n*, 307
Tara, 79
Tennyson, Alfred Lord, 293
Theodore Flournoy, 254, 399
Theosophical Society, 353, 397, 406
Theseus, 214
'third eye', the, 74, 318, *n*, 106, 318
Thorley, Anthony, xx–xxi, *n*, 264
thrice-born, 224
Tibetan Bardo, 204
timing for explorations, 19, 47, 273, 276, 371, 373, *n*, 276
Tippett, Sir Michael, 344
Tolkein, J.R.R., 212
'Training Manual', IGB, *n*, 253, 263
transcendent experiences, 7
transcenders and actualisers, 391 *n*, 150, 295

Transpersonal psychology, 14, 168, 181, 253, 273, 305, 379, 380, 400, 407
Transpersonal workshops, 272
  leaders, 273
  participants, 273
tunnel, 174, 410, 412
twice-born, 223, 224, 241
United Nations, 176, 289, 335, 353

Valhalla, 204, 218, n, 204, 362
Vich, Miles, 253, 405, 408
Vishnu, 156, 284, 287, 338, 340, 354
visualisation, 333, 335, 347, 352, 411
  and imaging, 18, 86, 259, 263, 275, 358
volcano, 38, 409, 413
von Franz, Marie Louise, 38
  n, 238

Watts, Alan, 245, 253, 281, 406
will, the, 62, 155–58, 185, 187, 284, 285–95, 325, 339, 346–49, 375
wise person, 20, 21, 33, 47, 137, 162, 248, 260, 283, 295, 419
Wood, Ernest, 308
words of power, 183, 352, 358, 361, n, 347
Wotan, 154, 218

Yggdrasil, 218
yin and yang, 72–75, 80, 150, 198, 236
yoga, 106, 219, 320, 328, 357 n, 410